C0-DKP-014

*Romantic Sobriety*

# *Romantic Sobriety*

## Sensation, Revolution, Commodification, History

ORRIN N. C. WANG

The Johns Hopkins University Press
*Baltimore*

Printed in the United States of America on acid-free paper
2 4 6 8 9 7 5 3 1

The Johns Hopkins University Press
2715 North Charles Street
Baltimore, Maryland 21218-4363
www.press.jhu.edu

Library of Congress Cataloging-in-Publication Data

Wang, Orrin Nan Chung, 1957–
Romantic sobriety : sensation, revolution, commodification, history /
Orrin N. C. Wang.
p. cm.
Includes bibliographical references and index.
ISBN-13: 978-1-4214-0066-2 (hardcover : alk. paper)
ISBN-10: 1-4214-0066-9 (hardcover : alk. paper)
1. Romanticism. 2. Senses and sensation in literature. 3. Marxist criticism.
4. Deconstruction. 5. Literature—History and criticism—Theory, etc. I. Title.
PN56.R7W37 2011
809′.9145—dc22 2010046803

A catalog record for this book is available from the British Library.



The Johns Hopkins University Press uses environmentally friendly book materials, including recycled text paper that is composed of at least 30 percent post-consumer waste, whenever possible.

*In memory of Betty S. Wang and Richard J. Conroy*

# CONTENTS

# ACKNOWLEDGMENTS

Unlike the Beatles, I had *a lot* of help from my friends. A number of individuals read and commented on portions of the book: Jonathan Auerbach, Marshall Brown, James K. Chandler, Jonathan Culler, David L. Clark, William Cohen, Marianne Conroy, Neil Fraistat, Colin Jager, David Kaufmann, Jon Klancher, Marshall Grossman, Brian McGrath, W. J. T. Mitchell, Patrick O'Malley, Daniel O'Quinn, Thomas Pfau, Marc Redfield, Hugh Roberts, David Wagenknecht, and Deborah Elise White. I especially want to thank David L. Clark, Jon Klancher, William Galperin, and Peter Manning for their timely interventions and support during different phases of the writing of the manuscript. I'm forever in debt to the smart and perceptive commentary that everyone gave me. All errors and shortcomings of the book are my own. I also want to thank Jonathan Auerbach, Marianne Conroy, Elizabeth Fay, Neil Fraistat, and Daniel O'Quinn for their advice and encouragement during various moments of the long trek that was this book. Ralph Bauer and Zita Nunes also cheerfully came to my aid in different ways as this project reached its completion. David Rettenmaier and Jeremy Horsefield did a splendid job helping me put the manuscript in order; the P. G. Cool Pool and Alex Paraskevas helped with the chakra side of things. Dan S. Wang was a friendly intellectual presence throughout the writing of the book. Marshall Grossman inspired this non-Renaissance project in ways that I'm still discovering; I miss him greatly.

My thanks to my students, to the Washington Area Romanticists Group, and to the University of Maryland Theory Colloquium for providing me audiences where many of the ideas in the book were first formulated and tested. A University of Maryland Graduate Research Board Award gave me the necessary push to finish writing and conceiving a large portion of the book. An earlier version of chapter 1 appeared in *Modern Language Quarterly* 60, no. 4 (December 1999); chapters 2 and 4 in *Diacritics* 30, no. 4 (Winter 2000) and 35, no. 2 (Summer 2005);

and chapters 6 and 10 in *Studies in Romanticism*. A version of chapter 3, "De Man, Marx, Rousseau, and the Machine," also appeared in *After Poststructuralism: Writing the Intellectual History of Theory*, edited by Tilottama Rajan and Michael O'Driscoll (© University of Toronto Press, 2002), and is used with permission of the publisher. My thanks to the Birmingham Museums and Art Gallery, the Bodleian Libraries, the British Museum, and Laurent Mannoni and *Cinémathèque française, collections d'appareils* for permission to reproduce the images in the book.

To Marianne Conroy, my gratitude for what we will always both know. To Margaret Limei Wang, my glorious little lark, whose entrance into our lives overlapped with a large part of this work, my thanks for the patience you'll someday come to appreciate, and for the impatience I in spite of myself can only treasure. This book is dedicated to the memory of Betty S. Wang and Richard J. Conroy, whose global peregrinations made up one huge swath of the last century's history, in all its poignancy and finality. That some things are never final is our burden, and our hope, if not this work's.

*Romantic Sobriety*

# The Sensation of Romanticism

Tiz dizziness to think of it.—John Keats, *Endymion*

Over the course of its ten chapters, this book stages a series of encounters among a number of key terms associated with the British and European Romantic topos: periodicity, revolution, commodification, materiality, and ideology, to name the ones that occur most frequently. Structuring most if not all of these encounters is the figure of *sensation*, a term whose relationship with the study of Romanticism is a storied one, both within and beyond the field. Literary scholars have extensively explored the topic of sensation, or the experience of the senses, in eighteenth- and nineteenth-century British culture, along with such attendant themes as sensibility and feeling. Sensing the world, the body, and one's own self has been a mainstay of our understanding of Romanticism in both its humanist and postmodern forms.[1]

This study of Romanticism and sensation attempts to distinguish itself in two ways. The first involves the counterintuitive exploration of Romanticism as an event equally fascinated by the rejection of sensation, equally caught up in a Romantic sobriety. As the term implies, however, such a sobriety can mean more than one thing. It can refer to a Romantic renunciation or policing of the senses; it can also mean a rejection of Romanticism as *itself* a literature, philosophy, or culture of misguided sensation. As much as late eighteenth- and nineteenth-century authors evince a suspicion of various modes of sensation and strain toward ways of ameliorating bodily and non-bodily forms of addiction, later thinkers will define their vision of literature, aesthetic, and world by the degree that it posits a cure from Romanticism. One can define Romanticism by its sobriety, but one can also demonstrate one's sobriety by judiciously abstaining from all that Romanticism offers. Romantic sobriety signifies an unavoidable doubling in the identity of Romanticism itself, one that also allows the very notion of Romanticism to come into being, not simply as a positive identity—the act of sobriety, say—but also as the negative other that results when another identity represents itself as decidedly non-Romantic—a Modernism, for example, no longer beholden to Romanticism's messy habits. The issue of Romanticism's very form, a mainstay question in the field of Romantic studies, finds itself entangled with the problem of Romantic sobriety, of staying sober about Romanticism. The dizzying effects of such logic become part of Romanticism, generating inflections to the meaning of Romantic sobriety that sustain but also go beyond instantiation of, or disidentification with, the Romantic event. This book is a tracking of such effects.

The second way *Romantic Sobriety* tries to distinguish itself has to do with a methodology that understands such semantic generation as necessarily involving the aporias of a tropological condition. Sensation in this book is neither a primarily psychological nor empirical phenomenon to be studied and shaped into a coherent history of various intersecting Romantic-era disciplines, say, between literature and science, or literature and economics. Rather, sensation is a figure, whose meanings profitably ground its use within a number of Romantic and post-Romantic narratives of political antagonism and social distinction. But the inevitable tropic drift of such meanings also results in an elongation of the term itself, so that sensation as the sensory finds itself also associated with sense as signification and sensation as the sensationalized.[2] More radically, this elongation necessitates a reimagination of sensation as a *non-physical* event also not necessarily understood in either mental or idealized terms. The middle portion of this book will especially be devoted to the argument for a Romantic *sensation of meaning*, now oftentimes counterintuitively understood by its disarticulation from phenomenal reality in a manner akin to that of Paul de Man's notion of a radical Kantian materialism. This sensation of meaning is ultimately about neither the perceiving subject nor the perceived object but about the workings—the imposition and deracination—of figure. As my engagement with Walter Benn Michaels and Steven Knapp asserts, such sensation can still be misrecognized as sensory corruption and can instigate a series of responses that uncannily reproduce a Romantic sobriety, this time aimed at a there-not-there Romanticism at the heart of a number of choices facing the postmodern left today.

A tropological understanding of Romantic sensation and sobriety necessarily stages the afterlife of Romanticism in current theoretical discourses as well as the operation of such terms in late eighteenth- and early nineteenth-century texts. Far from evading history, such an approach finds itself vigorously entangled with the question of history: of the meaning of periodicity for Romanticism as an era-bound identity, and of historicity itself as the space of figuration where the indeterminacies of deep history, uneven development, long centuries, and ambivalent prophecy play themselves out, and where the proposition of a Romantic discourse for a twenty-first century seems something besides a quaint, or embarrassing, question. *Romantic Sobriety* thus extends and complicates the many meditations on the intimate relation between Romanticism and history, insofar as its premise is that such a relation can only be approached by understanding history as historicity, as the imbrication of history's identity and non-identity—not the historical and ahistorical but, more properly, the historical and *transhistorical*, the form, shape, or sensation of history, which the historical, even after the putative end of all our meta-narratives, still demands for its intelligibility.[3] To call this the *radical* form of history in a way that speaks to both the nature of this form and how we signify its exceptionalism by denoting it *as* history, and to see the dramatization of this problem as a vividly Romantic one—these are some of the impetuses that drive this work.

To employ such a methodology and to invoke history as the place where our investments in the aporias of figure are markedly worked out is to align this book with the operations of deconstruction, above all with how that practice is inscribed in Paul de Man's well-known encounter with Romanticism as a rhetorical event. But it is also to feel the gravitational pull of yet another discourse, where the question of history's form as an ongoing narrative remains both the most intransigent and compelling, the analytical categories of Marxism that still remain as we feel our way past, or through, the ostensibly forever post-history of global capital. That both deconstruction and Marxism have a complicated, intimate relation with Romanticism, and that both, like Romanticism, now seem to exist in a permanently fragmented, anachronistic present time that from different angles can signal the discourses' timeliness or irrelevance, their topicality or datedness—this is the non-coincidence subtending much of the intellectual mood of this book. To be sure, the readings generated by such a mood do not cohere into any ultimate grand blending of these two great negative critiques of our *epistēmē*; indeed, at times implicitly and explicitly parataxis is as viable a denotation of their relationship as any synthesis. Still, in this book, the physics of the relation between these two discourses is not only about their repulsion from one another; it is also about their attraction. This work can be understood as a thought experiment that extends some of the basic figurations of de Man's reading of Romanticism to vocabulary and territory usually understood through Marxist categories—ideology and materiality, for example, as well as revolution and commodification.[4] Whether, however, *Romantic Sobriety* really is *that* or an allegory, in the de Manian sense, *of* a thought experiment—it is precisely the force of such a question, and of the answer's indeterminacy, that fuels the approach of much of this book.

This is not to say that there are no moments of critical distance from de Man; it is also not to say that when I extend his thought defamiliarizations and complications do not occur, as if reproducing the singularity of a de Manian reading was ever a real possibility. The larger point is simply then that a number of other writers and theoretical dispositions inform both the critical approach and objects of study in this work, especially as the book turns its gaze in its latter half to the primary writings of Romantic and early Victorian writers. Psychoanalysis, especially conceived in terms of Slavoj Žižek's reenvisioning of Lacanian theory, appears in a number of different registers as foil, object of critique, and analytical partner throughout the book's chapters. To a lesser degree, although quite explicitly, an engagement with Deleuzian thought supports portions of the chapters on Shelley and Keats. Arguably, a book on Romanticism and sensation must encounter in some way Deleuze's wide-ranging work on sensation. But Deleuze's intellectual affiliations with the genealogies of natural philosophy, as well as his interlocutors' own investments in the physicality of motion and force, diverge in many ways from this study's particular use of de Man to separate the sensation of meaning from any aboriginal tie to the phenomenal world.[5] Chapter 7's reading of "Ode to the West Wind" attempts to rethink that divergence, although the main theoretical encounter in the book remains between deconstructive and Marxist thought.

*Romantic Sobriety* organizes that encounter through the relation between Romantic sensation and historicity. Part I, "Periodicity," explores the meta-critical nature of Romantic periodization through figures of sensation and sobriety that appear in such writers as Wordsworth, Coleridge, and Kant. The two chapters in part I model for us a Romanticism that underwrites all our attempts at periodization, as the catachresis of historical thought that is as unavoidable as it is incredible, equally impossible to realize and to eliminate. Part II, "Theory," investigates a Romantic sensation of meaning that actively structures contemporary debates of the postmodern left, with four chapters looking at eighteenth- and nineteenth-century works by Rousseau, Wordsworth, and Marx and contemporary polemics by de Man, Knapp and Michaels, Derrida, and Žižek. The chapters develop the idea of a sensation of meaning whose oftentimes non-phenomenal, figural status is a point of entry into debates about the possibility of theorizing history today. The four chapters of part III, "Texts," examine how different forms of sensation and their abnegation operate in a set of second-generation Romantic and early Victorian writings. The post–French Revolutionary status of Shelley's "Ode to the

West Wind," Byron's *Don Juan*, Brontë's *Jane Eyre*, and Keats's *Lamia* by and large enables these texts to reflect on the historical problematic of troping revolution and commodification, both apart and together. Within these and other chapters, revolution and commodification are the two specific historical narratives underwriting the fantastic capitalist modernity that we continue to inhabit to this day. *Romantic Sobriety* tries to enact a Romantic understanding, or sensation, of the fantastic event of this modernity, whose implications for the study of literature are taken up in the coda to this book.

In many ways, revolution and commodification also enable us to make the relation between Romanticism and Marxism intelligible. Indeed, how we formulate the precise relation between revolution and commodification becomes a key problematic in Marxism itself, especially the Marxism that emerges after Marx and his own historical prophecies, the Marxism that encounters the world of postclassical capitalism. Similarly, the nature of Romanticism's relation to Marxism also relies on such questions as whether the *récits* of revolution in these two discourses diverge or converge, whether Marx's notion of the commodity form best explains Romanticism's own disruption of any monolithic sequential history that would relegate that era to one side or the other of the divide between modernity and postmodernity, and whether in retrospect commodity reification actually supersedes revolution as the key story that Romanticism conveys. A rendering of these questions unveils a more volatile relation between Romanticism and Marxism than that which interlocutors of the Marxist Modernist habitus, such as Georg Lukács and Fredric Jameson, usually tell.[6] Yet that is the point. The problematic of revolution and commodification in Romanticism helps limn the question of inscribing those events within a Marxist history committed to realizing a founding representation (*Darstellung*) where diagnosis and prognosis, critique and practice, analysis and prophecy all coincide. Romanticism *as* a problematic—a key troping in deconstruction's own encounter with Romanticism—becomes a spur to articulating as exactly as possible that commitment, in spite of, or because of, the irresolute, never-simple nature of that provocation.

Revolution and commodification thus also structure the specific historical identity of Romanticism itself, in ways as complicated as they are extensive. Most obviously, revolution has especially been a constant theme that has helped figure Romanticism as either a revolutionary or counterrevolutionary literature and political disposition, with the 1980s flowering of historicist Romanticist writing, emblematized by Jerome McGann's famous critique of the Romantic ideology, perhaps being the most vivid and fresh rearticulation of this topos for current scholars working in the field. In contrast, the theme of commodification is not as explicitly embedded in our sense of Romanticism, although the past several decades have seen key works in Romantic studies cohere around this topic, most notably Marjorie Levinson's *Keats's Life of Allegory: The Origins of a Style* and Jerome Christensen's *Lord Byron's Strength: Romantic Writing and Commercial Society.*[7] That Levinson and Christensen each choose one of the seminal second-generation, post-Revolutionary poets, and that both their works continue but also complicate the revisionist historicism begun by McGann, is more than a complete coincidence. For if McGann's *Romantic Ideology* can be understood as reformulating M. H. Abrams's own famous essay, "English Romanticism: The Spirit of the Age," transforming Abrams's Romantic transcendence of the trauma of the French Revolution into ideological evasion of the same event, both Levinson's and Christensen's studies can be seen as a further opening up of Romanticism to the complexities of a history first glimpsed, or remembered, by McGann's call to return our gaze to the Revolution as the site of our primal reading of Romanticism.[8] This is obviously an intensely schematic understanding of these works, but there is certain clarity to such a schema, where the sequential order of McGann's, Levinson's, and Christensen's works allegorizes the question of the relation between Romantic revolution and commodification.

One might, for example, consider how the indeterminate, or inconclusive, nature of Romantic revolution leads to a larger sense of radical social transformation in England and Europe, the increasingly unavoidable way that the market relations of capital dominate life globally and locally, in an utter fashion. Arguably, this is Marx's own sense of the great bourgeois revolutions of the latter half of the eighteenth century, a view that underlies his own prophecy of the increasingly untenable social relations produced by the market that will lead to genuine class revolution in the nineteenth century. Or one might retroactively see this sequential narrative upended by a more complex rise of the commodity form, with its attendant events of consumption, reification, production, and expropriation creating a more volatile timeline in which the certitudes of Marxist revolution are replaced by ontological and epistemological instabilities already glimpsed in the historical combustibility of Romanticism's historicities, and which demand a rethinking of the Marxist analysis itself. Can we not see Levinson's identification of the working-class antagonism at the core of Keats's poetry as an expression of this former tendency, and Christensen's study of the commercial strength of Byronic writing spectrally alienated from the aristocratic paternal name as an example of the latter disposition?[9] Such a proposition surely overlooks the full subtleties of both works' rich theoretical imaginings, but it does get at the fundamental problem that arises when we juxtapose the two studies. If one important version of the Romantic imaginary is in large part structured by the hypothetical event of radical social transformation, what is the precise form of that event? Does it begin with revolution and then open up to commodification as the rise of the commodity form, or is revolution still the proleptic *telos* of this narrative arc? The point of juxtaposing Levinson and Christensen would then be precisely *not* to choose between them, but to observe how the problematic they generate together is an open question that Romanticism poses, and that we are still asking today. That Romanticism reemerges as a vital discourse in our own grappling with this volatile predicament and, likewise, that Romantic-era writings especially model the unstable intensity of such historical questioning are two complementary claims explored in different ways throughout the book.

We can also add David Simpson's remarkable recent study of Wordsworth to Levinson's and Christensen's meditations on Romanticism and the commodity form. *Wordsworth, Commodification, and Social Concerns* does not so much choose either of Levinson's or Christensen's paradigms as tellingly select its vision of Wordsworth over that of the 1980s McGann-inspired ideological critiques of the poet, of which Simpson's earlier appraisals of Wordsworth might intriguingly be considered part. In doing so, Simpson implicitly reaffirms the allegory of Romantic historical knowledge that we've identified in the sequential order of McGann's, Levinson's, and Christensen's works, by arguing that the event of the commodity form better informs the complex poetic texture of Wordsworth's Romantic life than the poet's turn away from the radical promises of the French Revolution. Whether for Simpson the history of capital that enmeshes Wordsworth and twenty-first-century readers alike then leads to the radical transformation of something we might call revolution—we might say that is the open question that Simpson finds in Wordsworth's own struggles to decipher the reifying processes occurring around him, a question that very much informs the critical character of the present book as well.[10]

The shaping force of that open question, both liberating and oppressive, is not the only thing that *Wordsworth* and the present work share; readers will also see a similar consideration of the language of Derridean spectrality as a resource by which a certain knot of issues might be articulated—in Simpson's case the symptomatic presence of the commodity form in Wordsworth's poetry, and in ours in the ghostly shape of revolution that chapter 6 sees as one inheritance that the study of Romanticism receives from Derrida. The present book's interest in a Wordsworthian sensation of meaning also resonates with Simpson's focus on the mysterious, oftentimes spectral figures that routinely populate the poet's landscape, including one subject of my own reading in chapter 4, the Boy of Winander.

In my case, however, such sensation is more properly theorized through de Man's notion of a non-phenomenal materiality. *Romantic Sobriety* thus doesn't track the sensation of meaning in Wordsworth to the commodity form in the same explicit way that Simpson's work does—indeed, the very possibility of tracking meaning, historical or otherwise, from a resemblance, or figure, becomes the primary focus of my interest in Wordsworth in part II of this book. Yet the scandal of mind underwriting that possibility frames much of the discussion of commodification, revolution, and ideology that orients my readings in part III of the second-generation Romantics. Their post-Revolutionary status can thus also stand for a more literal encounter in their texts, especially in Byron's *Don Juan*, with things more readily understood as commodified objects than the ghostly figures of alienated capital proleptically haunting the consciousness of Simpson's Wordsworth. This is not to say that explicit encounters with commodity life are absent from earlier Romantic and eighteenth-century writing, or that the Wordsworthian sensation of meaning examined in part II is definitively cut off from the historical narrative that Simpson expertly limns. Nor does it imply that we understand the meaning of a commodified object simply because we have it in our grasp, or sight, like Juan's shoes in Donna Julia's bedroom. It is to say that the post-Revolutionary encounter with the commodity form especially affords in many instances allegories of what Slavoj Žižek has called a "parallax view" of the very question of the relation between commodification and revolution that Romanticism poses.[11] It is also to consider how the indeterminate nature of Wordsworth's, and Romanticism's, sensation of meaning might inflect, indeed transform, the intelligibility of dialectical history—to ponder how that history might be understood when coupled with a Romanticism that often as not realizes itself as an evasive, ghostly, and unreadable force.

In this book that coupling is expressed by how meanings of commodification and revolution are generated by the figural operations of sobriety and sensation. While such figures might especially appear to organize Romantic anxiety over and attraction to the commodity form, the same will also be found to hold for the narratives of revolution and post-revolution studied in this work. The latter dynamic operates at a number of levels: the maturation out of Jacobin identity; the sensation of meaning in contemporary postmodern leftist debate; the figural connection, and disconnection, between ideological critique and empirical analysis; and the sensing of a contingency beyond the iron laws of global instrumental capital, beyond what Jürgen Habermas labels *system* and Shelley close to two centuries earlier denotes through his figures of blood and gold.[12] Sensing revolution, like sensing commodification, becomes a sensing of history's direction (*le sens d'histoire*).[13] That this endeavor involves both a complex attending to and disavowal of the physical senses (*and* non-physical sensation) makes this a history that Romantic writings especially articulate.

As a sensation of meaning, this history's Romantic nature also lies in the urgency of its expression, a well-nigh-unthinkable formulation of the relationship between deconstruction and Marxism as both the imposition of figure and the figure of imposition. As much as deconstruction and Marxism diverge from one another, Romanticism forces us to consider how together they express this chiasmus—how the imposition of figure registers the necessary presence of figure during the making of the world while the figure of imposition specifically demands the inscription of value in its most radically challenging, unthinkable form, precisely that of the emancipatory, utopian kind. One main thesis of *Romantic Sobriety* is that the full force of this dynamic remains in many ways a Romantic one, in texts both primary and secondary in nature, written a mere two centuries apart. Thus, while necessary work has warned us against the presentist dangers of historicizing past literatures in perhaps too enthusiastic a fashion, the critical impulse of this study moves in another direction, toward a forward sense of ourselves caught in the Romantic mediation of a history that is, radically, terribly, and beautifully, *incomplete*.[14]

That being said, it's worth repeating that this book is not an empirical historical study of sensation during the Romantic period. *Nor is it a cultural history of Romantic sobriety*, in any comprehensive sense of the term, although the question of history haunts much of its pages. Chapter 1 does somewhat perversely take on the guise of such an analysis, only to destabilize the precepts of this type of inquiry at the chapter's conclusion. Yet if *Romantic Sobriety* does not emulate the narrative coherence of a comprehensive historical study, the sequence of the work's three main sections does describe several formal and thematic arcs: part I investigates how Romanticism both upends and realizes the idea of historical identity, part II introduces the non-phenomenal character of sensations of meaning, and part III draws upon both of the earlier sections' concerns for its analyses of revolution and commodification in second-generation, post-Revolutionary writings. The tropology of sensation and sobriety thus changes from a focus in part I on figures of physical senses, to an exploration in part II of the non-physical dimension of sensations of meaning, to the variegated troping in part III of sensation as both phenomenal experience and non-phenomenal event. We might also note the differing yet complimentary aims of parts II and III: part II intervenes in a number of theoretical debates going on today, while part III focuses mainly on literary works associated with the Romantic period. As the chapter titles in both sections and my own reference to Wordsworth attest, this division is porous, with primary and secondary (or critical) writings juxtaposed in both sections. Still, the purpose of part II is mainly polemical, with its chapters using Romanticism to engage with a number of contemporary theoretical positions, while the intent of part III is critical, insofar as its chapters primarily try to gain new insights into the Romantic literature being read.

Despite these organizing principles, readers might notice a countermovement in this work, where the investigative energies of each chapter seem to reside especially in the individual analyses of each separate study, to the point that each chapter appears to rework—indeed, allegorize anew—the tropology of key terms that structure the book. I don't want to downplay this trait of *Romantic Sobriety*. One might recall de Man's famous prefatory remarks about the "melancholy spectacle" underlying the failed attempt of his collected writings in *The Rhetoric of Romanticism* to cohere into anything like a literary history of Romanticism.[15] I don't mean to trade on the supreme critical confidence underlying de Man's mordant confession, but I do want to observe a similar resistance to any unproblematic dialectical progression in the present book. Or one could say at the very least that this work leaves open the question of where the force of its inquiry lies, in the recognition of its sequential transformations *as* sequential, or as constant—indeed, compulsive—returns to one of the main scenes of writing that composes Romantic modernity. Which of these recognitions is the more sober choice for the study of Romanticism?—that is the question that this dissonance in form highlights.

The dialectic was an explicit key figure in my earlier work, *Fantastic Modernity: Dialectical Readings in Romanticism and Theory*. Despite the present book's attention to a variety of chiasmic structures in the Romantic texts read, I have eschewed the consistent enframing use of *dialectical* precisely because of the tension between Marxist dialectical thought and deconstruction that *Romantic Sobriety* both works off of and scrutinizes. Yet *Romantic Sobriety* also follows in the wake of my earlier book, in terms of the national and institutional context of *Fantastic Modernity*, which explored the relation between Romanticism and contemporary theory by looking at key critical readings in the North American study of Romanticism. Like *Fantastic Modernity*, the focus of *Romantic Sobriety* is primarily (although by no means exclusively) English Romanticism. Another study of Romanticism, concentrating on either British or European critical genealogies, could have profitably engaged with many of the same themes of sensation and sobriety that *Romantic Sobriety* does.[16] In both *Romantic Sobriety* and *Fan-*

*tastic Modernity*, then, the North American focus is exemplary rather than totalizing. Like my previous work, this work makes the further wager that its exemplary character says something not only about the academic study of Romanticism, and Romanticism itself, but also about the world, or worlds, in which that study is situated, no matter how exorbitant, or Romantic, that connection appears to be. In the book's coda that connection is further allegorized as the predicament of the North American academic study of *all* literature (and its vexed cousin, the literary), at a time ever more defined by the instrumentalities of a global capitalism increasingly uninterested in the studying of literature at the university level.

On a related matter, readers will note a further trait of the English Romantic texts that I study, the secure status of many of the authors as members of the high Romantic canon. This situation is not always the case, as chapter 9's attention to Charlotte Dacre's novel, *Zofloya; or, The Moor*, shows. Still, there's no denying the canonical character of much of the Romantic literature—English and non-English—that this work explores. Arguably, such a canon can now only be simulated rather than conceived as a genuine entity, given the decades-long rediscovery of the vast array of authors writing in the eighteenth and nineteenth centuries. But that is exactly the point. Running through a number of my chapters is the thesis that the expansion, or dissolution, of the Romantic canon does not necessarily confront all the problems about literature and history that Romanticism poses, and that a self-conscious, critical use of the high Romantic canon might better dramatize these issues in a vivid manner. These issues include whether Romanticism itself exists as a viable historical category after the emergence of the long eighteenth (and long nineteenth) century in literary studies and, likewise, whether we can say that *literature* retains any kind of intrinsic identity separate from the numerous cultural practices existing during and after the late eighteenth and early nineteenth centuries. Similar to how Modernist writers will later define themselves against Romanticism, literature during Romanticism oftentimes realizes itself by noting precisely what it is not: the sensationalized productions of mass viewing and reading, for instance. The Romantic institutionalization of literature as an elite form of cultural experience is thus entangled with one form of sobriety, the ritualistic disavowal of commercialized forms of print and non-print sensation. This book specifically attends to this disavowal but also complicates this trope by its association of both Romanticism and the *literary* with a Wordsworthian sensation of meaning, a dynamic that further involves sobriety at two dizzying levels: as the rejection of phenomenal perception as the unproblematic basis for this sensation, and, paradoxically, as the shunning of this sensation, a reoccurring feature of our conception of literary and social history to this day.

This complicated scenario clarifies present debates over the implication for studying literature—in terms of not only its institutional fate, but also whether it should be subsumed by other terms such as history, philosophy, or, most importantly, *culture*—by demonstrating how literature and the literary not only converge but *diverge* in their meanings and effects.

The idea of the canon, then, functions in these predicaments not so much as the sign of priestly constraint but, like Romanticism and literature, as the aporetic possibility of an identity. This is not to say that this possibility doesn't engender its own politics, but it is to assert that the acuteness of such implications can be especially discerned in the singularly reflexive character of certain canonical works. In the present book this textual self-awareness is located in how much writers thematize their *own* relation to canon making and to instituting literature as an elite form of aesthetic experience, particularly in a Wordsworth intensely alive to the gross and violent stimulants that he positions his poetry against, and in a Keats wryly acknowledging how the vilification of his Cockney discourse turns largely on the accusation that the sensation he records isn't really literature at all. But reflexivity about the canon also resides in the specific ways that certain texts have been received and valorized: how by the mid-twentieth century "A Slumber Did My Spirit Seal" comes in the North American academy to stand for the very act of, or test case for, interpretation itself, and how *Jane Eyre* exists all at once as a Romantic and Victorian, and gothic and non-gothic, novel. The very "metacommentary" that distinguishes a text *as* canonical lends the work an especially sharp reflexivity about the meanings of Romanticism, literature, and history that I want to investigate (Jameson, 9–10). There is certainly a form of authority here, but one whose intelligibility is by no means clear; indeed, that pressing, imposing sensation of ambiguous authority, in all its linguistic and historical inchoateness, is one key subject of the book. The canon might then be understood as simply one more metonym for this identity—or, more precisely, for the catachrestic imposition of this spectral identity, which more thoroughly is metonymically coupled in this study to the term *Romanticism*, and even more so to the designation *history* itself.

Finally, let me say a word about the title. As I have tried to indicate, readers will find *Romantic Sobriety* misleading if they assume this work to be a comprehensive history of sobriety during the Romantic period. (Indeed, readers will notice that only chapter 1 studies the literal appearance of the word in various Romantic texts.) Neither is the book a comprehensive theory of sobriety in any way that we might understand the notion. Rather, the work registers a series of moments where by and large dialectical thought *and* linguistic figure encounter one another, characterized in complex ways by both the presence and rejection of, in its diverse forms, sensation. The claim of this book is that this refusal is Romantic, not only because of the many texts involved, but also because of how much the event of Romanticism and the event of its reading are structured by the confrontation between dialectic and figure—because of how much the fantastic modernity of Romanticism overlaps with the fundamental *récits* of both Marxism and deconstruction. Yet this formulation doesn't foreclose the possibility that Romantic sobriety might also mean something else besides the gesture of a renunciation, that it might also signify a desired critical temperament, regardless of whether—*or because*—such a temperament depends on an encounter between dialectic and figure that can only resolve itself in a scandal of thought. Of course, the distance between that desire and one's own reading disposition can also be considered a Romantic problem, one that, as chapter 7 records, Shelley's "Ode to the West Wind" dramatizes in excruciating fashion. Likewise, the aporetic nature of such a critical temperament cannot help but recall the exorbitant workings of the sublime in Romantic writing, a condition that in this book is linked most strongly, although in diverse ways, to Kant's writing on the subject. De Man's notion of a non-phenomenal materiality comes from a reading of Kant's work on the sublime, of course, and so my own formulation of the sensation of meaning in part II comes in part from an analysis of that engagement. Chapter 2's consideration of Kantian genius and chapter 7's reading of Shelley both also address the sublime, as either implicit theoretical backdrop or explicit object of inquiry.

In all these ways the title of *Romantic Sobriety* remains generative, more an ongoing provocation about the meaning of criticism, about and influenced by Romanticism, than any totalizing historical, or philosophical, conception. Whether we can't help losing our sobriety; whether we can't help being sober; whether we can't help being Romantic—these and a host of attendant questions permutate exponentially within the term, held together and unbound at once. Wherever we are led by such transformations—*whether* we are led—this book begins an accounting of such a flight.

PART ONE

# *Periodicity*

The two chapters in part I are introductory in a way that both supports and troubles much of what follows them. They examine the rhetorical dimensions of historical periodization, how representational aspects of language allow us to consider Romanticism as a historical period. A study of this topos not only illuminates Romanticism as a historical entity but also characterizes that history in its impossible founding as indelibly Romantic. Chapter 1 studies a variety of British and Continental Romantic writers, including Wordsworth and Coleridge, to see how the trope of Romantic sobriety organizes aesthetic and ideological distinctions both within and beyond the Romantic period. But the mode of that study also becomes the problematic object of the chapter's own inquiry, insofar as the realization of Romantic periodicity is structured by both a sober suspicion of Romanticism's seductive mystifications and, simultaneously, a critical bad faith inherent in any attempt to realize the sober knowledge of Romanticism, historical or otherwise, in a positive manner. Or, at the very least, these are the consequences modeled for us in texts by Hazlitt and Coleridge that help compose our present understanding of Romanticism. Arguably, the chapter's influence on the rest of the book resides not so much in its historical cataloguing of figures of Romantic sobriety as in its inscription of the unstable energies of figuration that exemplify the trope of sobriety, and that then appear in a variety of formulations throughout the book. In that sense the relation of chapter 1 to both the book's title and the other chapters is metonymic rather than metaphoric, one relay among a chain of articulations on the meaning of Romantic sobriety rather than the definitive expression of a central idea.

Chapter 2 reworks in a meta-historicist mode the aporetic claims about Romanticism in chapter 1 by elaborating how Romanticism underlies the exceptionality of all historical identities. The chapter does so by focusing on the tropological knotting of Romanticism, modernity, and Enlightenment, this final term denoting the event of philosophical and historical identity that Kant surprisingly dramatizes through the light of genius that appears in his third *Critique*. In doing so, Kant models for us a Romanticism that underwrites all our attempts at periodization, as the catachresis of historical thought that is as unavoidable as it is incredible, equally impossible to realize and to eliminate.

This reading of the *Critique* acts as the counterpoint to its own framing device, a consideration of how much the field of Romantic studies has been structured by forms of a critical sobriety signaled in chapter 1, the suspicions of both deconstruction and ideological critique, with the latter especially asserting the disappearance of Romanticism as a mystified historical designation. Sobriety is also present at another level of chapter 2's analysis, implicit in the very notion of Kantian Enlightenment, although in a manner paradoxically infused with the vertiginous play of light, a troping of phenomenal sensation that says less about that experience and more about the aporetic operations of figure. A dizzying Romantic sobriety can therefore stand for this less than sober tropological rendition of sensation-infused Enlightenment. It is thus cannily appropriate that this dynamic is played out in that part of the *Critique* most famous for vividly showing the hypervolatile dimensions of reason itself, the "Analytic of the Sublime." The question of how a Romantic sobriety and the sublime might overlap will inform my discussion of the sensation of meaning in chapter 5 and return with even more explicit force in chapter 7's study of Shelley's "Ode to the West Wind."

CHAPTER ONE

# Romantic Sobriety

> In the wonderment of this taxonomy, the thing we apprehend in one great leap, the thing that, by means of the fable, is demonstrated as the exotic charm of another system of thought, is the limitation of our own, the stark impossibility of *that*.
>
> —Michel Foucault, *The Order of Things*

Legitimation, as Jürgen Habermas has long argued, is at the heart of modernity, and the same applies to Romanticism.[1] The Renaissance is now denoted by the term *early modern* in part because of an ideological critique. Still, as a historical and cultural entity, the *early modern* retains the brute existence of the real; while the phrase does have its problems, especially when contrasted with non-Western notions of history, no one spends much time discussing whether it actually happened, much less whether it should have. In contrast, the study of Romanticism has always encountered debates about its periodicity, its reality, and its value—whether it is over and, if not, where it or its study is going. This distinct hermeneutic structure becomes part of what we consider in Romanticism and gives it a certain epistemological currency that is not yet exhausted even in the postmillennial age. Difficulties that are insistent yet evasive confront any attempt to image Romanticism in a new way, to return to its primal scenes and to allow, as in Los's creation of Urizen in *Milton*, a new figure to emerge.

Whether through images of opium, inebriating Hippocrene, hock and soda water, or even the crescent moon of Peter Bell, it is a commonplace to associate British Romantic literature with figures of delirium and psychotropic activity. This association has remained remarkably consistent, even as the study of Romanticism, like all literary fields, has undergone intense methodological and topical transformations, from Northrop Frye's imaging of Romantic creativity as the "vehicular form" of the "drunken boat" to various New Historicist, materialist, and language-oriented studies of Romantic addiction.[2] Yet running through a number of Romantic texts is a counterdiscourse of Romantic sobriety. Developing a taxonomy of sobriety, however, does not simply mean reconceiving the a priori and innate traits that define Romanticism as a cultural and historical abstraction. Such a reconceptualization merely replaces Romantic hysteria and drunkenness with the structural effect of sobriety, or of sobriety and intoxication combined. Rather than simply trade one monological view of Romanticism for another, which assumes progress toward the truth of Romanticism, this chapter reads the discourse of Romantic sobriety tropologically. In doing so, we emphasize how the literary and philosophical truth of Romanticism is always reified. We reflect on historical thought about Romanticism and thinking romantically about history.

When attached to a high Wordsworthian set of themes and concerns, the figure of Romantic sobriety reflexively showcases the normative material of British Romantic literary history, such as the division between the first and second generations of Romantics, and the sociohistorical spectrum of conservative, Reform, and revolutionary Anglo-European politics. Sobriety throws into relief the relation between such material and received constructions of Romanticism. It especially comments on recent historicisms that have moved away from associating Romanticism with only the French Revolution to subsuming it within such larger historical entities as that of the long eighteenth century. Historical identity, and non-identity, is what Romantic sobriety is about, even if it is not, in any a priori, ultimate sense, what Romanticism essentially is.

As is well known, the modern temperance movement did not gain momentum or visibility in Great Britain until the 1830s; studies of the various abstinence societies usually represent themselves as scholarly contributions to *Victorian* social history. Conversely, eighteenth-century England is typically associated with a culture of drink and excess, starting with the notorious gin craze of the 1730s and 1740s.[3] Joined together, these familiar historical narratives make a distinctly Romantic sobriety a superfluous, phantom event. Thus, attempting to periodize Romantic sobriety through the changing medical, political, and recreational habits of British society actually reproduces the problems of periodicity and of the event that mark Romanticism's own century-straddling identity.

More promisingly, historians have linked sobriety to Protestant ideology in its new role as supporter of nineteenth-century England's growing labor forces, a development that suggestively overlaps with Romantic-era reconstructions of the idea of "work." Reading *The Prelude* through the "self-authorizing power of professionalism," Clifford Siskin argues that it was largely through Romanticism that the concept of work "had to be rewritten from that which a true gentleman does not have to do, to the primary activity informing adult identity; the tales that tell of it and the features associated with it were altered to produce a myth of vocation. This was not just a work ethic, for it made work more than necessary: it made work desirable—and necessary for personal happiness."[4] Robert in *The Ruined Cottage* (1797–98), for example, is first described as an "industrious man/ sober and steady"; his fall from sober grace to dissolute inactivity allegorizes something close to Siskin's subject, the moral urgency of a universalizing laboring self-sobriety that motors the pathos of this particular Wordsworthian text (lines 120–21).[5] Indeed, we might use the sobriety of Robert's prelapsarian industrious self to gauge the complex circuitry of activity, inactivity, rest, waste, wandering, and hysteria that marks the actions of Robert, Margaret, and the other characters in the poem.[6] The exemplary lesson that the Wordsworthian poet draws from the Wordsworthian rural imaginary might be historically particularized as the story of sobriety, labor, and the Romantic self.

Given the purposes of this chapter, however, I want to turn to a work of Wordsworth's that connects sobriety, even more so than *The Ruined Cottage,* to the fundamentals of high Romantic self-realization. Again, history touches on this analysis, although in oblique, asymmetrical ways. Most immediately, perversely, and crucially, the now often-embattled clarifications of literary periodization remind us that the figure of sobriety traditionally asserts the *boundaries* of Romanticism. Witness Andrew Elfenbein's account, regarding one Victorian literary rite of passage, of how the "development away from a youthful, immature Byronic to a sober, adult 'Victorian' phase became one of the nineteenth century's master narratives, the *Bildungsroman* of the Victorian author."[7] Or there are the statements of Modernists like T. E. Hulme and others, who defined themselves against a sloppy, drunken, and immature Romantic excess by invoking a *Modern* literary ethos of poetic sobriety. As Hulme opined in his famous piece on Romanticism and classicism, the "awful result of Romanticism is that, accustomed to this strange light, you can never live without it. Its effect on you is that of a drug."[8] In both the Victorian and the Modern instances, breaking away from Romanticism's "strange light" includes the compulsive figural assertion of a sobriety that resonates with aesthetic, moral, and political implications, depending on what associated ideas are stressed in the anti-Romantic narrative. While these ideologemes might vary—ranging from tropes of hygiene to those of desire or of epistemological pathology—they are all incorporated in a narrative of teleological growth. For both Victorian and Modern subjects, a new cultural self-knowledge is won at the expense of a former Romantic self marked by error and delusion of the philosophical, aesthetic, or political kind. What has rarely been observed, however, is that this well-known critique of Romanticism, the progression toward a critical and moral sobriety, is precisely the narrative trope structuring one of the urtexts of high Romanticism, Wordsworth's "Tintern Abbey" (1798).

Readers of Romanticism have long recognized in its writings one elementary narrative, the recognition and overcoming, tentative or otherwise, of a temporal scission in either cultural or individual terms. Regardless of varying responses to this meta-story—from laudatory to skeptical to demystifying—"Tintern Abbey" stands in our critical habitus as one of the best-known monuments to the Romantic narrative drive. It conceives of this drive, moreover, in terms of a process of maturation toward adult sobriety. Unlike Robert, who *begins* in *The Ruined Cottage* in a state of industrious sober grace, Wordsworth's former childhood self is anything but a figure of corporeal abstinence or discipline. Haunted by the "sounding cataract" and perceiving the "colours" and "forms" of mountain and woods as an "appetite," this remembered younger self connects the state of childhood to one of sensory diversion, hallucination, and overload (Gill, 133; lines 76, 79–80). Of course, the present narrator recognizes his distance from that former epistemological state—the "coarser pleasures of my boyish days"—while also asserting the more profound relation he has attained between himself and mind and nature (line 73). Abstaining from, growing out of, the allurements of eye and ear, Wordsworth claims an imaginative knowledge that he can project onto sister Dorothy's own future development, the anticipated reconciliation of past and present selves that will occur when "these wild ecstacies shall be matured / Into a sober pleasure" (lines 138–39). From a coarse to a sober pleasure: that is the arc of the text that defines the high Romantic lyric and the high Romantic life. That the "mind is capable of being excited without the application of gross and violent stimulants"—that is the poetic experience that Wordsworth would create.[9]

Indeed, this high Romantic aesthetic of sobriety may well speak to the wraith-like, anorexic figures that also populate the Wordsworthian imaginary.[10] The poet's fascination with the Leech Gatherer and the Discharged Soldier might then be perceived as the affect of a hyperbolic sobriety, a flirtation with that zone of human life where moral and physical self-sufficiency blurs into corporeal annihilation. Wordsworth's well-known strategy of indulging in vicarious experience through poetic doubles would then be not simply a meditation on the liminal but also a scrupulous acting out of the logic of the normative that leads to the unknowable point of exchange where health and sobriety turn into stillness and death. Dorothy's sensory agitation in "Tintern Abbey" would then find its ultimate complement not in her anticipated adult sobriety but in William's anticipated diminishment, literalized as the still dead figure of the Lucy poems. As in Freud, sobriety's attainment brushes up against maturation as death.

Within the confines of a still-healthy Romantic sobriety, we can also say something about the politics of this trope. As familiar as my reference to Wordsworth's "Preface" and much of this reading of "Tintern Abbey" is, so too would be a rehearsal of all the complications and qualifications that color the supposed success of the poem's Romantic transcendence. Suffice it to say that since Geoffrey H. Hartman it has been difficult to see the poem's performative attainment of "abundant recompense" as *simply* a fully realized dialectical progression.[11] Especially relevant is how readings from the last several decades, which focus on the blockages and displacements of "Tintern Abbey," signal another intersection between Romantic sobriety and historical analysis. The context of the aversion to "gross and violent stimulants" in Wordsworth's "Preface"—the popularity of "sickly and stupid German Tragedies" in London—intimates the nationalist and antiurban associations of this analysis (599). More immediately, the well-known arc from "wild ecstacies" to "sober pleasure" comes to us politically embedded in the equally familiar 1980s return to history critiques of the poem, where the progress toward a sublime adult sobriety is more urgently the sign of William's apostasy from the Jacobin—or, more exactly, Girondin—sentiments of his youth, his fall into a more politically evasive Romantic ideology.[12] The high Romantic blend of sobriety and apostasy is by no means limited to "Tintern Abbey." For example, *The Prelude* recounts the imagination's liberation from the usurping tyranny of the eye, a story that very much connects sensory sobriety to Wordsworth's own perspective on historical and personal transformation. More apparent, although perhaps even more complex, is Coleridge's retroactive diagnosis of the Anglo-European spirit of the age in chapter 10 of the *Biographia Literaria* (1815), itself a precursor to Irving Babbitt's warning against the "vague emotional intoxications" of Romantic democracy:

> Now that the hand of providence has disciplined all Europe into sobriety, as men tame wild elephants, by alternate blows and caresses, now that Englishmen of all classes are restored to their old English notions and feelings, it will with difficulty be credited how great an influence was at that time possessed and exerted by the spirit of secret defamation (the too constant attendant on party zeal!) during the restless interim from 1793 to the commencement of the Addington administration, or the year before the truce of Amiens. For by the latter period the minds of the partizans, exhausted by excess of stimulation and

> humbled by mutual disappointment, had become languid. . . . The youthful enthusiasts who, flattered by the morning rainbow of the French revolution, had made a boast of *expatriating* their hopes and fears, now disciplined by the succeeding storms and sobered by increase of years, had been taught to prize and honor the spirit of nationality as the best safeguard of national independence, and this again as the absolute pre-requisite and necessary basis of popular rights.[13]

Unlike the ostensibly apolitical relation between mind and nature in "Tintern Abbey," the sober state attained in Coleridge's passage is an unassuming political moderation that can be opportunistically projected back into the 1790s to distinguish his early activism from the "excess of stimulation" of both Jacobin radicals and reactionary government agents. Like the sober economy of "abundant recompense" in "Tintern Abbey," however, the full passage purchases the "restored" subjectivity of "old English notions and feelings" at the cost of the historical nightmare just experienced by England and France. After this excess of civil conflict, the people have reached a "national unanimity unexampled . . . since the reign of Elizabeth," a collective self-sobriety equated with the political moderation that Coleridge claims he embodied even during the 1790s (189). Explicitly political and politically quietistic in its tale of moderation, explicitly apolitical and politically exploitative in its assertion of a Christian national imaginary transcending partisan politics, sobriety is troped as the historical force structuring the changing zeitgeist. Indeed, as the consequence of the disciplining "hand of providence" and the "tam[ing of] wild elephants," sobriety becomes the very condition of Christian civilization that Coleridge's fellow English have at once attained and regained.

While chastened British reactionaries participate in this script, Jacobin "youthful enthusiasts" tellingly conclude the paragraph's Burkean passage out of a state of nature that is intrinsically delusory as the revolution's "morning rainbow." Thus, like our contemporary interpretation of "Tintern Abbey," Coleridge's text ultimately narrativizes the realization of sobriety as the reversal of a Jacobin pathology, providing readers, as it were, with the hermeneutic code—or, more precisely, with its mirror opposite—that has made the "historicization" of Romanticism formally intelligible since the 1980s.

This totalizing homology between Romantic sobriety and Romantic ideology needs qualification, however. Following Alan Richardson, one might suggestively distinguish the first generation of high Romantics from the second by arguing that the former were especially taken with the topos of "childhood," whereas the latter were more specifically, in both the textual and the psychobiographical senses, inscribed in the topos of "youth."[14] Because of the supposedly discrete identity of childhood, the move from childhood to adulthood has a fairly stable narrative structure, particularly when compared with the more indeterminate moment of youth, defined by the adolescent blurring of innocence and experience, latency and sexuality, immaturity and maturity. Consequently, childhood invites its retrospective qualification, celebration, and critique, whereas youth presents itself and its indeterminacies as an immanent condition, eschewing the possibility of youth's abandonment or dialectical rejection. As Julie A. Carlson points out, the biographical trope by which we know the second generation is in fact this condition of non-progression: the perception that such poets "did not live to regret their youths" (597). Thus, insofar as Romantic sobriety seems tied to the recognition and rejection of a prior state of sensory delusion, this more ascetic mode of narrative intelligibility is arguably the provenance of such first-generation figures as Wordsworth and Coleridge, rather than of a Keats self-realized by the youthful articulation of his senses and his belief in negative capability. The failure of the "story of progress" in *Hyperion*, the thwarted evolution of the "crudest sensory manifestation . . . into an autonomous, embodied subject," might be read in this light.[15]

William Blake problematizes these distinctions in ways that limit not only their efficacy but also the unity of the first generation's attainment of adult sobriety and its retroactive disavowal of French revolutionary politics. For in emphasizing the innocence of the child, Blake calls into question the nature of the progress into experience. Sobriety for him comes first, and far from a politically conservative advocacy, he describes mature creative wisdom as the state of being "drunk with intellectual vision."[16] There is also a measure of tropic drift in other first-generation usages of childhood, for example, the degree to which the incoherencies of youth underwrite the figure of Wordsworthian childhood: the displaced mingling in "Tintern Abbey" of latency and sexuality in Dorothy's "wild eyes" or, more to the point, the reduction of childhood to a mere figure for a literally older Girondin Wordsworth. The mature attainment of sobriety is a papering over of the fracture between childhood and youth that exists not simply between the first and second generations of Romantics but also within the dynamics of childhood that drive the ostensibly more secure dialectical progressions of the first generation. It signals the virtual presence of what sobriety endeavors to deny, the blurring of childhood and youth, of progress and blockage, what resists the narrative intelligibility circumscribing and consolidating the first generation's identity.

The question of stabilizing a particular narrative meaning also arises at the level of Romantic sobriety's specific ideological nature. Fissures in that identity emerge when the paradigm of a politically conservative sobriety is contrasted with statements that historically frame and support the more "central" texts of high Romanticism and that are contemporaneous with or later than those of the first-generation Romantics. For instance, in an 1812 letter to William Godwin, Percy Shelley writes that he hoped "in the course of our communication to acquire that sobriety of spirit which is the characteristic of true heroism."[17] Immediately referring to a balance between intellectual self-confidence and an openness to critique, Shelley's "sobriety of spirit" also invariably associates itself with the figure of Godwin and, by extension, with the older writer's Enlightenment-inflected, politically progressive philosophy. Indeed, decades before Shelley's letter, Godwin himself uses sobriety to contrast successful, non-violent social change with the "inflamed" feelings of disappointment and betrayal among reformers that cause violent revolution: "Revolutions are the produce of passion, not of sober and tranquil reason."[18] Thus, like the reactionary narrative of political maturation, Godwin also associates revolution with an excitable, immoderate state; yet he *also* connects the process of sobriety with the radical potential of Enlightenment reason, whose enactment governments can either help or hinder: "Man is in a state of perpetual mutation. He must grow either better or worse, either correct his habits or confirm them. The government under which we are placed must either increase our passions and prejudices by fanning the flame, or, by gradually discouraging, tend to extirpate them" (253). Explicitly warning government to wean its people off a Burkean addiction to "prejudice" and "habit," Godwin's own rational anarchist concept of perfectibility is itself a narrative of sober maturation.

Similarly, but in a perhaps even more direct and startling fashion, a statement by the French radical Louis de Saint-Just reflects how the political connotations of sobriety expand beyond exclusively conservative, counterrevolutionary meanings. Saint-Just's topic is what constitutes the perfect citizen of the French Revolution: "A revolutionary man is inflexible, but sensible; he is frugal; he is simple, but does not display the luxury of false modesty; he is the irreconcilable enemy of all lies, all affectation. A revolutionary man is honorable, he is sober, but not mawkish, out of frankness and because he is at peace with himself; he believes that grossness is a mark of deception and remorse, and that it disguises falseness under exuberance."[19] Here sobriety helps describe a national masculine identity based on a set of related oppositions: between truth and deception, modesty and excess, self-possession and self-affectation. David Simpson has identified these very oppositions as justifications for the Romantic self-interpellation of a British culture of common sense and experiential directness over and against a French subjectivity of deluded Enlightenment revolutionary theory.[20] But Saint-Just startles us, of course, because the sober virtues of his "revolutionary man" mimic exactly those celebrated by the "sensible" *English* in their fantasized, self-validating negation of French alterity. Both the British nationalist and the French revolutionary, it seems, just say no.

While sobriety thus helps both to demarcate and blur national difference, it organizes the fractures in British domestic politics as well. Reflexively representing the constitutionalist Reform movement, Samuel Bamford delivers this account of the preparations for the 1819 Peterloo demonstration: "It was deemed expedient that this meeting should be as morally effective as possible, and that it should exhibit a spectacle such as had never been witnessed in England. We had frequently been taunted in the press with our ragged, dirty appearance . . . with the confusion of our proceedings, and the mob-like crowds in which our numbers were mustered. . . . 'Cleanliness,' 'sobriety,' 'order,' were the first injunctions issued by the committee, to which . . . was subsequently added that of 'peace.'"[21] Like many in the Reform movement, Bamford knew that those involved in Reform activities were depicted as a drunken mob; the movement was also associated with revolutionary France, whose "Temples of Reason were brothels" from an anti-Jacobin, and anti-Reform, point of view (Thompson, 741). Thus, British Reformers and Radicals were themselves invested in a self-constituting rhetoric of sobriety, supported by the articulation of artisan identity with sober labor and by postwar calls in the 1810s for abstinence from taxed items, such as beer, that would "feed the Maggots of Corruption."[22] For E. P. Thompson, in fact, "moral sobriety was . . . demonstrably a product of the Radical and rationalist agitation itself; and owed much to the old Dissenting and Jacobin traditions" (740).[23] In many ways anticipating the symbolic antagonisms that support Simpson's study, Thompson's words point toward a Romantic sobriety that actively structures a political troping of both national identity and difference that preempts any simple, hegemonic perception of sobriety as a sign of Wordsworth's and Coleridge's first-generation political revisionism.

Such first-generation writers are also not the only ones interested in narrating the attainment of sobriety. Shelley writes to Godwin that he explicitly hopes "to acquire that sobriety of spirit which is the characteristic of true heroism." In doing so, Shelley's letter self-consciously plays off the first-generation structure of conservative revisionism: "Southey the Poet whose principles were pure & elevated once, is now servile champion of every abuse and absurdity. . . . He says

'You will think as I do when you are as old.' I do not feel the least disposition to be Mr. S's proselyte" (160). Shelley's anticipation of a sober maturation under the guidance of Godwin is thus simultaneously the narrative double and the ideological opposite of Southey's self-perceived acquisition of social wisdom. In seeking an adult, heroic sobriety, Shelley himself, like Southey, narrativizes the attainment of political knowledge; in rejecting Southey's prophecy, however, he transforms the content of that narrative into the ideological opposite of Southey's beliefs. He thereby distinguishes his realization of social merit from Southey's in one important way. Contrary to the division detected by contemporary scholars between first-generation revisionism and second-generation narrative indeterminacy, Shelley's desire for sobriety asserts a topos that does not regret its youth; rather, the attainment of sobriety is in proleptic continuity with an earlier self, the very self writing Shelley's piece. The letter to Godwin both acknowledges and resists the conservative, revisionist attainment of social and cultural sobriety. For Shelley, you can be sober and still young.

Wordsworth's poetic growth away from sensory diversion and epistemological error also surprisingly echoes Mary Wollstonecraft's Enlightenment-inspired, English radical argument for the reasons behind the uneven development of girls and boys in British society. In an even more explicit and complex manner than Godwin, Wollstonecraft resembles Wordsworth in terms of not only maintaining a teleology of sobriety but also building it around the image of an early, youthful self deluded by error. For Wollstonecraft, this schema most vividly occurs when she demonstrates how boys are allowed to indulge in the negativity of their passions and thus outgrow them, while Albion's infantilized daughters are never permitted such bodily and mental maturation: "One reason why men have superior judgement and more fortitude than women, is undoubtedly this, that they give a freer scope to the grand passions, and by more frequently going astray enlarge their minds. If then by the exercise of their own reason they fix on some stable principle, they have probably to thank the force of their passions, nourished by *false* views of life, and permitted to overleap the boundary that secures content."[24] I argue elsewhere that this diachronic narrative, geared toward the English middle-class radical attainment of Christian reason, is placed by the language of *A Vindication of the Rights of Women* (1792) in a radically indeterminate relation with a synchronic model in which the blurred borders between passion and reason, and error and truth, disable any immediately transparent, teleological progression (*Fantastic*, 134–40). Here I want to consider instead the consequences of viewing Wollstonecraft's diachronic narrative as an uncanny structural doppelgänger for the 1980s historicist versions of Wordsworth's teleological arc toward a poetic and ideological sobriety.

There are, of course, differences. Wollstonecraft's telos of Enlightenment reason is precisely the state of error that Wordsworth's Jacobin child must leave behind. Still, both narratives chronicle the gaining of wisdom after a period of excess and delusion, figured either corporeally, mentally, or spiritually. Perhaps more problematically, the latter stage of reason in Wollstonecraft *depends* on the initial, genetic force of "going astray." The interdependence between the two stages is radicalized in Wollstonecraft's very next words, the Pisgah vision of chapter 5, where the complex, overlapping relations between reason and passion are most visibly worked out. The vision in fact begins with Wollstonectaft hypothetically summoning the clarity of mental analysis that elsewhere in the book marks the telos of reason, a faculty she describes as "soberly survey[ing] the scenes before as in perspective, and see[ing] everything in its true colors" (110). The vision ends with Wollstonecraft descending from her sober view into the "lying dreams" of passion, accepting the negativity of the latter as the genuine vantage point for political praxis (112). From one angle, Wollstonecraft's vision admirably critiques her own political theory and its assumptions about the progressive attainment of political knowledge.[25] Rather than gain the sobriety of reason, she falls into the negative epistemology of the passions, which she nevertheless embraces as a necessary condition for political and critical thought. Beginning with sober reason and concluding with passion, Wollstonecraft's vision reverses the teleological framework of her statement about the advantages that men have over women. The reversal is so jarring as to suggest a limit to the very concept of a progressive teleology in *The Rights of Women*; it implies instead a more complex predicament, in which the negativity of passion and the sobriety of reason coexist.

Yet their simultaneity is made intelligible by an explicitly linear passage from a mistaken trust in sensory perception, "soberly survey[ing] . . . and see[ing] everything in its true colors," to an acknowledgment of the partial sight of the passions. If Wollstonecraft's vision allegorizes the instability of progressive teleologies and the indeterminate relation between passion and reason, it does so through the movement from the delusion of clarity to the truth of limited sight. The Pisgah vision is thus structured around *two* moments of sobriety. The sobriety of reason, which is linked to the activity of confidently "survey[ing]" things as they really are, begins the narrative. This confidence is then implicitly superseded by another sobriety, reason's self-critique, the figurative action of giving up the falsehood of sensory clarity for the more genuine, limited epistemology of passion. Like the sober maturity in Wollstonecraft's earlier, less complicated passage, this second sobriety is defined by its movement away from an initial state of delusion—in this case, the delusion of sensory clarity. This is the very figure that underlines the anti-Jacobin troping of sobriety in the Wordsworthian *Lebenswelt.*

It is worth recalling that both Wordsworth and Coleridge are unable to maintain an absolutely clear distinction between youthful error and mature sobriety in their own writings. In the *Biographia* the "excess of stimulation" of the late 1780s and the 1790s induces in the minds of erstwhile partisans a mental languor that *positively* makes them forget their volatile past divisiveness and encourages their openness to the new "national unanimity" that Coleridge records. Wordsworth's disavowal of his youth's "coarser pleasures" also does not diminish the compulsive energies of the middle of "Tintern Abbey," in which the descriptive memories of childhood erupt with an obsessive force equaling the sensory passion of his former self. Thus, in two contradictory ways the interdependence between passion and reason in Wollstonecraft brings her narrative of sobriety closer to Coleridge's and Wordsworth's. First, a diachronic model disavowing the deluded promises of sight can be retrieved from Wollstonecraft's synchronic destabilization of her Pisgah vision. Second, this synchronic derealization paradoxically highlights what the tension between childhood and youth already shows, and what has often been said about the arc toward a conservative Romantic maturity: the borders between past and present selves in Coleridge and Wordsworth also often blur, and the teleological rendering of a soberly realized self is also always already the occasion, submerged or otherwise, for a temporal questioning of that self's professed independence from an earlier life.

What should we make of all the figural echoes of sobriety across the span of Romanticism's political imaginary? There are two basic options. We can conclude that the trope was historically a violently unfixed term, with opposing parties struggling over its ideological meaning, or we can see sobriety providing a set of shared, if complex, formal and rhetorical patterns that consolidate the terms of struggle. In one case, sobriety is an empty vessel for the clashing political and cultural meanings of Romanticism's social history; in the other, it formally delimits the interpretive options that make its cultural signs intelligible and becomes the ultimate meaning of that social history. This is therefore not a choice between non-meaning and meaning; both readings depend on a conceptual abstraction, the differing signifieds of their critical orientations: either, in the second case, something called Romantic sobriety or, in the first, something delineated by the *Romantic ideological spectrum.* From a historicist's viewpoint, accepting either the formalist troping of sobriety as a historical referent or the Romantic ideological spectrum as a conceptual abstraction presents difficulties. What needs special attention, then, is how fundamentally impossible it might be for us to decide which choice presents less trouble for historical thought, although, paradoxically, we make that choice all the time.

There is one possible objection to this predicament: the impossible choice between history and tropology is based on its own recent historical reifications, the 1980s historicist narratives of Wordsworthian apostasy that mediate contemporary political knowledge of the Romantics. The paradox of thought involved in the specular doublings of Jacobin and anti-Jacobin sobriety would then resolve itself through a more capacious view of history, absorbing Wordsworth's and Wollstonecraft's, if not Saint-Just's, rhetoric into a larger, more complex historical formation of, for example, eighteenth-century civic republicanism, where sobriety would be part of a number of political virtues that included modesty, simplicity, labor, and thrift.[26] Similarly, in his lecture "On the Living Poets" (1818) William Hazlitt ponders the Lake School's commitment to simplicity and aversion to artifice in a cultural formula that denudes the shock of Wordsworth's and Saint-Just's shared language. Crucially, Hazlitt does so in the historical service of what will come to be known as Romantic rupture, not Pocock-inspired continuity:

> The change in the belles-lettres was as complete, and to many persons as startling, as the change in politics, with which it went hand in hand. There was a mighty ferment in the heads of statesmen and poets, kings and people. According to the prevailing notions, all was to be natural and new. Nothing that was established was to be tolerated. . . . Authority and fashion, elegance or arrangement, were hooted out of countenance, as pedantry and prejudice. Every one did that which was good in his own eyes. The object was to reduce all things to an absolute level; and a singularly affected and outrageous simplicity prevailed in dress and manners, in style and sentiment. A striking effect produced where it was least expected, something new and original, no matter whether good, bad, or indifferent, whether mean or lofty, extravagant, or childish, was all that was aimed at. . . . The licentiousness grew extreme. . . . The world was to be turned topsy-turvy.[27]

Hazlitt's essay is fascinating, not the least because of its mixture of "simplicity" and "licentiousness" and its account of sobriety-linked traits that is given in a tone of vertigo. For Hazlitt, Great Britain's "native writers [adopt] a wonderful simplicity" that, paradoxically, is part of a time of revolutionary excess (5:162). The context of this zeitgeist is thus prior to any revisionist maturation; it is a time when the “new and original” might mean the “lofty, extravagant, or childish.” Indeed, with the image of a “singularly affected and outrageous simplicity” Hazlitt holds out the possibility of a stylized Puritanical sobriety that is more simulation than virtue, more in tune with a cultural “topsy-turvy” psychedelia than opposed to its regnant forms.

Most important, however, is the explicit historical narrative that organizes Hazlitt’s description and that he will apply specifically to Wordsworth seven years later in *The Spirit of the Age* (1825). Both analyses depend on a narrative *coupure*; they dwell not on prior historical determinations but on a perception of romantically beginning “*de novo*, on a *tabula rasa* of poetry” and, by extension, of history (11:87). Such a historical context, with its revolutionary mingling of sobriety and delirium, reasserts the origins of Lake School poetics “in the French revolution, or rather in those sentiments and opinions which produced that revolution; and which sentiments and opinions were indirectly imported into this country in translations from the German about that period. . . . [Our poetical literature] wanted something to stir it up, and it found that something in the principles and events of the French revolution” (5:161). Of course, the Wordsworth produced in “On the Living Poets” and *The Spirit of the Age* is also the *pre*-1980s Romanticist historicist Wordsworth, whose early high Romantic works espouse rather than betray the populist leveling effect of the Revolution. Thus, in his sociology Hazlitt, like the long-eighteenth-century view of Wordsworth and Wordsworth’s ostensive civic republicanism, circumscribes and contains the implied volatility of the ideas and figures that collide in Wordsworth’s and Saint-Just’s sober language. He does so, however, by conceiving of a historical identity at odds with the formal properties of continuity that inhere in the larger historical formation of civic republicanism: a historical identity of populist and aesthetic revolution, whose subtending similarities are the structural symptoms of intense political and cultural change.

It would be a mistake to assume that the juxtaposition of the two historical identities implies a simple, formalist relativization of these contrasting perceptions of Wordsworthian—and, by extension, Romantic—politics. Doing so would involve the historicist’s, or the theorist’s, own linguistic reification of the choice between history and tropology. The point is instead to recognize the inevitable interference of formalist properties in the very procedures of distinguishing among these historical identities, the absence of recourse to a pure mode of historical thought that could simply and absolutely perform the adequation of historical material to the historical real—a rather formalist proposition at that. *Civic republicanism* and Hazlitt’s “spirit of the age” are each, at some point, as much a conceptual abstraction as the *Romantic ideological spectrum*. This does not mean that they do not exist or have consequences; indeed, Hazlitt's topos might very well connect to and comment on the articulations between Shelley's 1812 letter to Godwin and the Reform movement's own investment in a symbolic of sobriety.[28] But while *civic republicanism* and Hazlitt's "spirit of the age" may both qualify the asserted volatility of a *Romantic ideological spectrum*, one by absorbing differences and the other by abolishing them, they both also occasion at another level precisely the same question of the relation between their self-evidence and the evidence for their existence. Whether the figures of Romantic sobriety refer to them or they refer to this process of troping remains the predicament with which we began, the uneasy knowledge of the Romantic object, or event, that the Romanticist constantly and impossibly sidesteps. Paradoxically, the resolution of the aporia between the Romantic ideological spectrum and Romantic sobriety leads to this keener sense of the blockage underlying their relation.

The choice between history and tropology is thus not so much a concern as a prior, more exact opposition that collapses the boundaries between methodology and epistemology, as well as between the historical and the linguistic. These effects are symptomatic of the impossibility implicit in the problem of telling figure from content. After over forty years of post-structuralist discourse, the blockages of thought that accompany this old chestnut have the familiarity of *doxa* that are at once universally accepted and immediately bracketed. Yet benign critical neglect does not diminish what is in fact most challenging and valuable about attending to Romantic sobriety, first- or second-generation Romanticism, or Romanticism, for that matter. The historical problem of sobriety as the problem of the metaphor for the stability of metaphor, of the steady relation between figure and content, is what the circuit of ideology and figure in Romantic sobriety most forcefully and unevenly marks.[29] Insofar as understanding Romanticism means conceiving what Romanticism stands for and what stands in for Romanticism, the problem of Romantic sobriety also allegorizes what we consistently retrieve from Romanticism as an exemplary studied object that might yield the particulars of literary, cultural, and sociohistorical thought.

That this retrieval still seems to concern especially Romanticism merely indicates, in de Manian terms, a resistance to Romanticism by literary and cultural studies. There has been, for example, little or no awareness of how the subsumption of Romanticism by the long eighteenth century may well be an intensely Romantic proposition, as well as an intensely Romantic problem. This lack of awareness is only partly institutional, in the same way that the predicament of

Romantic sobriety is only partly historical, insofar as history is conceived separately from tropology. Chapter 2 will further explore the specific implications of this situation for the field of Romantic studies, by identifying Romanticism as the very problem of a *period* metaphor. We can lay the groundwork for that analysis by considering how, if Romantic sobriety highlights the radical dialectic between figure and content that defines the Romantic object, it also provides the register for differing responses to that dialectic. Two such responses are proleptically embedded in this chapter's concluding examples, two final primary Romantic texts.

The first is the conclusion to "On the Living Poets," which problematizes the sociology of the essay's Lake School section and the later "Mr. Wordsworth," in *The Spirit of the Age,* by complicating Hazlitt's affiliation with a pre-1980s Romanticist historicism. Hazlitt's lecture ends with a short meditation on Coleridge, a bittersweet estimation of a being whose failed genius comes to stand for the *full* spirit of the age, the compromised "progress of human happiness and liberty in bright and never-ending succession" (5:167). This estimation brilliantly ends with a citation of the "Intimations Ode" (1802–4), Wordsworth's own response to the lost possibilities of temporal existence, his affirmation of "what remains behind . . . the philosophic mind" (Gill, 302; lines 183–89). But Hazlitt's ironic point is that Coleridge's "philosophic mind" is not enough, that Wordsworth's temporal ameliorations and the "spell" of Coleridge's past voice do not overcome the nightmare of history. In Hazlitt's refusal to succumb completely to a Romantic past figured sensually as "never-dying sound" lies a critical sobriety that anticipates our own forty-odd years' resistance to the promises of high Romanticism (5:167). Hazlitt's sober intelligence assumes a stable clarity for Romanticism's figure and content, for what must be denied. This imperative to recognize, delimit, and disavow the Romantic object motivates not only Jerome J. McGann's 1980s exemplary demystifications of the Romantic ideology but also an earlier de Manian rigor ever vigilant against the professed plenitude—sensual and existential—of Romantic being and Romantic aesthetics. Both ideological critique and deconstruction reflect Hazlitt's desire for a cure from high Romanticism, as differing as that term may be for each critical plot.

The next chapter explores the force of that theoretical difference and its implications; chapters 4 and 5 also explore the inability of the literary critic Walter Benn Michaels to recognize this ascetic side to de Man. For now, I want to return to our second example of sobriety's reaction to the possibility of Romanticism, Coleridge's poem "To William Wordsworth" (1807), where we can identify a perhaps readily familiar de Manian dynamic. A poetic rendition of a literal moment of reader response, it dramatizes the power of what will come to be known as high Romanticism to change a life. Recording his response to Wordsworth's recitation of the growth of his individual mind, Coleridge positions himself as the first significant reader of *The Prelude.* As such, he provides future generations of Wordsworth students with a canonical reaction to the poem, and to Romanticism, a newly found resolution to swerve away from error and self-destruction: "That way no more!" (line 76).[30] Blending the rhetorical and the autobiographical, Coleridge's repentant hermeneutic reveals the structural assertion of a newly felt sobriety that, contrary to Hazlitt, is also a new Romantic life.

But the complexities of the Coleridgean symbolic exceed the parameters of this poetic education. There is, for example, the repetition of the paradigm in the *Biographia,* with its convoluted attempt to transform Wordsworth from mentor into philosophically vulnerable equal, and its own version of repentance and resolve that traces Coleridge's philosophical education from associationism to German critical thought, from Hartley to Kant.[31] Kant's usurpation of Wordsworth is not, however, a simple thing; indeed, its constitutive self-discontinuity emblematizes the oxymoronic qualities of anything that might be called Coleridgean action. For considered by way of Kant's well-known fastidiousness and abstention from excessive food or drink, Coleridge's reworking of "To William Wordsworth" into the *Biographia* is appropriate to the point of an overdetermination: what is then so striking about these two works is their similarity, where first the man of sober poetry and then the man of sober reason hold out to Coleridge the cure *of* high Romanticism.[32]

There could, of course, be quite a gap between the reasonableness of sobriety (*Nüchternheit*) and philosophical reason (*Vernunft*). But the relation between this gap and the unitary sense of Kant as a sober thinker might itself be a double for the one between the coherence of "reason" and "Kant" as unitary identities and the multiple meanings that both term and name emit in relation to the arc between eighteenth-century Enlightenment thought and Hegelian idealism. Kant's biographical abstinence and Wordsworth's poetic sobriety thus provide the uncanny hinge for a set of associations that at once overlap and contradict one another. Within this dynamic, Coleridge's high Romantic cure of Kantian logic, with its resonances of Enlightenment reason, could just as well be the invidious solution that Wordsworth's "sober pleasure," especially when inflected with its anti-Jacobin meanings, rejects.[33] Read back into "To William Wordsworth," this contradiction shows that the paradigmatic quality of the poem is its instability, the degree to which Coleridge is caught in a repetitive structure that does not even afford the security of repetition: the contrasting senses of sobriety and reason in Wordsworth and Kant become the conflicted material of Coleridge's high Romantic vow for a sober life.

Given that in various writings Coleridge parts ways with the severe dimensions of Kant's ethics, it might be said that an ascetic sobriety was precisely one of the portions of Kant's thought that Coleridge did not accept.[34] Yet the good faith behind such a philosophical disagreement exists alongside the larger senses of contradiction and irresolution that characterize the question of sobriety in what we understand by Coleridge's life. That the Coleridgean symbolic is not even intelligible without the repetition of the promise of sobriety, that "To William Wordsworth" is as much a poem about its non-finality as its vow, speaks to the wider set of meanings that inflect the poem's performance of reading, and realizing, high Romanticism. Because of that symbolic, this performance simultaneously entails the curtailment of its staying power, the immediate derealization of its conception and closure. If Kant's logical sobriety prevents him, at least in the *Critique of Pure Reason,* from proving the existence of God and the immortality of the soul, Coleridge's cannot stop him from exploring the "higher gift of reason," a mystical inebriation that entangles philosophy and faith.[35] If "To William Wordsworth" asserts Coleridge's vow for a sober life, it does so through the intoxication of a familiarly Romantic lyricism that reproduces Coleridge's own response to Wordsworth's poem: "My soul . . . now a tranquil sea, / Outspread and bright, yet swelling to the moon" (lines 96, 100–101). We would not know Coleridge otherwise.

Read along with De Quincey as the literal and figurative Romantic addict par excellence, *Coleridge* becomes the alchemical site where the Romantic profession of interpretive sobriety becomes the equally Romantic staging of bad faith epistemologically and ontologically embedded in any promise concerning the performative and constative effects of Romanticism's words and images. This bad faith has perhaps most strongly been understood through the issues of canon making and unmaking, but its conceptual force outpaces the historical clarity assumed in such projects. Sobriety's failure, keenly announced in sobriety's words, highlights the volatile interstice between knowing Romanticism and knowing romantically. Coleridge's Romantic sobriety is also at once the impossibility of sobriety and of Romanticism, high or otherwise, the unavoidable aporia between figure and content that conditions the reading of Romanticism's texts and narratives. That this impossibility is itself merely a figure is certainly the case. That it exists as much as the phantom figure of Romanticism is certainly part of the challenge of any truly sober reflection of and on the Romantic event. Indeed, as Marx and Engels famously write, uncannily echoing Hazlitt in his descriptive powers, if not simply in terms of the revolutionary *epistēmē* being analyzed, "All that is solid melts into air, all that is holy is profaned, and man is at last compelled to face with sober senses, his real conditions of life, and his relations with his kind."[36] What is our task today, but to reflect on the conditions and possibilities of such "sober senses," as we attempt to face our own terror-filled, vertiginous Romantic moment?

# Kant All Lit Up

## Romanticism, Periodicity, and the Catachresis of Genius

We might say that in deconstruction history is always posed as a question, at once urgent, ubiquitous, and insoluble, whereas ideological demystification conceives of its relation to history as an answer, a solution, to its critical hermeneutic. Certainly, this critical truism has special force in Romantic studies, a field very much shaped by the complex relation between deconstruction and ideological critique over the last forty years. But it could just as well be said that the full implications of this relation are especially clarified by the field of Romantic studies, not least because its object of study replays the tensions between these two modes of inquiry. Studying Romanticism means knowing it as a historical period but also knowing it as a figure that stands for something else: an aesthetic practice, a form of consciousness, a political aspiration, an ideology, the possibility of historicity itself. That as a figure Romanticism can be either transhistorical or tied to its historical identity makes its situation all the more complicated, and compelling. Romanticism especially dramatizes the interlocking relation between period identity and trope, and the investment of literary studies in that dynamic. In chapter 1's concluding reading of Coleridge, we used the figure of Romantic sobriety to elucidate the problem of Romanticism's identity, where the impossible task of steadfastly affirming the truth of Romanticism becomes a figure for the inescapably fantastic event of Romanticism itself. Here we can extend the paradoxical energies of that reading by reformulating the problem of realizing Romanticism as one specifically about conceptualizing historical periodicity and assert that Romanticism is the period metaphor that both stabilizes and disrupts the very concept of period metaphors.[1] The deconstruction and demystification of Romanticism is very much about the deconstruction and demystification of history, its existence as either question or calculation, trope or immanent being.

But even as Romanticism asserts its special relation to history, it must also confront an opposite trajectory, how its meaning is best understood through a constellation of other larger historical identities, such as the Enlightenment and modernity itself. We can, then, continue probing the relationship between Romanticism and the long eighteenth century begun by chapter 1, by considering how the potential disciplinary reorganization of Romanticism into the long eighteenth century becomes one vivid academic expression of the question, where does the historical specificity of Romanticism reside, within itself or something larger, or both?

Sorting this issue out is certainly a historical proposition, but as Romanticism's special relation to history reminds us, it is also, in Paul de Man's sense, rhetorical. Which is to say, Romanticism's relation to history is, paradoxically, *not* special—or, more precisely, it is a trope for something pervasive among all the period fields of literary studies, insofar as they remain particular and distinct from one another. This includes those historical entities that might subsume or entangle with Romanticism itself, that would enact historicity by absorbing a field so intent on both the enabling and worrying of historical thought. Approached tropologically, the relation of Romanticism to these larger historical periods is not simply about events and formations that constitute the boundaries of historical identities. It is also about best identifying and clarifying the workings of figure that create the intelligence of such periodicity.

Such labor, what de Man designated innocently enough by the term "reading," calls for its own crossing of a particular set of boundaries. A philosophical text, generated by the entanglement between Romanticism and the eighteenth-century Enlightenment, might contain sections exemplary in their recording of the interstice between trope and historical periodization. Immanuel Kant's short meditation on genius in the third *Critique* is, like the rest of his book, about the limits and possibilities of the judging subject; his words on genius are also specifically about the artistically creative subject. In resolving the contradictions between aesthetic judgment and creation, Kant transforms the solar light of human genius into the historical genius of the Enlightenment, which is very much the linguistic genius of Romanticism. In this reading the force of Kant's genius becomes the "strange light" of Romanticism opined by T. E. Hulme in the last chapter, the historicity of which we "can never do without," whose intractability is like the entrenched "effect of a drug" (127). This all occurs, however, in a register not of consciousness or of historical truth, but of something else before either's constative realization.

Kant's text is especially telling in its reflexive expression of this situation, so much so that it helps illuminate the sharp distinction between deconstruction and ideological demystification. For if deconstruction always poses history as the pressure of an insoluble, omnipresent question, it does so through figure, before truth. In contrast, ideological demystification, with its answers to the questions of history's meaning, always feels the gravitational pull toward truth and falsehood. Insofar as the relation between deconstruction and ideological critique in Romantic studies helps elucidate some of the intellectual circumstances behind the field's present engagement with the long eighteenth century, Kant's meditation on genius and its light clarifies one consequence of Romanticism's potential absorption by the larger historical identity, the extent to which that subsumption *cannot* happen, regardless of whether *Romanticism* the term survives. That subsumption will not happen if it is meant as the truth of a purely historical comprehension, because the historical in Romanticism is always something besides that act.

If, indeed, such a period reorganization was simply and purely to occur—that would indicate a disciplinary narrative tantamount to the conflation of deconstruction in Romantic studies with its leftist cousin. We could conceive of such a narrative fairly easily, one that in its own way would describe the arc of Romantic studies since the 1970s.[2] It would begin with Paul de Man's deconstructive readings of Wordsworth, Rousseau, and other Romantic writers, in which a number of themes associated with them, such as the power of symbol over allegory and the organic unity of mind and nature, were radically problematized. It would continue in the 1980s with Jerome McGann's ideological critique of such Romantic concepts and others, such as the celebration of Romantic genius, imagination, and transcendence of history. It would further continue into the 1990s, where with the especially added impetus of feminist concerns, such traditional Romantic terms are perceived to be not only ontologically but also, more importantly, ideologically suspect, limiting our understanding of both the history of Romantic writing and the social concerns of an array of authors other than the six major poets. Such a disciplinary narrative might also note how de Man's work stressed the ontological and epistemological bad faith of the Romantic topos; the social consequences of such a focus implicitly hovered around his arguments but remained elliptical and open-ended. In contrast, the work of McGann and others stressed articulating those ideological consequences as precisely and completely as possible.

Acknowledging the bad faith of the Romantic topos was a means to securing the ends of this more sociohistorical inquiry. It was also a bad faith that was calculable. Using a de Manian distinction, we might say that McGann's Romantic ideology expressed the intelligibility of a mistake, as opposed to the more complicated deconstructive condition that de Man called error. For many since then, it might be observed, this distinction has, for the most part, disappeared: we understand the deconstruction of the Romantic topos to be basically the demystification of the Romantic ideology; deconstruction is a means toward exposing and rectifying an ideological mistake.

It could also be noted that de Man's deconstruction of Romanticism was more precisely a critique of the conception of Romanticism that was held by such twentieth-century scholars as M. H. Abrams and Earl Wasserman. In arguing with these critics, de Man's proof was the work of the Romantic writers themselves. The 1970s deconstruction of Romanticism was never a simple dismissal of Romanticism; indeed, in much of de Man's work there exists the desire not only to question but also to preserve, in no matter how vexed a historical or linguistic form, something called *Romanticism*.[3] McGann also argued that Romantic-era writings could many times provide the best critiques of the Romantic ideology that was also found in such works and later generations of Romantic readers. But if McGann, like de Man, also keenly engaged with twentieth-century Romanticists such as M. H. Abrams, the larger consequence of McGann's scholarship and other sociohistorical work following him was to equate the Romantic period with the Romantic ideology. This would lead to the main point of the disciplinary narrative, that, consequently, the demystification of Romanticism has always implied, even more so than deconstruction, the dissolution of Romanticism, into a multiplicity of Romantic ideologies or some new historical identity altogether. Until the rise of the long nineteenth century, the most visible candidate for this new identity was, of course, the long eighteenth century.[4] The transformation in Romantic studies of deconstruction into demystification would thus converge with the dissolution of Romanticism as an ideological and historical entity, as well as the absorption of its writers and texts by the larger, historically more capacious field.

The first part of this short account needs major qualification, insofar as it overlooks the continuing number of Romanticist scholars who have in fact combined historicist and deconstructive work, while staying keenly aware of their difference. (To the degree that critics assume deconstruction to *serve* a historicist inquiry, of course, the opposite is true.) Likewise, the first part minimizes how much critics understand ideology as something more complicated than a mistake or falsehood, the rectifiable condition of false consciousness.[5] Still, the transformation in Romantic studies of deconstruction into demystification has a certain persuasiveness, not least because of its exemplary nature as an allegory for *all* literary studies since the 1970s, as it retells how the deconstruction of literature evolves, or falls, into the sociohistorical study of literature and culture. And, as a 1990s Blackwell anthology of Romantic criticism illustrates, there are institutionalized accounts of the field that very much allegorize its return to history through the marginalization of deconstruction in the study of Romanticism.[6] Yet the instructive value of the disciplinary narrative really inheres in its second part, in the putative convergence between the appearance of the long eighteenth century and the conflation of deconstruction with demystification. For if that convergence is true, deconstruction should have nothing to say about the proposition of the long eighteenth century, something that Romanticists will confront as simply an issue of history, and not of figure, regardless of how much the long eighteenth century might now find itself superseded by the long nineteenth century in Romantic studies. Not surprisingly, the situation turns out to be more complicated than that.

Of course, there are no "simple" issues of history, with or without figure. The reasons for the possible reorganization of Romanticism into the long eighteenth century were many and complex, and they had as much to do with limited resources for the study of literature in a global economy as the research of scholars in either field. The consequences of this reperiodization are equally many, not the least being the professional question of how best to train and prepare students to work in a field that is, at a number of levels, being transformed. At the same time those students and their teachers have, through the perspective of the long eighteenth century, been given the opportunity to rethink and reconfigure a number of issues: the concerns and literary styles of late eighteenth-century female authors, the ongoing presence in British Romantic culture of earlier social formations, such as Pocock's civic republicanism, and the connection between Romantic writing and the larger global history of the British empire, to name a few. The study of Romanticism continues to confront all these issues, and it is safe to say that the field will be dealing with them for some time.[7]

The politics of such a study become especially complex. For if the demystification of Romanticism conceives of its relation to history as an answer, the shorthand name for that solution for much of the 1980s and 1990s was the French Revolution, the key term for understanding the domestic and foreign concerns, the social texture, of especially British Romantic writing and culture. Playing off this view of McGann and others, Alan Liu did complicate the Revolution as ultimate referent through a French revisionist historiography that made the Revolution the sign of indeterminacy between culture and text (138–63).[8] Still, the Revolution was a weighty presence in the field, in many ways the organizing principle behind it. It still is today a central tenet in late eighteenth- and early nineteenth-century studies. But the equivalence between the Revolution and the Romantic period, the way in which one acted as a sign for the other, is not as dominant as it once was in our historiography.[9] The Revolution is now being contextualized as part of a larger set of sociohistorical processes; instead of viewing it as a primal scene inaugurating a new Romantic spirit of the age, we are now beginning to consider it and its effects on Great Britain in continuity with a number of social formations already at work in British history. As much as this recontextualization has engendered attempts to expand Romanticism's historical boundaries, other historical formations, such as the long eighteenth century, have also been proposed as a replacement for the Romantic period.[10] This is one answer to the critical hermeneutic implicit in the demystification of Romanticism: a more complex and capacious historical identity that explains the culture and society of late eighteenth- and early nineteenth-century England better than Romanticism itself.

Coincidentally, a certain *Jacobin* disposition underpinning the work of McGann and others has become less dominant as the French Revolution has been absorbed by the long eighteenth century's larger historical span. While in part the welcome consequence of the broadening and deepening of political issues involving this larger historical period, this occurrence has also meant a certain dilution of one normative assumption of the earlier historicist work, the equivalence between the critical activities of historicization and politicization that characterized the late twentieth-century Romanticist scholar as both Revolutionary sympathizer and contemporary oppositional critic.[11] Ironically, the dissolution of the Romantic ideology has affected the political assumptions behind the demystifying goals of the 1980s ideological critique, since the long eighteenth century, for example, is at once more socially complex and historically distant, insofar as the study of this period is no longer so intensely structured by the question of our own political connection to the Revolution, of whether in our present that seminal event is ongoing or indeed "over."[12] The long eighteenth century is oddly more global, more nominalist, and less totalizing than the more concentrated Romantic period.

This is also the case at least in part because of one way that both Romanticism and the eighteenth century currently register the volatility of modernity. This concept has always been violent because, like Romanticism, the historicity of modernity is both a figure and a period. Indeed, I explore elsewhere how modernity is the very trope of historical difference, a condition that actually enables history through its fantastic, or tropological, character (*Fantastic*, 3–4). But, of course, modernity is also preeminently Enlightenment modernity, the far-reaching period term that in many ways enables Romanticism's historical coordination with the long eighteenth century. What needs particular remarking is how this period term has increasingly grown in complexity and contradiction; *as* a period term Enlightenment modernity has come to stand for a history that is radically nominalist, multiple, and untotalizable. As *simply* a period it now already is volatile. The dispersion of the Romantic ideology into many Romantic ideologies, and into such new historical formations as the long eighteenth century; the dissolution of the political role of today's oppositional critic as simply Jacobin opponent to the Romantic ideology—all these events reflect this new historical understanding of modernity itself.

It would be tempting to see this historical situation in all its radical indeterminancy as the convergence of tropology and periodicity, of deconstruction and ideological critique, of, in fact, the boundaries between Romanticism and Enlightenment modernity. To some degree this is true. But as powerful a model as this situation is, it and its attendant historical knowledge also operate in a different valence than the concept of Romanticism as both simultaneously period and trope. Enlightenment modernity is the historical period that in its complexity resists the uniformity, the very identity, of periodicity. Romanticism is the period metaphor that as a trope makes history into something besides simply history. This distinction is crucial. It is also, paradoxically, highly problematic.

The difference is problematic not simply because Romanticism, as a historical period under reorganization, functions within the historical multiplicity of Enlightenment modernity. The difference is also problematic to the extent that Enlightenment modernity, for all its radically nominalist historicity, still at some level coheres around the figure, or figures, of a particular identity. For that is what especially marks the tropological character of Romanticism: not simply, as one might suspect, the decomposition of sign and meaning, but, more vertiginously, the performance of sign and meaning at the simultaneous moment of decomposition. Romanticism is historical because it is figural, because it *stands* for something, because it insists on the metonymic relays of signification, prescription, and description. Romanticism is the trope of a fantastic modernity as well as a period term. Enlightenment modernity is that fantastic trope as well, which means that it, like all historical periods, no matter how complex or indeterminate, is also a Romantic proposition.

Romanticism is the figure of our investment in history, of history as a cathexis. As Marc Redfield keenly observes, this explains in part how overdetermined the disciplinary title of McGann's seminal work is, why it had to be about the Romantic, and not the eighteenth-century or Victorian or Modern, ideology, even though similar ideological critiques occur in those and other numerous literary fields (149).[13] Romanticism's strange status also explains why, paradoxically, debates about its historicity *are* ideological, why, as I observed in the previous chapter, we argue about not only whether Romanticism did happen but also whether it should have happened, whether, politically or ethically, we should consider it to have happened.[14] The extent to which a historically objective position cannot make sense of these propositions is the degree to which the operations of figure underwrite the assumptions of historicity embedded in Romanticism's ideological critique. Romanticism is the trope of a particular identity, and value, in history.[15]

Conversely, if Romanticism can indeed be simply folded back into the long eighteenth century of a non-totalizing Enlightenment modernity, if deconstruction now, like demystification, simply serves the goal of historical comprehension, this peculiar dimension to Romanticism will likewise disappear, as it will have only been a specific sociohistorical condition of Romanticism's own study. If this is not the case, however, the study of figure should have something to say about the period reorganization. Certainly, the question of Romanticism's relation to what came before it—the Enlightenment, the eighteenth century, long or otherwise—is fraught and unwieldy, already in only historical terms. In terms of figure the challenge is no less complex. But such a study can begin to formulate its own grounds of inquiry by recognizing how much figure indelibly marks the period relation, not only Romanticism but also both other terms—*modernity*, certainly, but also the *Enlightenment*, in an especially manifest, almost awkwardly obvious way, in English at least. The Enlightenment is the period of light, the act of light on, and as, a period.

To move away from Enlightenment modernity toward a discussion of Romanticism and the Enlightenment is already a troping of sorts. But while within historical terms this abstraction might too easily simplify the problem of the larger, more complex field, as a move about rhetoric it has the merit of providing a point of entry for an analysis fundamentally contrary, but also inextricably linked, to the historicist approach. Certainly the topos of Enlightenment is rich in ideological and sociohistorical meaning.[16] But *as* a topos, it also vehemently demonstrates the logic of manifest meaning itself, of the enactment of ontological and epistemological clarity that defines the agency of Enlightenment as both human consciousness and historical era. Indeed, the enactment of that clarity is the very historical action of that era, a condition of knowledge that also models the clarifying force enabling all historical periodization. To understand that force both *as* and *through* figure is to approach the Enlightenment's historical nature as precisely a Romantic idea.

In a philosophic text appropriately famous for troubling the divide between Romanticism and the Enlightenment, the name for this enactment of manifest meaning is genius, a term long central to the study of the high Romantic subject, although now often dismissed as one idol of that same subject's ideological mystification. Exemplary in their precision, several short passages from Immanuel Kant's *Critique of Judgment* inscribe genius within the workings of sun and luminosity. In doing so, the *Critique* connects genius to light's phenomenal blending of identity and action. Genius implicitly becomes (the) Enlightenment, the predication of human cognition as a discernible human endeavor and collective historical event. The text's account of genius is not, however, philosophic, much less historic, or phenomenal, truth. What occurs *is* an illumination, nevertheless, something resistant to the simple dampening power of an ideological critique; if Romanticism is the trope for history's value, Kant clarifies the genius behind that trope.

> Must one consent in the end (or at the beginning) that the "consciousness" that pure reflection is, i.e., sensation, is unconscious like "nature"?
>
> —Jean François Lyotard, *Lessons on the Analytic of the Sublime*

Regardless of the previous chapter's distinction between Kantian *Nüchternheit* and *Vernunft*, we might respond to Lyotard with this formulation: the genius of the Enlightenment is the emergence of a calm, sober intelligence that is paradoxically figured through an overwhelming solar sensation, which tells us less about any phenomenal state than about the drive of figure itself. While one could certainly talk about the sober dimensions of Kant's definition of beauty—of the separation of beauty from the perceptually pleasing—within the context of this chapter our focus lies elsewhere. Fittingly, then, Kant's discussion of genius occurs within his thoughts on the sublime, whose machinations arguably constitute the Kantian candidate for yet another sense of Romantic sobriety, a dialectical show of reason both steady and dizzying at once. Chapter 7 will exploit this sense of the vertiginous in our own extraction of Shelley's revolutionary sublime from his "Ode to the West Wind," which is characterized especially by the poem's sober attempt to perform a historical intelligence ultimately independent of phenomenal experience. The concluding section to the present chapter will likewise recall the sublime's encounter with dizzying infinite thought, as well as its oftentimes antagonistic relation to the senses, insofar as Kant's examples of genius are beholden neither to the phenomenal world nor to the mind, but to the luminous violence of language. But we begin in this section with another dimension of the problematic of the sublime (and the beautiful) in Kant, the dilemma of human art, which frames the question of how exactly the notion of genius fits into the third *Critique*.

Coming late in the first part of Kant's work, in the discussion of aesthetic judgment, the five short sections on genius do not seem central to the thinker's overarching argument. Then again, the structure of that argument is notoriously difficult to identify, especially with regard to resolving how different portions of Kant's book relate to one another in terms of importance and argumentative development.[17] The third *Critique* invites us to ponder the meaning of its main split between aesthetic and teleological judgment, as well as the significance of the divisions in aesthetic judgment between the beautiful and the sublime and nature and art. Much critical and narrative energy has been spent explaining the relations among these different topics in Kant's work. Indeed, we usually evaluate interpretations of the third *Critique* by the persuasiveness of the narratives created out of these different portions of Kant's book. That we have so many narratives of the third *Critique* speaks to how much its philosophical richness coincides with the reoccurring possibility of its discontinuous nature.

One conventional narrative separates Kant's chapters on genius from the first part of his book, the discussion of taste in the "Analytic of the Beautiful." Traditionally, thinkers have been interested in both sections of Kant's aesthetics, but have rarely studied them together. The reason for this separation is easy to see, as the theory of taste refers to the world of nature while the theory of genius refers to the world of art. But, of course, the relation between nature and art becomes, in spite of Kant's prose, one of the key themes of his work. Commentators of the third *Critique* have noticed the fitful, almost reluctant way its discussion of aesthetics moves from nature to art (Cohen and Guyer, 7–10). It's tempting to see this textual clumsiness as a moment when biography and philosophy coincide, as Kant's own notorious antipathy toward all the arts except poetry has been well documented. Still, Kant does move his discussion from nature to art; the process begins almost imperceptibly in the "Analytic of the Sublime," the section of the book in which the sections on genius reside.

Like the beautiful, the sublime is mostly discussed through examples of nature. But while a natural object can be beautiful, it can't, strictly speaking, be sublime. Rather, the sublime describes those powers within us that rise above what threatens us from the outer world: "All we are entitled to say is that the object is suitable for exhibiting a sublimity that can be found in the mind."[18] Even as it focuses on the power of the outer, natural world, the Kantian sublime shifts the aesthetic discussion away from perceptual forms to a more explicit consideration of the human mind, to, as Eva Schaper adumbrates, "ideas of reason and aesthetic ideas" (385).[19] Like his sections on the sublime, Kant's later discussion on human art also confronts the possibility of aesthetic *conception*, even as art is defined by its beauty, precisely that which resists conceptualization. A consideration of artistic beauty invariably leads to the matter of its creation, which leads to questions of intentions, rules, and concepts; like examples of the sublime, beautiful art cannot avoid the explicit workings of the mind. But examples of artistic beauty, like those of natural beauty, are also perceptual forms whose judgment *as* beautiful eschews understanding them conceptually as beautiful things—indeed, just as for Kant sublimity does not reside in the natural object, neither does beauty reside in the concept.

The work of art challenges, perhaps scandalizes, the categories and oppositions that underpin Kant's prior discussion of the beautiful and the sublime. The discontinuity between beauty and conception is one of the key claims of the "Analytic of the Beautiful": judging something as beautiful means judging it without the aid of a concept that would a priori designate that object as beautiful. As Kant argues, judging something as beautiful involves a claim to "subjective universality": "since a judgment of taste involves the consciousness that all interest is kept out of it, it must also involve a claim to being valid for everyone, but without having a universality based on concepts" (sec. 6, 54). As difficult as this claim regarding "subjective universality" might be, Kant is quite clear in defining it by what it is not, a universality based on objective concepts. The judgment of the universal beauty of an object occurs independently of our concept of that object. Much later, during his discussion of art and nature, Kant does not back down from this earlier claim: "For we may say universally, whether it concerns beauty in nature or in art: *beautiful is what we like in merely judging it* (rather than either in sensation proper or through a concept)" (sec. 45, 174).

This reiteration is crucial, since, unlike natural objects, artistic objects are the results of human creation. Beautiful natural objects are products of nature; hence, they can exhibit, in Kant's famous phrase, a "purposiveness without purpose"—a design or form without intention (sec. 10, 65). Indeed, the second half of the

*Critique*, its study of teleological judgment, is primarily concerned with the dangers of assuming that humans can authoritatively know that intention in nature exists. Any such attempt invariably confuses human purpose with nature, letting a human concept stand in for a natural object. As Kant says much earlier in his "Analytic of the Beautiful," a purpose is the "object of a concept. . . . We think of a purpose if we think not merely, say, of our cognition of the object, but instead of the object itself (its form, or its existence), as an effect that is possible only through a concept of that effect" (sec. 10, 64–65)—hence the radical appeal of Kant's aesthetics to some readers, whereby to judge something as beautiful is to confront dramatically the error of "subreption," the confusion of human conception with objective truth, the very limiting nature of human thought.[20]

But art objects, as products of human creation, cannot free themselves completely from human design, conception, and purpose. As Kant bluntly states, "If the object is given as a product of art, and as such is to be declared beautiful, then we must first base it on a concept of what the thing is [meant] to be" (sec. 48, 179). Kant is referring to the specific character of mimetic art, but his statement encapsulates a more general predicament about art and taste that his larger argument must also confront. Making something beautiful certainly means judging something as beautiful, but the process also paradoxically means considering the presence of purpose and conception in the art object, negating the defining trait of a judgment of beauty. As Kant says in his famous comparison, "Nature . . . is beautiful [*schön*] if it also looks like art; and art can be called fine [*schön*] art only if we are conscious that it is art while yet it looks to us like nature" (sec. 45, 174). The sentence is not as dialectical as it first appears. In both clauses art remains associated with a purpose before purposiveness. In the first clause we only know nature's beauty by a purposiveness that resembles the human intentionality that makes art; in the second clause we must be aware of this intentional character in art even as it resembles the purposiveness without purpose of the beautiful in nature. Nature might simulate art, but art's simulation of nature is kept in check by art's reflexive relation to itself.

The emphatic reiteration in section 45 of the discontinuity between beauty and conception highlights the paradoxical and fitful connection that art has to Kant's study of taste. How can art and art's creation be beautiful, if the making of art brings back the relation to conception that beauty eschews? If our awareness of art as art keeps in check art's dissolution into nature, what keeps in check art's dissolution into itself, into a circumscribed identity of rules and concepts totally alienated from the beauty of nature? What prevents human aesthetics from being an impossibility, an acute moment of subreption, in Kant's own *Critique*?

The answer, of course, is the human talent of genius. With it Kant creates an entirely new backdrop for his discussion, upon which the threatening contradictions of his analysis seem to disappear:

> *Genius* is the talent (natural endowment) that gives the rule to art. Since talent is an innate productive ability of the artist and as such belongs itself to nature, we could also put it this way: *Genius* is the innate mental predisposition (*ingenium*) *through which* nature gives the rule to art. (sec. 46, 174)

The artist's genius allows his or her art to be made through a rule, to be conceived artistically. In fact, art's rule is conceived through genius. For genius is always original, quite like beauty's judgment, in that both are independent of any prior rule or concept. Through genius something like a rule or concept, but not a rule or concept, is given, thereby realizing the artistic creation of beauty. Genius allows Kant to distinguish between judging an object as beautiful, which requires taste, and making a beautiful object, which requires genius.[21] Moreover, for Kant, the difference between original genius and original *nonsense* is the exemplary nature of genius's creations: "hence, though they do not themselves arise through imitation, [such products of genius] must serve others for this purpose, i.e. as standard or rule by which to judge" (sec. 46, 175). As the bearer of such a standard, Kant's genius might inspire the genius of other artists or, just as likely, influence less-talented individuals who will codify the creations of genius into a school of precepts and rules that invite emulation. Kant's genius thus gives rule to art in two ways: first, as the originary non-rule that allows beautiful art to resolve the contradiction between its conceptual and non-conceptual character; and second, as the non-rule that becomes an ordinary rule for artistic schools of imitation.[22]

There is also a third way that genius gives rule to art, which Kant points to when he reformulates genius as the "innate mental predisposition (*ingenium*) *through which* nature gives the rule to art." Nature gives rule to art through genius, since the human artist and his or her talent already belong to nature. Kant's reconciliation of the conceptual and non-conceptual traits of artistic beauty is repeated in this rapprochement between the purposive rule of art and the non-intentional design of natural beauty, with the former actually being an effect of the latter, a dynamic mediated by human genius. This mediation by genius anticipates the conclusion to the first part of the *Critique*, which resolves the antinomy of taste, itself a revisiting of the problematic relation between taste and conception. Kant's solution is the "indeterminate concept" of the "supersensible substrate" of all phenomenal reality on which judgments of taste are based (sec. 57,

213). The indeterminate concept resolves the conflict between the conceptual and non-conceptual in the judgment of beauty while also, like genius's mediation of nature, shifting Kant's aesthetic discussion from epistemology toward metaphysics and ethics, a process completed in his concluding claims about beauty as a symbol of the good in this first part of the *Critique*—hence the conservative appeal of Kant's aesthetics to some, who see in the rule given to art by genius a theme reiterated in a number of places of the *Critique*, the active presence of a morally grounding nature in human life (Zammito, 283–84). Far from being an ancillary moment in Kant's discussion, the synthetic role of the genius replays one of the professed central projects of his work, connecting through aesthetic judgment the realms of pure and practical reason, or of philosophical understanding and ethics.

Whether this argument ultimately belongs to Kant or to just some of his readers, many have also been skeptical of it, either citing the artificial and forced progression toward the resolution of the antinomy of taste, the somewhat strained symmetry between this section's inclusion in the third *Critique* and the "Dialectic" of the first *Critique*, or wondering why Kant makes the indeterminate concept a claim about the "supersensible substrate" rather than of the harmony of the cognitive faculties, which would have more neatly defined the epistemological, rather than ontological, boundaries of Kant's discussion.[23] This tension is already signaled in Kant's two formulations of genius, as that which gives rule to art and that by which nature gives rule to art. For it could be argued that genius's grounding in nature merely begs the question of genius's ability to give rule to art. (Indeed, distinguishing between taste's judgmental powers and genius's creative abilities can already be seen as a deferral of this problem.) If we are not convinced of genius's ability to solve the epistemological conflict between the conceptual and non-conceptual aspects of artistic beauty, we are not likely to be satisfied by Kant's transcendental recourse to nature either. If genius resolves this conflict by mediating nature, the question still remains as to how nature can overcome the very distinctions between artistic and natural beauty that make those notions intelligible. Rather than simply grounding the epistemological, the ontological finds itself placed in the same trying predicament as the epistemological, while also highlighting the ontological instabilities of Kant's epistemological argument. Securing genius through nature does not secure nature, just as securing artistic beauty through genius does not secure genius.

There is thus a tautological sense of rhetorical imposition, rather than of constative reasoning, that characterizes Kant's invocation of genius and nature, an act that both affirms and makes friable the ontological quality of his argument.

(What enables artistic beauty?—genius. What is genius?—that which enables artistic beauty.) The implications of this rhetorical sense have not been thought through fully enough, probably because of its limited role in helping us decide what would seem to be most pressing about Kant's resolution of the problem of artistic beauty, the true or false existence of genius. If we accept Kant's solution of genius and nature, we ignore this tautological sense in order to secure the ontological and ethical dimensions to Kant's aesthetics. If we disagree with Kant's claim about genius, the imposed quality of his claim becomes a sign of occulted thought, Kant's own lapse into subreption, that then can be dismissed as falsehood, a gesture that very much connects philosophical argument with forms of ideological demystification in Romantic studies and elsewhere. Genius and nature are idols of the mind that the tautological sense of Kant's thought accidentally helps to unmask. As such, this rhetorically imposed quality is *simply* that, one step in a much larger project, whether that be ascertaining the larger values of Kant's philosophical argument or discovering the socially constructed character of his, or Romanticism's, vocabulary.

However, the rhetorically assertive nature of Kant's use of genius allows for another response to his text, one that sidesteps the central philosophical question of whether to accept his claims as true. Genius might very well not secure artistic beauty through the synthetic manner that Kant describes. But its role as an answer to a problem that Kant's system of thought cannot otherwise overcome also implies a reorganization of that system, in which the demands for ontological, epistemological, and ethical certitude are themselves the a posteriori compulsive effects of rhetorical, or linguistic, performance. Within this reorganized system the non-truth of Kant's definition of genius does not simply mean that term's falsehood and its subsequent rejection. Genius cannot be so easily dismissed.

The relation between Kant's two definitions of genius clarifies this predicament. It is difficult not to see the first formulation sublating into the second. Granted, this process need not simply mean the foundational presence of an ethical nature. One could view nature's giving rule to art through genius in a more radical manner, whereby nature's non-conceptual particularity—its rule—extends to the artwork, making the originality of genius a sign of thought-against-itself (or, indeed, making the origin of thought *in* thought-against-itself). But insofar as this activity centers on the dialectical recuperation of a certain generative insight, this condition still occurs within a constative mode, regardless of its strong form of defamiliarization as a negative dialectic.[24] Another maneuver against thought, at least as equally vehement, would insist on a certain discontinuity between Kant's two definitions, in which the very need to define genius a second time implies a tension between the two that the second's introduction of an all-encompassing nature cannot fully erase. For as much as the first definition might seem to slide into the second, the question of originality resists the completion of that sublation.

Insomuch as nature gives rule to art through genius, genius mediates the originary power of nature for human art. But insomuch as genius gives rule to art, genius is the originary human force that allows the making of beautiful art to reconcile the conceptual and non-conceptual character of that act. Genius is at once original and a mediation. It is precisely this problem of, or solution to, human creativity that makes Kant's discussion of genius emblematic of numerous works that construct for us the high Romantic conception of the Romantic artist. To accept simply this situation as the confirmation of a traditional high Romantic aesthetic is to ignore once again the imposed nature of a claim about the truth of what genius is. The more urgent question is whether we can then dismiss genius outright because of this constitutive self-conflict as both a mediating and originary identity.

The answer is no, insofar as genius's paradoxical status as an originary mediation is the imposed force of precisely that which cannot be dismissed. As a mediation of nature, genius involves a dynamic of continuity, substitution, and representation that marks genius as a *figure* of nature. But what type of figure, what notion of figurality, simultaneously asserts itself as originary? To ask that question is to insist on a certain gap between Kant's two formulations that then characterizes their continuity as a mutual interference. The result of that interference is a figurality that cannot be dismissed, that comes before epistemology and ontology. Simultaneously, the result is an origin that cannot explain itself, that must always remain secondary insofar as it is a figure for itself, not the truth of itself. Genius is a *catachresis*, a figure for the imposed character of figure, independent of, inexplicable by, and separate from not simply the semantic field that it inhabits but, more radically, any non-figural, any epistemological or metaphysical, mode of being. Genius solves the problem of artistic beauty in the *Critique* because it makes that problem one not of truth, but of figure. As Jacques Derrida notes, "The original agency here is the figure of genius" (10). More emphatically, genius is an originary figure *for* originality. It solves the problem of art's originality, of art's originary rule, by imposing itself as figure's origin for origin's truth.[25]

Kant's answer to the problem of artistic beauty is *genius*, insofar as the answer is a figure for a truth claim that Kant's system depends on but cannot know, explain, or accommodate, except as a paradoxically non-signifying, radically exterior figure, a catachresis. His answer *is* genius, in the sense that it is also a catachrestic action that lies at the very heart of signification. It is genius because it is nothing else, because nothing else could stand within Kant's system and make sense. *Genius* is the figure of making sense as opposed to nonsense, a differentiation that Kant specifically identifies as a duty of genius, except that, as a catachresis, genius is first and foremost the material of non-sense, of meaning unable to reside anywhere except as the performative violence of a figure that exists independently of the system of signification—Kant's aesthetics—that it saves.[26] Genius is a catachresis for signification, and thus the figure for its impossibility, insofar as it is impossible for Kant's discussion of aesthetic beauty to say what genius is, except that genius allows Kant's discussion to say what *it* is. Genius is the nonsense that makes sense.

Section 49 of the *Critique* forcefully illustrates this situation. The heady character of this dramatization actually makes the location of genius in Kant's discussion of the sublime an appropriate one. As my discussion of resemblance and the sensation of meaning in part II further elaborates, the linguistic character of genius's light also supports the canniness of placing these sections in the "Analytic of the Sublime." Not coincidentally, then, section 49 explicitly discusses genius through a theory of expression, or signification. Genius is first associated with the "spirit" (*Geist*) of an artistic creation, a putatively idealist move that seems to contradict the status of genius as figure. But Kant introduces this term in order to relate it to the representation of an aesthetic idea, the "counterpart (pendant) of a *rational idea*" (sec. 49, 182). This binary further clarifies the troubled relation between artwork and conception. An aesthetic idea is a "presentation of the imagination which prompts much thought, but to which no determinate thought whatsoever, i.e., no [determinate] *concept*, can be adequate, so that no language can express it completely and allow us to grasp it" (sec. 49, 182). Conversely, a rational idea is a "concept to which no *intuition* (presentation of the imagination) can be adequate." In other words, an aesthetic idea is something that a concept cannot explain, whereas a rational idea is a concept that cannot be imagined.[27]

While apparently emphasizing the gap between art and conception, Kant's distinction actually allows for a connection between the two. For, as the *Critique* explains, there can be *no one* image or intuition that imagines the concept of a rational idea. There can exist, however, a dynamic between a rational idea and *a set* of images or intuitions. Indeed, the generation of this dynamic and the structural relations among the rational idea and those images constitute the aesthetic idea that, conversely, *no one* concept or rational idea can explain. The aesthetic idea is the form of the generative, dialectical interplay between these images and the rational idea. Thus, Kant cites the example of Jupiter's eagle, which, with "lightning in its claws," is an "attribute of the mighty king of heaven," one image of the rational idea of the "sublimity and majesty of creation" (sec. 49, 183). Kant's point is that there is no simple one-to-one correspondence of meaning between Jupiter's eagle and the rational idea of majesty; rather, the image of the eagle participates in the prompting of the imagination "to spread over a multitude of kindred presentations that arouse more thought than can be expressed in a concept determined by words" (sec. 49, 183). The implicitly sublime experience of this multitude is the aesthetic idea of what we might call "Jupiter," something that both outpaces and exists in relation to the rational idea of majesty. For Kant *genius* is the term for the human incitement of an aesthetic idea out of the relations among a rational idea and a number of images or attributes.

For Lyotard, Kant's genius is thus "crazy with forms and crazy about forms," a site of no longer pleasant free play but of melancholy anguish, in which "the powers of presentation strain almost to the breaking point; their ratio ceases to provide a feeling of the beautiful, and the object, which occasions the feeling, seems in the end unrecognizable to the concept" (75–76). In contrast, the Kantian philosopher Paul Guyer sees in genius's dynamic a holistic argument against a simply formalist comprehension of the *Critique*, insofar as genius unites form and content through its ability to create the richness of aesthetic ideas, meaning animated, or given "spirit," through the formal interplay of the ideas' images and intuitions.[28] Certainly, Lyotard's view of genius as a "figural aesthetic of the 'much too much' that defies the concept" threatens the stable union of form and meaning in Guyer's argument, in that form's "boundless" proliferation could very well imply a basic hostility toward content's restrictive articulation, the meaning of the aesthetic idea's structure, the relation among its attributes (76). But as intriguing is the way that Guyer's synthetic analysis also clarifies the radical paradox explicit in Lyotard's analysis, of an infinitude of forms chaffing at the finitude of the concept. For what could it mean even to speak of an infinite *set* of attributes, an infinitude still structured around the expression of a specific identity?

Derrida describes this radical paradox in Kant as the "immaculate commerce" of "economimesis," a "pure productivity of the inexchangeable" that marks how the infinite forms of the imagination are determined by the economy, the laws and principles, of analogy from which such forms must also be free (9). Unlike Lyotard, both Guyer and Derrida see Kant's text doing more than simply expressing regret over the impossibility of this dynamic. Surprisingly, Guyer more than Derrida gives us a specific way to understand the precise action of figure in section 49, even as Guyer's putative synthesis of form and content does away with the vertiginous generosity of economimesis as a radical trait of aesthetic creativity.

Central to Guyer is Kant's description of genius as the "happy relation" between how imagination discovers a number of images of a given concept and how it communicates those attributes in a synthetic expression; the happy relation, in Guyer's view, is between content and form (sec. 49, 185). Others have understood Kant to be actually referring to the happy relation between imagination and understanding in the aesthetic idea, that which then allows imagination to uncover a plentitude of attributes mobilized for the concept's expression, as opposed, in the rational idea, to simply the concept's cognition. That commentators of the *Critique* cannot agree with any precision on to what the "happy relation" of genius refers, except that there *is* a happy relation, is already both telling and troubling.[29]

But insofar as the happy relation between understanding and imagination enables the rational idea's successful expression by the aesthetic idea, we can still use Guyer's categories, his understanding that "genius . . . lies in the ability to produce both form and content and the 'happy relationship' between them which makes the former especially successful for the expression of the latter" (360). Unlike Guyer, we can specify this "happy relation" even further, as that which makes the opposition, and interaction, between form and content intelligible from the get-go: figure. More exactly, genius is the sign of a happy figure, a figure that works—a figure that successfully enables the retroactive distinction between, and combination of, form and content. Kant's argument for aesthetic expression can thus also be understood as a theory of signification, of the operation of tropes. Similarly, his section's earlier opposition between the words of a rational idea and the images of an aesthetic idea can be subsumed under this larger, more capacious linguistic inquiry into how figure effects form and content, and meaning. Kant's reminder that this is a poetic as well as pictorial predicament punctuates this point.[30]

But how, exactly, does genius occur—how do we realize a happy figure? Kant's three specific examples of how aesthetic ideas represent themselves suggest an answer. Together they make up what Richard Klein has wittily called the "most aesthetic, poetic, the sunniest, happiest page in the whole flinty volume" of the *Critique* (28). Kant's first instance is the expression of the rational idea of the "majesty of creation," the aesthetic idea of "Jupiter." His second example is the "animation" of the rational idea of keeping a "cosmopolitan attitude" even in the face of death, achieved through conjoining this idea with the poetic rendering of a beautiful summer day's end:

Let us part from life without grumbling or regrets,
Leaving the world behind filled with our good deeds.
Thus the sun, daily course completed,
Spreads one more soft light over the sky;
And the last rays that he sends through the air
Are the last sighs he gives the world for his well-being. (sec. 49, 184)

Kant's third example refers to how an intellectual concept can also act as an attribute of an aesthetic idea, as virtue does in a poetic description of a beautiful morning: "The sun flowed forth, as serenity flows from virtue." For Kant the line's aesthetic deployment of virtue helps create an ensemble of meanings, the elevated sobriety of a "multitude of sublime and calming feelings," that the rational idea of hopeful anticipation cannot by itself exhaust (sec. 49, 184–85).

Starting with the first example's focus on the lightning in Jupiter's eagle's claws, all three instances noticeably dwell on the articulation of light. The next two examples characterize the precise nature of this image. Light operates in a formalized manner through the setting and rising of the sun, an entity that, as Derrida famously observes, we and philosophy know as the "most natural, most universal, most real, most luminous thing."[31] Light suffuses both passages, inside and out. The natural cyclical movement of the sun marks a structure of continuity between both examples, as the very idea of animation and *Geist* is enacted through the third example's revivification of light by the dawn sun. In Kant's second example light is everywhere and then nowhere; its movement enables the very intelligibility of this spatial distinction, as well as of a natural temporality that is itself the cosmopolitan lesson of earthly acceptance that the stanza conveys. Echoed and enhanced by the introduction of serenity and virtue in the third example, the orderly procession of sunlight is *Geist* itself, the natural ability to "apprehend the imagination's rapidly passing play"—to identify and expand upon cognition's affinity with phenomenal, affective, and moral reality. Kant's light is, as both Derrida and Klein indicate, *logos* itself: analogy as identity, signification as pure, non-contingent being, figure as a natural entity.

Light as logos is not only pervasive; it is generative as well, a condition made explicit by the sun in the last two examples. But the presence of this trait in the extended passage is far from unproblematic. That the light of the first example, the lightning of Jupiter's eagle, is in dialectical interplay with the rational idea of the *majesty* of creation already signals this more complex predicament. This situation requires a reformulation of Derrida's sense of Kant's sun as the radical generosity of economimesis. It also suggests another reading option than Klein's, where he concludes with a thought experiment outside the *Critique* about a different type of reflecting light whose uncertain shimmer deflects the logocentric bias of Kant's luminosity (39–40).[32] Indeed, the very articulation of *bias* within Kant is at once more ineluctable and uncertain than first perceived. For if light in all three examples points toward the generative power of figure as a natural entity, light also delineates more specifically the apodictic, self-authorizing character of this power. All three examples involve the performance of a radical command that cannot be reduced to the comprehension of either an intention or thought.

The third example's analogy between the flowing of the sun and the flowing of serenity from virtue both hides and exemplifies this performative, apodictic moment. To see flowing sunlight as the generation of serenity from virtue is to see it achieve the certitude of an ethical mode of being different from the mindlessness of mere physical existence. But that assurance itself depends on the intrinsic character of nature, the naturalness of an ethical life that replicates the natural flow of the sun. More precisely, for the simile to work, the sun flows from the sun as serenity flows from virtue. The analogy between these two processes thus enables another figure that the light of the sun also hides. Serenity is different from virtue but can also signify it; the figural reorganization of their separate meanings into genetic continuity is allowed by the coincidence between the sun and the sun, the ability of light to command an origin by its assimilation of difference, by the way sunlight is still the sun wherever and whenever it appears. The figural connection between serenity and virtue, enabled by the one flowing sun, is also the figure for the command of figure, for the successful reordering of identity and non-identity, difference and similarity, into the intrinsic signification of a trope.[33]

But the command is empty; there is no prior agency or authority behind it, since in these lines the sun borrows its design from an ethical process that depends on that very same sun for the intelligibility of serenity and virtue's meaning. In intensely condensed form Kant's third example gestures toward some of his writings' most daunting themes within and beyond the *Critique*: how ethics, or virtue, can be something besides an external, arbitrary injunction and, more immediately, how the natural and ethical worlds can be anchored in the same purposiveness, or design. Here, however, the solution of the aesthetic is explicitly presented through the highly problematic function of a sign. Neither sun nor virtue can quite escape the heteronomy of their mutual existence as a figure for the other. Yet it is as an intrinsic, autonomous entity that each paradoxically still insists on the authority of the example's natural meaning, incontestable as the flow of both light and serenity from solar world and virtuous mind.

The tension between arbitrary command and natural authority is foregrounded even more emphatically in the second example of the setting sun. Regardless of the passage's cosmopolitan tone of resignation, the intelligibility of the example is still based on the apodictic form of a command ("Let us part from life . . .") that also exists in the German of the *Critique* ("Laßt uns aus dem Leben . . . weichen . . .") and the original French of the poem's writer ("Oui, finissons sans trouble . . ."). The incontestability of the statement comes from one aspect of the analogy structuring the quote, the unavoidable finitude of our lives and the inevitable setting of the sun. Yet the sun also sets with a grace that signals "his well-being" at the moment of his extinction, which is the basis for the same grace of an ethical life well lived "without grumbling or regrets." This pathetic fallacy is itself the result of the lines' imposition of a certain symbolic order: we are told to act like the sun, which only makes sense if the sun acts like us, like we are told to act. Kant's second example is thus more than simply a repetition of human authority inscribing itself within a natural process (of, for example, a king commanding the sun to set or rise); it is equally and more problematically the expression of an incontestable force that does not reside purely in nature. That we *are* talking about something like an authoritative command becomes clear when we also consider who the writer of these lines is, Kant's "great king," the late Frederick the Great of Prussia, patron to artists and philosophers of Europe's Enlightenment movement (sec. 49, 184).

The kingly presence of Frederick II (and, to a lesser degree, the academic authority of the third example's writer, J. Ph. L. Wilhof, Duisburg professor of morals) surely signals the sociopolitical character of what up until now might have been perceived as only a philosophical set of problems. Such a sociohistorical approach might not simply note Kant's notorious self-positioning as a shill for his late monarch; it might also consider Frederick the Great's contribution to modern state authority as well as, at another level, the difference between a command by him and his successor, the reactionary Frederick William II.[34] But a full treatment of such an analysis must also recognize the degree to which the politics of thought—the specificities of its institutionalization, codification, and authorization—refer to neither simply a natural nor a human quandary. The symbolic generation of the eighteenth-century Enlightenment from Frederick II's poetic command, from his regal expression of a cosmopolitan French imaginary, certainly speaks to the interpenetration of mind and human social history. But that dialectic has another crucial, although asymmetric, coordinate within the context of Kant's three examples.

When the *Critique* describes how the "king . . . animates his rational idea of a cosmopolitan attitude," Kant's text refers to something more than simply Frederick II's poetic acumen, something that speaks to the constitutive state of "animation"—of inciting meaning or inspiring life "even at the end of life," in the mute cycles of nature and the dead objects of language (sec. 49, 184). All three of Kant's instances of how the aesthetic idea operates revolve around various images of a higher authority—Jupiter, Jupiter's eagle, Frederick II, the sun, and virtue—that condition the semantic action of the examples. Interacting with the lightning and solar imagery, these images enact the apodictic command behind the self-authority or "majesty" of natural meaning. They reveal the origin of the "happy relation" of genius, or figure, to be a capricious fiat that cannot account for itself in any fundamentally non-contingent manner, a situation that explains the ambiguous reference of the happy relation in Kant for Guyer and others, insofar as figure is its own referent and imposition. Kant's three examples are the attributes of genius, demonstrating the genius of genius to be what we have earlier called its catachrestic nature. The genius of the animating king is that genius *is* the king.

Frederick II's poetic speech act allegorizes the genius of cognition, of enlightened subjectivity. But the existence of his genius as a nominalization, as the *act* of enlightenment, also allegorizes the performance of historical action, the coherent intelligence of a historical event or period. Cognition, action, and event: the light of genius, the genius of signification condenses these meanings within itself, the drive of *Geist.* Frederick II literally speaks, or authorizes, the Enlightenment. But this literality is itself the outcome of the drive of figure. To the degree that the Enlightenment rests on such figure, its periodicity is indelibly Romantic, in a manner neither simply proleptic nor anachronistic, if these traits function only as transparent, historical terms. The apodictic genius, the light of the Enlightenment *is* Romantic insofar as Romanticism signifies the figural operation of the subject in, as well as *of*, history: the light of the sun as cognition as well as the temporal action of a distinct historical period. The distinction between subject and historical period is itself the result of the linguistic force that Kant's examples of aesthetic expression convey.

Kant's three examples are not simply instances of how an aesthetic idea might work; they are also *part* of an aesthetic idea, insofar as Kant's formula for such an idea is also a theory of signification. Together Kant's examples aesthetically express the rational idea of genius as the reliance of identity on a catachresis, of synthetic meaning on the non-meaning of an imposed command, with *command* itself a trope for the founding semantic intrusion of an external alien figure upon a field of signs. Lyotard's characterization of the melancholy state of genius in Kant as form's ultimate *ressentiment* regarding content would thus be one more self-reflexive notation of this more difficult condition, which could just as well be troped through the success of a command as by the estrangement of simply failed form. Indeed, this failure could itself be seen as another moment of the aesthetic expression of the rational idea of catachresis, but only to the degree that that failure is read as a trope, and not as an unquestioned moment in the economy of philosophical truth. *Failure* can no more be the truth of form's inability to mean than *majesty*—capricious, beneficent, or otherwise—can be the truth of the unconditional, princely power (here or in Heaven) that secures form's and content's "happy relation." Neither can failure and majesty be simply the same, a point that sets the narrative course for any sociohistorical interrogation of philosophy's constative effects.

As Kant's own categories insist, the rational idea of catachresis is not, strictly speaking, genius in and of itself, insofar as "no [determinate] concept can be adequate" to the aesthetic idea that expresses it (sec. 49, 182). Neither, however, is genius simply that aesthetic expression. The dialectical interplay of Kant's examples, or images, of genius, its aesthetic expression, distributes genius throughout the section (indeed, throughout the *Critique*) while simultaneously preventing any ultimate access to this "happy relation." The concept of figure is not figure; neither is the figure of figure. Genius cannot capture itself. Genius does not simply mark the truth of figure as content or of figure as form; nor, as Guyer suggests, does genius simply enable the natural synthesis of content and form. Rather, genius records the impossible bridging between these two conditions of meaning, the unavoidable gap, in Kant's terms, between conception and aesthetic judgment that his sections on genius and nature are meant to resolve. That genius, or figure, is everywhere in the specific examples of the rational and aesthetic idea in section 49, that genius saturates Kant's text as the object and subject of writing, points to this bridging. That genius is also nowhere purely present in either the rational or aesthetic idea, that genius is also the mutual antagonism between content and form that prevents the truth of such a presence, points to the simultaneous impossibility of this act.

Let us *historically* characterize the aesthetic expression of genius generated, at least in part, by the *Critique* and its formulation of the relation between the rational and aesthetic idea. Consider how other solar expressions, attributes, or images of the rational idea of genius include the *Critique* itself, as well as the very name *Immanuel Kant*, whose strange, complex inscriptions of light entwine the Enlightenment and Romantic Anglo-European subject in a very precise way for our own historically specific, disciplinary moment. If history is today's clarity, its illumination is not simply the certitude of a hermeneutic turn. If *Romanticism* itself is the aesthetic expression of genius, if Romanticism as both cognitive subject and historical period is the aesthetic idea of the rational idea of the genius of figure, then genius also explains why the impossibility of the Romantic subject and period is not the same as the demystification of Romanticism and Romantic subjectivity, their dissolution into a larger, more accurate form of historic truth.[35] The genius, or catachresis, of Romanticism is very much like the "*necessary* and simultaneously *impossible* logical construction" that Slavoj Žižek describes as Kant's subject of apperception in the first *Critique*, the "void called subject."[36] We cannot get rid of this condition, since it exists before truth and falsehood, before epistemology and ontology. But, of course, such a prior state is itself simply a figure for the more exacting, ineluctable delineation of any one particular historical identity. We can no more rid ourselves of the impossibility of genius than we can rid either the long eighteenth or long nineteenth century of Romanticism. Romanticism's name might no longer be used, but what Romanticism is is not simply relegated to Romanticism. As one valence of the long eighteenth century, Romanticism assures that the long eighteenth century never exists, neither simply nor absolutely. Not recognizing this predicament is surely a mystification, although that does not necessarily imply the option of simply recovering the demystified historicity of a larger era. Beyond Romanticism, beyond Kant, knowledge's answer, its illumination, is still genius.

PART TWO

# Theory

Arguably, de Man's rhetorical reading of Romanticism becomes even more intelligible as a form of critical sobriety as he shifts from exposing the ontological instabilities of a mid-twentieth-century conception of Romanticism to arguing vigorously against the constant confusion of language and phenomenal experience that lies at the heart of what he calls the aesthetic ideology. Yet his ascetic warding off of sensory experience from what he calls language's materiality has another consequence that part II develops, the idea of a sensation of meaning whose non-phenomenal, figural status is my point of entry into contemporary debates about theorizing history today.

Thus, crucial to chapter 3's analysis of the figure of the machine in de Man is a rereading of his distinction between the figural and the literal, where I assert that the latter is not necessarily linked to the phenomenal. The chapter also contains its own argument about a common technological unconscious shared by Marxism and deconstruction and, consequently, its own allegory about the problematics of revolution and commodification in Rousseau's *Confessions* and Marx's *Capital.* But it is the chapter's delinking of the phenomenal from the literal that is most explicitly taken up in chapters 4 and 5, where I formulate in opposition to Michaels's pragmatic polemics about language and politics a sensation of meaning based on the aporia of resemblance, a condition that, while radically complicating its relation to the sensory, also explains Michaels's implicit, sober rejection of the cognitive inchoateness of Romanticism. Michaels is not usually associated, of course, with the North American study of English Romanticism. But chapters 4 and 5 argue that his negative assessment of de Man is founded on an unacknowledged critique of Romanticism, which illuminates not only what de Man gets out of Romanticism but also what problems inform Michaels's own position on political and artistic issues in U.S. literature.

The Romantic inchoateness of nonphysical materiality, first registered in de Man's readings of Kant, can also be troped through the figure of the spectral that appears in Derrida's equally well-known engagement with Marx. Revolution thus returns in the guise of the spectral in chapter 6's consideration of Derrida's relation to Romanticism, where I now link Marxism and deconstruction not through a shared technological unconscious but rather through a future-oriented Romanticism, a ghost theory that unsettles the assumed divide between idealist thought and concrete material (in the Marxist sense) practice. Chapters 5 and 6 are consequently also connected by their responses to, respectively, Michaels and Žižek, each of whom in his own way is adamantly opposed to a political belief in ghosts. Insofar as the linguistic sensation of ghosts is itself a resistance to simple sensory experience, Romantic sobriety, as that resistance, paradoxically becomes the fantastic entity that Michaels and Žižek both soberly want to exorcise. Thus, running through the chapters of part II are tropes of the gothic, the sublime, ghosts, fanaticism, and ideology—various, oftentimes conflicting permutations of sensations of meaning that all still articulate a politics of the non-phenomenal. In their different ways the chapters of part II try to show how this politics of the non-phenomenal, of sobriety and sensation, is, in all its complex dissonances, at once contemporary and Romantic.

# De Man, Marx, Rousseau, and the Machine

If eternal means, not transcendent to all (temporal) history, but omnipresent, trans-historical and therefore immutable in form throughout the extent of history, I shall adopt Freud's expression word for word, and write *ideology is eternal*, exactly like the unconscious.

—Louis Althusser, "Ideology and Ideological State Apparatuses"

The writings of Paul de Man are fundamentally entangled with Romanticism. Yet, an offhand comment by an equally formidable figure from our recently past-but-not-past *epistēmē* of theory places de Man not in a Romantic but in an eighteenth-century context, one that profitably defamiliarizes our assumptions about not only deconstruction but also Marxism, as well as the relation between these two discourses. Paradoxically, this new assignation also means a further encounter, or new near miss, between Rousseau and Marx; without ever resorting to the term, this phantom confrontation necessarily registers itself as a Romantic event in a way akin to the procedures delineated by our previous study of Kant. Here, however, the dynamic of catachrestic identity is about the imposition of not so much periodicity as a larger historical narrative about the commodity form. To trope the approximation between Rousseau and Marx, or de Man and Marx, or deconstruction and Marxism, is invariably to write such a history, as well as to write *through* it, although the Rousseau texts read here are not the familiar pieces on political thought that one might immediately seek for such a juxtaposition. In the manner described at the conclusions of both chapters 1 and 2, this history will invariably announce itself as bound to what we today call Romanticism—not only because of the names and tropes that specifically outline its form, but because of the fantastic way this history both resists and inaugurates its own epistemological and ontological inscription.

During his one sustained commentary on his former colleague, Fredric Jameson states that de Man

> was an eighteenth-century mechanical materialist, and much that strikes the postcontemporary reader as peculiar and idiosyncratic about his work will be clarified by juxtaposition with the cultural politics of the great Enlightenment philosophes: their horror of religion, their campaign against superstition and error (or "metaphysics"). In that sense, deconstruction . . . can be seen to be an essentially eighteenth-century philosophical strategy.[1]

What does it mean for both deconstruction and Marxism to consider de Man as a postcontemporary version of eighteenth-century mechanical materialism? Jameson provocatively situates deconstruction within his larger argument for the immanent and nominalist nature of postmodern theory. But in doing so he unleashes analytic energies that extend beyond his own strategies for absorbing deconstruction within the overarching conceptual frameworks of a Marxist analysis of capital (181–259). Dialectically, Marxism's own valence changes from one emphasizing the hermeneutic coordinates implicit in Jameson's investment in narrative and representation (*Darstellung*) to a more uncertain topos, configured not in terms of an interpretive solution but instead as a tropological problematic, here in this chapter signaled by the conceptual irresolution of abstract labor and value in Marx's *Capital*.

Jameson argues for the continuity between de Man and eighteenth-century intellectual thought by recovering from *Allegories of Reading* a Kantian-inflected dilemma regarding generalizing from particulars and a likewise noumenon of "what language cannot assimilate, absorb, or process" (246). *Allegories* is actually as tough on the integrity of the particular as it is on the process of general, conceptual abstraction. Similarly, Jameson's argument for the noumenon as the repressed *non-dit* of de Man's book is complicated by the later, explicit use of the Kantian noumenon in de Man's *Aesthetic Ideology*, in which the term specifically expresses the "inward experience of consciousness" and functions as a counterpart to the phenomenal world (74). De Man does recover from Kant a certain non-phenomenal materiality, of course, but one whose relation to language goes very much beyond Jameson's notions of both Kant and eighteenth-century mechanical materialism, a point that this chapter emphatically makes and the following chapters explore in depth.[2] But especially compelling for our immediate argument is the way that Jameson's analysis notes but does not dwell on the most overt evidence for de Man's eighteenth-century mechanist materialism, the figure of the machine that runs through the essays in *Allegories* on Rousseau.

Contrary to Jameson's implied subsumption of de Man's mechanical materialism under the larger exigencies of a dialectical materialism, the machine demonstrates how both de Manian deconstruction and Marxism share a *technological unconscious* knotted around the mental antinomies of instrumentality, *technē*, and simulacra.[3] These issues intertextually connect de Man and Marx through Rousseau's *Confessions* and Marx's *Capital.* In Rousseau's work the machine marks a historical literalization of self, contingency, and value that opens up the question of the literal and the figural congealed in deconstruction's own economy of equivalence. In *Capital* the machine allegorizes the robotic catachresis underwriting abstract labor and value, making Marxism more than a transparent historicism even as deconstruction becomes something else besides an attack on history's literality, whose indexical imperatives might actually have nothing to do with assumptions about history's phenomenal nature.

First, a qualification: my point is not that the machine in de Man provides better proof of his affiliation with eighteenth-century mechanist philosophy. Rather, by responding to Jameson's proposition, we reorient analysis around the machine in de Man, a topos that both overlaps and diverges from a more traditional concept of mechanist materialism. It is worth remembering, for example, that philosophic mechanism is not simply tied to non-philosophic, prosaic ideas of what a "machine" is. But it soon becomes clear that the machine in de Man is also much more than such a definition.

In the essay in *Allegories* on the *Social Contract* the image of the machine operates in two ways. First, citing Rousseau's description of the *Social Contract* as a "machine ready to go to work," de Man argues that Rousseau's political creation is less a "piece of property or a State" than a text, a grammar that operates "like a logical code or a machine."[4] Such a "quasi-mechanical pattern" has less to do with any recognizable, intelligible structure on the part of the text than with the way the functioning of grammar is independent of referential meaning, much as an abstract law does not depend on any one of its particular applications for its existence (268). This gap between grammar and referential meaning also occasions the essay's second usage of mechanical language, how Rousseau's analogy between the "wheels of the State" and the "principle of inertia of machines" is best understood as a "debilitating entropy [that] illustrates the practical consequences of a linguistic structure in which grammar and figure, statement and speech act do not converge" (272). This predicament appears to be for de Man a second-order repetition of the initial divergence between grammar and referential meaning, insofar as de Man earlier defines figure as precisely that gap: for him, rhetoric, or figure, cannot unite with grammar to overcome that division (try as it might, as in the case of metaphor); consequently, the complicated, asymmetric, and mutually disabling relations among all of de Man's linguistic categories—grammar, reference, figure, statement, and speech act—function in a "quasi-mechanical pattern," a logic that constantly blunts or displaces its own constative or performative force. The final example of this mechanical logic would be the promise of the *Contract*. Equally empty and inevitable because a promise always rejects the particular present for a future moment when grammar and reference might converge, this linguistic act dramatizes the functioning of the text as a machine, in the service of neither itself nor any external referent.

The implications of the machine in de Man's essay are several. The machine underscores a certain linguistic dynamism that sublates the mechanical "entropy" illustrating the gap between grammar and figure. This dynamism, or set of forces, vehemently effects the mixed sense of aimless repetition and random patterning that de Man reads in Rousseau's mechanical references and asserts the inevitability of language's self-evacuations (as in a promise), distinguishing self-constitutive error from avoidable mistake. This dynamism also coincides with one characteristic of traditional mechanism, insofar as both eschew Aristotelian final causes, or teleological thinking, as explanations for their functioning. In de Man this rejection takes the further radical step of rejecting organic meaning altogether. As such, the machine also describes how language and the phenomenal world constantly diverge, and how language through reference and figure constantly try to erase that bifurcation.

In de Man's essay on the *Confessions* this final key issue carries a particular resonance, insofar as the importance of the machine lies not simply in the machine's ubiquity but in what it explicitly suppresses: the figure of the text as a body and, by extension, the human body itself. That for de Man the metaphor of the text as body in Rousseau refers not simply to a general, phenomenal organicism but to the specifically human form is made clear by de Man's stress on the moments of bodily mutilation—nearly broken heads and crushed fingers—that punctuate Rousseau's writings. The machine of grammar threatens the body, ultimately replacing the latter and all its possible desires and emotive meanings with language's own implacable, unmotivated logic. This displacement reaches the violence of a metalepsis. For "as soon as the metaphorical integrity of the text is put in question, as soon as the text is said not to be a figural body but a machine," this predicament occurs:

> Far from seeing language as an instrument in the service of a psychic energy, the possibility now arises that the entire construction of drives, substitutions, repressions, and representations is the aberrant, metaphorical correlative of the absolute randomness of language, prior to any figuration or meaning. It is no longer certain that language, as excuse, exists because of a prior guilt but just as possible that since language, as a machine, performs anyway, we have to produce guilt (and all its train of psychic consequences) in order to make the excuse meaningful. (299)[5]

These sentences climax a discernible narrative in de Man's chapter on the *Confessions* and, in a sense, his book's entire section on Rousseau. For if the human self stands for an exemplary moment when language and phenomenology, text and body, coincide, de Man's machine of language tears at this synthesis, first refusing to obey the vagaries of human intention, then turning upon the human form, and finally demonstrating how human subjectivity is itself a mere symptom of language's mechanical action. This radically perverse instrumentality, in which language first disassociates itself from and then endangers human purpose, and then displaces that purpose altogether, is described elsewhere in a famous quote by de Man: "Literature as well as criticism—the difference between them being delusive—is condemned (or privileged) to be forever the most rigorous and, consequently, the most unreliable language in terms of which man names and transforms himself" (19).

Given that non-literary or non-critical language, like the phenomenal world, is acknowledged but never encountered by de Man, his definition of literature can stand for what especially defines language: its existence as that "most rigorous and . . . unreliable" tool for human realization; one that not only rebuffs its own role in naming and transforming human existence but also exacts a chiasmatic exchange, in which the result is one with Kleist's inhuman marionette, a reoccurring image in de Man, the machine as the "anamorphosis of a form detached from meaning and capable of taking on any structure whatever, yet entirely ruthless in its inability to modify its own structural design for nonstructural [i.e., aesthetic or formalistic] reasons" (294). As a human extension, or prosthetic, language actually dramatizes the absence of any human animation or purpose behind the prosthetic. It is in that sense that language is a radically perverse instrumentality, an instrument divorced from the human aim that defines it as a tool, a *technē* that displaces any higher, non-contingent aim, any human truth or meaning, which are in fact products of its machinery. De Man's mechanism is first and foremost an obsession with this problematic, a topos of robotic simulacrum and mutilating instrumentality that deconstructs the intelligibility of language as a tool, a sign or extension, of human intent.

We are thus faced with a predicament equally impossible and aboriginal: that which defines us, our ability to extend ourselves, to make ourselves and our world, what can equally go by the name of either tool-making or language, is that which is radically disjoined from us, from human motivation and being. Within this *anthropological* context, one that paradoxically but also emphatically disarticulates its own object of analysis, de Man's well-known references to the "inhuman" nature of language gain their full force.[6] Language is not simply a tool, a thing, that we use to know our world and ourselves. It is that breach into the stable oppositions between making and knowing, means and ends, instrument and intention, machinery and human identity, that underscores the degree to which human nature is realized by its prosthetic character, by its dependence on the machine of language. As a repetitive patterning, simultaneously traversed by the aberrant and arbitrary, the machine of language is the logic of the inhuman. As an effect of language, the human is a non-human, inhuman, thing.

The mechanist materialism in de Man's deconstructive writings is something more than simply Jameson's interpretation of eclectic philosophical nominalism, just as de Manian deconstruction in general is something else besides a radically linguistic skepticism, insofar as that skepticism also reorganizes the distinction between the human and the non-human (that is, language) as the problem, or condition, of instrumentality. This view not only defamiliarizes de Manian deconstruction by giving it an anthropological cast; it also cannily hails Marxism as a body of discourse largely imbricated by these newly highlighted de Manian concerns.

Such an interpellation not only reiterates how Marx's dictum about freeing humanity from the necessity of nature resonates with a desired liberation from instrumentality. It also more specifically stresses and clarifies the degree to which Marxism's persuasive cognitive force, what Jameson in another context calls a "kind of shock to the mind," rests on a chiasmic violence that dramatizes how in bourgeois life humans are things and things are living beings.[7] The apotheosis of this reversal is the commodity fetish in *Capital*, a non-human thing putatively in the service of human life, but that in truth reorients human means in the service of its ends.[8] As a supernatural being, an idol of our mind, the commodity fetish displaces human intention much in the same way that Rousseau's inhuman grammar replaces the sovereignty of human desire. And, as in de Man, human existence is not merely shunted aside by this displacement; it is transformed, unveiled as part of the machinery of instrumentality. The status of the commodity fetish is inversely reflected in the plight of the worker, now made a machine to serve the production of the living fetish. The machine defines the human, as in Marx's case of the child laborer, outfitted with machinery specifically tailored to its size, so as to increase the efficiency of its production: "The machine accommodates itself to the *weakness* of the human being in order to make the *weak* human being [the child] into a machine."[9] "Human being" becomes a simulacrum of itself as human labor becomes an extension of the machine. Radically separated from human identity, the child laborer's actions take on the linguistic dynamism, the formal patterning, of Kleist's marionette, the "anamorphosis of a form detached from meaning," locked within "its own structural design," the non-human design of capital.

To understand Marx's argument as the assertion of capitalism as non-human, as fundamentally *without* meaning, is to approach the conceptual force behind Marxism's and deconstruction's shared investment in instrumentality, what, poaching from both Jameson and de Man, we might call the asymptotic point of their metonymic contiguity. From another level of Marxist analysis, of course, capitalism is fraught with the meaning of dialectical materialism. The prosthetic objectification of Marx's child laborer is not simply the sign of a condition of a radically perverse instrumentality that goes by the name of language; it is the symptom of a set of social and economic relations, whose intelligibility depends on the historical analysis that Marxism both presupposes and interrogates.

Marx also distinguishes between good and bad machines, tools and machines, and single machines and systems of machinery. But these and other crucial differences of contrasting affect and political prescription should not stop us from considering the implications that a shared focus on the machine and instrumentality have for the two discourses.[10] De Manian deconstruction, for example, has often been identified by a certain proscription of the literal, an activity oftentimes associated with the energetic exposure of how language constantly confuses itself with the phenomenal world.[11] The images of machines in Rousseau complicate this injunction in two ways: by their literal status as machines and, paradoxically, by their simultaneous existence as figures for language. The consequence is a movement by deconstruction toward the literal and the historical, although, paradoxically, the literal and the phenomenal no longer simply coincide in any immediately transparent, or comfortable, way.

*Literalizing* the images of machinery in Rousseau means that his encounters with machines are just that: encounters with instruments that thwart his plans, threaten his body, and challenge his subjectivity as the origin of his own agency and value. Such a challenge resonates, of course, with the many scenes of psychic self-conflict in Rousseau, such as the famous episode of Marion and the stolen ribbon in the *Confessions*, the very episode that de Man transforms into an allegory of how human intention and subjectivity depend on the contingency—the machinery—of language. The point is, however, that such psychic self-division also reflects Rousseau's interaction with a world of deadly man-made objects, instead of simply the other way around.

Conceivably, the ribbon in the Marion episode is itself a tool or machine that in the unpredictability of its purpose and effect splits Rousseau from his intentions, his subjectivity from the fiction of an originary desire. Indeed, Derrida has through the image of a typewriter ribbon wittily connected Marion's own trimming to the implacable, mechanical force of language in de Man's writing ("Typewriter," 284–359). But a later anecdote in the *Confessions* also vividly confuses the vagaries of machinery with the mercurial nature of Rousseau's desires: his account of the toy Hiero-fountain. This episode is less immediately structured in an ethical mode than the guilt-saturated theft of the ribbon and framing of Marion. The absence of such an ethical context is actually an advantage, insofar as it allows us to recover from the *Confessions* another series of coordinates. Rousseau relates how this toy figured in his designs with his friend Bâcle, when they planned to leave the home of Rousseau's benefactor, Mme de Warens, for a journey across the Alps:

> As a result of making this fountain work and of speaking about our trip, [we] thought that the former could serve the latter very well and prolong it. What was there in the world as curious as a Hiero-fountain? This principle was the foundation upon which we built the edifice of our fortune. In each village we would assemble the countryfolk around our fountain, and there meals and good cheer would fall on us with all the more abundance. . . . [Our fountain] could defray our expenses in Piedmont, in Savoy, in France, and all over the world. . . .
>
> I made this extravagant trip almost as pleasantly as I had expected, however, but not exactly in the same manner; for although our fountain amused the hostesses and their waitresses in the taverns for a few moments, it was no less necessary to pay upon leaving. But that hardly bothered us, and we thought of making real use of this resource only when money failed. An accident saved us

> the trouble; the fountain broke near Bramant, and it was time for it; for, without daring to say it to ourselves, we felt that it was beginning to bore us.[12]

Trivial and useless, the Hiero-fountain is also the "foundation" on which Rousseau builds the "edifice" of his fantasized fortune. The changing meanings of the fountain become an accurate index for the impractical and peripatetic nature of Rousseau's journey, as well as for his own inconstant attitude toward the trip: from being bored with the toy, and thus the grandiose plans associated with it, to laughing at his and Bâcle's foolishness as their clothes and shoes wear out, and to brooding over the outcome of his return to Mme de Warens. Within such a confusion of affect, of means and ends, the fountain could be said not only to reflect but also to generate Rousseau's journey and desires. Actively adding days to the planning of the travel, the "foundation" of Rousseau's excited imaginings, the fountain is at once what refers to the trip and what the trip refers to, the "it" that gradually bores Rousseau; literally and figuratively, the toy and its abrupt destruction structure the contingency of his journey, organizing his desires as well as serving them. The fountain is radically instrumental in the perverse sense that we have applied to de Man. At once at the center and the periphery of Rousseau's narrative, the fountain foregrounds the conflation of aim and pointlessness, of desire and apathy, that underwrites his wanderings. By laughing gaily as their plans for the fountain disintegrate, Rousseau ostensibly asserts a discontinuity between the toy and his emotions; yet the *meaning* of that laughter depends on that very discontinuity, on the very ineffectiveness of the fountain. Rousseau's narrative is as much a reaction to the fountain as what the toy reflects.

The indeterminacy of the fountain as either instrument or motive also tellingly takes place within two explicit systems of exchange: Rousseau's imagined exchange of the toy's performance for food and lodgings, and the actual money economy that rejects the toy as part of its system of substitution. Rousseau's journey is thus a continuous encounter with objects—toy and money—that stress not only the threatening unpredictability of their effects but also the degree to which those effects are questions of exchange and value. That Rousseau also specifies these systems of exchange in terms of class and gender—the imagined economy with peasants and the real one with landladies and their servants—is no coincidence. For the question of the toy's performance, of its value and what it does, could just as well be applied to Rousseau and his relation to Mme de Warens. Entertaining but impractical, of what value or use is Rousseau to his patron? As de Man argues, Rousseau is not simply threatened by the actions of objects; his subjectivity is itself objectified, made a thing. But to equate Rousseau with the

Hiero-fountain is also necessarily to detail the relation between Warens and Rousseau in terms of class and gender difference, terms that in their specificity are, for want of a better term, historical. If Rousseau is a toy whose value and purpose is unclear, that volatility is also at once the historical uncertainty of Rousseau's situation, of a petit-bourgeois man in the ambivalent service, and keep, of his "Maman," the wealthy Mme de Warens.

Both Rousseau's and Warens's positions could be particularized in even more complex fashion, but that is exactly the point: seeing Rousseau as the Hiero-fountain of Mme de Warens occasions this historical, indexical specification. Conversely, the question driving this indexical specification—what function Rousseau and the fountain serve—has a paradigmatic power that structures the entire book. Indeed, the *Confessions* can be understood as an extended response to the question of what value, what use, is *Rousseau*, a name that is almost always associated with the assertion of the interiority of Romantic imagination, the fantastic expression of a Hiero-fountain. As de Man argues, however, that interiority is paradoxically the consequence of a perversely instrumental world, what he describes as the machine of grammar and what we have depicted as the literal world of machines. In that sense the Hiero-fountain is not an "authentic" mode of Romantic expression, as conceived by Romanticism's mid-twentieth-century interlocutors, but an eighteenth-century mechanist work. But, more important, Rousseau's interiority is *itself* a machine in that, like the Hiero-fountain, it is marked by the question of its use and of the system of relations—the economy—that gives it "genuine" value. Understanding that economy means comprehending that system historically, which means seeing how the question of Rousseau's objectification is simultaneously the question of Rousseau's vocation in life, the question of a career, any career, that cannot be answered without first determining what makes such a question possible: in Rousseau's century the spread of market forces in Europe and the advent of other leveling events, one of which after his death Rousseau will retroactively become the emblem of, the French Revolution. Born the son of a watchmaker, Rousseau might become something else, a fact that is grounded in this historical moment, as well as one that is the occasion for his book: the possibility, the opportunity and crisis, that his vocation, the writing of his life and desires, might be something else besides the making of a watch. The perverse instrumentality recovered from de Man's reading of the machine in Rousseau can thus be linked to the historical instrumentality that resonates with the move from *Gemeinschaft* to *Gesellschaft*, the increasing dissolution of so-called *organic* society under capitalism.[13]

The apparent hyperbole of such an analysis seems less an issue when juxtaposed with an episode from the *Reveries of the Solitary Walker*, one made famous by de Man's reading of it in *Allegories*. The scene is Rousseau's encounter with a machine that crushes the ends of two of his fingers. De Man does not mention what the machine specifically does. Instead, his quote from Rousseau emphasizes the machine's formal properties, as seductive to Rousseau as they are empty to the reader of any apparent purpose or meaning: "I looked at the metal rolls, my eyes were attracted by their polish. I was tempted to touch them with my fingers and I moved them with pleasure over the polished surface of the cylinder."[14] De Man goes on to stress how the machine's power of suggestion

> reaches far beyond its illustrative purpose, especially if one bears in mind the previous characterization [in Rousseau] of unmotivated, fictional language as "machinal." The underlying structural patterns of addition and suppression as well as the figural system of the text all converge towards it. Barely concealed by its peripheral function, the text here stages the textual machine of its own constitution *and* performance, its own textual allegory. (298)

But what is the "illustrative purpose" of the "textual machine"? Rousseau's anecdote actually refers to a calender owned by an uncle who operates a calico works business. The "textual machine" is, literally, a textile machine. The intelligibility of both machines comes from the common Latin root of what they both produce: *textus*, a "woven thing." The status of this "thing" is, of course, precisely the issue. But while the two machines' commonality in this thing, *textus*, suspends any clear resolution to this issue, it also becomes impossible *not* to point to, or index, what the machine is. Indeed, by resolving this predicament in favor of his deadly machine of grammar, de Man cannot avoid clarity of meaning for the machine. Yet that referencing also at once paradoxically denotes the suppression of a certain history. Indeed, the clarity defines, points to, what the suppression is.

The contours of this suppressed history become clearer when we remember not only the famous role of linens and coats in *Capital*, but also how its discussion of machinery and large-scale industry begins with a number of references to the spinning machines and looms of Europe's eighteenth- and nineteenth-century textile industry (131–50, 493–96). Marx notes how the spinning machines of the Industrial Revolution create an odd dislocation in scale between the embodied human subject and the productive capacities of the machine, which leaves "the worker, in addition to his new labour of watching the machine with his eyes and correcting its mistakes with his hands, the merely mechanical role of acting as the motive power" (496). The spinning machine is at once human size and something much larger, a predicament that speaks to the inevitably hyperbolic nature of any narrativization of one individual's experience of capitalist history, as well as the odd combination of triviality and menace that Rousseau's encounter with machines thematizes. Indeed, if the machine in de Man comes from both the eighteenth and nineteenth centuries, from the random patterning of vertiginous clockwork and the dynamism and entropy of steam locomotion, that spectrum is imbedded in a historical set of social relations that the "literalization" of Rousseau's machinery reveals. The uselessness of the Hiero-fountain and the mutilating power of the calico calender—these are the linked symptoms of a historical horizon that coincides with the structure of Rousseau's texts.

It might appear that this "literalization" of the machine completely diverges from de Man's focus on language in *Allegories*, as well as from deconstructive proscriptions of the literal. Parataxis is at work here, and the ubiquity of this scission for critical thought will be a key focus of chapter 8's reading of *Don Juan*. But separating the literal from the figural also becomes a much more complicated proposition when, paradoxically, Rousseau's machines are seen as de Manian figures for language. Far from simply inscribing language within the definitive closure of the figural, such an articulation occasions the question of language's literal meaning: its purpose and value, which, like the machine's, inhere in the deconstruction of its subordinate role to the presumed originary force of human intention. A combination of the arbitrary and the formal, machine-like and like a machine, language *is* a machine.[15] The mechanical and the linguistic are thus caught in a metonymic relation of mutual displacement, an oscillation of referential properties that exposes how Rousseau's mechanical references are at once figures for machinery and figures for a language that is literally a machine. Signs of machinery can refer to both machine and language, which refer to each other; the machine is language, while language is a machine. That both could be figures for each other, that both could *be* each other, signals the tension of a metonymic displacement rather than simply a metaphoric subsumption that would allow the figural and literal to exist in naive opposition. Rather, the mutual displacement between machine and language asserts a condition that repudiates the a priori, separate existence of the figural and literal. This predicament prevents, or resists, the existence of de Man's allegories as the literality of figure as pure essence.

Contrary to such a pure existence, the literal is the foreign semiotic that deconstruction's own constative performance cannot quite subsume. We might then wonder whether this reformulation of de Man's terms resonates with the way that the Lacanian real cannot be assimilated by the symbolic; the answer depends, of course, on what Lacan we use, and how, more generally, we formulate that condition: on whether the real's resistance to signification recalls Jameson's neo-Kantian noumenon, for instance, or whether the real might actually converge with de Man's later notion in *Aesthetic Ideology* of the materiality of language as, in Derrida's suggestive phrasing, a "materiality without matter" ("Typewriter," 350).[16] In the latter case, which involves an aspect of de Man's intensely singular reading of Kant that Jameson doesn't really address, *foreign* would designate a resistance that could just as well be troped as an *internal* impediment, rather than as only an external interference. The rest of the chapters in part II will pursue this very issue from different angles. More immediately, as either an internal or external resistance, the literal is still held out as a possibility within a discourse that seems vehemently organized around the constant exposure of the literal as a false or blind figure. This by extension reinterrogates the certitude of the error of confusing the figural with the literal *as its own* error, as believing in the literality of the metaphor of pure essential figure. Deconstruction's resistance to such literality, or belief, would be, paradoxically, the foreign, unsubsumable, *opportunistic* element of the literal in deconstruction, the possibility of historical narrative.

This possibility, rather than any converse, simply positive realization of the literal, structures the aporia between the figural and literal that makes the literalization of machinery in Rousseau, along with the attendant historical specification, something else besides a pure, complete break from de Man's readings. There is a break, but one might also say that the machinery of the literal also breaks through this gap. Whether, however, this more fantastic recuperation of the literal completely restores the adequation between the literal and the phenomenal is another matter entirely. For if the historical specificities of Rousseau's machines appear to assume some type of empirical reality as one coordinate for the fabulist narrative of the move from *Gemeinschaft* to *Gesellschaft*, the literal existence of language as a machine is quite comfortable not relying on any phenomenal condition for its pronouncement. That, however, both moments of the literal might not be so easily separated; that, as our reading of de Man's *Allegories* shows, they can exist in some complex overlapping fashion together; and that this more problematic state is precisely the opportunity for history in de Man to emerge—all these observations point to a predicament where the literal, or the indexing *force* of the literal, what we might say our reading designates *as* the historical, is not only, or even necessarily, phenomenal. The literality of language as a machine prevents deconstruction from being closed to the historical, but the formal logic of this new identity is something besides a simple phenomenal recuperation. Paradoxically then, this non-phenomenal literality might be understood as a singular type of figure, although not like de Man's definition of metaphor, as a figure who has forgotten that it is a figure. Rather, this literality is singular because its referential denotative performance resists the ideology of figuration as pure essence. To literalize a figure is thus neither to essentialize nor to unmask it, but to index it. But, as such, this literality also depends on the constant generation of figure, or resemblance, a condition of meaning, historical or otherwise, that the next several chapters, both obliquely and explicitly, further explore.

For now I want to ask instead whether the aporia between the figural and the literal has any other consequence for the intelligibility of historical thought in terms of the way that deconstruction and Marxism relate; whether the machine conversely affects Marxist discourse in a way that is more complex than simply conceiving of Marxist historicity as the phenomenal literalization of deconstruction's instrumental concerns. If the presence of the machine in Marx clarifies the social character of the dilemma of Rousseau's value and use in the *Confessions*, how might the machine also complicate the conception of those very terms in Marx?

One could respond by considering Marx's many explicit statements about machinery and automatons in *Capital*, the *Gundrisse*, and elsewhere. A surprisingly more pertinent approach plays off one reading of Marx's theory of value in the first volume of *Capital*, what Gayatri Spivak might call a "continuist" version of the Marxist relation between use value and exchange value.[17] Within this reading use value is not blind radical instrumentality. Rather, it is the self-evident usefulness of a product or object, fundamentally separate from the value of something that occurs within a system of substitution, or exchange. With the advent of capitalism and the ubiquity of the commodity form, use value is shunted aside by the increasingly corrosive powers of exchange value. Thus, for example, Horkheimer and Adorno actually see exchange value as the most vehement sign of instrumentality in modern capital (157–58).[18] In dissolving the organic integrity of use value, exchange value, with its mystifying social relations among commodities rather than people, subverts the stability of means and ends that use value underwrites; the result is the general loss of organic meaning that is the invidious signature of capitalist, bourgeois exchange.

This scenario can, of course, associate Marx with a nostalgic longing for foundational use value. Such is the basis for Jean Baudrillard's well-known critique of *Capital*, where he attacks this apparent nostalgia, deconstructing use value by way of a supplementary exchange value that he claims always contaminates use value's pure originary force. For Baudrillard capitalism, rather than mystifying genuine social relations, most perfectly emphasizes a constitutive ontological fissure that always places "authentic" value and identity within a system of exchange, unmoored from any ultimate referent, adrift within an economy of signs. Use value and production are hollowed out, made phantasms of the equally surface phenomenon of commodities, consumption, and, in Baudrillard's later works, simulacra.[19] Like Kleist's marionette, Baudrillard's simulacrum, a copy with no origin, evinces the radical non-human instrumentality of the machine: an object that not only is unable to account for itself within any system of human reference or design but also has replaced that system, made it a simulacrum effect. Marx's commodity fetish is normalized, with the intelligibility of human affect and subjectivity becoming one more non-human thing.

This familiar argument depends, of course, on the truth of Marx's nostalgia, his investment in a metaphysical essentialism. Gayatri Spivak's meditation on Marxist value comes up with a very different *Capital*, one composed of a much more radical textuality, a vehemently "discontinuist" performance that foregrounds the "invagination" of use value's spatial relation to exchange value, and the moments of parataxis that interrupt the dialectical bindings of the transformation of value into capital (159–66). Such blockages turn *Capital* into a very different text than the one that Baudrillard deconstructs. Another tactic is possible, however, one that stays within the boundaries of a text that develops a continuous, architectonic argument about value, or more specifically, an argument about the relation between value and labor. But rather than supporting Baudrillard, this move demonstrates the degree to which *Capital* anticipates the question of the simulacrum, a predicament that says much about the roles of machine *and* figure in Marxist thought.

As Marx explains, exchange value does not occur simply through a set of relational differences, unmoored from the ultimate referent of use value. Exchange value occurs because of Marx's theory of equivalence, his belief that different commodities still share a fundamental commonality that allows them to form relations of value that are both quantitatively *and* qualitatively equivalent. That commonality is "human labour in the abstract," homogenous objectified labor, as opposed to heterogeneous concrete labor that produces use value (128). Indeed, a "use-value, or useful article . . . has value only because abstract human labour is objectified (*vergegenständlicht*) or materialized in it"—a commodity might have a certain utility, but its value lies in the amount of abstract labor, the labor time, that was expended in making it (129). This identity, value as abstract labor, comes to structure the equivalence among commodities that allows them to circulate within the realm of capitalist exchange.

While supporting Marx's entire theory of value, abstract labor has been the source of a continuing controversy, since the concept begs two thorny, interpenetrating questions. How do we define abstract labor, and when does it occur? *Capital* does conceive of abstract labor in a physiological sense, the "productive expenditure of human brains, nerves, and muscles" that allows for the temporal measurement of "identical . . . labour power" (129, 134). Of course, to *measure* one homogenous identity is to insert questions of relation and difference within the very objective nature of that identity. More troublesome is what this definition also implies, that abstract labor as embodied labor need not be restricted to the human production of a capitalist society. Paradoxically, Marx is also quite emphatic as to how the uniformity of abstract labor occurs only through the exchange of commodities; exchange value might not make sense without the equivalence of abstract labor, but abstract labor cannot happen completely without a society within which exchange value dominates. At the very least, then, abstract labor becomes a constitutive quality of human production that only gains hegemony during the capitalist era. Some readers of Marx have gone further, however, arguing that abstract labor is completely a symptom of capitalist exchange, an abstraction of quality that is in fact alienated labor, the reification of human subjectivity under capitalism. Thus, Marx's text, even its continuist version, occasions two competing conceptions of abstract labor that clash over the metalepsis between abstract labor and historical periodization, and abstract labor itself as either embodied being, constitutive property, or historical effect.[20]

Several passages from *Capital* forcefully convey these tensions. They occur toward the end of Marx's discussion of "The Equivalent Form of Value," where he unpacks the consequences of achieving an equivalence between coats and linens by turning the specific concrete labor of tailoring into a measure for weaving through the concept of undifferentiated, abstract labor:

> But because this concrete labour, tailoring, counts exclusively as the expression of undifferentiated human labour, it possesses the characteristics of being identical with other kinds of labour, such as the labour embodied in the linen. Consequently, although, like all other commodity-producing labour, it is the labour of private individuals, it is nevertheless labour in its directly social form. It is precisely for this reason that it presents itself to us in the shape of a product which is directly exchangeable with other commodities. Thus the equivalent form has a third peculiarity: private labour takes the form of its opposite, namely labour in its directly social form. (150–51)

The organization of this paragraph implies a certain uni-direction, with the transformation of private, concrete labor into social, abstract labor being the "third peculiarity," the final consequence of the equivalent form of value. Such a teleological movement would intimate the logic of perceiving the exchange of commodities as being a prerequisite for this transformation. Yet, at the same time, the commensurability between coat and linen through abstract, or social, labor results "in the shape of a product which is directly exchangeable with other commodities"; far from simply being the effect of exchange, such commensurability seems to present *itself* as the prerequisite for the exchange of commodities.

This chiasmus is exacerbated by the language earlier used to describe the first two peculiarities of the equivalence form, how "use-value becomes the form of appearance of its opposite, value"; and how "concrete labour becomes the form of manifestation of its opposite, abstract human labour" (148, 150). In contrast to the third peculiarity, terms associated with private labor ("use value" and "concrete labour") are described as vehicles for core identities associated with social labor ("value" and "abstract human labour"). To complicate matters more, the "mysteriousness" of the equivalent form and its first peculiarity, the manifestation of value through use-value, is solved by the second peculiarity, the manifestation of abstract labor through concrete labor (149–50). The equivalent form of value thus produces several conflicting, asymmetric relations between abstract labor and its converse identity. The third peculiarity of equivalent form seems to narrate the transformation of private labor into social labor. At another level, however, the very "riddle" of value in the equivalent form seems to be explained by the already existing presence of abstract labor in the form's second peculiarity (150). Finally, in the first and second peculiarities value and abstract labor are embodied in their opposites; they are not simply what their opposites teleologically become. Indeed, the "expression" of abstract labor through concrete labor appears to initiate the transformation of private labor into social labor. At the very least these different scenarios stress the huge complexity in *Capital* of abstract labor's theoretical and historical conception. More radically, this complexity dramatizes a scandal of, rather than a challenge to, thought. The meaning of private labor not manifesting but "tak[ing] the form" of social labor, the question of what refers to what, is simultaneously foregrounded and stalled at the very moment that that transformation's relation to commodity exchange is asserted in the text.

Trying to order these varying levels of conflicting cause and effect, of primary and secondary identity, is exactly what the controversy over abstract labor has tried to adjudicate. Marx himself appears to offer his own solution, with his discussion of Aristotle that immediately follows the description of this third peculiarity of the equivalent form. The question of abstract labor's relation to exchange is once again engaged, this time in terms of the difference between precapitalist and capitalist societies. Marx relates how Aristotle's *Nichomachean Ethics* at first seems to understand how an equivalence between unlike things is possible, how five beds equaling one house is indistinguishable from five beds equaling so much money, but then denies their fundamental commensurability. Marx argues that Aristotle's denial was the result of the "lack [in his analysis] of a concept of value":

> What is the homogenous element, i.e. the common substance, which the house represents from the point of view of the bed, in the value expression for the bed? Such a thing, in truth, cannot exist, says Aristotle. But why not? Towards the bed, the house represents something equal, insofar as it represents what is really equal, both in the bed and the house. And that is—human labour.
>
> However, Aristotle was unable to extract this fact, that in the form of commodity-values, all labour is expressed as equal human labour and therefore as labour of equal quality, by inspection from the form of value, because Greek society was founded on the labour of slaves, hence had as its natural basis the inequality of men and of their labour-powers. The secret of the expression of value, namely the equality and equivalence of all kinds of labour because and insofar as they are human labour in general, could not be deciphered until the concept of human equality had already acquired the permanence of a fixed popular opinion. This however becomes possible only in a society where the commodity-form is the universal form of the product of labour, hence the dominant social relation is the relation between men as possessors of commodities. Aristotle's genius is displayed precisely by his discovery of a relation of equality in the value-expression of commodities. Only the historical limitation inherent in the society in which he lived prevented him from finding out what "in reality" this relation of equality consisted of. (151–52)[21]

In this difficult passage the "common substance" of abstract labor seems to inhabit both the identity of a constitutive embodied property and a historical effect. By stressing Aristotle's historical inability to understand this idea, Marx appears to reiterate the degree to which abstract labor is fundamentally tied to capitalist society. But in stressing this inability as a question of historical *understanding*, Marx also implies that the objective nature of abstract labor was something that Aristotle *could* have perceived except for the invisible social inequalities of the Greek world. Indeed, only the advent of the "fixed popular opinion" of human equality allows abstract labor to be "deciphered" by modern understanding. This tension is further complicated by the cause of this opinion: the moment in capitalist history when the dominant human relation inheres in those that occur among commodity owners. Commodity production and exchange do seem to enable abstract labor, but only as a second-order effect, by creating the popular opinion that paradoxically allows us to see through the heterogeneity of concrete labor, what itself had been codified by such precapitalist modes of social inequality as slavery. The mediating terms that determine abstract labor's presence are thus themselves of differing ontological weight. This situation destabilizes any simple narrativization of Marx's historical comparison: what is the status of an abstract labor unavailable to Greek antiquity because of the historical fact of slavery, as opposed to that of an abstract labor available to modernity because of the fixed popular opinion of equality? What is the status of the historical difference that inheres in Aristotle's "historical limitation"? Furthermore, abstract labor is itself *exteriorized* from commodity exchange as a second-order effect of that phenomenon, exactly what abstract labor, within those societies in which the capitalist mode of production prevails, should subtend. Yet abstract labor is also unable to secure simply the identity of a universal property: if such labor was " 'in reality' " at the bottom of the equality that Aristotle theorized, its constative effect is inscribed within a phrase whose scare quotes stress rather than elide the figural disjunctions of the passage, the degree to which abstract labor seems at once to occupy and displace itself from both historical moments of Marx's story.[22]

Given the complexity of such passages, solving the controversy of abstract labor seems less pertinent than considering why Marx's text describes this idea in such emphatically ambiguous terms—why his writing creates this controversy in the first place. *Capital* installs within its analysis the concept of abstract labor as a problem of the relation between abstract labor and *something else*: between an entity and its abstraction, homogenization, or objectification, an entity that has been diversely interpreted as the heterogeneity of a concrete labor subtended by the pure physiology of undifferentiated labor and as the prolepsis of an unalienated labor negatively defined by the present expropriation of reified labor. The ambiguity of abstract labor is simply a sign of the ambiguity of its referent, what it abstracts, what we might try to circumscribe by the term *labor* except for the fact that that idea has no analytic force in Marx's theory of value without the initial divisions between abstract and concrete labor, and labor and labor power. Indeed, depending on what moment of analysis is occurring in Marx's theory, it is unclear whether that entity is abstract labor's referent or abstract labor is *its* referent. One could chalk this up to the mobility of dialectical positioning that characterizes Marx's thought. But one could also see this referential indeterminacy inserting a bar between abstract labor and what it abstracts, an absolute separation that would disrupt their putative mimetic grounding in one another. An abstraction of something else, abstract labor does not need anything else to be itself, to organize and generate Marx's theory of value. This sense of tautology is exactly what Gayatri Spivak criticizes in the continuist version of "Marx's scheme of value": "Yet even in this . . . version value seems to escape the onto-phenomenological question: what is it (*ti esti*). The usual answer—value is the representation of objectified labor—begs the question of use-value" (155).

To operate within a historically continuous argument of Marxist value, abstract labor does not need what it historically abstracts. What *Capital* marks by such terms as "concrete labour" and "use value" *does not need to exist*. An abstraction without a referent, abstract labor functions like a copy with no origin. Baudrillard's deconstruction of Marx is beside the point, insofar as Marx's theory of value is already underwritten by the simulation, the simulacrum of abstract labor. It is no coincidence that Marx so often explicitly or implicitly describes one trait of abstract labor, its homogenization, in mechanical terms. In doing so, Marx also signals abstract labor's robotic independence from what it abstracts, an independence that coincides with the metaphysical unmooring of the simulacrum.

When Marx places abstract labor within the realm of a "phantom-like objectivity," he could just as well be describing that concept's rhetorical effect on his text (128). Accounting for Marx's theory of value, abstract labor as a simulation cannot account for itself. It is a catachresis at the core of Marx's theory, a figure that cannot account for its figurality in non-figural terms; it cannot be simply absorbed by the exigencies of concrete labor or use value. If the machine in deconstruction produces the possibility of the literal in a discourse that seems only to assert the deracinating power of figure in texts, abstract labor is the machine of figure that enables the analysis of the literal in Marx. Indeed, the historical literality that emerges in de Man reveals itself to be the machine of history in Marx's thought. This condition is far from disabling: if one sees in abstract labor the historical fact of expropriation, the question still remains as to how that basic antagonism becomes something akin to a *history* of expropriation. The answer, in a word, is the machine of abstract labor. But this predicament is also not simply enabling, insofar as that possibility assumes we are in control of, or responsible for, this action. Abstract labor is thus material, but in neither the physically quantifiable nor socially ascertainable way that it has been interpreted. Rather, it is the catachrestic imposition of the literality of dialectical history in Marx, one specific rendering of the material event of history gnomically referred to in de Man's last writings, and explicitly connected to the de Manian machine in Derrida's own "Typewriter." As a catachresis, abstract labor is also a preeminent figure *for* the machine, an example of language's robotic quality, the component within a pattern that cannot be accounted for even as it generates a network of constative and performative effects. Far from simply literalizing deconstruction's figural application of the machine, Marx's theory thus demonstrates its textual awareness of a radically perverse instrumentality based on the simultaneous articulation of figure as machine, and machine as figure. Such simultaneity demonstrates that any vision of history is at once a rendering of its non-identity, or form. That this form is itself the effect of a radical instrumentality beyond value, instrumental or otherwise, means simply that no history can fully account for this condition. The form in history that "has no history": that is the machine, as much as the literal in deconstruction that is not pure figure, history in Rousseau.[23]

# Against Theory beside Romanticism

## Mute Bodies, Fanatical Seeing

> Then there will be readers who can read.
>
> —Friedrich Schlegel, "Über die Unverständlichkeit"

If in the preceding chapter Romanticism functions obliquely as the catachrestic nature of history in Rousseau and Marx, its role in this discussion is much more direct. Indeed, our main point in this chapter is to recover Romanticism's presence in an argument that is a well-known part of theory's academic institutional history. To do so, we begin with a somewhat contrary remark, that it appears that the theory wars are over, replaced by new forms and ways to articulate the current intellectual debates of our time. In that sense we can say that Steven Knapp and Walter Benn Michaels's 1982 essay, "Against Theory," succeeded, so much so that the reason to return to the dated but nonetheless fierce topicality of its polemic might remain far from clear. Still, as theory's role in the university has explicitly shrunk over the years (becoming, some might say approvingly, less hegemonic, less centralized, and more dispersed), the implications of "Against Theory" are worth revisiting. Such a return especially profits a field of study that Knapp and Michaels's New Historicism helped dethrone from its eminence in the late 1960s and throughout the 1970s, a Romanticism then defined by the deconstructive scrutiny of the Yale School.

Deconstruction, of course, was and sometimes still is a synonym for theory, especially when the nature of the characterization is critical, as in Knapp and Michaels's piece, although Paul de Man is just one among several targets in the essay. One could actually say, contrary to the concerns of another of its targets, E. D. Hirsch, that "Against Theory" helped inaugurate the academy's turn away from theory toward history in the early 1980s, with the observation that the essay—and hence once again the peculiarity of its status—is a central piece of the New Historicist canon that has no history in it (which might also explain partly Hirsch's reaction to it, regardless of the differences between his and the New Historicism).[1] Surprisingly, there is a lot of Romanticism in the piece, especially given how New Historicism moved the focus of literary studies away from Romanticism to the Renaissance and nineteenth-century U.S. literature. The predicament seems especially glaring within the framework of reading the essay over twenty-five years later, as the presence of Romanticism in "Against Theory" was never a major part of the controversy that ensued after its publication.

The core of the essay's argument is literally about Romanticism, a bizarre thought experiment involving a universal reader's encounter with "A Slumber Did My Spirit Seal" on a sandy beach. Ostensibly crystallizing the piece's argument about the coincidence between authorial intention and textual meaning, this strange version of the philosophic example, the wave poem, as it was called, actually takes the essay in another direction, one also embodied in the very lines of Wordsworth's poem: not the issue of the authorial intention of the text, but that of the intention—the meaning, form, or design—of mute nature.[2] In expressing a predicament most emphatically formulated in the second half of Kant's third *Critique*, "Against Theory" outpaces the moment of its own topical New Historicist and New Pragmatic intervention. As this and the following chapter argue, Knapp and Michaels's essay actually outlines the character of our modernity as it takes shape in the field of literary and cultural studies. "Against Theory" performs the proposition of a triangulation that we cannot let go of, resolve, or overcome: that the intention of the text is the intention of nature, which is the intention of history. That is why we read.

This action certainly involves the de Manian sense of reading, although not in a simply straightforward manner. Indeed, the question of reading can be approached from a fresh perspective precisely because "Against Theory" especially positions itself against deconstruction, although more apparently against New Criticism, Hirsch's historicism, and Stanley Fish's own version of pragmatism. The odd non-meaning of the essay's paradoxical resemblance to deconstruction echoes one crucial way the essay incites the compulsion of reading, through the formal structuring, or figuring, of the resemblance of non-meaning to meaning. The generation of that aporia also incites the very question of the relation between reading Romanticism and reading romantically, insofar as we cannot be immediately sure whether in that formulation Romanticism occupies the role of non-meaning, meaning, or the resemblance between them, a dilemma emblematized, and confirmed, by the role of "A Slumber" in Knapp and Michaels's essay, but also proleptically realized by the *sensation of meaning* recorded by a character in another Wordsworth poem, the Boy of Winander.

In formulating this action, this and the next chapter develop a dynamic of repudiating the physical senses that operates at a more complicated level than what we witnessed in chapter 1. Knapp and Michaels's essay involves the rejection of sensory experience as non-language that does seem to utilize a sobriety very much akin to what chapter 1 describes. But this chapter's response to "Against Theory" and the next chapter's to Michaels's recent book, *The Shape of the Signifier*, assert a profitable muddying of Knapp's and Michaels's categories, a sensation of meaning whose own relation to the phenomenal is complex and strained. Similar to how in the last chapter historical knowledge does not necessarily rely on the phenomenal, the sensation of meaning actually performs its own disarticulation from the physical senses. But, in turn, much of what is familiar in our literary and cultural history is characterized by the repeated attempt either to repudiate or to minimize this more complicated form of sensation. Emblematized by the uncompromising force of Knapp's and Michaels's categories, this particular type of critical sobriety is once again a struggle with the confusions, and promises, of Romanticism.

With remarkable astringency Knapp and Michaels define theory as "the attempt to govern interpretations of particular texts by speaking to an account of interpretation in general" (11). Theory is first and foremost, as some might call it, a meta-theory, specifically about the interpretation of a text—or an utterance, which, for Knapp and Michaels, is the same thing. More precisely, theory tries to govern interpretation by arguing how and whether, first, intention and meaning interact and, second, knowledge and belief interact. For Knapp and Michaels there is no need for this argument—and thus no need for theory—since intention and meaning are the same thing, as well as knowledge and belief. Those who theorize textual meaning without authorial intention, like the now not so New Critics, and those who theorize the need for intention to adjudicate meaning, like Hirsch, are equally mistaken because meaning is already intention. Those who theorize a meaningless language, like de Man, are also wrong in believing that such a language exists, since language is always the meaningful utterance of an intention.

The wave poem's purpose is to force us to admit the choices that we ignore in order to have either meaning without intention or language without meaning. The escalating silliness of each phase of the example—first we see squiggles in the sand that look like those of the first stanza of "A Slumber"; then we see a wave wash up and recede, disclosing the second stanza; finally we see a submarine of scientists looking at us and proclaiming the success of their experiment—forces us to realize how counterintuitive it is to maintain the existence of intentionless meaning when we encounter language, something that one might be able to do during the first stage of the example, but which becomes increasingly difficult with the intervention of the wave and then the submarine. If we respond to Knapp and Michaels's scenario the way that they think we should, we must admit that either the marks on the sand are language or they're not, either there is some intentional agency—author, pantheistic sea, or research submarine crew—behind the poem or what we see has no meaning and is therefore neither poem, writing, nor language.

Reversing one definition of Kant's sublime, however, we can say that comprehending the example is not quite the same as apprehending it. Matters of tone and allusion seem more elusive than stable. Is the increasingly ludicrous setup a parody of theory's own narcissistic abstraction, or a by-product of the ratcheted-up, traditional intensity of skeptical American pragmatic inquiry?[3] What does it mean that intentionless meaning becomes explicitly counterintuitive only when the scenario becomes especially bizarre? And what of the exemplary status of the wave poem itself? Ostensibly a hyperbolic replay of an example used by P. D. Juhl, a student of Hirsch's, the setup of coming upon writing in the sand seems to invite but also withhold its precise relation to numerous possible predecessors, including, in the eighteenth and nineteenth centuries alone, Defoe's Crusoe coming upon a footprint on the beach, Kant likewise coming upon a hexagon, Wordsworth's Dream of the Arab, and Shelley's Rousseau's "brain be[coming] as sand" (line 405); and, more close to the wave poem's inception, Foucault's concluding image in *The Order of Things* of a future where "man would be erased, like a face drawn in sand at the edge of the sea."[4] The philosophical, anthropological, and colonialist question of human identity; the frailty of text and cognition when confronted by temporality or some other inescapable force—these are some of the themes evoked by various scenarios of what occurs between sandy beach and ocean wave. How much do such issues abut on the question of intention? How much is intention simply about intention? Is the wave poem part of some larger textual iteration, or is it itself newly sprung from Knapp and Michaels, its identity fully whole and autonomous in terms of its own polemical occasion within the essay's argument?

*Iteration*, of course, is one of the key contested terms between John Searle and Jacques Derrida in their famous debate over speech acts and intention, an Anglo-

American/Continental dispute that also seems to hover proleptically over the parts in Knapp and Michaels that engage with de Man.[5] Peggy Kamuf has suggestively made Searle and Derrida's debate one of the main subtexts of "Against Theory," while charging that Knapp and Michaels represent the wave poem as completely within the autonomous, hermetically sealed state of the philosophic example.[6] Yet the very fact that Kamuf can extract Searle and Derrida from Knapp and Michaels demonstrates the permeability of the essay, a heteronomy itself echoed by the present-not-present iterative form of the wave poem. Knapp and Michaels might say, of course, that Kamuf and I are really simply quibbling over their intention for the wave poem—something with which, as Kamuf observes, Derrida would not really disagree (9). Yet that is the point: the possible iteration of the wave poem suspends, rather than resolves, the question of its, or Knapp and Michaels's, intention. Claiming that that irresolution *is* the real intention of Knapp and Michaels does not solve things either, since that situation can be repeated ad infinitum, becoming, in fact, the iterative structure of the wave poem's hermeneutic. As we might somewhat inelegantly ask, is the irresolution of intention the actual intention of the wave poem, or is the question of the intention of the irresolution of intention the true intention of the poem?

The wave poem, therefore, exemplifies not only a key idea of the polemic of "Against Theory" but also the character of the argument as a whole. For all the precision of its language, and the cogency of its message, that theory should stop, it's not quite clear what "Against Theory" is about. Knapp and Michaels in fact use this against their detractors, noting how the essay rattles a host of readers who understand the consequences of the essay in conflicting ways. In his introduction to the collection of writings on "Against Theory," W. J. T. Mitchell nicely summarizes this quality of the work, "its spare, laconic, almost enigmatic style. . . . The clarity of Knapp and Michaels's argument . . . is accompanied by a studious reserve about motives. The essay gives the impression that its authors are in the grip of an insight that is quite indifferent to questions of value, interest, or power. . . . Perhaps the most paradoxical and intriguing feature of 'Against Theory' is that an essay which argues that meaning and intention are essentially the same thing should be so clear about its meaning while remaining so inscrutable about its intentions" (3).

In describing Knapp and Michaels as being in the "grips of an insight," Mitchell employs the early de Man's terminology of blindness and insight, a radical dialectic that famously challenged the constative claims of literary cognition even before de Man advanced the term "deconstruction" in his later *Allegories of Reading* (x). Mitchell's application of such language to Knapp and Michaels is more than simply fortuitous. The reference tells one institutional story, signaling the reigning critical vocabulary that Knapp and Michaels's New Historicism will in fact supplant; yet the situation is even more complex than that. For all the ways that "Against Theory" seems to distinguish itself from deconstruction—through its own severe estimation of the idea of meaningless language and the way the essay replays, as Kamuf suggests, the debate between Searle and Derrida—Knapp and Michaels's essay also mirrors much of the troubling, entrancing, critical energies that characterize Yale School theory. Indeed, the essay's intellectual—if not theoretical—ascendancy appears to come as much from how "Against Theory" models those energies as it does from how the piece argues against them. Mitchell can apply the language of de Man to Knapp and Michaels because of the similar interpretive effects that these writers incite.

The very notion in "Against Theory" of interpretive practice over theory actually sounds quite like the position in de Man's contemporaneous essay, "The Return to Philology," which describes theory as merely the practice of reading, the simple but difficult endeavor of attending to what really happens in a particular text (*Resistance*, 21–26).[7] In this case, and in others besides deconstruction, theory evinces an antinomian side that Knapp and Michaels's definition of theory ignores.[8] Theory can actually argue against global perspectives as much as "Against Theory." This antinomian character of deconstruction supports, and is supported by, the uncomfortable question of deconstruction's (non-)application. If the previous chapter considered how both deconstruction and Marxism identify a radical instrumentality separated from human design, a comparison of deconstruction and "Against Theory" gestures toward an equally intense non-instrumentality, also disarticulated from any apparent or clear purpose. Part of deconstruction's power to unsettle is thus precisely a radical sense of non-instrumental practice, the endeavor of putting practice itself under interrogation. As our students constantly remind us, understanding a deconstructive argument, even agreeing with it, is not the same as knowing what to do with it. Knapp and Michaels in fact diagnose this as the problem of theory: "Since . . . there is nothing left for theory to *do*, what is there left for theory to *be*?" (26). Oddly enough, however, this is quite like the effect that "Against Theory" incites, what Mitchell's description so succinctly captures. While the argument of "Against Theory" is clear, its purpose is not, which paradoxically makes the essay's clarity an opacity all the more unsettling because of the essay's forensic precision.

This odd mixing of clarity and opacity conveyed by Mitchell is exactly what "Against Theory" shares with deconstruction. Of course, as with Kamuf, Knapp and Michaels might say that Mitchell's characterization of their essay doesn't so much contradict them as simply offer his view of what their intention is, the enigmatic character of their polemic. Regardless, the essay's perplexing semantic status, equally frustrating and entrancing, also points to the significance of the specific work in the wave poem example. If Knapp and Michaels get the wave poem from Juhl, Juhl gets the poem in the wave poem from Hirsch, whose *Validity in Interpretation* gets "A Slumber" from the 1950s debate between Cleanth Brooks and F. W. Bateson over the poem's meaning.[9] Knapp and Michaels themselves cite the iconic nature of "A Slumber" as an object of interpretation for twentieth-century critics (5, 7). Qualifying my earlier statement, then, we could say that history does seem to be imbedded in the wave poem and, by extension, "Against Theory." But like so much that hovers around both example and essay, this history seems both there and not quite there, implicit but not explicit, or even noticed by any commentator of the essay, including Knapp and Michaels themselves. In "Against Theory" the history of twentieth-century critical reading becomes the history of reading a Romantic poem, of defining Romanticism as the necessary, opaque literary object that makes the institution of literary criticism possible.

At a practical level that pragmatists Knapp and Michaels might appreciate, this critical history makes perfect sense, since "A Slumber" is a deceptively simple work, a notoriously, or wonderfully, difficult poem to read. Like the wave poem example, this trait of "A Slumber" is a question of tone as well as of comprehension. Is Wordsworth's narrator devastated or buoyed by Lucy's present place in the earth? Who or what is "my Spirit" (Gill, 147; line 1)? These are, of course, very traditional questions, but that is the point.[10] "Against Theory" retroactively highlights "A Slumber" as the reserve of Romantic poetic meaning initiating critical reading for the next two centuries to come, the uncanny proleptic moment for the essay's own enigmatic character. Of course, this apparently overdetermined role of "A Slumber" is appropriate for another reason, since the poem is about interpretation, about our comprehension, or incomprehension, of what rolls round with rocks, stones, and trees. This might be Lucy, or what Lucy has become, or the narrator's own self-knowledge of his experience of Lucy's passing, if we could be sure what that passing means. Read through "Against Theory," "A Slumber" becomes part of an expanding geometrical pattern, which includes its own dynamic, its place within the wave poem, the wave poem itself, and "Against Theory," where each component repeats the incitement toward and resistance to meaning that defines the interpretive act.

Indeed, the poem's cognitive action nicely anticipates, among other things, the categories that Knapp and Michaels argue about, and use. Referencing the second half of their essay, where the two dispute any separation between belief and knowledge, we might ask whether the poem's narrator really knows what "she" is doing, or not doing, in the second stanza. Or is that simply the narrator's belief? Or, does that distinction really exist? And if it does not, is that because it never did, or has the division been healed by the speaker's synthesizing imagination, as a mid-twentieth-century Romanticist might argue? Is there indeed anything to understand, is there in fact a reserve of meaning to Lucy, sealed inside her as she is encased within the earth? Or is she actually nothing—or, as Knapp and Michaels might say, something (some thing) that simply impersonates meaning without meaning anything, like the unintentional marks on the sand that cause us to fool ourselves into believing in intentionless meaning by merely resembling, not really being, language?[11] Is the presence of death an utterance, or only the illusion of an utterance? Bluntly put, what, if anything, does death—the dead body, the dead poem—tell us, and who, or what, tells us of death?

Paul de Man also speaks to these questions during a decidedly gothic moment of his own well-known treatment of "A Slumber," when he casually observes how "Wordsworth is one of the few poets who can write proleptically about" death, including his own, and "speak, as it were, from" his own grave ("Rhetoric," 225). From such observations comes de Man's later sense of prosopopoeia, a metaphor of face, body, and voice as oddly unavoidable during the textual hermeneutic as Knapp and Michaels's intentional agency (*Rhetoric*, 67–81, 93–123).[12] Knapp and Michaels do not, however, critique de Man directly through "A Slumber," although de Man's reading seems to haunt the wave poem example, through how de Man imagines Wordsworth speaking from the grave and how both essays exploit the iconic character of Wordsworth's piece. (De Man's reading is, of course, part of an essay explicitly about the study of Romanticism ["Rhetoric," 187–208].)[13] De Man also focuses on the idealized, temporal break between the two stanzas, which strangely resonates with how Knapp and Michaels make the receding wave unveil the second stanza. Each critical scenario narrativizes the attainment of a certain wisdom—the demystifying power of death or the necessary intention of meaning—by the latter stanza. Kamuf has cannily discussed this dynamic in "A Slumber" as the illusion, and then disillusion, of human presence: in the first stanza, the speaker and Lucy are seemingly alive; in the second, the speaker must acknowledge Lucy as the ghost, trace, or "seal" of his own death (12). For Kamuf, the wave poem actually imposes a tripartite structure onto the reading of "A Slumber," with the techno-administrative glee of the submarine scientists representing a willful forgetting of our readerly disillusion, a falling back into the illusion of continuing human presence, what allows us to "mistak[e] a (living) agent for a (dead) author" (13). But the odd interplay among these different critical explanations of the form of "A Slumber" can also have a more irresolute effect. Like the very relation between "Against Theory" and deconstruction, this interplay might represent an internecine academic conflict, a struggle over a critical truth, or, as has been suggested, a larger historical battle over the emerging cultural landscape of early 1980s Reaganomics.[14] But the formal resonances of this interplay might also mean nothing at all. They might be arbitrary or, as Knapp and Michaels might say, unintentional, although whether that condition always excludes meaning still remains to be seen. In that sense, it's more than appropriate that one concrete link between "Against Theory" and deconstruction should take the form of a poem. At question is the very status of form itself as a meaning, and whether such a meaning always means the presence of an intention. At question is the meaning, or non-meaning, of a resemblance. This is precisely the predicament thematized in, and thus formally set up by, Knapp and Michaels's actual critique of de Man.

"Against Theory" engages de Man through a pre–*Le Soir* reading of his well-known deconstruction of Rousseau's *Confessions*, in particular the infamous scene when Rousseau apparently accuses the servant girl Marion of the theft of a ribbon that he himself stole (*Allegories*, 278–301). While de Man sees Rousseau's arbitrary mouthing of "Marion" as a pure, contingent signifier, a moment of intentionless and meaningless language, Knapp and Michaels claim that the "Marion" in this case is simply white noise, not language.[15] Like squiggles in the sand bereft of any intentional agency, the sound "Marion" merely resembles meaningful, and thus intentional, language. For Knapp and Michaels, such a resemblance is definitely not the same as language; meaningless, intentionless language is thus for them an emphatic impossibility.

In making this claim, Knapp and Michaels attribute to de Man an interest in meaninglessness (whether it be language or not) conveyed by unintelligible, physical sensation—either visual marks in the sand, or white noise. De Man does increasingly employ the term *materiality* in his later works, which we could overhastily apply to "Against Theory," and thus strengthen Knapp and Michaels's understanding of what de Man means by meaninglessness. But, of course, de Man's whole point about materiality is that it is not phenomenal; it is, as others have said, a materiality without matter.[16] So one question to raise is the exact nature of the unintelligible sensation in Knapp and Michaels's essay, and whether it is best understood as the undiluted experience of physical phenomenon. Indeed, to say that such unintelligible sensation *resembles* language is rather to situate it within a linguistic dynamic, albeit a radically unstable one. Indeed, a better candidate for de Manian materiality than simply physical sensation would be something connected to this resemblance between non-meaning and meaning, this intensely strange mimetic drive that both generates and erodes the composition of figure. One might then say that the marks in the sand are figures for how non-figuration (no language) figures figuration (language)—or the reverse, since if white noise resembles an utterance, an utterance could also resemble white noise, which means that language's own figural drive might actually veer toward, or return to, the non-meaning of non-language, to an empty dynamic or non-human quiescence. Since, however, non-language also resembles language, we might also wonder whether this state could be a kind of meaningful sleep, a human slumber, as it were, instead of a meaningless death.

The problem of Rousseau's "Marion" thus returns us to "A Slumber": as J. Hillis Miller has shown, Wordsworth's poem is riven by a series of oppositions (between the male and female; ignorance and knowledge; stillness and motion; and containment and penetration) that collapse into and pull away from each other, which means that "A Slumber" is a work whose poetic dynamics are set spinning by a set of resemblances—like those among sleep, death, and ignorance, for example ("On Edge," 101–3).[17] Indeed, the very diurnal forces rolling the earth of "A Slumber" can be seen as the gravitational drive of resemblance, a materiality without matter, in this case the figural coordination of how alike, and thus how unalike, time and space, still death and dynamic nature, ignorant life and knowledgeable death are. This coordination could also be discussed as a pattern, or form. And in producing figure it could also produce meaning. But is it meaning? Not quite, nor simply, as arguably it itself more precisely replays the aporia of resemblance's fraught connection to meaning, how the empty structure of resemblance resembles meaning, which means that it is not meaning, except that it does mean resemblance.

Another way to talk about this indeterminacy, this resemblance of non-meaning to meaning, is through the idea of the uncanny.[18] Freud's notion perfectly captures the unsettling mixture of strangeness and familiarity, of remembering and forgetting, that the (non-)recognition of (non-)meaning incites. Indeed, what could be uncannier than coming upon marks in the sand that *seem* to be a written poem? Only, perhaps, coming upon a text that seems to be a text, or a text that seems to be the words of an author—the gothic nature of de Man's comment about Wordsworth speaking from the dead applies here. Exorcizing the uncanniness of the wave poem example is necessary in "Against Theory" because all authors ultimately speak from the dead; all texts are gothic; intention itself is uncanny in its very demotic assumptions. Like the uncanny, the resemblance of non-meaning to meaning threatens to spill over into *das Heimliche*, the territory of the normative. Non-meaning, or nonsense, takes on the solemn authority of the constative, while meaning congeals into a thickness that resists full understanding, or belief. Literary communication itself becomes uncanny, a commonality that has been either forgotten or ignored, something so obvious that it becomes fantastic, a dream whose canny intention can only be restored through the athletic precision of pragmatic argument.

Indeed, the uncanny, with its volatile blending of *das Heimliche* and *das Unheimliche*, occupies the very nether zone between the intent of human habitation and the non-meaning of nature. Lucy resides in this region, a space of stones, rocks, and trees that *seems* to mean something—a home or final resting place, for example. Or, perhaps, the speaker's *description* seems to mean something: an attainment of peace, a negative knowledge, or the poet's own self-dissolution. But this state of apparent transparency, of seeming meaning, would also then mean a seeping of the uncanny into the intent of the poet, whose cognitive action suddenly takes on the strangely inaccessible familiarity of Lucy's own motionless revolutions. The work's ambient strangeness—some might argue poetics—would be a result of this dynamic.

Knapp and Michaels would, of course, dismiss any attempt to couple this strangeness to a consequence of language. To do this, they must especially distinguish between sensory experience and semantic meaning—they must adamantly separate "Marion" as a meaningless sound from "Marion" as a heard name and, in the case of the wave poem, seeing squiggles from reading a text. For while Knapp and Michaels might agree that intentional resemblance exists, they're more interested in the putative confusions caused by accidental, and thus meaningless, resemblance. In their essay, meaningless resemblance is the object of sensory perception, while recognizing an intentional utterance entails a more complicated, non-phenomenal moment of cognition. This is the role of meaningless physical sensation in "Against Theory"—to oppose sensation to meaning and to keep sensation yoked to the phenomenal. The wave poem's force thus rests on a distinction between seeing marks in the sand and reading a poem on the beach. In the wave poem reading is more than simply seeing squiggles, even if it takes a submarine full of scientists to make us realize how counterintuitive it would be to understand the act of reading otherwise.[19]

More precisely, especially before (but also with) the submarine, the jeopardy of the wave poem involves using reading to contain what happens when we accidentally see patterns in the world, when our senses confront, for want of a better term, nature. Knapp and Michaels might say that since the pattern is accidental, it really isn't a pattern. But they've admitted that a pattern can be accidental since they've allowed for—indeed, insisted on—the existence of accidental resemblance. (If the marks weren't accidental, they wouldn't resemble, they would be language.) Seeing nature involves seeing its pattern, which is the paradox of unintentional form, even if that form is simply the resemblance of non-meaning to meaning. Contrary to the claims of the wave poem, however, it might actually seem counterintuitive *not* to call this seeing a reading, not to say we *read* the resemblance between non-meaning and meaning. Indeed, as so much of Romanticism suggests—think of the strange scrawls of Blake's book of Urizen—the opacities of seeing seem embedded in reading, while the meaning of reading constantly seems to beckon within the unintentional patterns of nature discerned by seeing. But this indeterminateness is precisely what the wave poem seeks to banish: either you see unintentional pattern accidentally created by the physical forces of a meaningless nature or you read a poem created by an intentional agency, even if it be the natural script of a pantheistic sea. As emphatic is also the wave poem's erasure of the act of seeing as a figure for a much more energetic problematic than "Against Theory" imagines, one involving a more complicated estimate of the sensory world than Knapp and Michaels allow, in which resemblance and figure might actually in some cases structure the sensory, thus making the *purely* phenomenal—the *bête noire* against which "Against Theory" needs to argue in its own quest for the clarity of read meaning—a radically complicated, if not fictional, event.

This problematic need not simply associate the question of the sensory with the visual. Indeed, given their rejection of Rousseau's mouthing of an unintelligible "Marion" as having anything to do with language, it's logical to assume that Knapp and Michaels would apply the same distinction between image and script to any *sound* of nature that might also stand for a, as Marx would say, sensual apprehension of form. Within this context, Wordsworth's "There Was a Boy" tells its own version of the story of the possible intelligence of a sensory engagement with nature. The poem's confrontation with alterity can be read in a number of ways that include both the theological and rhetorical.[20] Yet even more so than the poetic action of "A Slumber," the opening exchange between boy and owls is a test case for Knapp and Michaels's pragmatic requirements for meaningful communication—an unnecessarily repetitive phrase, of course, from their point of view. Chapter 5 will return to "A Slumber" when confronting Michaels's further argument about the misleading allure of one's subjective relation to the physical shape of linguistic signification. But more immediately we can ask of "There Was a Boy," using and testing Knapp and Michaels's terms, are boy and birds actually having a conversation, or simply simulating one?

Employing Knapp and Michaels, the solution seems straightforward enough: the boy famously blows "*mimic* hootings to the silent owls / That they might answer him" (lines 9–10; my emphasis).[21] Mimicry structures the entire exchange, which could more precisely be described as the mimicry of an exchange.[22] It is impossible to know the meaning of the mimicked hootings, or, more exactly, whether the hootings only mimic meaning, without knowing the meaning of the owls' hooted response, something also, in this poem at any rate, impossible to know. Are the owls mistakenly responding to some unknown meaning mimicked by the boy's hooting, or to that very mimicry? Are they mimicking the boy? Is their silence a judgment on the failure of the boy's mimetic skill, a thoughtful response in and of itself, or something altogether contingent? The impossibility of answering these questions means that no meaning takes place between boy and owls. True, either he or they might believe—or, according to Knapp and Michaels, know—that they are having a meaningful conversation; the more pointed question, however, is whether the reader can say the same thing. Without being able to cordon off simulation from meaning, the reader's pragmatic answer would be no. The mimicked hooting might appear to be a conversation between man and beast, but it is actually meaningless, another example of the resemblance of non-meaning to meaning, the white noise that Knapp and Michaels argue characterizes Rousseau's utterance of "Marion." From the vantage point of "Against Theory," a simulacrum of conversation is no conversation at all.

Of course, such negation of meaning goes against a long-standing critical tradition of reading Wordsworth's poem. Half a century ago, Lionel Trilling cited "There Was a Boy" when he discussed how the poet "conceived of the world as semantic."[23] Yet Trilling also specifically remarked about the work that "chances are we will be rather baffled by its intention" (143). If the pragmatic reader sees no meaning in the (non-)conversation between owls and boy, Trilling also suggests that the representation of that exchange lacks a clear-cut intention. Yet Trilling then places this lack alongside an argument about the semantic quality of the Wordsworthian world. Trilling soon does find in Wordsworth the intention of a Hegelian sense of soul, or *Gemüt*. We, however, can still use Trilling's ambivalent language to forge an even more uneasy reading of the poem, one that focuses on the radically tense binding of non-meaning to meaning. Something semantic does seem to be generated by the hootings of boy and owls, despite, or because of, the lack of a clear-cut intention both among the participants and about the episode itself. This meaning might simply be the resemblance of non-meaning to meaning, of inchoate sound to a conversation. Or it might even be the meaning of non-meaning, of a "jocund din" as white noise (line 16). But in a reading where the semantic is at once ineluctable and inaccessible, a simulation of conversation doesn't necessarily negate the meaning of simulation, the aural resemblance of noise to conversation.

Meaninglessness, in other words, cannot escape resemblance, even if it is the resemblance to non-meaning, or (as is more often the case) to resemblance itself. "There Was a Boy" shows this through a dynamic that at first simply seems to anchor the episode of the owls in a plentitude of meaning. In doing so, the poem appears to answer Knapp and Michaels by giving them what they ask, evidence of intention. Specifically, the poem seems to describe the intention of both the boy's and owl's "halloos" as mutual addresses of pleasure and play (line 14). The episode is, after all, one of "mirth and jocund din," happy noise (line 16). Likewise, the silence of the owl is structured as an intention, a "mock[ing]" of the boy's skills (line 17). We might then come up with another pragmatic reading that argues that the boy and owls address each other with the intention of mirth; that they indeed have a conversation about happy play.

Such happy meaning becomes complicated, however, when we ask what, exactly, is happy: does a happy sound necessarily mean that the maker of the sound is also? Something, or someone, is happy here (the poet knows, or believes, that), but what or who it is is not entirely clear. The affect is free-floating, like sound itself, equally attached to, and thus equally disengaged from, the owls, boy, "wild scene," and poet's memory, as unmoored as the "uncertain heaven" that replaces lake with heavy sky (lines 15 and 24).[24] The issue is not so much about both knowing and believing in the intention of mirth as it is about the exponential number of potential listeners and speakers of mirth—the owls, boy, poet, and Winander itself—who dislocate happiness by placing it in a number of conflicting scenarios. Insofar as the emotion of mirth is the meaning of the conversation between the boy and owl, meaning itself becomes as unanchored as it is omnipresent in the exchange between self and, paraphrasing Trilling, semantic world.

Another way to approach this dilemma is, of course, through the problem of the literal and the figural, although not by way of the previous chapter's focus on historical indexing. Rather, the issue before us is more about the meaning of the sensory itself. Happy sounds could mean that the owls are literally happy, and likewise are literally mocking the boy with their silence. They could indeed be intelligible participants in a mirthful conversation. But if the din is not literally jocund, if the owls aren't literally mocking or answering the boy, what is happening here? If the happiness is simply figural, the din itself could simply be jocund, in the sense of loud or raucous. Figurative happiness might mean no happiness at all; an answer might not literally be an answer. Such raucous sound could itself be a figure for the boy's own internal experience, but that leaves the possibility of no real conversation between him and the owls, whose noise could simply be that, noise. Of course, one could also say the reverse, that the owls' literal mirth does not guarantee in any way that the boy is himself really jocund. We could go further and note that the literal happiness of the birds is itself the outcome of reading the jocund din in one particular, figurative way. Indeed, the only thing a truly literal grammatical reading guarantees is the happiness of neither boy nor owls but of the din itself.

We are then confronted with the somewhat unthinkable proposition of a sound that is happy in and of itself, an assertion whose forceful imposition of meaning is equaled only by the degree to which we can make no sense of the claim. We have, in effect, a literal rendition of the dynamic of figure: a formal imposition of meaning—the sonic resemblance to happiness—that simultaneously can go no further than the structural form of that claim, which, in both cases, is resemblance. Resemblance can only give us resemblance, much in the way that de Man once remarked that reference can only give us reference, not the real world (*Resistance*, 11).

In "There Was a Boy," this point is simultaneously made with another, commensurate but also paradoxically incongruent claim: that the world, real or not, cannot stop giving us resemblances, or figure. The world produces, and is produced by, resemblances, including those of conversation, mirth, and meaningful exchange. The world produces a semblance of a lesson, which could also help explain the poem's later appearance in the discussion about pedagogy in book 5 of *The Prelude*. The world also gives us the resemblance of an intention, which becomes codified in the poem through tropes of anthropomorphism and personification. These particular figures certainly organize the encounter with the owls, but as the address of the poem's first lines indicates ("ye knew him well, ye Cliffs / And islands of Winander!" [lines 1–2]), the scope of such action extends well beyond the birds, just as play and mirth are subsumed by some larger, more mature affect initiated by the avian silence, which, of course, is also synecdochically the silence of everything else. Indeed, such emotion is triggered by the fact that the deep mocking silence could very well be that of everything, instead of simply literally the owls. Figure effects the coming-to-be of profound feeling, even while limiting the significance (in both senses of the word) of such deep emotion. Nature—everything—is given a certain import, or, more specifically, the resemblance to a meaningful meaning. Yet, insofar as a resemblance is not absolutely what it resembles, as Knapp and Michaels (among others) insist, the poem's personified world is unable to secure the very intention that it incites. Yet again, this time contrary to the view expressed in "Against Theory," resemblance by its very nature cannot mean the complete elision of the semantic. The world resembles a lesson and an intention, which is less than those things in themselves, but also something besides the pure white noise of non-language.

The move from play to a more mature feeling is a familiar story in Wordsworth, although "There Was a Boy" does not necessarily make this the sober tale of maturation that chapter 1 witnesses in "Tintern Abbey." "There Was a Boy" distinguishes itself instead by rooting the "shock of mild surprise" in the realm of both bodily and mental sensation, "the voice / Of mountain torrents" and "visible scene" in the boy's mind and heart (lines 19–21). In doing so, the poem both anticipates and refutes Knapp's and Michaels's distinctions—its world communicates to the boy with a sensation that does not achieve the clarity of articulate intention but still retains the figural assertion of meaningful exchange. Reading, as enacted in "Against Theory," does not occur; sensation of some kind does instead. However, sensation's mere resemblance to meaning does not simply block access to language or meaning, as it does in Knapp and Michaels. Instead, this resemblance has its own particular, vertiginous power. Unintelligible physical sensation abuts against this other power, intelligible as the sensation of intelligence; sensory meaninglessness intractably and hauntingly exists alongside the sensation of meaning.

J. Mark Smith has perceptively noted how this sensation of meaning occurs by accident on the boy's part; he does not intentionally look for meaning beyond play, a contingency of experience that Wordsworth seems to laud.[25] We could go further and say that the world with its silence, sights, and sounds might convey something to the boy, but also accidentally, with no intention behind it. Yet this doesn't mean that intention disappears completely from the scene. It haunts the episode through the energetic dialectic between an animistic, anthropomorphic figuration and its exposure as such, as a calcified trope that turns figure toward the meaning of nothing. All the figures, from "answer" to "silence" to "mock'd," turn toward nothing (lines 11, 17). They turn toward nothing, which, however, as the *meaning* of nothing, turns, falls, and floats—like sound, like an "uncertain heaven"—toward something else.

This double movement emphatically announces itself in the last third of the poem, which shows the piece's tripartite structure to be a proleptic parody of the wave poem in "Against Theory."[26] If the wave poem gives us three episodes that increasingly show us the unavoidability of intention, "There Was a Boy" gives us three moments of meaningful exchange that increasingly render intention a fantastic, if not phantasmic, proposition. Wordsworth's poem moves from a conversation between owl and boy, to the sensory communication between Winander and boy, and finally to the episode between boy's grave and speaker. Here the figural animism of the living cliffs is replaced by its own demystifying trope, the inanimate grave. The surface of the reflecting lake changes into an even more inchoate screen, the grave's ground. The poem thus arrives at the same uncanny place as "A Slumber," where death has transformed, or simply made explicit, the boy's existence, like Lucy's, as a thing. The poet is told something about death, from death, but in a manner that repudiates any sense of the living intention of death, unless life itself is simply one dimension to the figural rendering of a dead object.

Of course, no real exchange could be occurring here, as nothing could have actually happened between the owls, mountain torrents, visible scene, and boy. The last episode in the poem could simply be one of extreme poetic solipsism or of simple meaninglessness, both familiar past estimations of Romantic writing. Yet "There Was a Boy" seems to anticipate such dismissals, with the poet's silent hovering over the grave both acknowledging and defying the emptying out of meaning in the scene. He stays because he hasn't been told anything yet. He stays because the grave has something to say. He stands mute a full half hour, compulsively resisting the pure divide between meaning and non-meaning.[27]

Such compulsion names a mode of reading different from the one Knapp and Michaels outline through the experience of the wave poem. This mode attaches itself to a negative knowledge of the impossibility of intention, which is not the same as an absolute rejection of intention. Indeed, intention becomes the term for the unavoidable intrusion of the semantic, even when meaning seems meaningless. This mode of reading also does not simply transcend sensation through a larger, more constative sense of itself, but instead complicates physical sensation by becoming caught up in the production of figure, through the resemblance of non-meaning to meaning. Indeed, if anything, the sensation of meaning actually devolves into an even more unintelligible version of itself: an insensate *aphanisis* of meaning at the boy's grave, with jocund din, mild shock, and Lucy's orbit transformed into the utter stillness of boy, speaker, and time. (From this perspective, the plaintive notice of the boy's youth in the last line is a moment of Freudian *Nachträglichkeit*, a retroactive assignation of meaning to a past scene whose semantic powers are at once more overwhelming and opaque than the poet's concluding recollection.) All attention has been turned to the dead boy; everything has been turned to nothing, which turns to something. The sensation of meaning is the death of meaning and, consequently, all that death means. If the mute poet does see, standing still before the grave, his is a reading that is not reading in the way that "Against Theory" envisions. This is literally the case as it is unclear whether he even faces the grave; likewise, no mention is made of the signs that would make this the boy's specific resting place, neither tombstone nor words carved upon its slab.[28]

Arguably, the boy's actual epitaph occurs earlier. The poem's statement about self and language happens when the boy blows his mimic hootings; in doing so, he blows together the non-meaning and meaning of language, of himself and nature. He blows the convergence of aural sensation and de Manian materiality, insofar as the sound does not exist by itself, but also unavoidably through the formal acoustics of figure and resemblance. In "There Was a Boy" the sensation of meaning is therefore not aboriginally phenomenal.[29] The sensation of meaning is not simply, or even, meaning's physical sensation. Troubling Knapp and Michaels's own categorical distinction between linguistic meaning and sensory experience, the sensation of meaning more precisely marks the moment when linguistic unintelligibility nevertheless becomes a semantic event, and resemblance determines the physical and phenomenal as that event. Occurring linguistically, this action figures the compulsive nature of both physical sensation and semantic meaning, of sense and sense, while frustrating either in its pure form. "There Was a Boy" circumscribes the sensory through a sensation of meaning that paradoxically makes the poem all the more dizzying through the radically indeterminate character of figure's intrusion into, or through, the physical world.

Appropriately, then, the boy blows "*as through* an instrument," making this action a trope about troping, a trope that produces more tropes: something like an instrument that produces the mimicking of a hooting (line 9; my emphasis). Figure sounds more figures, including the prosopopoeia that undergirds intelligence of self, world, and their exchange, an encounter now based on self's and world's (non-)resemblance, instead of simply a resemblance to conversation. Indeed, conversation itself becomes another figure for this exchange of (non-)resemblances, a boy both continuous with and separate from nature, a poet both part of and cut off from death.

Through such exchange the poem both divides and keeps together—what? That seems to be quite literally the question of the poem's penultimate line: "I believe, that near his grave / A full half hour together I have stood, / Mute—for he died when he was ten years old" (lines 30–32). What is "together"? Poet and grave? A full half hour of time? The poet by himself? The contingency of poetic meter? "Together" is a mimic hooting, a simulation of formal resemblance. Embedded in the poem's final action, it is the catachresis of constative action, both imposition and effect of the instrument of figure. To say that the world cannot stop giving us resemblances is to say that the world cannot stop showing things—poets and graves, boys and owls—together. We cannot stop seeing or hearing things together, conversation or no.

Such resemblances spiral beyond any boundary we might use to shape something like a hermetically sealed reading of the text. They not only include works that can function as the proof that Hirsch asks for in discovering a writer's historical intention; their effect can be much more indeterminate than that of such evidentiary material.[30] For example, in a 1798 letter to Wordsworth, Coleridge famously writes about his own experience when reading "There Was a Boy":

> That
> Uncertain heaven received
> Into the bosom of a steady lake (ll. 24–25)
> I should have recognized any where; and had I met these lines running wild in the deserts of Arabia, I should have instantly screamed out "Wordsworth!"[31]

Exchanging desert for beach, Coleridge proleptically enacts his own version of the wave poem. While he does not say whether what he discovers is found on a single parchment, carved in stone, or traced in the sand, the Orientalist locale and Coleridge's own "wild" state set up this encounter as another thought experiment, imagining the lines to be as far removed from their Lake District, Wordsworthian origins as possible. And still, Coleridge recognizes them—but is this the same unavoidable intuition of intention that Knapp and Michaels create with their submarine full of scientists? What is being recognized? And what does such recognition consist of, the mere seeing of a landscape or a face, or the particular reading of meaning that "Against Theory" authorizes? Coleridge's one word answer—"Wordsworth!"—exacerbates rather than resolves this situation. Is this the communication of a received intention and meaning—"William, I recognize these lines as the meaning of you, Wordsworth"—or the contingent mouthing of a non-meaning and non-language, another pragmatic version of Rousseau's cry of "Marion"? Or, as with the boy's simulated conversation, is Coleridge's cry the incitement of meaning through a set of resemblances—to those of a hooting, the name of a poet, or the lines of a poem—which don't necessarily yield any further meaning or intent? Like all one-word answers, does it stand for all that we know—of, in this case, Wordsworth—or, simultaneously, of all that we really don't know, or know how to explain? Can it be paradoxically both a communication and a placeholder for such (non-)knowledge? What is the meaning of lines from "There Was a Boy" found in the desert, when that meaning is simply *Wordsworth*?

Coleridge's answer is really not too different from the ultimate lesson that dominated the teaching of Romanticism for a large part of the twentieth century, when being a Romanticist meant learning to be a Romantic, which oftentimes meant learning the meaning of *Wordsworth*. Coleridge's apparent satisfaction with his 1798 answer thus also characterizes a later pedagogical formation in literary studies, one that we in the twenty-first century have yet to surpass, insofar as we are still not entirely done with literary history. The necessity of Romanticism's aporetic character, delineated in previous chapters, can be narrativized through the plot about meaning and non-meaning that Wordsworth's poems write and Coleridge's anecdote underscores. For if Coleridge could just as well have hooted the boy's call, someone else could have cried "Romanticism!" instead and been faced with the same questions of meaning and non-meaning that Rousseau's "Marion" provokes, the same unstable dynamic of resemblances that Wordsworth exploits in his engagement with death and nature. In Romanticism's case, the question of the resemblance to meaning becomes one of a resemblance to any number of historical identities, from Jacobinism to the Romantic ideology, from fascism to communism. That this indeterminate quality characterizes other historical and cultural formations as well simply underscores the degree to which our understanding of most, if not all, of history is Romantic. The portent of Romanticism, aesthetically and ethically as well as historically, is the meaning's own incitement as well as end point, a condition that links Coleridge, boy, and poet standing over grave to a mode of reading unrecognized in "Against Theory."

To sense meaning when nothing might be there, or, perhaps more unsettling, when something might be: this is in many ways a traditional understanding of what Wordsworth does—indeed arguably the reigning one before the model of ideological repression that revitalizes Wordsworthian (and Romantic) studies in the 1980s. Before the more linguistically severe estimation of de Man, or the still phenomenologically rooted diagnosis of Hartman or Bloom, or even the humanist affirmation of Abrams, this view can be seen in others such as Trilling, a sympathetic but baffled appraisal determined to understand Wordsworth's strangeness, one anchored in the poet's refusal to separate in any easy fashion meaning and non-meaning.[32] Of course, as traditional are the unsympathetic dismissals of this refusal. There are Romantic readings that make this critique such as in Byron, but also, as significantly, readings from Arnold to the Modernists whose appraisals represent themselves as distinctively and reflexively non-Romantic.

The aporia that both "There Was a Boy" and "A Slumber" exploit, the resemblance of non-meaning to meaning, constitutes a strong version of the putatively distinct, Romantic cognitive confusion that plays a major role in many of the *récits* that compose post-Romantic literary and cultural history.

The point of such narratives is to free us from such confusion, precisely what Knapp and Michaels attempt to do by liberating us from theory. At the polemic center of "Against Theory" is a canonical Romantic poem, which makes perfect sense, since the essay is indeed a reading of Romanticism, a non-Romantic reading that attempts to clarify precisely what so many Romantic texts, or the representations of such texts, have muddied. "Against Theory" tells us how to read "A Slumber" unromantically, or, in the case of marks that merely resemble the poem, not to read it at all. We can thus place Knapp and Michaels in a tradition of readers that perhaps reaches its apotheosis in the Modernism of Leavis, Pound, and Elliot, but which, of course, also structures the earlier writing of Romanticism itself. Knapp and Michaels's radical version of American pragmatism is part of the larger historical form of Romantic sobriety, in this case a sobriety that wants to free Romanticism from itself, from the Romantic claim of problems and confusions that do not really exist.[33] Romanticism, as dramatized by the boy's aural engagement with the owls, is a fascination with meaning when only a resemblance to meaning might exist, when intention might be rooted in the uncanny instead of simply the intuitive obviousness of common sense. "Against Theory" argues against such a fascination, our compulsive standing before a silent nature, text, or history—before Romanticism itself. Knapp and Michaels's radical pragmatism argues against an understanding of the world that cannot quite let go of the aporias generated by resemblances—figures—that do not easily separate meaning from non-meaning, or contingency from intention. They argue against a sensation of meaning that can only become something even more fantastic, the *aphanisis* of meaning, the semantic as the implacable stoniness of death, the implacable surface of a grave. In that sense, "Against Theory" is against Romanticism.

> Must you be able to see light around a chad in order for that chad to indicate intention? . . . Yes, the chad exhibits intention, is perhaps pregnant with intention.
>
> —Rick Moody, *The Diviners*

One might assert, of course, that such an argument actually proves Knapp and Michaels's point. To say that their essay is against one version of the cognitive confusion long associated with Romanticism is simply to say what their meaning, and intention, is. If the consequence of their essay is to repeat a certain dismissal of Romanticism (whether we call it Romanticism or not), that is the essay's purpose, and their intention. The more difficult issue, however, is whether such an intention can then fully demystify the essay's own sensation of meaning, the number of uncanny resemblances among wave poem, other wave examples, "A Slumber," and "Against Theory," as well as the resemblances between the essay and works of theory, most notably those of deconstruction.

If it is appropriate that a canonical Romantic work lies at the center of the essay's argument, is that indeed evidence of the authors' intention, or merely a fortuitous coincidence, and therefore appropriate in only a bad faith sort of way? Or is the presence of "A Slumber" overdetermined in a manner that eschews the series of either/or interpretive choices that "Against Theory" insists we make? This final option is, of course, exactly the fuzzy bent of mind that Knapp and Michaels want to free us from; it is also precisely the insistence of the volatile syncretism between intention and contingency, meaning and non-meaning, that informs the compulsive attention of Wordsworth's poet before the dead, buried bodies of Lucy and the boy of Winander. The radical incompatibility of such views might indeed signal an impasse. But this antagonism might also be the sign of something fantastically genetic: more than simply the imputation of intention, interpretation itself would then be the ongoing, uneven interplay between intention and the sensation of meaning. Interpretation would be the generation, and negotiation, of resemblances that can be subsumed under intention, as well as those that disorient intention by imposing a compulsive value upon meaning's reflexive sensation.

Far from limiting intention, this situation actually shows how immense and unavoidable the problem of intention is. "A Slumber" might very well appear in "Against Theory" because of its status as a canonical object of interpretation, a status itself indebted to the way that Wordsworth's poem—and, by extension, Romanticism—invokes a certain poetic strangeness, a hermeneutic dissonance, that generations of readers have tried to explain, if not scorn. This engagement with Romanticism might very well be Knapp and Michaels's intention, regardless of the fact that neither they nor anyone else made this part of the polemic following the publication of "Against Theory." We might then have to admit that in all likelihood a confrontation with Romanticism is not Knapp and Michaels's intention, and not really the purpose of the essay—although it could be of ours. Or, if we eschew their pragmatic argument, we might argue nevertheless that this engagement is actually the essay's larger, unintentional purpose. But that simply means that we have distinguished between the essay's larger meaning and Knapp and Michaels's now diminished authorial intention. This distinction does not mean, however, that we are really done with the question of intention, which still haunts the putative "larger meaning" of the text. That meaning, of how the reading, institutionalization, and transmission of Romantic texts relate to the argument in "Against Theory," is intelligible only as the possible coherence of a set of larger historical discourses, or forces: the intention, or design, of history.

If intention constantly finds itself entangled with sensations of meaning, the uncanniness of such sensation depends on the possibility that resemblance's contingencies might actually be revealed as evidence of a determinate design. Knapp and Michaels are right in a way that they don't really consider: the sensation of meaning is uncanny precisely to the degree that it is also the *sensation of intention*. We are all familiar with narratives in psychoanalysis and historicism, particularly Marxism, which both exploit and evince this condition, but they are not the only ones. The power of the wave poem example does not so much lie, for instance, with the submarine of scientists, but with the pantheistic sea. We might experience the possibility of the writing sea as uncanny, in the literal way that Freud associates his term with the return of repressed superstitions. But such supernatural beliefs might also be symptomatic of a more relevant uncanniness, the end-point aporia that occurs when intention is as implacable and unavoidable as Knapp and Michaels insist and, simultaneously, human agency is drained of any organizing, constative power. The natural supernaturalism of Romanticism is thus not simply a secular humanist negotiation with a theological past, but the sign of a more unsettling condition: the uncoupling of the human from intention, the existence of intention in a non-human, or post-human, world.[34]

Pantheism, of course, also does return us to a traditional Romantic (and Romanticist) vocabulary, indeed exactly what Hirsch uses to give the nod to Bateson's optimistic biographical reading of "A Slumber" over Brooks's bleak New Critical analysis, where Wordsworth's pantheism in the late 1790s is cause enough to read "roll[ing] round" with "rocks, stones and trees" in a positive light (*Validity*, 238–40; lines 7–8). In terms of "A Slumber," we might also discuss this predicament as the agon, or dialectic, between nature in death and death in nature. Is death infused by the life forces of a greater nature, or is nature's vitalism simply an empty dynamic, either mechanical or vegetative, the mindless motion of death? Can the narrator actually read something in Lucy's still but spinning mute body, or does his mind simply see the grand, cosmic scale of unmotivated force and contingent, kinetic pattern?

Such Romantic concerns do not simply appear in Wordsworth, of course.[35]

Prominent among figures involved in such debates would be Immanuel Kant, whose third *Critique* could have entered this discussion at a number of earlier points, in terms of the beach hexagon, the pure signifier of Kant's pure beauty, and the possible resonances among his famous definition of beauty as "purposiveness without purpose," deconstruction's non-instrumental practice, and the question of unintentional resemblance. Indeed, the second half of Kant's work is all about the difficulty of ascribing an ultimate intention, a final cause or author, to nature. Kant's solution does seem to anticipate the strategy of the wave poem: while neither reason nor empirical practice can lead us directly to God, the patterns of the world and our own understanding make it impossible for us not to consider that such a being exists. But Knapp and Michaels's vehement conflation of belief and knowledge runs roughshod over the discriminations that motivate Kant's strategy, the cautionary line drawing between faith and reason, and a moral analogy to and direct cognition of God.[36] Indeed, Kant makes clear what happens to religion and theology if they are allied with an unrestricted reason asserting a direct knowledge of the world's ultimate author: they become idolatry and fanaticism.

An earlier reference to fanaticism in the first half of the *Critique* is pertinent here: "*Fanaticism* . . . is the *delusion* [*Wahn*] *of wanting to SEE something beyond all bounds of sensibility*, i.e. of dreaming according to principles (raving with reason)" (sec. 29, 135).[37] Kant is literally discussing a positive idealism that contrasts poorly with the negative presentation of the moral law in the sublime—as he says elsewhere, Plato was the cause of all fanaticism in philosophy. But, juxtaposed with the figurative use of physical sensation in "Against Theory," what might such a literal idealism signify, figuratively? What might it mean for seeing to go beyond its own phenomenal condition, to rave with reason? What might such a mad intuition figure? The distinctions in the wave poem suggest that the answer is reading. Reading is seeing seeing beyond itself, seeing as the sensation of meaning, which is a kind of fanaticism.[38]

More precisely, in "Against Theory" at least, fanaticism is seeing the resemblance between non-meaning and meaning in the world and, unlike Knapp and Michaels, not being able to leave that distinction alone; fanaticism is reading intention into that resemblance, the erasure of sensation from the sensation of meaning. But Knapp and Michaels do not really leave the difference between non-meaning and meaning alone either, since they put so much energy into solving, or forgetting, it. They do away with resemblance and accept the pantheistic sea. For them there is no fanaticism, only the choice between intention and non-intention, language and non-language. We might say, however, that this is a fanatic's choice: there is something fanatical about preserving intention at all costs, even if meaning must reside in a pantheistic sea or research submarine.

The message might, of course, be that the sentient sea is a ridiculous option and so, logically, the marks in the sand are not language. But the bizarre scenario of the receding wave might also simply point to how equally strange and unavoidable the drive, explicit or not, toward intentional agency is. The receding wave is a burlesque allegory of the aporia of accidental resemblance, the way contingency both resists and demands meaning. The point, then, would be not to dismiss Knapp and Michaels because of their fanaticism, but to note how pervasive the fanatic mode of reading is—as ubiquitous, in fact, as the fanatic, but altogether persuasive, pragmatist's melding of knowledge and belief. Indeed, if Knapp and Michaels really make no distinction among revived author, sea, and submarine, if all will do as proof of how we intuit intention when reading what looks like a poem on the beach, reading in general begins to take on a fanatical character.

There is certainly something fanatic about the narrator in "A Slumber" standing over a buried still body, narrating his cognition or non-cognition of this experience. There is surely something fanatic about our reading of this strange, difficult Romantic poem, how we mull over our comprehension and incomprehension of its words, what in "Against Theory" becomes narrativized as the history of twentieth-century criticism. There is something fanatic about reading the world, which means there is something fanatic about reading.

The implications of such fanaticism go beyond yet another contemplation of the madness of reason, as important as such reminders remain, even, or especially, today. Fanaticism calls us to return to the question of intention while also characterizing the nature of that demand. Fanaticism exposes the bad faith underlying the avoidance of the question, even while reminding us that there is no simple comfort, no commanding resolution, to confronting the question in a self-congratulatory, forthright manner.

This uneasy logic informs the nature of critical reading, and teaching, today. Since "Against Theory" the academy has arguably moved from debates over interpretation to ones over value, arguments not only about the viability of non-instrumental practice but more pervasively about the uses of certain kinds of reading canons. This has been represented as a move from theory to history. In doing so, we now hardly ever talk about intention, but in fact we really do, constantly. This involves the archaic question of authorial intention haunting, like Hamlet's father, the postmodern historicisms that we routinely employ to ward off the dated early 1980s debates that "Against Theory" signaled were coming to an end. The issue is one of both pedagogy and, as Stanley Fish would say, community.[39] When *Wordsworth* appears in our discussions of "A Slumber" or any of his poems today, a slippage of meaning routinely occurs. At any given time, *Wordsworth* can be the sign of an assumed post–New Historicist model steeped in the implicit vocabularies of a Foucaultian author-function or de Manian prosopopoeia, to name two well-known examples. But, in numerous conversations, *Wordsworth* can also mean simultaneously the intention of the biographical poet. This slippage not only makes intention an issue of community but characterizes the institution of critical reading in a particular manner, one whose very community of exchange depends on such implicitly assumed, (mis)understood transcodings of critical . . . intention. As a practice this logic is also ongoing, which means that it is also an issue of transmission, or of pedagogy. At stake is the very simple but nevertheless daunting question of what kind of historicism we are teaching our students. That what occurs between owls and boy, or grave and poet, might indeed model the answer to that question is a mordant irony altogether appropriate in terms of disciplinary conceptualization, as one singular example of the 1980s academic fall into historicism is, of course, Romantic studies. Because of writings like Wordsworth's, the field also has an intimate relation to the literary compulsions evinced by the sensation of meaning. Romantic studies has also, in terms of both its objects of study and its own history of methodologies, a singular relation to the great, biographical subject.[40] For all these reasons, the study of Romanticism should be one exemplary site where the critical and pedagogical logic of authorial intention works itself out, because of, or in spite of, its readers.

But if the author continues to function in critical literary discussion as what Barthes calls an *alibi*, intention and history also go beyond the author, and the academy, to cathect around the knottier problem of the resemblance of history to nature, of the accidental resemblance between non-meaning and meaning, and around how this sensation of meaning paradoxically incites the unavoidable possibility of history's intention. Because of Romanticism's own meta-historical status, it should be present during any substantive discussion of this problem. The agon in one supremely Romantic poem, "A Slumber," is now between history in death and death in history, which means that an entire politics waits to be, or continues to be, generated from that agon, and from confronting the degree to which reading history, like reading nature, is a fanaticism. Trite, profound, or offensive, it is also necessary to say the obvious, that the term *fanatic* carries a special burden today. Yet the further point would be to begin discussing such a term beyond the limited moralistic vocabulary now ineluctably coloring it, to begin to sort out the implications of an intention, or the resemblance of an intention, that still remains after the end of all our meta-narratives. Like the Romantic participants of that earlier Age of Terror, we might start to understand our responsibilities toward today's specific burden of fanaticism, by acknowledging how intimately history is linked to the disjuncture and simultaneity between seeing and reading, to the sensation of meaning.

# The Sensation of the Signifier

Her mouth was open as if she had something to say;
But maybe my saying so is a figure of speech.

—David Ferry, "Lake Water"

Twenty-five years after its publication, we now know the intention of Knapp and Michaels's "Against Theory," something that, as the previous chapter showed, was not at all apparent during the furor that followed the piece's claims about the irrelevance of theory and the unavoidable fact of meaning (or intention) in a text. Michaels's 2004 work, *The Shape of the Signifier: 1967 to the End of History*, retrospectively connects this argument in "Against Theory" to the social commentary of another of Michaels's books, *Our America* (1995). The result is a wide-ranging critique of postmodern (or, using Michaels's preferred term, "post-historical") left writing and artistic culture, along with a number of polemical observations about a variety of contemporary cultural and political issues, ranging from the meaning of recent sci-fi literature and contemporary photography to the arguments behind deep ecology and the movement to secure reparations for slavery.

This retroactive connection, however, involves a paradox, since Michaels acknowledges that his present understanding of "Against Theory" depends on a different temporal relation to the essay—what he later calls a different "subject position"—than what he had had previously.[1] But *The Shape* connects "Against Theory" to *Our America* by precisely attacking the overwhelming presence of the "subject position" in critical thought today, which it claims is the theoretical consequence of transforming texts with intentional meaning into sensory objects that we experience from different subject positions. The primacy of "subject positions" is also alleged to be the historical consequence (as recorded by Francis Fukuyama) of the triumph of liberal capitalism over communism, which signaled the end of struggles based on adversarial beliefs (what Michaels means by ideologies). The result is a literary and political landscape in which one inhabits a culture or subject position that can only differ from, rather than disagree with, other cultures or positions; there is no way to say that one position is more true, or more false, than another.

Yet Michaels's own intention rests on a difference. Michaels understands the purpose of "Against Theory" by seeing it from the vantage point—the subject position—of *The Shape*. (This is not to consider even the difference, or similarity, between Michaels's and Knapp's intentions. Does Michaels's retrospective articulation of the intention of "Against Theory" also include the latter's, so that Knapp's intention can only be gleaned through a book that he did not write, twenty years later?[2]) "Against Theory" is therefore haunted by the future writing of *The Shape*, whose own political argument depends on its preexistence in the now-understood intention of the essay's more than twenty-five-year-old argument.

A certain logic to this future writing has ramifications beyond Michaels's works. Discussions of language and meaning are always haunted by what is already implicit within them, the political and social world, with that haunting presence generating, as well as being made intelligible by, tropes of spatial and temporal difference. But Michaels would dismiss such language, as one further purpose of *The Shape* is to do away with ghosts, with the phantasmic nature of postmodern politics and culture: the ghostly memory of history in New Historicism, as well as in recent literature and social controversies. In a word, ghosts and a universal riven by difference (as opposed to being shored up by disagreement) are examples of sloppy thinking, of illegitimate forms of sensation. By dint of its very pervasiveness in post-history, its contamination of the constative, the sensory comes to be defined *as* the illegitimate. We can then agree with Michaels that the stakes involved in *The Shape* (as well as "Against Theory") are indeed quite large. For the question is what form *any* critique of politics will take—whether there are such things as ghosts, and whether an uncanny politics exists.

The response to this question depends on how we register the intersection between sensation and meaning. Michaels's tack in both "Against Theory" and *The Shape* is to disavow, or regulate, as much as possible that relation, to argue against any suggestion that one might imbricate the other. Unspoken in either work, although present in a number of ways, is how much this policing is a certain argument about Romanticism: about a non-Romantic understanding of literature in "Against Theory" and a non-Romantic politics in *The Shape*, about a Romantic generation of the literary that the previous chapter called a *sensation of meaning*. As I argued, the sensation of meaning is neither simply nor even necessarily phenomenal, something that Michaels does not consider in his account of the sensory experience of different subject positions. This is itself part of another, more fundamental misunderstanding by *The Shape*, of the materiality of the signifier—and, specifically, de Manian materiality—as phenomenal experience. Misreading that term as the sheer meaninglessness of a sensory object, Michaels does not see how materiality is more the meaningless imposition of meaning *through* difference, and *in* disagreement. His distinction between meaning and the non-meaning of materiality, or sensation, does not allow for the possibility of materiality as the sensation of meaning, the sense of sense, the materiality (or shape) not simply of the signifier but of figure: of non-meaning's *resemblance* to meaning, or to *resemblance per se*.

Extending the argument of the previous chapter, we will see that attending to such a dynamic, either to dramatize or soberly deny it, structures much of literary history's self-representation after the Romantic era's own texts. As Michaels's polemics inadvertently clarify, the structuring of history, and post-history, is also involved. Indeed, the literary history underwriting the very polemics of *The Shape* comes from such a *récit*. Far from a Fukuyama-inspired postmodern condition, Michaels's scenario actually adumbrates a basic problem between Romanticism and Modernism-as-modernity.

In a very odd way, Michaels's book reworks Fredric Jameson's classic study *Postmodernism, or The Cultural Logic of Late Capitalism*, a text whose earliest incarnations were contemporaries of Knapp and Michaels's "Against Theory." The oddity of this reworking comes from several sources: the replacement of Marxist Ernest Mandel by neo-conservative Francis Fukuyama as the founding theoretical visionary of capitalism at the end of the twentieth century, the discontinuity between the theoretical and historical conceptions of Michaels's argument, and the neo-vulgar Marxist use of class that Michaels implicitly employs to argue his case against identitarian politics.

This is not to say that Michaels endorses or aligns himself with any of Fukuyama's particular political convictions so much as to note that *The Shape* bases its diagnosis of postmodernism not on an economic but a political model of history. Jameson uses Mandel to outline the hyperbolic abstraction of value that inheres in late capitalism, a condition that underwrites a host of oftentimes contradictory cultural phenomena in postmodernism: the simulacrum, schizophrenia, the loss of historical consciousness, and so forth. Michaels, who has little to say about Jameson (or, curiously, the other left figure his polemic for modern universal argument most resembles, Jürgen Habermas), utilizes Fukuyama to see capitalism as a belief system that has won out against its most intractable nemesis, communism.

For Jameson, the historical event that defines postmodernism is the ubiquitous penetration of global capital into the mind and nature. For Michaels, the historical event that defines post-history is the fall of the Soviet Union, and thus the end of any real, sustained argument with capitalism. That one might analyze that fall through a Marxist model is not a question that Michaels, following Fukuyama, raises, as the point seems to be that the disintegration of the Soviet bloc ends, for good or ill, the communist argument and, therefore, Marxist analysis. In other words, Jameson's is a Marxist account of capital, whereas Michaels's is capitalism's own self-representation of its triumph over the anteriority of Marxism.

Michaels does not share in this triumph (nor, truth be told, does Fukuyama, simply). For if modern history has in effect been an argument for capitalism, capital's triumph means the end of both argument and history. Not that people have stopped arguing now, or that they avoided identity difference during the Cold War; still, the end of the Soviet Union becomes the "occasion to assert at the level of politics . . . the end of or the irrelevance of or, in its purest form, the impossibility of disagreement" (184).[3] This position also seems odd from a left materialist vantage point, insofar as political argument is made synonymous with ideological disagreement; post-history is also the neo-conservative end of ideology, or, more precisely, of "mankind's ideological evolution."[4] Of course, both Marxist and post-Marxist critiques have dispensed with ideology as a form of false consciousness. But Michaels understands ideology as a conscious set of beliefs, and its purpose as the choate articulation of those convictions. Michaels's own argument against capitalist hegemony thus ignores a history of ideology—from Jameson to Slavoj Žižek to even de Man—that in a variety of ways positions ideology against the coherent, self-transparent statement.[5] Whether ideological analysis even in its more complicated forms is a viable mode of inquiry in and beyond Romantic studies—this is a query the present book does take up, already in chapter 2 and again most notably in chapters 6 and 9. More immediately, I simply want to note how, for Michaels, ideology has to be a coherent set of beliefs because a more volatile yoking of the coherent and incoherent in language means a fatal (as well as mistaken) conflation of meaning and meaninglessness in language, as well as the collapse of language and belief into one another.

This insistence is connected to another odd way Michaels and Jameson compare. If for Jameson his theoretical argument is the dialectical expression of his historical argument, for Michaels the connection is not as clear. As Michaels seems to put it, the theoretical argument of "Against Theory" succeeded but needs to be revived in the form of a historical intervention:

> But even if it is true that no one any longer thinks that capitalism is wrong, it is not true that no one thinks that anything is wrong, and it is certainly not true that anyone—except, perhaps, in theory—thinks that there are no more misinterpretations. Which is just to say that, if history has ended, it has only ended in theory. Theory is already over in history. (*Shape*, 81)

As "Against Theory" argued, people argue and disagree, which means that they necessarily interpret and understand meaning, which also means that theory as the meta-conception of interpretation is not needed. But the end of the Cold War and the onset of post-history mean that argument, or ideological disagreement, is in some key sense over. But this is only true in theory, as "it is certainly not true that anyone . . . thinks that there are no more misinterpretations." Allegedly theory is already over, at least in the history of post-history. Yet it really isn't if that history is defined by the political argument against disagreement and the theories of identity and culture that understand discord not as disagreement but as difference. So theory is both over and still persistent, inciting *The Shape* even as the book reaffirms the polemical trajectory of "Against Theory," that theory is no more. Historically and theoretically, *The Shape* is against nothing. The historical argument of *The Shape* is haunted by "Against Theory" either because theory is over or because it's not.[6]

One might also say that if people are still disagreeing in post-history, if Michaels himself is counting on people (or academics and artists, at least) disagreeing with *The Shape*, his polemic is needed as much as theory was in the world of "Against Theory." The problem isn't so much whether there's too much difference and not enough disagreement as whether the difference between difference and disagreement, or between ideological difference and other forms of difference, is as unconditional as Michaels would like. Strangely enough, difference in this relational instance carries the possibility of absolute distinction that Michaels only confers onto disagreement, since the disagreement between difference and disagreement means that they might also agree more than Michaels wants to acknowledge. Things get no less complicated if we allegorize this as the relation between Michaels and those he critiques in *The Shape*. If Michaels disagrees with readers who (as he would describe it) only differ with each other and himself, what is their relation to him? If they disagree with him about difference, why does he need to argue for disagreement in the first place?[7] If they and he differ over disagreement (and agreement), how does he overcome the way disagreement continually finds itself faced with something exterior to it? Put temporally instead of spatially, how do he and they avoid the infinite spiral of differing about disagreeing about differing about disagreeing, and so forth?

I call Michaels's relation with those readers of difference an allegory, since it expresses through the trope of individual agents an opposition that could also be figured as what occurs between two different discourses. This is exactly what Michaels argues against, of course, since in his formulation people can disagree while discourses, or languages, can merely differ. That is his point about Richard Rorty and Jean François Lyotard, who have sacrificed argumentation—and thus belief—for gaming:

> Hence the difference between losing a game and losing an argument: you don't lose at chess when you are convinced you cannot move your king out of check; you lose when, whatever your views, you cannot, within the rules of the game, move him. . . . Beating someone at chess has nothing to do with changing his or her mind. . . . That's why the redescription [by Rorty and Lyotard] of people who have different beliefs as people who are playing different "language games" amounts to a repudiation of the idea that people actually have any beliefs. (189)

Beating someone at chess has nothing to do with changing his or her mind, which would more properly be beating him or her at an argument. For Michaels, then, a statement like "beating someone at *an argument* has nothing to do with changing his or her mind" would be nonsensical, which could very well be, except that what it describes happens all the time; as Hume once observed, people lose arguments and still don't change their minds. (If *Dialogues Concerning Natural Religion* won't do, academics can consider the last faculty meeting they attended.) Arguably, if the end of history exists only in theory, so does the changing of minds, or beliefs, by argument. In contrast, history is full of the discontinuity between an argument's success and a change in belief, between the constative and the performative. There are many ways to approach this situation, of course, with one notable avenue being through the very Marxist tradition of ideology, as varied as it is, that Michaels ignores in his narrative about the end of communism and the post-history of capitalism's triumph. From the perspective of that tradition, ideological analysis actually begins with the end of ideology, as Michaels knows the term.

This formulation is itself part of a larger issue about the way language and politics work in *The Shape*. Before facing this question through de Man's own particular sense of aesthetic ideology, let us consider one final way the book seems oddly Marxist: how Michaels counters cultural and racial difference with class difference, the social discord of economic inequality. Here Michaels does seem to be making an economic argument, or a political argument about the economic, since class difference is perceived to be more readily of a weightier ontological texture than cultural difference:

> The difference between these problematics is, as we used to say, essential, since insofar as exploitation is at the core of class difference, class difference is ineluctably linked to inequality, where cultural difference, of course, is not. Cultures, in theory if not always in practice, are equal; classes, in theory and in practice, are not. From this standpoint, the rise of culture, or of the so-called new social movements, or of the problem of identities and identification, or—more generally—of the problem of the subject, has functioned as the Left's way of learning to live with inequality. (17)

As Jameson himself noted a while back, this has been a debate in, beyond, and beside Marxism since Eduard Bernstein in 1899.[8] This is not to say that the argument does not have its own force in contemporary postmodern left politics. The debate's extended history does highlight, however, the question of Michaels's own polemic, whether class analysis is a means or an end in relation to his assertion about universal disagreement. That the answer to this question is not explicitly part of Michaels's argument creates a dissonance in his book's analysis, insofar as we are asked either to agree or disagree with his polemic, without quite entirely knowing what it is—a situation made all the more strange by the apparent precision of Michaels's language and one that also quite famously, as we have seen, characterizes "Against Theory." By in this case gesturing toward Marxism without really engaging with Marxism, Michaels also ignores arguments against the ontological purity of class, as well as treatments of social antagonism that don't simply see economic inequality and the conflict between two different classes of individual agents as given essences.[9] But class inequality and class conflict have to be ontologically more stable than other relations that characterize the "problem of identity," since for Michaels inequality and conflict are in seamless continuity with the constative action of (dis)agreement, whereas those others only evoke the experience of difference.

Hence, Michaels concludes *The Shape* by critiquing Michael Hardt and Antonio Negri's *Empire*, where their putative "politics without beliefs" accedes to an "empire of the senseless" (or meaninglessness) and the poor are transformed into a culture that can be appreciated instead of a class whose inequality one can argue against. That Hardt and Negri are seizing upon in their particular way Marx's own sense of the difficulty of the poor becoming a class is not Michaels's concern. More pressing for him is how class inequality is in continuity with adversarial class beliefs. Cultures are all equal, and thus their beliefs are also, whereas the opposite is true for the relations, and beliefs, among classes.[10]

The sharp contrast in this formula explains the necessary role of class in *The Shape* by pointing out what is conspicuously absent in Michaels's adumbration of identitarian politics: gender. Michaels does discuss sexual identity by way of Samuel Delany's novels, but again in a way that demonstrates how, in this instance, masochism functions like a cultural or ethnic identity. (Michaels also does engage with Judith Butler, but most keenly over Butler's argument against hate speech laws.) Feminism, however, is notably absent from the variety of discourses of different bodies, languages, and histories explicitly critiqued in *The Shape*. This is to be expected, given how much of the book's critique about race and culture replicates the historical study of identity in *Our America*.[11] But another logic might also be at work, as the putatively stark, ontological contrast between class and cultural (or ethnic or racial) identity becomes immediately complicated by gender identity. Indeed, if *economic* inequality is not a given, that's first and foremost because of how opening up analyses to *gender* inequality registers a more thorough (if not complete) sense of social antagonism. Likewise, of course, the study of gender has been exactly where the fact of essential identities has been most vigorously critiqued. The infelicity of characterizing gender as either ideological (in the way that Michaels defines class) or cultural (in the way that Michaels defines race and ethnicity) highlights this predicament. In theory and practice gender identity has marked the aporia of the equal and unequal, as opposed to their evenly calculable distribution.

This is also a question of figure. If the troping of race allows Michaels to argue against the role of race in arguments for social justice, that's because a trope for Michaels means an ontological fiction, insofar as we don't so much argue whether a figure is real as simply experience it. Troping is, in fact, what culture is, what makes an ethnic or racial identity an identity, and why Michaels thinks such forms of subjectivity can be undone by the real of universal argument. Culture is in turn the very trope (or experience) of the hegemony of subjective identity over objectively real, social discord. This is thus less about the reality of race than an argument about the limits of figure for political argument and analysis. Troping, however, is more the volatile interface between ontology and fiction than simply a fiction that stands in for, and thus crowds out questions about, reality. Bluntly, one dismisses tropes of gender, and the troping of gender, at one's risk, something *The Shape* implicitly acknowledges by not following through with such an interrogation. This is not to say, of course, that other tropes such as race cannot dramatize this condition, or that all tropes equally articulate this situation in a homogenized manner. In theory and practice, all tropes interrogate the trope of equality, which means that all tropes are *not* equal. This does not imply, however, that one can then dismiss a particular operation of figure for simply being irreducibly figural.

That is what Michaels is doing, since for him you don't argue with a figure, much in the same way that you don't argue with a culture or language.[12] You instead identify it as such, expose it as something that is distracting us from arguing about what really exists, such as class inequality. If figures do hold our attention, it's not because we're arguing with them, or simply understanding them in order to comprehend the meaning, or intention, of an author. It's because we're enthralled by their unregulated spectacle, which means that we're enthralled by our subjectively different reactions to writings, art, and politics, which now constitute sensory objects linked to neither the constative nor the cognitive. Strictly speaking, for Michaels, such objects are no longer even figures, or components of language, but instead things of sheer sensation.

Hence, we have the final overdetermination for the basic absence of gender in *The Shape*: it has been subsumed under the cultural body of a phenomenal materiality that does not evoke thought about the object but the particularity of experience by the subject. *The Shape* avoids the juncture between an explicit critique of feminism's relation to identitarian politics and a (gendered) argument for disembodied thought over thoughtless sensation by . . . avoiding it. Appropriately, then, feminism is made missing while figure is rectified and sensation resisted.[13] Rather than through an engagement with feminism, Michaels's exorcism of sensation is by way of a de Manian materiality that comes to stand for the linked postmodern mistakes of theoretical reading and identitarian politics. The choice of de Man is not simply a prestidigitation, however. A narrative about the politics of postmodernity does emerge from Michaels's consideration of de Man's terms, but one that exceeds the possibility of a simple end of sensation and a concomitant return to history and argument.

Writing on de Man, Michaels asserts that

> it is the single-mindedness of de Man's commitment to the mark instead of the sign—to the "purely material" as the "purely formal," "devoid of any semantic depth"—that distinguishes *Aesthetic Ideology*. Indeed, the replacement of the sign by the mark articulated in (although by no means unique to) *Aesthetic Ideology* is foundational for and constitutive of the aesthetics of posthistoricism just as the emergence of the subject produced by the same process is—once

> the subject has thoroughly grasped itself as a structure of identification—constitutive of its politics. (18)

To place de Man at the center of a serious discussion about postmodern left politics is all to the good. And "single-minded" does capture something of the relentless nature of reading that unfolds in de Man's writings. That all said, it's somewhat stunning to come across an account of de Man that makes him the exemplary figure for the instantiation of an aesthetic subject at the start of the twenty-first century, as one of the main arcs in *Aesthetic Ideology* is how the aesthetic records its own disarticulation as a founding principle of mediation in, among others, Kant and Hegel. As Andrezej Warminski points out in his introduction to the book, this dynamic certainly has implications for the efficacy of their notions (and ours) of a closed system of successful meaning (5).[14] But this does not mean that the aesthetic is meaningless because it's intentionally opposed to meaning, or that that is the case because the aesthetic is not about understanding but sensory feeling—far from it. The aesthetic is rather for de Man the attempt to unite such understanding and feeling; as Jonathan Culler puts it, aesthetic ideology "imposes, even violently, continuity between perception and cognition, form and idea."[15] As such an assertion, aesthetic ideology is neither a belief in nor an argument for the aesthetic as the positive identity of meaninglessness.

Michaels seems, however, to understand meaninglessness in de Man (if not the title of de Man's book) in precisely this way. There is the signifier and then there is the material of the signifier, which is meaningless. De Man and others valorize this material over signification, which means that we as readers are left with only experiencing this material in different ways, from different perspectives, instead of understanding, and arguing over, meaning. Similarly, the celebration of the many meanings of multiculturalism is in fact the fetishization of experiencing many cultures differently, as that is all we are left with after giving up on meaning and disagreement. On one side lies language as the understanding of meaning; on the other lies the physical materiality of language, which is not to be confused with language. The two are not the same because such materiality can only be experienced, neither read nor understood. It is not language but literal matter, meaningless by definition. For Michaels's de Man, the aesthetic is constituted precisely by the valorized experience of this materiality.

It is certainly true that many understand the materiality of the signifier in ways that resemble its exposition in *The Shape*. It is also true that, in the resurgent textual studies of the last two decades, materiality is indeed about matter (paper, ink, or screen), although a matter that is thought to be integral to language and meaning. But, as the last chapter already notes, de Manian materiality is not in any simple way a materiality of matter, especially not phenomenal matter.[16] Indeed, "Phenomenality and Materiality in Kant," the essay from which Michaels quotes the phrases "pure materiality" and the "purely formal, devoid of any semantic depth," argues that the "material vision" of the sublime remains aggressively unreconciled with the desire in Kant's third *Critique* to adequate the sublime's inner noumenal generation with its exterior, phenomenal expression (*Aesthetic*, 83). This resistance is itself part of a larger blockage. As de Man concludes the essay, "The bottom line, in Kant as well as in Hegel, is the prosaic materiality of the letter and no degree of obfuscation or ideology can transform this materiality into the phenomenal cognition of aesthetic judgment" (90). The *prosaic* is not the quotidian fact of matter but language's resistance to its own sublimation, its disarticulation of the achievement of phenomenal cognition, and thus of the aesthetic experience of the object that organizes Michaels's polemic in *The Shape.*

Of course, Michaels's aesthetic experience is not simply Kant's, as the latter's association of the universal with aesthetic judgment actually grounds the world of agreement that Michaels wants to champion against the relativity of sensory experience that defines his own sense of the aesthetic. Michaels gestures toward these connections himself when he approvingly uses W. K. Wimsatt and Monroe Beardsley's example of how Coleridge's waterfall distinguishes between the questions of deciding whether something is really sublime and merely considering how something makes you particularly feel (72). Both questions, however, invoke a phenomenal dimension that de Man argues Kant's materiality disrupts. As de Man says elsewhere in *Aesthetic Ideology*, the "formalism" of Kant's materiality is not only "a-referential" but also "a-phenomenal" (128). The material in *Aesthetic Ideology* is not something one simply feels.

For Michaels, however, de Man's material demonstration of the failure of phenomenal cognition as meaning must dramatize the triumph of sensory feeling over cognition, the instantiation of materiality as phenomenal meaninglessness. Thus, when de Man begins his key reading of Kant's architectonic description of the sky and ocean as examples of the sublime and wonders how that account relates to other "allusions to sensory appearance" in Kant that try to describe the sublime, Michaels uses de Man's phrase "sensory appearance" to authorize his understanding of Susan Howe's analysis of an Emily Dickinson facsimile (sic) as "not just . . . convey[ing] the meaning of the text to the reader but also . . . reproduc[ing] the experience of its physical features" (4). For Michaels's de Man, "the purely material . . . is everything [e.g., a blank page or border] that can be seen by the reader" (6). Is the experience of such physical properties really the same, however, as regarding Kant's ocean the way that the philosopher says poets do? For de Man, Kant's description conveys "how things are to the eye, in the redundancy of their appearance to the eye and not to the mind, as in the redundant word *Augenschein*, to be understood in opposition to Hegel's *Ideenschein*, or sensory appearance of the idea; *Augenschein*, in which the eye, tautologically, is named twice, as eye itself and what appears to the eye" (82). De Man's point is to describe a material vision discontinuous with any cognitive or semantic action. But as the discontinuity between eye and mind escalates in his passage, it also becomes increasingly difficult to attach the eye to Michaels's experiential subject. The eye stands alone, explicitly divorced from solar meaning but also detached from any seeing reader (or poet, for that matter), simply the "formal mathematization or geometrization of pure optics" (83).

This might be nonsensical to Michaels, but if that is the case, the reason is because the subjective experience he decries, the visual or tactile perception of a blank page, is still attached more to Hegel's "sensory appearance of the idea" than to what de Man's Kant describes. Materiality in de Man is by no means a simple notion. That Michaels translates the term into a physical substance speaks, however, to the very fact of different discourses that Michaels wants to deny. In the language of *The Shape*, Michaels neither understands nor disagrees with de Man so much as he differs from him. More than any sustained argument with what de Man actually says, this predicament enables Michaels to cast de Man in the central role of the book's polemic.[17]

This difference can be measured in another way. As much as Michaels actually argues for meaning and intention in a text, he actually seems uninterested in what de Man might have intended or meant in *Aesthetic Ideology*.[18] There is no indication in *The Shape* as to how much Michaels's reading of de Man diverges radically from what *Aesthetic Ideology* argues about aesthetics and materiality, or from what others have said that argument to be. Michaels's own reading of de Man's intention achieves an odd state of being, less an unavoidable condition of what's right arrived at by an inevitable line of reasoning and more a phantom form of denotation underwritten by the catachresis of what *The Shape* calls "mak[ing] sense" (47). Michaels labels this phantom form "meaning," but it seems more about his difference from de Man than anything else.

Michaels's and de Man's difference does enable the severing of "sensory appearance" from "allusions to sensory appearance," a mutilation quite like the severed Kantian human limb that *Aesthetic Ideology* uses to argue for the non-organic and non-teleological nature of materiality. (To the degree that Michaels restores to the severed phrase the semantic wholeness of human perception, he actually enacts the aesthetic ideology that the book describes.) That act transforms an allusion to sensory appearance into, literally, sensory appearance. As de Man asserts, however, Kant's materiality is neither literal nor figural, precisely because of its supreme uninvolvement with either transference or exchange, especially as part of the key economic circulation between mind and nature. De Man makes this clear by contrasting the third *Critique* with recordings of the sublime in Wordsworth, where "exchange or anthropomorphism" allows the poet "to address, in Book 5 of *The Prelude*, the 'speaking face' of nature" (82).

Wordsworth's ability to address nature adds another register to the materiality that de Man discovers in Kant. This dimension also comments on the argument about nature tentatively begun in "Against Theory" and categorically developed in *The Shape*. (As my previous chapter and this chapter's concluding section claim, this is also implicitly an argument about Wordsworth.) The story also has another key coordinate: Knapp and Michaels's decisive moment in their dispute with de Man in "Against Theory," how they argue that Rousseau's mouthing of "Marion" in *Allegories of Reading* is not an instance of unmotivated, meaningless language, but meaningless "white noise" that simply *resembles* language. "Marion" in "Against Theory" has nothing to do with language; it's a moment of sensory static that is a precursor to the meaningless experience of sensual materiality that *The Shape* identifies as the defining problem of de Manian aesthetics characterizing post-historicist politics. In terms of the argument of "Against Theory," the white noise of "Marion" means that de Man is wrong to use Rousseau's mouthing to assert the coincidence between language and meaninglessness, as "Marion" has literally nothing to say about language.

"Against Theory" itself has nothing extended to say, however, about the status of the *resemblance* of "Marion" to language, of the resemblance of meaninglessness to meaning. As the previous chapter asked, isn't resemblance itself a form of signification? Without posing the problem in quite those terms, *The Shape* answers this question by chiefly critiquing the role of nature in recent science fiction literature and the politics of deep ecology. Specifically, Michaels looks at several recent works of sci-fi that take up the question of what it might mean for the planet Mars to speak. This is first understood as the possibility of an indigenous people speaking for a place, where a planet (or nature) confers onto a people (or culture) an essential dignity and identity. But then, in Kim Stanley Robinson's *Mars* trilogy, a more radical proposition is explored, where the equation of nature and culture implies the possibility of an uninhabited planet speaking a language. In Robinson's works there are thus not only moments when settlers from Earth feel that their new planet allows them to speak culturally as Martians, but that the rocks of Mars—its very landscape—seem to speak. As in deep ecology, nature quite possibly is a culture with its own language, independent of any human coordinate.

For Michaels, of course, the key detail is that Robinson's uninhabited Martian landscape only appears to convey meaning. Mars seems to speak because of the "natural accident" of the shape of its rocks, which from different vantage points (or subject positions) look like they might be something one could understand, a language (*Shape*, 57). Mars is the shape of the signifier, a physical materiality whose resemblance to meaning is only the effect of different perspectives, and whose replacement of meaning by meaninglessness incites the post-historicist trumping of sensory experience over understanding. Mars, or uninhabited nature, is the end point of deep ecology: the post-historical text and culture, the place of difference over disagreement and sensory effects over meaning. This is the predicament that Michaels refers to when he argues that the current post-historicist primacy of the subject position "is based on a characteristically unacknowledged appeal to nature" (15).

To drive home the point, Michaels reworks another key moment in "Against Theory," the wave poem, the example of coming across what appears to be Wordsworth's "A Slumber Did My Spirit Seal" in the sand. In *The Shape* what resembles the lines of Wordsworth's poem are now in Martian sand, or a formation of Martian rock. In "Against Theory" the discovery of the apparent lines forces us to choose between understanding them as lines, as writing "entirely determined by the intention of their author" (*Shape*, 57), and seeing them as marks of non-language that only accidentally resemble meaning. Transposing them to the dead Martian landscape, Michaels foregrounds the impossibility of seeing such squiggles as language, something that occurs only by mistaking the shape of such marks as language, when, in fact, shape's sole presence evinces the absence of language. On Mars, the sense of that impossibility is so great that you don't even need to see anything but what resembles the first stanza of Wordsworth's poem to know that no one wrote it. In contrast, "On Earth . . . you might immediately think that someone had been before you writing" (*Shape*, 57). Indeed, as Knapp and Michaels "suggested" in "Against Theory," "it was only when, seeing these shapes on a beach [on Earth], you then saw a wave wash up and recede, leaving behind [what appeared to be the second stanza of "A Slumber"] . . . that you realized no person made these marks" (*Shape*, 57).

The retrospective nature of this realization actually creates a dissonance between Knapp and Michaels's argument and the one in *The Shape*, however. For, as with the change in Michaels's own understanding of "Against Theory" before and after his writing of *Our America*, this realization depends on the temporal change of one's subject position, now, in the second stage of the wave example, a position oriented around the strange viewing of what appears to be the second stanza of Wordsworth's poem, instead of around the more prosaic discovery of the first. Retrospective meaning is always in some irreducible way a matter of temporal perspective, which is simply another version of the interdependence between meaning and spatial perspective that *The Shape* attacks. The retroactive structure of Knapp and Michaels's wave poem, the example's ongoing reaction to changing empirical evidence, allegorizes this very situation, the unavoidable relation between meaning and positioning, temporal or otherwise.

The question of temporal location is also present in how the 1982 essay is understood through the vantage point of Michaels's 2004 book. In the Earth of "Against Theory," you might actually *not* immediately think someone had written the alleged first stanza—that's the problem, your belief in an intentionless language. If, however, by the second stage of the wave poem you no longer believe in intentionless language, that's a separate issue from believing in a specifically *human* "someone" responsible for the intentional meaning that putatively separates the writing of Wordsworth's second stanza from accidental squiggles. *The Shape* uses "Against Theory" to force the choice between an assumed human author and no human author (and thus no meaning) at all. But the question of human authorship is actually neither simply assumed nor fully resolved in Knapp and Michaels's earlier, more complicated argument against intentionless language.

*The Shape* thus neglects to mention the starkly absurd but also unavoidable character of the wave poem's second-stage choice, as at that point in the example our only options for the marks' genesis are Wordsworth's ghost or a pantheistic sea somehow capable of authoring a poem, or the cosmic accident of squiggles resembling a poem being produced by the unintentional roiling of ocean wave and sandy beach. *The Shape* also leaves out the third stage of the wave poem example, the appearance of a submarine full of scientists watching our reactions to the squiggles, whose presence gives us (presumably, to our great relief) the empirical option of human intention. The coercive nature of such a pedagogical structure aside (given the choices, who would not accept the ontological authority of Michaels's technocrats?), the deletion of the third stage is telling, as its absence highlights the incredible, imperative nature of the second stage's demand: choose between intention and nothing, even if intention is disconnected from human agency.

Choosing intention, of course, could just as well be about *not* choosing the cosmic accident of wave and ocean that merely produces resemblance. The whole point of the Mars example, that we *should* choose nothing when faced with an uninhabited landscape, becomes much more difficult to assent to when the example becomes a wave first rolling up and then revealing what appears to be the second stanza of "A Slumber" in the sand. As Knapp and Michaels describe, choosing nothing, the mere resemblance of the marks to words, means choosing "some subtle and *unprecedented* process of erosion, percolation, etc." (16; my emphasis). Choosing this process means agreeing not only to what Knapp and Michaels call the "mechanical operation" of the waves, but to the mechanical as the genesis of an unprecedented singularity, an "astonishing coincidence" that transforms our sense of what contingency actually is (16). The radical nature of such a contingency can only be conceived through its non-identity as well, as a contingency that is also at once a process or pattern with some yet-to-be-understood purpose or design. Contrary to Knapp and Michaels, we are "amazed" not because something we thought was language turns out merely to resemble language. We are amazed because resemblance has happened at all, and we cannot help but feel the uncanny intention of that accident. The extreme nature of their example points us in a direction altogether different from their normative definitions of intention, meaning, and language.

Intention is not rationed to one side of the second stage's choice but distributed on both sides of the decision, although in such an unthinkable way that intention itself becomes transformed. Faced with the cosmic accident of the wave, of, indeed, resemblance, we are faced with an intentionality more like what de Man in the terminology of an early essay calls the "structure" that establishes the unity of a work; our very distance from that unity or design, however, places us in what de Man describes as a Heideggerian "hermeneutic circularity," where the presence of such an intention can only be felt in terms of a "negative totalization" with which we can never quite coincide (*Blindness*, 25, 29, 35).[19] Knapp and Michaels's wave poem experiment leads to this same unsteady situation of contingency knotted with the form of design. The point of both "Against Theory" and *The Shape*, of course, is to cut that knot, to separate accident from intentional form, or to force the choice between such form and form as the accidental resemblance of shape. But the book's own understanding of the essay freezes the latter around the impossible choice of what to think about the wave's unveiling of the apparent second stanza. De Man's early Heideggerian use of temporality as the aporetic element inciting endless hermeneutic circularity finds its counterpart in the temporal staging of the wave's activity, a staging that makes the question of intention deeply unthinkable in terms of its unavoidable necessity, especially when compared with our relatively easy dismissal of intention when facing the static, uninhabited rock formations of Mars.[20] The very activity of the waves, their mechanical operation, incites, keeps alive, the question of intention.

The waves are a figure for some animating agency, or more exactly, a figure for an awareness of that figure. They are a figure for a temporal action, and therefore of temporality itself. But temporality is also a figure for a basic problem about meaning that de Man of course will elaborate in his other early essay, the seminal "Rhetoric of Temporality." Likewise, all the phenomenal and spatial motifs that de Man and Derrida at times employ, the "sound" of "Marion" or "surface" of the mark, are themselves figures for, different avenues into, the problem of language that deconstruction has explicitly tried to think through over the last forty years. Michaels, however, takes such language literally as evidence of an argument for an immanent physicality, so much so that he is left with as the object of his critique the literally impossible belief that texts, bodies, and cultures operate as objects purely experienced in a sensual manner. This invisible domestication of the figural reaches its apotheosis in his critique of recent sci-fi and other types of literature that envision language as a code, information, or somatic transmission, a pure communication of sensation that dispenses with language as mediated meaning. Michaels asserts this pure sensation as the post-historicist end point of the physical tropes in deconstruction, without considering how such idealized physical sensation is simply another version of the self-present autarky of consciousness freed from the materiality of writing that the early Derrida interrogated so scrupulously in works such as *Of Grammatology* and "Plato's Pharmacy." That moments of idealized physical transmission would still leave a material remainder, now *not* figured as the physical character of language exiled by consciousness, and that *that* would be the mark of a deconstructive inquiry—these are not possibilities in *The Shape.* To say explicitly but also simply that invocations of the physical are not always actually about the physical is to change profoundly what Michaels reads, and targets, in his text.

Resemblances of non-meaning to meaning, on Mars, Earth, and anywhere else in the universe, are sensations of meaning that are neither the pure meaninglessness of sensory experience nor the pure meaning of a language. Such sensation, neither simply nor even necessarily phenomenal, registers the yoking of meaning and meaninglessness, in a way that paradoxically extends the complications of a meaningless language that *The Shape* wants to dismiss, as the sensation of meaning also remakes such language as the site of intention, the second unthinkable stage of the wave poem. Sensation is the figure for the possibility of such a meaningless, intentional language, where that possibility *is* the very sensation of such language. This is the sensation of sensation, the figure of figure, which resemblance intones. For Michaels, this is precisely the epistemological mistake that his argument against a physical sensation separate from meaning is supposed to dismiss. Conversely, however, the sensation of meaning is that dimension of figure that disarticulates figure's generation from the absolute confines of Michaels's human author. Such a separation opens up figure to the predicament of a dizzying, incalculable generation, which is why so many scenes in Robinson's trilogy (and the wave poem's choice, in its own parodic way) seem to touch upon the sublime—as well as the gothic—in terms of the possible choice of the return of Wordsworth's ghost as author. The hyperbole of Michaels's wave example is therefore exemplary *as* hyperbole, the excess of figure.

For Michaels, resemblance as the sensation of meaning is precisely the erroneous triumph of physical shapes and the experiential perspective of the subject position. Resemblance is a subjective effect, depending on one's position in relation to the perceived object. For Michaels, however, meaning never changes, no matter from what perspective meaning is viewed. Hence, Michaels uses the artist Robert Smithson to assert the idea of a map as a model for both texts and paintings, since a map's (authored) meaning doesn't depend on your subjective relation to it; it just is.[21] We might wonder, however, if misreading and then arguing over a map isn't also a matter of perspective—who hasn't tried to bring a map closer to their face when lost? And if we are mistaken, disagreeing over the map's meaning when we're actually just viewing it differently, how much might that epistemological lapse actually structure the arguments (as opposed to differences) we have over texts? And what is the status of being lost, when reading a text? How much does such a model, or figure, of map-as-text simply operate as a resemblance?[22]

More fundamentally, there is the question of whether resemblance really even functions within the differential calculus of the objective meaning of an authored work and the identifiable view of an opposing subject position. The point of the resemblance of non-meaning to meaning is that it is in fact impossible to determine whether such resemblance rests within the empirical object or the phenomenally perceiving subject. We don't know if it is there or if we're imagining it to be; it is a relation radically dislocated from the constative underpinnings of each option. Resemblance is figure genetically unbound from the categories of human reader, viewer, *and* author, which is one way to understand de Man's observation about the "inhuman" nature of language (*Resistance*, 86, 94–97, 99–102). This scission is itself simply another way of expressing the figurative nature of both object and subject, as well as that of the spatial and temporal distance between them; the impossibility of locating resemblance absolutely in either is itself a trope for a specific condition in language and figure. That condition not only includes the separation of resemblance from a human agency who is either the recipient of subjective experience or the author of objective meaning. That condition is also the simultaneous sensation of meaning or intention, the phantom pattern of "negative totalization." The resemblance of non-meaning to meaning might actually be meaningful and, inconceivably, authored. The (literary) affects associated with this sensation, of the uncanny, sublime, and gothic, are therefore in continuity with a more accurate correlation of de Man's inhuman language and deep ecology, with the simultaneous evacuation of human meaning and instantiation of resemblance to meaning in the natural object.[23]

Michaels anticipates the problematic of this more vertiginous generation of signification by distinguishing between meaning and effect, the latter already present in "Against Theory" as the choice of seeing the squiggles in the sand as simply the "nonintentional effects of mechanical processes" (16). In *The Shape* effects are further aligned with the physical materiality of sensation and non-meaning.[24] Properly speaking, meaning is always intentionally caused, while effects are not. Since for Michaels meaning is always equated with intention, meaning will always be confined to intention and found nowhere else. But, as much as both "Against Theory" and *The Shape* assert the fundamental wrongness of finding meaning in resemblance, the acknowledgment of effect sets off a dynamic that Michaels's distinction between meaning and effect can't quite control. Thus, in arguing with Derrida's substitution of "intentional effect for intention" (*Limited,* 66), Michaels opines,

> We don't in general identify the meaning of an act with the effects it has; we don't think that the act performed by the assassin of Archduke Ferdinand at Sarajevo was the act of starting World War I, even though we may believe that World War I was indeed a consequence of this act. And we certainly don't identify the meanings of texts and speech acts with their effects. We don't treat the fact that it bores or amuses you as part of the meaning of my utterance; we don't treat the fact that it makes you think of one thing instead of another thing as part of its meaning; we don't even think the fact that it makes you think what I want you to think (that it communicates what I mean) or that it doesn't is part of its meaning. (127)

Effects are caused by the tyranny of the experiential subject: our ability to feel amusement and boredom, or to have thoughts we associate with a text, even a thought that correctly reproduces the meaning of the author. Indeed, a "reader's understanding of the text" is an effect of the text, but separate from the "meaning of the text," even if they coincide (128). Resemblances would certainly be an effect, but, as the epistemological escalation of the passage indicates, so might almost everything else that passes for practical knowledge, or practical interest, in literary studies. Effects don't even seem to be confined to the subject, if we are asked to consider the difference between an act starting World War I and World War I being merely an unintentional consequence of an act. (What intentional act did start World War I, then?) Such a distinction seems less about what we might individually think and more about a debate over historical causality. Conversely, if this really is about only us, the subjective effects of texts or utterances we experience, it's difficult to see how post-history will end and we can begin once again to argue over the meaning of texts, if our separate understandings of a text are still just effects of the text. Michaels's determination to separate meaning from the sensation of meaning basically turns everything into sensation, into a series of Derrida's intentional effects. In that sense, everything becomes a resemblance. This overrunning of effect, or resemblance, into the world would then itself simply be a trope for the sensation of meaning as *not* being about either the subject or object in any aboriginally prelinguistic way.

In order to keep meaning distinct from effect, and the text separate from everything else, Michaels cedes everything to effect. This might seem less an askesis than simply, and somewhat ironically, the end of argument, as most might feel inclined to give Michaels his meaning and then go study everything else, the effects of the world. But, from Michaels's standpoint, a text *isn't* everything, an argument he associates with Michael Fried's late Modernist appeal for the need to frame artwork (hence the full title of Michaels's book, "*1967*" being when Fried published his influential essay, "Art and Objecthood," about postmodernism and art).[25] To disarticulate artwork and texts from framing is to open them up to the vertiginous generation of effects and thereby end their status *as* artwork or text. Alluding to a story about artist Tony Smith's nighttime highway drive, Michaels comments, "As a producer of effects, the text is like the unfinished New Jersey Turnpike and like everything else in the world: you can't put a frame around it" (127).[26] Without a frame, you have neither text nor the text's meaning—just everything else.

Earlier, Michaels makes clear that this is once again the problem of fetishizing physical materiality. Concerned with a frame as the "sensuous appearance of a text," we don't simply read the text. Indeed, trying to do so suddenly seems, *is*, arbitrary, as contingent as frames really are: "Conventions *are* arbitrary; if it is only conventions that keep us from taking the surface of the paper . . . into what Derrida calls 'our calculations,' then every frame we place around the text, every limit we impose on it, will seem just that, an imposition—something that may be necessary but that cannot be justified" (112–13). And once we have dismissed frames for the contingent conventions that they are, or made them part of what we are experiencing, the text or artwork becomes part of everything else, simply another object whose variety of perception by different subjects is identical with the multiplicity of experience, instead of the univocality of interpretation.

The whole point of *The Shape* is, of course, that we shouldn't make this mistake. But it's unclear from Michaels's argument how preserving frames that separate texts from the world might change the contingent nature of such entities. As Michaels himself seems to indicate, Fried's entreaty for the " 'innumerable conventions both of art and of practical life' " is not an argument against perceiving the convention of the frame as something arbitrary (112). Framing a work might avoid the dire consequences of an out-of-control subject position that Michaels outlines; it might also be the outcome of shunning the sensuous appearance of a text in the first place; but it is also just *that*, an "imposition . . . that may be necessary but that cannot be justified" (113).[27]

In Michaels's terms, moreover, frames ensure the status of a text or artwork as a "representation," insofar as the piece as Modern art is distinct from everything around it (113). Representation is, of course, another way to talk about figure, although here in *The Shape* such figure operates in an intensely stable, functionalist manner. Figure as representation conveys the one meaning or intention of the author of the work. Indeed, one could in fact understand figure in Michaels as explicitly about representation, not resemblance. Yet what about that same figure, or representation, understood as an imposition? The contingent character of framing, not quite extinguished in Michaels's argument, brings representation and resemblance into each other's gravitational pull. Likewise, the distance between intention and imposition collapses. Indeed, Michaels's discussion of framing inadvertently provides us with a perhaps more advantageous candidate for de Manian materiality, rather than Michaels's incorrect use of the term as the physical property of language. Materiality is in fact the very imposition of figure, an action whose radical arbitrariness blunts the realization of figural representation as simple, intentional meaning. But figure, as the very site of transference and exchange, retroactively confers onto materiality the sensation of meaning, or the resemblance of an intention. Such temporal language would itself be an allegory for a condition of language that spatial images, especially of the sublime, also try to evoke. Kant's ocean would then coincide with Knapp and Michaels's sea, now however roiling and inciting (or unveiling) figure, the imposed meaning of non-meaning's resemblance to meaning.

Such a predicament is indeed often narrativized as an appeal to nature, explicit or otherwise, as Michaels notes. But if *nature* in all its nonhuman sensation is a placeholder for what can be, as de Man notes with Wordsworth, "addressed" in this situation, *history* can also occupy that position, as Marx's famous dictum in *The Eighteenth Brumaire* reminds us.[28] And the appeal to silent history is not as easily dismissed as a non-human Martian landscape that does not speak—although, as Robinson's trilogy makes clear, understanding what Mars has to say is very much related to discerning the momentum of a planetary history encompassing both Earth and Mars.[29] For Michaels such a desire again incites a choice, between knowing history as history and experiencing it as memory. Indeed, the problem of post-historical historicism in his book is not the absence of historical consciousness, as it is in Jameson, but the transformation of history into lived memory, a presentist lapse once again informed by the hegemony of the subject position. Such a miscue characterizes not only the argument for reparations for slavery and other issues about ethnic and racial identity, but also academic discourse as well, including both New Historicist studies and deconstruction's own engagements with history.[30]

The figure of history as experienced memory is the ghost, present in such diverse works as Toni Morrison's *Beloved* and the New Historicist technology that critically enables that very experience. Michaels argues that the ghost is not actually needed in deconstruction, as it is merely a figure for what deconstruction actually does, the withering of the historical sign into the performative mark, a physicality denuded of meaning and thus open to the experiential, subjective politics of difference. Thus, while a critique of presentism certainly does inform the complex politics of historicism, Michaels's own version relies on once again a limited understanding of deconstruction as an argument for the phenomenal, as well as a strict separation between the physically immaterial (the ghost) and material (the sensory object as mark). He thus also separates the figural and literal—deconstruction literally does what the ghosts of New Historicism only figuratively do. Yet the sensation of meaning indicates a more phantasmic state than the regulated nature of this separation allows, a linguistic operation that focuses on the relation between the physical and non-physical, the literal and figural, *as* figure. Complicating Michaels's adumbration of post-history, then, the ghost is not always simply a figure for historical memory; more difficultly, history can also be the ghostly, phantasmic operation of figure.[31] Referencing chapter 3, we might say that history is made up of figures, or resemblances, which *as* history perform a non-phenomenal literality.

This spectral formulation of history, with all its implications, is obviously the concern of a number of deconstructive writings, although it is certainly not relegated to such works per se.[32] We can in fact apply this formula to the very historical knowledge that Michaels claims has been abandoned in favor of historical memory and that presumably informs his own book. We have already discussed the effects generated by the resemblance of his text to a more explicitly Marxist analysis, and how his own retroactive understanding of his 1982 essay seems based on resemblances left in the wake of a twenty-year gap, or difference, in temporal position. Knowledge of any author, necessarily past, brings intention and figure together; we do choose Wordsworth's ghost all the time, as Knapp and Michaels say we must. But we also choose the intention of history-as-nature, since to say that history is an operation of figure is to say that its design is made up of resemblances. The shape of *The Shape*, its own historical knowledge, is based on the resemblance between its "theoretical" and "historical" arguments, the pre-historical structures of sensory non-intention espoused by de Man and others, and the post-historical ideological triumph of capitalism. The design of the book, its intention, is in fact a clever tri-part structure (aside from its coda on Hardt and Negri), founded on the resemblances among history, pre-history, and historicism. This is not so much to say that the design isn't true (although I have been saying that about a number of its claims) as to point out that its own constative status rests on a relational structure to which Michaels's descriptive term of "historical knowledge" seems inadequate. But neither does Michaels's definition of memory as experience describe the history of *The Shape*. Walking on a beach and coming upon post-history, Michaels neither knows nor experiences the historical; he does read its intention, however, in the form of its sensation.

> She had fallen in love with Mars for the same reason that Michel hated it: because it was dead.
>
> —Kim Stanley Robinson, *Red Mars*

If *The Shape* is an argument over what form politics and historical understanding should take, it's also a fight over what literature is, and should be. More precisely, it's an argument about an epistemological lapse that literature consistently repeats, of finding meaning in non-meaning, of being obsessed by the gothic and uncanny structures of semantic generation. In that sense, *literature* would be the placeholder for precisely what in the design of *The Shape* exceeds the book's own self-representation as historical knowledge, what one might perversely admire as the book's formal organization. (Whether as such a placeholder literature can attain the disciplinary status of an exclusive *positive identity* is another question entirely; see my discussion of this issue within the context of the relation of the literary to the debate between high theory and cultural studies in the last section of chap. 8 and the study of literature under global capitalism in the coda to this book.) Examples of the coincidence between literature and its own ostensibly worse instincts are both prosaic and profound and abound in both our scholarship and classrooms.[33] The historical narrativization of this coincidence has its own name, of course, which is Romanticism. There are many versions of this *récit*, in the form of both opprobrium and identification, both within but also obviously beyond the era of Romantic writing itself, that make up literary history—that arguably make up the very object of that history. Michaels's own work can thus be approached not simply through a comparison to Jameson's *Postmodernism*, but also as the latest example of a Modernist appeal to repudiate the hold that the cognitive lapse of Romanticism has over literature, art, and politics. The narcissistic solipsism of Romanticism targeted by Irving Babbitt finds its corollary in the subject position of post-history critiqued in *The Shape*.

Michaels himself alludes to the Romantic underpinnings of fetishizing the subject's senses when referring to the German Romantic character of Richard Rorty's emphasis on feeling and "speaking differently," approaches that together will mistakenly transform written text into sensory object (75–76). The empirical crisis that Michaels thus describes finds its psychological and epistemological parameters already anticipated by Romanticism's own inquiries into the relation between subject and phenomenal world. But Romanticism also contains a larger, more complex description of this problem, through, among other trajectories, the one that de Man mentions between Kant's ocean and Wordsworth's address to nature, the latter a troping, or imposition, of the transference of mind and nature and therefore of an economy of figurative exchange. Critical readings of the volatility of that economy are different registerings of the sensation of meaning that Wordsworth poeticizes in his work, an activity in his writing that explicitly includes the (non-)resemblances within and between nature and history, as a Romanticist generation of historicist scholarship from the 1980s has exploited, for and beyond studies of the particular poet. As the subjects of both wave and Martian poem indicate, and as the section headings for Michaels's argument against post-history's covert "appeal to nature" cleverly demonstrate ("rocks," "and stones," "and trees"), "Against Theory" and *The Shape* are themselves allegories for one way to read Romanticism-as-Wordsworth.[34]

This is literally the case in terms of the canonical status of "A Slumber" as *the* poem that numerous critics have used throughout the past century to argue over what an interpretation of a poem might actually mean. But as the previous chapter argues, it is also the case because of the subject matter of "A Slumber" itself, one of many versions in Wordsworth of a poet facing the resemblance of non-meaning to meaning, of impossibly contemplating design in what Michaels dismisses. This chapter can return to "A Slumber" to consider how much the poem appears to dramatize the confusion between non-meaning and meaning in exactly the terms *The Shape* uses: a poet mistakes a dead body for a text to be understood, when in fact he is simply subjectively experiencing an object, confusing his position toward her as poetic meaning. Yet, in "A Slumber," the spatial relation between poet and Lucy is actually radically indeterminate:

A slumber did my spirit seal;
　　I had no human fears:
She seemed a thing that could not feel
　　The touch of earthly years.

No motion has she now, no force;
　　She neither hears nor sees,
Rolled round in earth's diurnal course
　　With rocks and stones and trees. (Gill, 147)

*Where* the poem's action takes place—at Lucy's grave, in the poet's mind, in the earth, or in the universe—is precisely one of the questions asked of the piece. Similarly, *when* the poem occurs is also highly unclear. The divide between the two stanzas creates a sense of spatial and temporal change that can be immediately complicated by asking whether Lucy is already in the ground at the start of the poem.

Neither the poet's physical nor temporal location is fixed in the piece. He is literally disembodied, apparently bereft of any particular subject position aside from his relation to Lucy, someone who has become, as de Man notes, a thing. *When* she became such an object, whether the speaker's perception of her or her death made her so, is also a question—one so conventional it defines in many ways the history of reading and teaching the poem. But the question also defines the very instability of subjective feeling and objective world that makes the sensation of meaning something else besides the despotism of the subject position. The objective status of Lucy as an object and the speaker's interior relation to this external predicament are also both predicated on the same action, or more exactly *appearance* of an action: "She *seemed* a thing that could not feel / The touch of earthly years" (lines 3–4; my emphasis). The speaker's relation to Lucy does not create a perception. Rather, that relation is evidenced by a resemblance, the sensation of Lucy as a thing. He felt a certain way because of what she seemed to be. Dead, she seems to become something akin to what she seemed to be in life. Both subject position and object are based on an appeal to figure, what both shapes and blocks our (one) understanding of the poem's action.

Even more emphatically than the aural engagement with the owls in "The Boy of Winander" that the last chapter examined, the sensation of Lucy is delinked from the phenomenal, with feeling itself reached either through figure ("The touch of earthly years") or feeling's negation: the speaker feels Lucy rolling round with the earth, which is him simultaneously feeling her neither seeing nor hearing anything. The combination of her utter stillness and intense movement at poem's end is thus also a figure for the a-perceptual sensation of meaning that more properly describes the working of sense in the poem than any literally physical, sensory experience. Neither seeing nor hearing, Lucy has become an object like a rock, stone, or tree. But that does not mean that she is either seen or heard, much less experienced purely as an immediate, physical presence. (The same could, of course, be said of the poem's own rocks, stones, and trees, metonymically realized by their proximity to Lucy.) Paradoxically, she is like Michaels's map, intransigent in her location buried beneath the ground. Wherever we move, whatever we feel, she is simply there. But she is a moving map, as the ground itself rolls diurnally. She is meaning based on figure, and forever in relation to the positioning—the imposition—of her own movement.

Meaning as a non-phenomenal sensation tied to figure and resemblance, and therefore to the effects of non-meaning—"A Slumber" allegorizes our (which is to say, language's) compulsive reading of this event, while *The Shape* and "Against Theory" narrate the sober, pragmatic end to such Romantic madness. Michaels's book and coauthored essay are not the first. It is not much of a stretch to say that the literary (as well as political) history of modernity is based on countless attempts either to constrain or to do away with the cognitive and ethical lapses of a solipsistic Romantic sensation. That Wordsworth himself famously asks us to be vigilant against the despotic eye simply shows how much Romanticism itself helps formulate this problem in countless diverse versions, including up to this day equations that confuse a sensation of meaning not in debt to the subject with a physical meaninglessness both enthralling and enthralled by the narcissism of subjectivity.

To say this in another way: postmodernism has to be understood through

Romanticism because that is how Modernism understands itself. Postmodernisms that understand themselves simply as part of a binary with Modernism (that would be Fried's and Michaels's, but also Jameson's) basically assume that Modernism has superseded Romanticism. But if Modernism is against postmodernism, the latter is beside Romanticism as well. Michaels's "theoretical" argument is already "historical," in that his argument about meaning is really about the history of literature as it is made intelligible by the (post)modernity of Romanticism.

This is not by any means to downplay the seriousness of the subject matter in *The Shape*, neither the complexity nor the urgency of the issues it tries to address. And this is not to deny the risks involved in the political inscriptions of sensations of meaning, the immense difficulty of navigating between Babbitt's narcissistic Romantic self and the interminable call of, say, Žižek's Big Other. But it is to say that political meaning—in, as Wordsworth himself shows, the interpersonal, the intelligibility of history, and the retroactive event of memory—is not simply meaning.[35] It is the sensation of intention, belief, understanding, argument, and conflict as well. There is a politics to sensation that ineluctably informs the politics of meaning. If the sensation of meaning can now only congeal in the commodity object of late capital, the sensation of a contingent future still demands a revolutionary meaning beyond capital's reach. Likewise, whatever impasses identitarian politics may evince, there is no going back to a politics that does not acknowledge the sensation of identity and the uncanniness of the same, that does not make room (however riskily) for sensations of meaning as composing a cynosure for political discussion and practice. As the next chapter argues, this spectral condition holds true even for the dialectical history that implicitly underpins Michaels's class polemics and that would somehow subsume or move beyond late capital. There is no simple way to have subjects instead of ghosts, meaning instead of resemblance, knowledge instead of the uncanny. To try and do so is to indulge in an aestheticism—one based, however, not on sensory experience but on the phenomenal cognition of truth.

CHAPTER SIX

# Ghost Theory

> As in *Hamlet*, the Prince of a rotten State, everything begins by the apparition of a specter. More precisely, by the *waiting* for this apparition. The anticipation is at once impatient, anxious, and fascinated: this, the thing ("this thing") will end up coming. The *revenant* is going to come.
>
> —Jacques Derrida, *Specters of Marx*

What is the legacy of Jacques Derrida for Romanticism?[1] There are, of course, many Derridas and many Romanticisms. And the structure of a legacy, even if it is one among many, is to obviate the many in favor of the one. Exponents of a legacy know the one *as* the one prior to any identity before contingency. As Gayatri Spivak also reminds us, this is as much an issue about gender and sexuality as it is about ontology, insofar as a legacy is what our father leaves, or should leave, us.[2] Legacies are as well oftentimes mixed up with ghosts; so much so that, inevitably, a legacy is also what a ghost leaves. Derrida explicitly confronts this predicament of ghostly entailment in one work from his voluminous writings, in a way that also allows us to say something about the relation between Derrida and Romanticism, and, as usually is the case with Derrida, much more. Derrida's text opens up a way for us to think about what I want to call *ghost theory*, whose significance lies not least in the redundancy of the term.

The text of Derrida that I refer to is his *Specters of Marx: The State of the Debt, the Work of Mourning, and the New International* (1994), a work whose reception showed it to be something less and something more than what many had hoped it would be, the definitive negotiation between deconstructive and Marxist thought. One thing that Derrida's book definitely is is *literary*, and not simply by way of reading Marx; there is also as crucially the contemplation of Shakespeare's tragedy, so dominant in the Romantic mind (as well as Marx's own),

*Hamlet.* Playing off of Marx's own particular love of Shakespeare, Derrida finds in this basic phoneme of Western culture one of the central tropes of his book: Hamlet's ghostly armored father, embodying what Derrida calls the "visor effect," the prosthetic ability of a ghost to see without quite being seen in any absolute fashion, while giving Hamlet the injunction to correct a primal wrong of family and state (7). The phantasmic as well as indeterminate nature of this injunction (Paternal law? Social justice? Dialectical inevitability?) is the father's legacy to Hamlet and, according to Derrida, Marx's legacy to us. In both cases the power of the injunction lies not in its certitude but in exactly the opposite, its constative inconstancy, upon which, nevertheless, future action and historical event—*revolution*—rest.

For Marx, of course, the injunction of his manifesto defines itself against the necessarily incomplete, great bourgeois revolutions of the eighteenth century, as well as the necessarily uninformed, myriad visions of reform and partial revolution of the nineteenth century. However, in Derrida's reworked version of Marx's legacy, spectralized and thus preemptively auto-immunized from its own phallic authority, the ghostly yet discernable injunction for social transformation need not stay resolutely sequestered on one side of Marx's epochal divide. Indeed, are not such codified but still infinitely charged terms as the "Age of Revolution" and "Marx and Romanticism" already metonyms for this historical problematic? Is not the legacy of Derrida's *Specters* to Romanticism the specter of Romanticism itself, the ghost of history as revolution, the fatal intersection between representational knowledge and political action? Are not the spectral poetics that Derrida discovers in Marx prefigured in the phantom periodicity, the trope of exceptionalism, of Romanticism itself? Is not the thinking through of the (non-)ontological nature of this situation, along with its ineluctable although by no means simply decipherable political articulation, one of Derrida's legacies to us all, the imperative of ghost theory?

Ghost theory is a theory about ghosts, theorized by ghosts—by a discourse structured around the de-ontologizing nature of the specter: spectral entities and phantasmic thought. The tangible intangibility of a ghost cuts across one key binary of both philosophy and political writing, a dichotomy historically linked to one of Romanticism's own numerous *récits*, the material versus the ideal. Ghosts are precisely not material to the degree that that term stands for an ontological certitude based on the reified hypostasis of physical reality. But they are also not ideal to the extent that that word also refers to an ontology this time based on the reality of the non-physical—of Spirit (*Geist*). Ghosts are neither material nor ideal insofar as the material is embedded within a materialism and the ideal within an idealism, ontological structures secured by the reifying tag of an *ism*. Ghosts are as real as everything else; everything else is real as a ghost. Ghosts delink the staging of the opposition between the material and the ideal from the ontological choice of one or the other, as well as from any Hegelian *Aufhebung* of the two.

If such ghostly disarticulations are present in the texts of Romanticism, readers of Romanticism have had difficulty always seeing it that way, choosing oftentimes instead to see the question of Romanticism and ghosts as a debate over what is more real, the material or the ideal. If we now read Romanticism and that debate differently, that's in large part due to Derrida and his fellow traveler, Paul de Man. The phenomenal as well as political question of materiality versus ideality was forever changed by their incursions into the study of language as something neither simply material nor ideal but actually prior to that distinction. If people today invoke the possibility, as the present book does, of a "materiality without matter" or of an "idealism without absolutes," that is in many ways because of the work of these two thinkers (Cohen, Cohen, Miller, and Warminski, vii–xxv; Rajan and Plotnitsky, 1–3).

Evoking the effects of Derrida's and de Man's writings inevitably calls to mind the consequences of theory, a term larger than but also metonymically tied (for good or ill) to the workings of deconstruction. Invoking theory also means questioning its relation to praxis, a logic that replays the dynamic between the material and the ideal, the substantial and non-substantial, the realm of action versus that of thought. Taking theory seriously doesn't necessarily mean, however, seeing thought as substance, or theory as praxis. It can also mean understanding theory as taking issue with the hypostatizations of thought and action, of unveiling the phantasmic character of each. Theory is also therefore no more idealist in the ontological sense than a ghost is; like a ghost, theory also disputes the nonmaterial essence of idealism. Theory *is* a ghost, the ghost of a theory whose spectral state makes it no less urgent or compelling as the *mise en scène* within which we read.

For Marx, or one Marx, theory is nevertheless the unreal, idealist state eschewed in favor of a socially transformative practice: "Philosophers have only *interpreted* the world, in various ways; the point, however, is to *change* it" (Tucker, 145). This speaks to one portion of Derrida's reading in *Specters*, his interrogation of a Marx, chiefly glimpsed in the critique of Max Stirner in *The German Ideology*, who is intent on exorcising ghosts from the world, with ghosts to be understood as the ontological truth of illusion, or false consciousness (120–47). And yet, Derrida argues, Marx cannot quite prevent the actions of ghosts and phantoms from contaminating key moments in his own prose, as the scene in *Capital* with the dancing table attests (161). One might note, however, that this tropic movement does not so much expose the fallacy of Marx's argument as set his claims spinning away from the centripetal force of their own metaphysics. The meanings of Marx are real, real as a ghost's. Derrida at times does seem to think that Marx finally falls on the side of exorcism rather than that of conjuration. But insofar as the intelligibility of Marx's writing depends on both the overt and subterranean exchanges between these two actions, Derrida's science of "hauntology" is itself already prefigured in Marx's handling of his own "pre-deconstructive" ontology (10, 170). In wrestling with the difficulty of ghosts, Marx's own discourse becomes one example of ghost theory.

(Derrida thus writes of Marx the exorcist, "Pre-deconstructive here does not mean false, unnecessary, or illusory. Rather it characterizes a relatively stabilized knowledge that calls for questions more radical than the critique itself and than the ontology that grounds the critique" [170]. But is not the question of the difference between the pre-deconstructive and deconstructive precisely the uncertainty of this "call" as either communicative action or ghostly injunction—the call of the call, as it were? Insofar as this call and its indeterminancy emanate from Marx, his theory is enmeshed in ghost theory, just as is this uncommonly sensible moment in *Specters* that tries to place Marx's critique in some stable, pre-radical space elsewhere than, "before," deconstruction. In that sense the opposition between the ontological and non-ontological does not simply subtend our discussion but also participates in the relay of distinctions—material versus ideal, praxis versus theory—that we've been describing.)

If Marx cannot exorcise ghosts, we cannot exorcise Marx. As "'Marx—*das Unheimliche*,'" he "remains an immigrant *chez nous*, a glorious, sacred, accursed but still a clandestine immigrant as he was all his life" (*Specters*, 174). Like Hamlet confronting *his* ghost, we cannot avoid Marx's injunction to change the world, words that literally come from (atop) Marx's grave and its epitaph. The injunction's very attempt to separate philosophy from action, or theory from praxis, paradoxically becomes a ghostly insistence that satisfies the demands of neither in their ontological incarnations, but whose call nevertheless cannot be ignored. Such language, of course, calls forth its own phantasmic doubling, since these are the very terms that have been used to commemorate Derrida since (and truth be told, before) his death. We cannot exorcise Derrida, whose memory many would like to expunge as feverishly, or wistfully, as Marx's. Without trying to occult or press this family resemblance further, we can still say that their phantom legacies involve our inheritance of the very vocabulary, affective and intellectual, by which such terms as legacy, propriety, and property are simultaneously known and drastically interrogated.[3]

The dynamics of exorcism, conjuration, and haunting also apply to another legacy, insofar as we might simply ask, as previous chapters have, whether Romanticism—putatively demystified, deconstructed, and dispersed into both the long eighteenth and nineteenth centuries—is over. Or does it haunt us in a way that also chases us, and projects us into the future? What of it cannot be or has not been exorcized? One answer to these questions involves the very formula in *Specters* for a haunting that is also a future projection, what Derrida's reading clarifies for Marx, but which also has all along been part of Romanticism: the *revenant* of revolution.

Romanticism is full of ghosts, ruins, and portents—figures of past, present, and future conflict; textual allusions of either indeterminate or exorbitant meaning; images of indistinct substance and mental visitation; signs of tremulous memory and inchoate anticipation. Ghosts are everywhere in Romanticism, to the point that Romanticism is arguably the very hauntology that Derrida outlines in *Specters*. This view of Romanticism has been contested in ways that simultaneously become part of that perspective, much in the same manner that exorcism is part of the logic of conjuration for Derrida, or the resistance to theory *is* theory for de Man. The case of the gothic, a mode or genre about ghosts, is exemplary in this instance, where Romantic writers (Wordsworth, Coleridge) and readers (Geoffrey Hartman most recently, and elaborately) have made the case for the separation of Romanticism and the gothic.[4] After the scholarship of Michael Gamer and others, however, it's difficult to see how a strict border between the two (historical or otherwise) can be maintained.[5] If, as Hartman might argue, much of Romanticism's (or, at least, Wordsworth's) power seems to come from this primal separation, an equal amount of Romanticism's energies appears to spring from the sublime failure of this distinction. A gothic Romanticism is as redundant a term as ghost theory.

The gothic nature of Romanticism places issues of alterity, of the uncanny and the Seen and the Not-Seen, in the foreground of our attention. Implicit obsessions of the gothic also dovetail with themes in Derrida's reading of Marx's argument about the commodity form (149–66). How much can the spectral nature of the commodity stay contained on one side of a history understood in terms of pre-capitalist and capitalist production? Was there really a time before the commodity when there were no ghosts? These are questions others besides

Derrida have asked of Marx, with interrogators including non-Marxists, post-Marxists, and Marxists. For our purposes, these are also questions that accompany the gothic's own self-representation, the experience of gothic literature, drama, or show as the commodity form of mass culture.[6] If we see the gothic as a reflexive tale about commodification and Romanticism as irrevocably bound to the gothic, we also confront Romanticism as a key moment in the spectral narrative of capitalist production; it is the moment when something definitely happens in the mutating acceleration of capitalism's realization, although that something also seems to have a prior life and story. This formula is itself a ghostly doubling: the paradoxical nature of Marx's narrativization of capitalism (When did it begin? How can we know since we've always been within it?) finds its *Doppëlganger* in the question of Romantic exceptionalism (Did it really happen? Can there really be a time without, or before, Romanticism?).[7] The question of whether to talk of a gothic genre or mode, of a historic or trans-historic model, with the latter paradoxically also able to say something about the nature of something as historically unavoidable as the commodity form, simply extends the gothic dynamic of this ghostly multiplication.[8]

Such parthenogenesis does not end there, since if we now study Romanticism as the age of commodification, we before studied it as the age of revolution. And if the gothic narrativizes commodification, it also, as many have pointed out, tells the story of revolution.[9] Indeed, to see the gothic in Romanticism is to see how in so many ways Romantic texts are haunted by revolution, a commonplace of our own Romanticist reading habits for quite some time. This haunting comes in many forms: of a revolution about to occur; of one that came and failed; of one that failed but that might still happen. The politics of such hauntings are as varied as the specters of social conflict. Not all works run from or (simply) fear images of revolution. This is especially true if we extend the gothic sense of the spectral beyond the gothic novel and even Jacobin fiction. *America* is about the conjuration, not the exorcism, of the violent, prophetic libido of William Blake's Orc, and the intangible, not-present consequence of Percy Bysshe Shelley's West Wind involves believing in, not dismissing, the ghost of future revolution.

Yet it is fair to say that, since the 1980s, we have mostly been involved with the intelligibility of Romantic narratives that attempt to contest, repress, or exorcise the power of such signs of historical change. That such phantasms still erupt within the representational space of the narratives is part of this very intelligibility. Hence, William Wordsworth, in book 10 of *The Prelude*, comes out of his bedridden thoughts in Paris shortly after the September Massacres to hear a cry that both remembers and describes both instants: "Sleep No More!"[10] In this uncanny moment of Romantic iteration, Wordsworth the poet of memory cites Shakespeare in order to encode individual history as waking up to the nightmare of revolutionary Terror. Wordsworth the Girondist is chased into consciousness by the ghost of a text and event that figures waking life as witnessing crimes as terrible as Macbeth's regicide and murder. The remembered inability of his Girondist "calmer mind" to quell fully such a terrible punctuation to the poet's thoughts becomes the very mechanism by which Wordsworth retroactively circumscribes and excludes the revolutionary sublime from his life.

The retrospective counterrevolutionary anxiety that characterizes this eruption and its management speaks to the congruence of a certain ghostly tropology and politics, the anti-Jacobin attempt to exorcise the phantom possibility, or choice, of revolution. Standing behind such moments is of course the writing of Edmund Burke, arguably the most developed and consistent expression of a spectral poetics of revolution during the Romantic period. Indeed, Burke has since the 1980s been perhaps the exemplary model for our own understanding of how the ghost of the French Revolution was both articulated and expelled, simultaneously. (Whether the retrospective narrative of Wordsworth's own exorcism of such trauma is in fact structured by Burke's more preemptive endeavor is arguably the key question that 1980s Romanticist historicism asks.) In Burke the phantasm of modernity is at once ferociously contested and strikingly embodied; Burke tries to exorcise Romanticism as revolution even before it comes to be and haunts all the nineteenth century and beyond.

Burke's great counterrevolutionary work, *Reflections on the Revolution in France* (1790), in fact shapes its historical argument around a gothic plot of entailment. The English people are what they are because of their inheritance from the past. Putatively writing to a young friend enamored with the Jacobin cause, Burke's purpose is to remind his colleague of their English legacy and to save him from the spectral distractions of what is happening in France.

> You will observe, that from Magna Charta to the Declaration of Right, it has been the uniform policy of our constitution to claim and assert our liberties, as an *entailed inheritance* derived to us from our forefathers, and to be transmitted to our posterity; as an estate specially belonging to the people of this kingdom without any reference whatever to any other more general or prior right.[11]

Like his young friend, Burke's English readers follow *Reflections* in order to rediscover an inheritance from their "forefathers" that they had all along possessed, the traditions, habits, and customs of the English feudal past: "People will not look forward to posterity, who never look backward to their ancestors" (119).

As with the gothic narratives of Ann Radcliffe, the Burkean drama of discovering a legacy involves the attainment of a rectitude that is both ethical and epistemological. The illegitimacy of the revolution, its criminality, lies not simply in the atavistic impulses of its participants but also in the illusory nature of their claims. The French revolutionaries are not only depicted as nightmarish figures; their ideas are the misbegotten consequences of the nightmare of reason. And the abstractions of reason are at once deceitful and without content. They misdirect, distract, and lack substance. They are ghostly deceptions. As has oftentimes been remarked, Burke best makes this point through the optical figures in his language.[12] The revolutionaries' "new conquering empire of light and reason" is a phantasmic army that oppresses precisely to the degree that it blinds everyone to its own constative poverty, as well as to the Burkean truth of the necessity of feudal tradition (171). Burke asks us not to believe our eyes, to see beyond and banish instead the visual deceptions of a revolution fatally in debt to the social experimentation of the Enlightenment. Perceiving correctly, getting past the revolutionaries' superstitious use of the Enlightenment, becomes an ethical and political act.

As has also been observed, an epistemological and ontological argument likewise underwrites Burke's attack on France's paper currency economy.[13] For Burke, the speculative nature of paper money is exactly that of the spectral: unmoored from the weighty fact of feudal land, paper makes value itself a ghostly proposition, as unreal as the abstract claims that French reason makes about humans and society. Burke thus anticipates Marx's own critique of the spectral character structuring the commodity form in modernity. Their solutions, of course, are mirror opposites. Marx wishes for modernity to break dialectically out of itself, into a non-capitalist future. Burke desires to halt modernity in its tracks, and for society to return to the foundational values of the chivalric past.

The Marx that *Specters* criticizes assumes the ontological soundness of that future, the Other of a capitalist present permeated by the illusory nature of ideology and the commodity form. The Marx that *Specters* recuperates from Derrida's readings is the more radically complicated figure, whose metaphysical assumptions are belied by the spectral rhetoric that underwrites Marx's own polemics and analyses. Yet, this very doubling, what for Derrida makes Marx's work both an exorcism and conjuration of specters, is also intrinsic to Burke's argument for the conservation of a feudal past.

Specifically, the English's legacy from their forefathers is as phantasmic as Hamlet's from his; the logic of Burkean entailment is twinned with the off-putting term (then and now) that Burke contrasts with reason, "prejudice":

> Instead of casting away all our old prejudices, we cherish them to a very considerable degree, and, to take more shame on ourselves, we cherish them because they are prejudices; and the longer they have lasted, and the more generally they have prevailed, the more we cherish them. (183)

The timeless, foundational nature of England's ancient constitution is so because of its inheritors' ongoing, active *disposition* to read it in that manner; as J. G. A. Pocock argues, the "immemorial" in Burke is ineluctably mixed with the "customary" (*Politics*, 227).[14] Foundation and choice, the "immemorial" and "customary," are thus locked together in a heteronomy that hollows out either's claim to an aboriginal essence. Burke's prejudice is not simply based on the truth of the feudal past; that truth also depends on the habit of retroactively choosing to enact the values of such a previous time. Burke's spectral descriptions of revolutionary reason are juxtaposed with his expression of the phantasmic logic of prejudice's supplementary relation to the feudal era.

In Jerome Christensen's famous description of this dynamic, Burke's fidelity to custom is also an apostasy, since it admits to the degree that the nation's entailment depends not simply on the forefathers' wishes but also on the sons' desire to choose—indeed, conceive of—such an inheritance: "Descent succeeds to a primordial detachment of son from father, reader from writer, which inscribes contingency in the relation between the present and the past, thereby requiring that any necessity in the connection between past and present be adduced retrospectively" (775). Apostasy and fidelity are mirror doublings of social linkages based on contingency rather than on any ultimate essence. The prejudice of choosing the past is therefore also never simply an individuated, existential act, but always part of the performance of a larger network of social meanings. In terms of both its contingent and social character, Burke's prejudice actually describes the non-ontological structure of hegemony two hundred years before Ernesto Laclau's own *New Reflections on the Revolution of Our Time* (1990).[15]

Christensen later refigures the "primordial detachment" between father and son in terms of the son's own conflicted subjectivity, with a gothic image that ironically separates the present English reader's prejudice for the past from his knowledge of his own distance from such a prior era: the inherited text of England is "*constituted* by the head's bloodless detachment of itself in order to read the history of the mystical body . . . in order to return and metaphorically 'frame a polity in blood' " (776).[16] The detached bloodless head of the English son, coolly suspended over and reading its severed national body, which emotionally asserts a continuity between past and present; the metonymic (dis)articulation of hegemony that both contemplates and performs the metaphoric desire of nation building—such are the ghostly dynamics of a de-ontologizing fealty to a past English history as phantomlike as the allegedly terrible future of revolution that Burke's *Revolution* contests. In a lurid confrontation, the detached head of England faces the guillotined head of France. This is Romanticism as revolution as ghost theory.

Using Burke as the exemplary figure for a Romantic hauntology of revolution would seem to do neither Derrida nor Marx any favors. Indeed, noting a connection among all three writers appears to support the harshest critics of *Specters*, who charge that Derrida and deconstruction have given succor to the political right.[17] This is a charge not to be simply dismissed, if just for the practical observation that, as Stuart Hall's analysis of Thatcherism and, arguably, U.S. politics for some time have shown, the right can do hegemony as well as, if not better than, the left.[18] That very well might be, although one might wonder if that is actually an argument for a return to metaphysics. Indeed, by highlighting the phantasmic structures of hegemony in arguably the most prominent counterrevolutionary writer of the last two centuries, ghost theory dialectically reenvisions itself as a field of possibility of which the left has yet to take advantage; in an odd chiasmus, Derrida's Marx points the left toward how to catch up to Burke.

Another related criticism (so familiar in debates about deconstruction) might see the continuities among these writers as effacing their differences, subsuming everything into yet another example of the aporetic character of language. One could argue that this critique of subsumption is a strangely incomplete charge for a discourse that always returns to issues of alterity and otherness. One might also recognize the independence of such differences from the security of an eternal truth as precisely the start of politics. Yet one might also simply note that other examples besides Burke from across the political spectrum could have been used to demonstrate the ghost theory of revolution in Romanticism. If the figure of Burke seems especially exemplary, that is so not simply because of the undeniable semiotic thickness of his writing, but also for two other reasons, one that has to do with what Burke specifically highlights about the Marx in *Specters* and one that speaks to our own academic and institutional moment in Romantic studies.

First, Burke's unabashed allegiance to a feudal vocabulary of entailed inheritance foregrounds Derrida's own reflexive, ironic decision to have Marx speak to us via the Prince of Denmark's ghostly father. The increasingly phantasmic question of getting beyond (late) capitalism becomes, in other words, inextricably tied up with the always already ghostly question of where capitalism *came from*, the when of the momentous shift from feudal land to bourgeois market value. And those questions both reflect the further reflexive difficulty of what language might form these very queries. Hamlet's father lays something on us, an injunction or claim that might or might not take the form of a legacy or inheritance. Burke would know this act irrevocably as one of chivalric entailment; as such, however, it is also a fantastic proposition, insofar as feudalism is already by the Romantic era, indeed by Shakespeare's, *over*. And if we can surely demonstrate that feudalism was over for quite some time, Romanticism becomes the site where we see it enacted nevertheless in political and aesthetic practice and thought; Romanticism becomes the ghostly reflexive moment where capitalism breaks out of the feudal era, *but not really*—not really because it was already over; not really because the language of legacy and inheritance signals that it's not. The question concerning Marx's own claim on the present is therefore one that cannot be answered without the interrogation of this prior moment, the exemplary Romantic—that is, indeterminate—reception of modernity's past.

Second, the congruence of an anti-Jacobin politics with the language of ghosts speaks to how Romantic scholars for the last thirty years have by and large understood the story of revolution in Romanticism. A Nietzschean *fable* of that study might go something like this.[19] The Romantic exploration of the relation between mind and nature generated in the 1950s and 1960s a phenomenologically oriented study of Romantic literature. Both Derrida's and de Man's overlapping interrogations of Jean Jacques Rousseau deconstructed that perspective's orientation around an inside and outside, transforming the phenomenal question of Rousseau's inner expressive self into the elaborate predicaments of Derridean writing and de Manian reading. The 1960s and 1970s dissolution of Rousseau's consciousness into *écriture* and allegory, for all its excess of signification and ongoing relevance, was then codified in Romantic studies and elsewhere as primarily the deconstruction of individual (Romantic) subjectivity, and not really about a collective or social event. The 1980s critique of the Romantic ideology and return to historicism follow the deconstruction of Romantic consciousness and explicitly foreground the social world as their arena of inquiry. The multivaried historicism of the 1980s critique coexists in a complicated fashion with the de-ontologizing impulses of the earlier deconstructive readings of Rousseau and others. One clear point of intersection is the adversarial stance both modes of critical reading take toward earlier Romanticist habits of reading, if not toward Romanticism itself. The Romantic ideology is in fact associated with a humanist understanding of Romanticism as the ameliorating transcendence of revolutionary disappointment, a perception that implicitly condones the counterrevolutionary perspective of a number of Romantic writers.[20] In the 1980s the age of revolution was primarily understood in terms of its resistance to that event.

This institutional fable could of course be complicated much more—by de Man's intense engagement with history in his Romanticist writings, for example.[21] But it is safe to say that the main and most extensive studies coming out of 1980s historicism worked off of the exemplary logic of a Romanticism defined by the anti-Jacobin impulse. This is the case even though an earlier Romanticist historicism existed from the 1950s through the early 1970s, a body of scholarship that actually identified itself with a Romanticism then defined as the spirit of revolution, with, for example, a populist, radical Wordsworth yet to be perceived as either the consistently ideologically repressed or politically apostate figure that comes to dominate Romantic studies in the 1980s.[22] This earlier revolutionary historicism very much overlaps with Derrida's and de Man's readings of Rousseau, but the two bodies of criticism could just as well have been two different fields. The earlier literary historicism does not trouble the metaphysics of history in terms of periodicity, origins, teleology, or human experience. The French revolution of that historicism, as well as the historicism itself, is securely ensconced within the same categories of ontological thought that Derrida argues bind the Marx who attacks Stirner in *The German Ideology*. The spirit of that earlier historicism's revolution is not a phantom. Its relation to empirical evidence aside, the spirit is the idealist essence of an authentic identity in history.

The topic of revolution has arguably taken a backseat in Romantic studies of late, for a variety of reasons that range from the rise of new historical themes (empire making, consumerism) and perspectives (the long eighteenth and nineteenth centuries) to the more prosaic fact of the professional oversaturation of such arguments—we *all* know what the Romantic ideology is.[23] Perhaps, also, working through the trauma of historical change does not seem as urgent a duty for scholarship today when every waking moment of contemporary life already feels involved in that process—which is not to say that either empire or consumption, then or now, escapes such trauma (far from it!). But the fact remains that the study of revolution in Romantic studies has basically taken two forms especially in the North American academy after World War II: a 1950s, 1960s, and 1970s historicism, unconcerned with questioning its ontological grounding, that sympathetically takes as its subject a Jacobin Romanticism agitating for revolution; and a 1980s (new) historicism that disconnects the identities of Romantic and Romanticist, and that takes as its subject, if not its object of critique, an anti-Jacobin Romanticism intent on suppressing the revolutionary impulse.

This then is one legacy that the Derrida of *Specters* leaves Romantic studies, if we choose retrospectively, like Burke's alleged English contemporaries, to make such a hegemonic articulation. ("Choice" itself would of course be a figure for the spectral practice—Burke's "prejudice"—that simultaneously remakes and enacts prior articulations.) That legacy would be a study of Romanticism shot through with ghost theory, equally open to the question of revolution (ineluctably then and now) and to the possibly spectral, de-ontologized natures of such an inquiry and topic. It would be a study that identified Romanticism with that very openness to the fantastic event of historical change, a scholarship that would be written within the moment of what Derrida refers to in *Specters* as Walter Benjamin's concept of some "weak messianic force," a "certain messianic destitution, in a spectral logic of inheritance and generations, but a logic turned toward the future no less than the past, in a heterogeneous and disjointed time" (*Specters*, 55, 181).[24] Such a line of thought would mean thinking about the meaning, in terms of both form and content, of a past figure confronting the present—of feudalism standing before capitalism, of Shakespeare before Romanticism, and of Marx (or Derrida) before us. But, like Derrida's Marx (outrageously? vertiginously?) catching up to Burke, we would also be thinking and writing about a Romanticism ahead of, not simply behind, us.

The very political positioning of such scholarship presents itself in fact as the question of a ghost. Very few more powerful pedagogical moments exist in Romantic studies than the act of connecting contemporary invocations of the left and right to a two-hundred-year-old genealogy originating in the Jacobin and anti-Jacobin conflict. Very few genealogical claims can also be complicated as extensively, from Marx's own critique of past revolutions in *The Eighteenth Brumaire*, to recently past conservative accusations of the Jacobin nature of the neocons, to scholarly qualifications about presentist blind spots in academic oppositional criticism. And yet who can deny the existence of this claim as always somehow part, no matter how distant or invisible, of the intelligibility of Romanticism? The very force of this claim, this claim as force, exists as the phantom clarity of our own political (post)modernity. Romanticism describes the logic of its own exceptionalism *as* this clarity.

Such assertions tie the study of Romanticism in an exorbitant manner to future concerns beyond and outside the scholarly world; in doing so, they risk an undeniable hyperbole of claims—which is to say, they risk being Romantic. To blush at such a thought is simply to acknowledge how the ghost of theory, exemplary in the critiques and injunctions of *Specters*, dares us to be Romantic once again.

---

Thus, Romanticism in the wake of *Specters* simultaneously asks us: Do we believe in revolution? Do we believe in ghosts? These are serious questions to ask today. Indeed, as our previous chapter's engagement with Michaels shows, recent leftist and neoleftist arguments have actually based their claims on the sober, judicious repudiation of ghosts. One other particularly instructive example comes from Slavoj Žižek's own critical observations about Derrida's *Specters* in his essay "The Spectre of Ideology" (1994). Žižek's piece, with its particular blend of Lacanian and Marxist thought, is apposite precisely to the degree that it takes the discourse of specters seriously, only to fall ultimately on the side of a logic of exorcism defined against one of conjuration.

Žižek's main topic is one that certainly could have been woven earlier and more explicitly into this present discussion about ghosts, revolution, and Romanticism. He considers the spectral nature of ideology, a problematic generated by a discomfort held by many about ideology's collusion with the ontological distinction between truth and falsity (or false consciousness) and a gnawing sense still of ideology's indispensability as a critical term: "[Ideology] seems to pop up precisely when we attempt to avoid it, while it fails to appear where one would clearly expect it to dwell."[25] After a rich and tenaciously dialectical analysis of the implications of this and other attendant issues for theories of ideology, Žižek evaluates Marx's own relation to a constative metaphysics in a section that both resembles and differs from the argument in *Specters*:

> Although [Marx] may appear to fall into the trap [of such a metaphysics] (is not the entire *German Ideology* based on the opposition of ideological chimera and the study of "actual life"?), things get complicated in his mature critique of political economy. That is to say, why, precisely, does Marx choose the term *fetishism* in order to designate the "theological whimsy" of the universe of commodities? . . . Fetishism designates "primitive" superstition, the fear of ghosts and other spectral apparitions, and so on. And the point of Marx is that the commodity universe provides the necessary fetishistic supplement to the "official" spirituality: it may well be that the "official" ideology of our society is Christian spirituality, but its actual foundation is none the less the idolatry of the Golden Calf, money.
>
> In short, Marx's point is that there is no spirit without spirits-ghosts, no "pure" spirituality without the obscene spectre of "spiritualized matter." (20)

Like Derrida, Žižek sees the ghostly language of Marx's commodity fetish as resisting the duality between truth and illusion upon which ideology is based; the fetish is thus a more genuine barometer of the problem of ideology in Marx than ideology itself.[26] Unlike Derrida, however, Žižek does not see this resistance as the sign of a Marx drifting toward either a spectral poetics or science of hauntology. As Žižek's explanation of the superstitious nature of the fetish implies, the specter of "spiritualized matter" is still something to get beyond.

In Žižek's essay the symbolic's depiction of social reality is always incomplete; the real (as opposed to reality) is the failure of that depiction. Within this scenario, the "*real (the part of reality that remains non-symbolized) returns in the guise of the spectral apparitions*" (21). Derrida's problem, according to Žižek, is staying with (and thus fetishizing) the spectral guise instead of working toward, as Lacan allegedly might, an encounter with the real, or freedom. The specter actually runs away from this terrifying freedom, the "redefinition of the symbolic within the real."[27] Derrida's specter of revolution is actually a prophylactic, the "positivization of the abyss of freedom," "gentrify[ing]" and postponing the encounter with the real by always conceiving it as *avenir*: "Our primary duty is not toward the specter, whatever form it assumes. The act of freedom *qua* the real not only transgresses the limits of what we experience as 'reality,' it cancels our very primordial indebtedness to the spectral Other" (27–28). To cancel such a debt is to abjure the "logic of conjuration" that Žižek associates with the argument of *Specters*. It is rather to argue for a politics based on the exorcism of ghosts, of " 'leav[ing] the dead to bury their dead,' as Marx put it in the *Eighteenth Brumaire of Louis Bonaparte*" (28).

Of course, the insistence of the *Brumaire* upon leaving the superstitious, dead past behind is structured around the great future revolution of the nineteenth century, precisely the momentous non-event that Derrida's alleged "logic of conjuration" attempts to preserve in a paradoxically non-monumentalized or non-occult way.[28] If the revolution of the *Brumaire* now exists in such a de-ontologized manner, we might wonder if the same can actually be said of Žižek's encounter with the real. How can the injunction to dispense with the specter, so as to let freedom transpire, itself evade what Žižek elsewhere refers to as the call of the Big Other? Žižek's association of the real with "class struggle" in his specific handling of the Marxist analysis of ideology would seem to confirm this predicament, with Žižek's "kernel of the Real" taking on hermeneutically the same foundational intelligibility as Fredric Jameson's classic conception of history as the "absent cause."[29]

Yet a series of escalating moves in "The Spectre" takes class struggle in another direction. At first, class struggle is the negative identity in the history of capitalism, the inability of capitalism's symbolic to complete itself fully. Class struggle is the hole in the reality of that symbolic, even when there appears to be peace, which simply means one side has momentarily won over the other. Toward the end of the essay, however, class struggle startlingly becomes the negative identity in Marxism *itself*—less a positive essence and more an indication of a "gap [that] emerges in the very heart of historical materialism . . . [a sign that] something must be excluded, foreclosed, if social reality [as opposed to the real] is to constitute itself"(28). Class struggle in fact becomes simply one historical form of the fundamental predicament of *antagonism*, the structural impossibility of any totalizing social symbolic.[30] For Žižek, antagonism is at once the real—the inherent limit of symbolic reality—and what necessarily allows for the possibility of an encounter with the real as freedom, the breakdown of social reality's own self-possession.

Class struggle as social antagonism thus avoids its own metaphysical entrapment by a logic that is in fact phantasmic. Antagonism as the real is contentless but also the site of an incalculable number of effects; it is ultimately in Žižek a *formal* dysfunction of the symbolic, indeterminate and therefore also non-determinate, insofar as its relation to its effects never appears in a transparently clear, unproblematic manner. In another critical language we might call it a catachrestic intrusion in a field of meanings that nevertheless underwrites those meanings. Or we might say that antagonism is the internalized catachrestic dimension to metaphor, the non-erasable gap between Burke's English head and body. Žižek criticizes Derrida for confusing the fleeing messenger (the specter) with the message (the real), but the message is in fact the messenger, the spectral nature of language or meaning as its own self-incompatibility. For both *Specters* and "The Spectre" the political reading of this antagonism is primarily Marxism. Žižek's shorthand for the real in Marxism—"social antagonism ('class struggle')"—could very well be what the specter of Marx as Hamlet's father, with its visor effect, says to us (28). For that confrontation is not simply prior to the opposition between truth and illusion; it is also the operation by which meaning is structured by non-meaning. We simply don't know absolutely what this Marx is telling us aside from its significance as signification, or signification as significance. The phantasm stands for an indeterminancy that could be either the blurring of meaning or the meaning of non-meaning—the sensation of political meaning as the antagonism of the social real.

Žižek's own variation of his shorthand term—"class struggle *qua* antagonism"; "social antagonism (class struggle)"; and "social antagonism ('class struggle')"—conveys the main point of the term(s), its (or their) semantically elusive nature (23, 25, 28). The mixture of parenthetical and diacritical formulas speaks to the referential obliquity of the phrase, which is more properly a slot by which the very formal violence of that opening (an incompletion whose momentary occupation all the more forcefully stresses the real of the aperture) is conveyed. One cannot simply refer to the specter of ideology and then to the real of antagonism; the real as the antagonistic failure of the symbolic is itself spectral in meaning. While the multiplication of shorthand terms could very well indicate different conceptual moments in Žižek's dialectical argument, at the end of the day, the real, like ideology, is where it's always been: not here *and* here, nowhere *and* everywhere.

Žižek seems to understand the fantastic character of antagonism, so much so that he anticipates the charge of spectral alterity when he describes ideology and class struggle as radically displacing Marxism itself: "To those to whom this result of ours appears far-fetched, speculative, alien . . ." (28). To repudiate that inference, he cites the "concrete" Marxist analysis of class struggle and ideology by Étienne Balibar, who reaches a conclusion about those terms similar to Žižek's (28).[31] Coupled with his references to the "idolatry" of the commodity fetish and the "occult" nature of Derrida's project, "concrete" registers the degree to which Žižek's analysis of the specter is still entrenched within the vocabulary of an opposition between physically genuine materiality and simply mental idealism, hence also his understanding of Derrida's phantoms as examples of "pseudo-materiality" (20). Earlier, Žižek also resorts to the notion of a "concrete social analysis" that would determine whether class struggle is indeed the dominant form of antagonism today (25). Yet his point is that this is *not* the focus of his own analysis of the way antagonism functions as the real. If his focus is neither concrete nor something to be dismissed (like Derrida's alleged idealism), what is it? It is the spectral nature of antagonism as that which sidesteps the choice of the material and ideal, the phenomenal and noumenal, altogether.

"Concrete" also of course references Marxism's own contribution toward advancing beyond the cul-de-sac of this choice, the assertion of a materiality not primarily composed of physical properties but rather of social relations. Yet what is antagonism as the real but a de-ontologizing of this more pertinent materiality? The spectral nature of antagonism therefore also calls attention to how the historical materialism of Marxism might actually intersect with the linguistic materiality of deconstruction—what, as our studies in part II have noted, Derrida calls in the de Man of *Aesthetic Ideology* a materiality without matter. "Concrete" signifies a binding of the question of social materiality to the alleged reality of physical matter. The other possibility is to consider a materiality of the social not fixed by the aboriginal troping of a genuine physical world that ostensibly trumps the distractions of the mind. Abutting against our previous deployments of de Man's materialism, this alternate materiality would be the irreducible specter of antagonism. The politics of resemblances and ghosts that Michaels denied in the last chapter *would be* a politics precisely because its materiality is antagonism, the formal resistance to any symbolically closed social identity. Likewise, the transhistorical machine of abstract labor in chapter 3, the catachresis of history, *is* that history, is Marxism's own narrativization of antagonism, the key to the conjuration, contrary to Žižek, of expropriation as, paradoxically, an intelligible, decipherable, historical event. The obdurate opacity of abstract labor that we retrieved from *Capital* would then simply reiterate abstract labor's fundamental materiality, in Derridean terms the visor effect of its diagnostic and prognostic spectrality.

In terms of prognosis, for Žižek the supposedly idealist contamination of the specter also stands for how Derrida's text sequesters away social transformation in an occulted future (*avenir*) that dilutes radical change of its threat as well as possibility. Indeed, the specter flees in Žižek's essay precisely because it cannot stand up to the immanent prospect of truly encountering freedom *qua* the real. For Žižek, revolution—"genuine" revolution—would be one term for this vertiginous moment of the symbolic's redefinition in the real. Yet we might still ask of the existential force of this immanent scenario: when does it occur? The very fact of its possibility means that it has not yet happened, regardless of whether it might have already in the past—another issue that would also complicate the relation of this prospect to any "concrete" Marxist analysis of capitalism. (If freedom did happen, was *that* the great nineteenth-century future revolution of *The Eighteenth Brumaire*?) The immanence of encountering freedom is still necessarily proleptic, and thus an immanence not fully present to itself. Žižek thus rejects the phantasm of a revolutionary future for the phantasm of a radical present registered as the non-occult encounter with the real. As such, however, this present is as much a promise of the spectral Other as that of the Derridean future that Žižek decries.

An odd spatiality seems therefore to overpower any explicit temporal template in Žižek's theory, the one thing arguably that no Marxism can do without. (Consider, for example, Jameson's argument for the centrality of narrative in Marxist thought [*Political*, 17–102].) Yet the future returns covertly in a moment of transference at the conclusion of "The Spectre," when Žižek holds up psychoanalysis as the one mode of inquiry that can enable Marxism to get past the specter of ideology to the real of antagonism. Narrative is in effect transferred from Marxism to psychoanalysis. Psychoanalysis rather than Marxism becomes the structure of a forward momentum simultaneously holding politics in an immanent present while also providing Marxism with the interrogatory pressure to push beyond capitalism's social reality. The interminable nature of psychoanalysis becomes the interminable character of revolution, the Marxist project.

It is precisely the open-endedness of that interminability, however, that registers the impossible future from which Derrida's specter of Marx calls us. Like the titular figure in Paul Klee's painting "Angelus Novus," whom Benjamin describes, we rush into that future with our back to it, without any metaphysical guarantee, any determinate sense of resolution upon which we can rely during our flight (257–58). We are thus also chasing the future, one with which by definition we can never coincide, with only the specters of the past in our backward-facing view retroactively able to give us a sense, or sensation, of our momentum. We are ghosts chasing a ghost chased by ghosts. Of course, the future will never arrive; neither will the past nor the present. Žižek's distinction between an always-deferred future and an immediately graspable present (if only!) is itself a phantasm, a figure for the same condition of ghostly possibility that Derrida's writing (indeterminate as promise, injunction, or legacy) marks. We should thus take seriously the temporal vertigo that Shelley incites at the end of the "Ode to the West Wind": "Can Spring be far behind?" is not simply an attempt to create linear revolution out of its cyclical counterpart (Reiman and Fraistat, 301; line 70). Shelley's line is also a recognition of the necessary aporia of temporal and spatial figuration. Spring, the future, *is* far behind, and we are rushing toward it.

It should be clear that reading a deconstructive conjuration into Žižek's argument for ideological exorcism by no means sets deconstruction's legacy for Marxism over that of psychoanalysis, or even assumes that such a calculation is possible. Rather, the specter of antagonism ("Marx") delineates a set of choices about the politics of ghosts that is inescapably Romantic. For, instead of venturing far away in this last section from the concerns of Romanticism, we have considered a set of circumstances—the terror of symbolic death, the alterity of freedom as revolution—that should right away resonate with a number of narratives that constitute the Romantic event. (This is immediately the case with Žižek's conception of freedom, which he draws from his understanding of Schelling.) Such a resonance impacts not only upon our comprehension of that event circa two hundred years ago, but also upon what is happening today at this moment. Derrida enables us to continue, as well as recognize, a discussion within which we are still enmeshed: the *revenant* of Romanticism as revolution.

Not seeing that is to understand the pertinence of Romanticism today as at best a residual and reactionary formation, the anachronistic expression of, for example, ethnic and national identity within an intractable framework of transnational, globalized capital.[32] Romanticism as the *revenant* would then be precisely what has been foreclosed by the social reality of that framework, and what simultaneously pries open that closing. And if it appears that neither Marx's specter nor even the ghost term *revolution* itself seems able to contain the heterogeneity of all the emancipatory practices of an unknowable future, that very difficulty of totalization versus phantom identity comes to us already inscribed within the question mark of Romanticism as an, or the, event of history.[33] Let us then hail *Specters* with our own meta-version of Shelley's cry, a rendering locked in its own particular incongruence between rhetorical denotation and performative choice: Was there ever a time more out of joint than Romanticism?[34] Is there any other moment than that, self absent from itself, that we are now, so fatally and hopefully, in?

PART THREE

# Texts

If Romanticism is especially entangled with scandals of thought that characterize the problem of historical identity, that problem takes on a particular acuteness in a number of second-generation, post-Revolutionary texts. These texts worry the question of what specific history they convey—whether they are indeed texts of revolution or of something else entirely. There are, of course, a number of candidates for what these works might narrativize. But if one framing thesis of this book is that Romanticism, Marxism, and deconstruction are connected in a particularly intimate manner, a corollary would be that the problem of history in these texts coheres especially around their relation to revolution and commodification. The readings in part III test that corollary by focusing on how, in different and oftentimes conflicting ways, sensation and sobriety underwrite the post-revolutionary, second-generation reflexivity of these texts. Chapter 7 especially considers how a non-physical sensation of meaning might clarify the problem of political prophecy; chapter 9 does the same for the conundrum of ideology. Chapters 8 and 10 more readily consider sensation in its physical form, as an inescapable part of Romantic market life.

Chapter 7 focuses on how the lyric prophecy of Shelley's "Ode to the West Wind" relies on a dynamic akin to the sensations of meaning studied in part II, where the poem exploits the volatility of its own lyrical nature as it attempts to outpace both cognition and the physical senses in order to obtain a measuring of history beyond the phenomenal constraints of time and space. One meaning of Romantic sobriety and one instance of the sublime—both Kantian and post-modern—converge in the poem's vatic historicism, which eschews phenomenal experience as the basis for historical knowledge. But the chapter also contrasts the "Ode" with Keats's own famous post-revolutionary seasonal lyric, "To Autumn," whose embrace of the physical sensory world helps reveal the distinctly different ways the two poets approach the intelligibility of a historical moment caught between revolution and commodification. Much more than the Shelley of the "Ode," the Keats in this chapter and chapter 10 consistently exploits the physicality of the commodity form.

The same could be said of the Byron of chapter 8, whose major satire, *Don Juan*, comments on how a burgeoning Romantic commodity culture apparently qualifies our reading of Romanticism as a culture of sobriety. Byron's work is an exercise in proto-cultural studies, an anthropology of the commodity form, that anticipates the same tensions between commodity culture and philosophy, body and mind, and graphic image and figured word that mark the present-day divide between cultural studies and what we call high theory. Yet *Don Juan* also problematizes its apparent opposition to sobriety by allegorizing its own ambivalence toward the physicality of culture: the poem withholds a kiss between two of the poem's most famous characters, and in all the spiraling complications of that sober restraint we can glimpse the radically paradoxical nature of a divide that informs critical thought to this day.

The uncomfortable relation between the sensation of meaning and phenomenal experience returns in chapter 9's pairing of Dacre's Romantic gothic novel, *Zofloya*, and Brontë's early Victorian classic, *Jane Eyre*. The chapter tracks how a specific novelistic language against superstitious perception involves not only overtly anti-French revolutionary meanings but also more radically indeterminate ones about the intersubjective hypostatizations of commodity reification. In *Jane Eyre* the name for the problem of this intersubjectivity is love, and the possibility of a sober love free from the trickery of human perception becomes the place where the sensation of meaning as gothic idolatry, or ideology, is confronted. Idolatry appears to translate the sensation of meaning into perceptual misprision, but one gothic instance of *Jane Eyre* reveals how idolatry as ideology never actually coincides with empirical sensation.

In contrast, the empirical senses, especially sight, are of central concern to chapter 10, where Keats's poem *Lamia* reflexively meditates on pre-cinematic forms of mass entertainment that Romantic poetry both uses and disavows in its own understanding of itself as an elite social art form. Sensation thus again operates in this chapter as a figure for the physical senses, although phenomenal experience is also now unavoidably marked by the brute fact of social relations. Sensation is sensationalized, at once enthusiastically embraced by mass audiences and soberly rejected by Keats's critics, who attack his writings as something besides literature altogether. As his critics note, commercial sensationalism unavoidably appeals to the physical senses, much like the world of commodified things that Byron's Juan inhabits. But in *Lamia* the social mysteries of the commodity form do not simply enact an obdurate physical sensuality; they also radiate something similar to a sensation of meaning. The chapter formulates this predicament, however, not through a de Manian non-phenomenal materiality, but through the metrics of Lacanian desire, specifically the self-evasive operations of the *objet petit a*.

The shift in analysis is in large part due to how a Lacanian optics, theorizing especially the machinations of the Lacanian gaze, best conveys the workings of commoditized desire in Keats's pre-cinematic appeal to visual sensation. Yet chapter 10's reliance on the recognizable shape of a Romantic capitalist modernity and a dialectical approach equal parts Lacanian and Marxist also gives the chapter a critical distinctiveness that could imply a final arc organizing my work. While my introduction notes how the centripetal force of each chapter problematizes any apparent dialectical progression in the book's narrative, this final arc would assert otherwise: part I's initial interrogations into the impossible but necessary form of Romantic periodicity would then provide the unstable semiotic ground for the dialectically material analysis that the book narrativizes as its finally arrived at telos in chapter 10, a predicament that I further expand on in my coda on the sobering embarrassments of both Romanticism and literature in the present age of global capitalism.

But, one might ask, isn't this simply an elaborate way to describe a subsumption of deconstruction by dialectically materialist history? More starkly put, what is the relation between the dialectic and deconstruction—is it dialectical or deconstructive? If the stated methodological form of *Romantic Sobriety* explicitly asks this question, part of the book's thesis is that its tropological content—the figures of sensation, sobriety, revolution, commodification, and others that this study examines—also participates in this inquiry. Let us then return to and take seriously my introduction's initial description of this work as staging a series of encounters, where the question of the relation between the dialectic and deconstruction remains both ongoing and suspended, where the question of progress remains a fatally urgent one for both discourses, for a series of diverging and converging reasons explored throughout the book. Whether such progress can cohere into a moment of reading that exists as an instance of edification, whether reading can give rise to something besides simply a sensation of insight—confronting these questions is what motivates and compels this study's own allegory of the Romantic text.

# Lyric Ritalin

## Time and History in "Ode to the West Wind"

> If you have an idea, one will have to divide into two.
>
> —Mao Zedong

> The sense faints picturing them!
>
> —Percy Bysshe Shelley, "Ode to the West Wind"

Where is the wind in Shelley's "Ode to the West Wind"? We might very well respond with the answer that Slavoj Žižek gives about the location of ideology, one that likewise informed the light of genius in Kant: everywhere and nowhere. Such an answer also describes a trait explored by much of Shelley's writings. It's not much of an overstatement to say that Modernist irritation with and postmodern delight in Shelley are simply two different reactions to the poet's ongoing interrogation of a condition constantly asserted as everywhere and nowhere, as at once omnipresent, absent, invisible, and on the move. (To call such a condition an identity would, of course, signal a solution akin to Earl Wasserman's and others', which understands the wind and its compatriot figures as signs of a metaphysically weighty Shelleyan Spirit.)[1] Formulated differently, this predicament becomes not only about Shelley but also about poetry itself. Thus, the intangible yet undeniably felt measure of the wind in the "Ode" brings together two different culminating drives—that of Shelley's own feverish interrogation into the possible and impossible, registered in his lifelong opposing poetic vocabularies of, on the one hand, blood and gold and, on the other, wind, light, and shadow; and of the realization of the lyric itself, the ontological paradox of a permanent poetic expression shaped by its temporal shortness, its evanescence and ineffability.[2]

Virginia Jackson is correct in observing how this basic sense of the lyric is the consequence of a historical reification based on various interested readings of the particular genre.[3] But one place this reading takes place is in the reflexive inscription of the "Ode" itself, where the event of such historical and textual construction, and contestation, occurs. I say "contestation" because Shelley's poetic consideration of such intangible elements of the physical world as the wind can in fact be understood as a questioning of the very existence of the poetic, or lyrical, realm. If contemporary readers of the lyric—and poetry, for that matter—constantly butt against the sense of the lyric moment as having the tangibility of something both everywhere and nowhere, that is at least in part due to "Ode to the West Wind." In perhaps his best-known work, Shelley writes in a mode that he himself helps instantiate—the high Romantic lyric—even as the force of such writing also seems to point to the impossibility of that very event.

This is not quite the claim that the "Ode" ushers in the death of the lyric at the exact moment of its high Romantic (re-)birth. Such a view would actually be less ambitious than past assertions that have already radically problematized the Romantic-era lyric, along with other post-structuralist pronouncements about the end of the lyric per se. Within Romantic studies, Tilottama Rajan has perhaps articulated the most forceful version of this narrative, demonstrating how Romantic texts dramatize the fundamental instability of both lyric subjectivity and the lyric as a genre independent of other linguistic and literary sign systems.[4] As Rajan points out, Shelley's own *Prometheus Unbound*, which he subtitled a lyric drama, and whose third act was written during the same time as the "Ode," exemplifies the draw of Romantic lyric toward the volatility of more intertextual generic creations (201–6). In contrast, however, the very conciseness of the "Ode," its putative existence as a traditional lyric hymn, enables it to be the thought experiment of this chapter. My argument thus has more to do with seeing how the "Ode" exploits the impossibility of lyric for its own aims; the lyric is not so much dismissed outright or made a generic hybrid as pushed to the point of its own self-contradictions in order to generate something besides the phenomenal categories of time and space—in a word, history. This dynamic bears more than a faint resemblance to the negative dialectics that Adorno famously discovered in the tenuousness of the lyrical form, although my claim is that the "Ode" is actually more explicit, and more conflicted, about this movement in the text than the stringently elegant process that Adorno describes, precisely because the poem vehemently exposes the contrary impulses within *movement* itself, dialectical and otherwise, as an action that paradoxically involves both progression (what lyric makes its norm) and narrative (what lyric actively resists).[5]

This chapter thus joins other recent attempts, such as James K. Chandler's,

Thomas Pfau's, and Sarah Zimmerman's, that consider the soundings of history in the Romantic lyrics of Shelley and others, although my tack will be to do so by recording the way that the "Ode" actively employs the unmanageable and unthinkable dimensions of lyric in order to achieve this goal.[6] Shelley's interrogation of the impossible is thus also the contemplation of staging the impossible while not sacrificing in the least the scandal of mind underwriting such an undertaking. Perhaps more than anything, it's the serious attempt not only to express but also to preserve such a scandal that distinguishes the ongoing task of reading Shelley today. In the "Ode" the impossible fact of the wind becomes in particular the impossible question of its speed, of indeed lyric speed, a formal trait that William Keach and others associate especially with Shelley's poetry, and which becomes in this instance the question of the precise relations of time and space to history.[7] The wind's lightness of being also benefits from a comparison with Keats's own famous lyric of post-revolution temporality, and of the gap between seasonal change and history, "To Autumn." Both works trope history as their lyrical sensation of meaning, although Keats more readily envisions this event as the mutation of sensory experience under the iron law of commodity exchange, while Shelley more explicitly makes this a happenstance that leaves the phenomenal senses in their own wake, with the poem's event moving on to something else entirely, at least figuratively. Oftentimes twinned since Hallam with Keats as a poet of sensation, Shelley in the "Ode" pushes sensation past its physically perceptual coordinates.[8] If F. R. Leavis worried that in Shelley sensation would utterly outpace reflection, this anxiety itself a concise allegory of the contradictions that lyric's non-conceptual dimensions ineluctably generate, the first three stanzas of the "Ode" proleptically leave such Modernist anxieties behind, by recording the attempt of sensation to outpace itself.[9] In examining this dynamic, my reading of Shelley's lyric adds its own particular valence to the often-studied tale of the poet's relationship—in and beyond the "Ode"—to the revolutionary sublime.[10] The result is a sensation of historical meaning at once adamantly about its scission from the phenomenal and profoundly vertiginous in the specific message of its vatic pronouncement. The complexity of this sensation is not completely present in Shelley's first three stanzas, but it's with the first part of the "Ode" that the chapter necessarily begins.

> When it is a matter of this structure of the text, the concept of historicity will no longer be regulated by the scheme of progression or of regression, thus by a scheme of teleological process, but rather by that of the event, or occurrence, thus by the singularity of the "one time only."
>
> —Jacques Derrida, "Typewriter Ribbon"

Where, then, is the wind in the "Ode"? Everywhere and nowhere, although this is not quite true. There *are* places in the poem where the wind occurs as a distinct identity, although such appearances are most telling because of their inconclusive, unsatisfying nature. Indeed, one occurrence is notorious for its evidentiary role in Leavis's indictment of the limitations of Shelley's poem, the "blue surface of thine aery surge" of the second stanza (line 19); another is the little-remarked-upon personification of "Thine azure sister of the Spring" from the first stanza, insofar as the wind *is* its sibling whether it blows during the fall or spring (line 9). For Leavis, the infelicitous yoking of smoothness ("surface") with dynamism ("surge") speaks to the general incomprehensibility of the imagery in the "Ode," something the poem's own surging qualities don't allow the reader to dwell upon: "We let ourselves be swept along, the image doesn't challenge any inconvenient degree of realization, and the oddness is lost" (205). From Harold Bloom's mythopoetics to Jerrold Hogle's decentering transference, the post-Leavisite, post-Modernist reappraisal of Shelley has developed a rich critical vocabulary able to find poetic quality in exactly what Leavis could only experience as failed writing.[11] But I would like to stay with Leavis's position a bit longer, to consider what it might mean to judge such imagery of the wind as, indeed, infelicitous.

I would also include among such imagery "Thine azure sister of the Spring." As a perhaps even banal allegory, this description of the wind seems to escape Leavis's charge of unintelligibility that "aery surge" and other figures in stanza 2 invoke. However, the very conventional clarity of its personification makes "azure sister" a clumsy fit in the poem when juxtaposed with the much more figuratively ambiguous, and thus more commented upon, personifications of stanza 1, especially the mysterious "enchanter" whose surrogate nature to the wind is problematized as much at it is asserted by critics (line 3).[12] What, then, to say of these infelicitous and maladroit appearances of the wind in Shelley's poem? Quite simply, *appearance* itself, along with all its assumptions, becomes an awkward proposition for the wind. To appear means being given some type of physical definition and substance, which is why the narrator's oratory invocations of the wind as "Wild Spirit" and "Destroyer and Preserver" don't necessarily fall into the same category as "aery surge" and "azure sister," insofar as such addresses don't really locate the wind in any concrete manner; they resist the indexical, failing to pinpoint in any fixed way the spatial coordinates of the wind as an autonomous identity (lines 13–14). The emphasis in the poem's hailing would thus be on "Wild" rather than on "Spirit": on a radically indeterminate, destabilizing quality rather than on any idealized transcendent identity. The wind can't be spatialized precisely because it actually generates the poem's sense of space in the first three stanzas. It can't be placed in space because it *makes* space.

Leavis's claim that the "blue surface of thine aery surge" unhappily marries two disparate qualities is simply another way of noting this failure of discretely spatializing the wind—how can something that has no end or beginning have a surface? The question of how "blue surface" and "azure sister" convey the substance of the wind also emphasizes this empirical confusion, as both literally refer to a *blue wind*. Travelers to Florence might very well testify that a blue wind is an apt way of describing the clarity of the Arno region's atmospherics; yet attributing such a chromatic quality to the wind is still cognitively dissonant, insofar as we are left asking, somewhat embarrassedly, *where* is the wind blue? Two contrary physics clash, one that involves a blue surface, and thus a substance defined by its opacity, and another that implies an infinitely receding although ubiquitous blue on the other side of the wind, now characterized by its immaterial emptiness, or transparency. The questions of wherever the wind is and whatever the wind is collide, forcefully.

The blue wind is at once a density and an effervescence, surface and depth, translucent and clear. The Gilles Deleuze of *A Thousand Plateaus* would call adjudicating among such asymmetric relational intensities the task of recognizing the difference between the "molar" and the "molecular," with the former referring to the hypostatization of being and the latter referencing the ongoing, a priori dynamic of becoming, at an infinite variety of microscopic and macroscopic levels (3–38, 45–46, 272–75). Without hawking too exuberantly Shelley's and Deleuze's shared interest in ancient atomist philosophy, we can still note the proto-Deleuzian character of the first three stanzas of the "Ode."[13] As a number of readers have observed, the wind appears through the vertiginous catalogue of its effects, from those upon seed and leaf to cloud and rain to sea and ocean plant life; as Ronald Tetreault asserts, "Because the wind itself is like Intellectual Beauty an 'unseen presence,' it can be known only by its effects."[14] The point, however, would be to take the "Wild" in "Wild Spirit" seriously, *not* to see all these effects simply radiating from the first principle of the wind but to sense the wind instead as the incalculable collection of all these shifting effects impinging upon one another. The wind is everywhere insofar as everything is either hurtling, dropping, floating, spinning, or still, with some forms ushered to sleep and others to the explosion of storm. The wind is nowhere insofar as at no one moment can all these intensities and vectors of force, with their infinitely expanding effects upon one another, reciprocating and deflecting, be frozen into one calcified identity, or force field. To use another Deleuzian term, the wind is literally a "line of flight," away from and toward a multiplicity of identities, forms, and positions (*Thousand*, 9, 55).

For Deleuze, the line of flight marks the event of becoming, something registered in stanza 1 by the proleptic movement of seed as both winter corpse and spring bud, and in stanza 2 by the unfolding dynamism of the storm in the sky (232–309). This radical sense of *becoming-spring*, where immanent potentiality crowds out the telos of intelligible change, is especially registered in the quavering "sea-blooms and oozy woods" of stanza 3 (line 39), the undersea foliage swaying in the vibrating ocean, itself a medium of thickness and clarity, of light and solidity, like and unlike the wind. The moving flora and vegetation, "trembl[ing] and despoil[ling]" themselves (line 42), seemingly both more contained but also more concentrated and intense in their shivering than their counterparts on the land and in the air, especially appear to be on the verge of some transformation, whether it be within themselves or in the very entirety of the image of the underwater world that the third stanza presents, one constructed out of an optics that plays with the differing visual perspectives of reflected "azure moss and flowers" and submerged "sea-blooms" (line 35), a further blue surface and trembling depth, all of whose distinctions could be scrambled and reformed, reterritorialized, at a moment's notice, insofar as both "flowers" and "sea-blooms" occupy an overlapping space distinct from but also very much like the surface density and spatial emptiness of the previous stanza's "aery surge."

Arkady Plotnitsky has suggested a convergence between Deleuzian terminology and de Manian thought, and one might want to use the "Ode" to underscore Plotnitsky's approach (Rajan and Plotnitsky, 113–34). If previous chapters have explored the assertion that de Man's materialism can best be understood as conceiving of a materiality without matter, this proto-Deleuzian reading of the first part of the "Ode" reveals a meteorological substance that is in intense movement and flux; in the intensity of this matter's sheer becoming, the ever-changing (non-)relations among its multiple bodies in motion, one can glimpse a repudiation of both genetic and teleological meaning that is akin to the blunting force of de Man's non-physical, although also non-ideal, materiality. A radically formal immanence would seem to be a shared focus of de Man and Deleuze, and that could very well be one way to describe what we have read into the actions of the wind thus far; the very play between such terms as the surface, density, and intangibility of the forces activated by the "Ode" could be understood as the imposition of the wind as a materiality without matter. As chapters 4 and 5 argued about the Wordsworth of "A Slumber," however, there is also a Romantic fascination with the relations among such moving (and still) bodies, a sensation of such relations as meaning, emphatically unmoored from any determinate link to either the perceiving subject or immanent object. This scenario might parallel the predicament of Deleuzian becoming, with its a priori resistance to both necessarily reified, molar meaning and the subject-object divide. (Indeed, it would be a worthwhile venture to reread our earlier analysis of orbit, stasis, and semblance in "A Slumber" through a Deleuzian language of force, densities, and haeceities.)[15] But this Romantic fascination with the relations among such bodies or forms, what I would venture to call one dimension of the *literary*, also propels de Manian materiality toward the generation of figure that we saw the Kantian light of genius inciting in chapter 2, with resemblance and reference no longer simply tied to molar hegemonic meaning, in either its empirical or idealist mode, but also connected to the contingent, the unexplainable, the hyperbolic, and even the ludic.[16] This too the "Ode" as a hyper-reflexive—that is, high Romantic—lyric exploits.

As both Hogle and Chandler in different ways point out, the "Ode" is abundantly full of questions of resemblance and reference—of, in a word, figuration as the semantic expression of a relation (Hogle, 205–7; Chandler, 532–41). We can develop this further, insofar as the Deleuzian becoming of the first three stanzas can also be a means to foreground a particular question about the three stanzas, the issue of whether they are meant to be read sequentially or, somehow, simultaneously. This is where the trait of Shelley's lyric speed is relevant, something the poem exemplifies through, as many have noted, the use of enjambment, arrest, and cyclic imagery that leaves each of the first three stanzas pushing forward, ahead of itself to the next stanza (Wasserman, 240; Keach, 162–63; Tetreault, 213–14). To be, like the wind, in more than one place in the poem is to achieve a certain simultaneity, which, however, depends on a sequential progress through the poem. A traditional understanding of the "Ode" might try to assert how the poem resolves this tension through its classic hymnlike structure, or through its topos of the cycle or spiral (Wasserman, 240). Yet to take Shelley's speed seriously is to confront how much this speed seems to want to get beyond itself, how much sequentiality wants to establish simultaneity, something that seems less about a resolution and more about the insistence of a radical problematic. The very proleptic nature of the first two stanzas' narratives of regeneration repeats this dilemma, insofar as the anticipatory, temporal stretching of the fate of the seeds and sky actually spatializes the stanzas' narrative structures, making it possible to conceptualize the stanzas' thematic actions of death and rebirth at the same moment, an option condensed into one phrase with the narrative interpellation of the wind as simultaneous "Destroyer and Preserver." This situation also encapsulates one dilemma of the lyric poem itself, as an utterance that endeavors to become *pure* lyric, as opposed to a poem, or prose piece, for that matter, with lyric moments. What, indeed, is the difference between a work with such moments and a work that defines itself *as* the simultaneity of such a moment? What is the lyrical relation—the figuration—between sequentiality and simultaneity?

From another angle this is a renewal of the problem of lyric subjectivity, as an expression of a consciousness existing in time, and a consciousness whose conceptual expression approximates the non-conceptual force of lyric's musicality.[17] The difficulty of sequential existence also being the instantiation of simultaneous conscious existence; the problem of pure lyric sensation as somehow avoiding the temporal dimension of reflection and narrativization—these and other formulations all articulate in various ways the problem of the sequential and simultaneous, which might more properly be understood as the formal aporia activating these other scenarios. We are, of course, talking about the problem between the diachronic and synchronic, which can also be approached through the phenomenal terms of time and space. Figures for these two phenomenal categories basically constitute the event of the wind in the first three stanzas: the temporal narrative of the seeds being ushered to rest and rebirth in a future spring, the unfolding of the cloudy storm bursting the dome of the sky, the travel of the seeds and clouds through land and sky, and the awakening of the Mediterranean, vibrating sympathetically with the wind from surface to lower depths. We could in fact argue that such action actually makes the categories of time and space intelligible in the poem; in its reach, the wind, as the formal action of the sequential and the simultaneous, makes not only space but also time throughout the first three stanzas.

*How* intelligible these categories are is another matter, however. The third stanza's memory ("Though who *didst* waken") of the reflected ancient villa ruins would imply a past optic moment occurring during the Mediterranean's "summer dreams" (line 29; my emphasis); however, the sea's awakening from, or passage out of, summer might also make the reflection part of an immanent autumnal present, the now of a becoming that's strengthened by the analogous "quivering" of the mirroring and the "tremb[ling]" of the sea plants (lines 34 and 42). Indeed, insofar as the subject of "saw in sleep" is not entirely clear—it appears to be the Mediterranean but could also be the wind—the past tense of that action is destabilized, possibly made simply the initial step of a present autumnal becoming, one that's immediately followed by the present tense "cleav[ing]" of the Atlantic's "level powers" and trembling of ocean flora (lines 37 and 38). Like the temporal connection between the autumnal wind and her "sister of the spring" and the dual meanings of "cleave," the spatial relation between the "Atlantic" and "Mediterranean" also brings up questions of continuity and difference—does "Atlantic" designate a further shift in geographic place, or are its depths "far below" simply those of the "Mediterranean" (lines 30 and 37)?[18] Similar issues structure the "closing night" of stanza 2 (line 24). The most immediate reading would also temporally divide this stanza into two parts, with the first half describing a present gathering of clouds and the second proleptically imagining the explosion of an evening storm; "closing night" would mark this temporal passage from the present to the future. But the pun on "closing" and "dome" spatializes this temporal predicament; night suddenly has to travel through space to seal the heavens from the earth (line 25). Connected to the earlier perception in the stanza's present of some liminal vista ("the dim verge / Of the horizon to the zenith's height") from which the "approaching storm" comes, the spatializing of "closing" is magnified further (lines 21–23). As a darkness that is either the literal or figurative reference for the storm, night is *already* in the present, approaching, *closing* upon the poet's perspective and position.

The temporal and spatial shifts in the first three stanzas thus underscore how much figures of time and space are ineluctably caught in a violently unstable interdependence. Indeed, Leavis's discomfort with the infelicity of "blue surface" simply intuits the fundamental aporia that the "Ode" vigorously tries to demonstrate, the unavoidable but nevertheless vertiginous way that space (the smoothness of "surface") and time (the dynamism of "surge") rely on one another. Time might be calculated by an approaching storm, except that that calculation relies on a movement through space. Space might be differentiated by the different weather of various locales, except that such climate change might be happening temporally, as a series of events. At another level, the poem's sequential narrativization of all these shifts exposes rather than simply masters the volatile nature of their heteronomy; this very sequentiality generates the fantastic demand for a simultaneous understanding of all these shifts that would make sense of what sequentiality quite cannot. The poem's outburst of atmospheric events, which instigate but also trouble a slew of temporal and spatial demarcations, parallels the poem's own recording of this action in its first three stanzas, a poetic utterance that replicates the insistence that the stanzas' sequentiality be somehow understood or read as simultaneity, as one lyric moment. In that sense, the reader finds herself affiliated not simply with the poet but also with the wind, whose simultaneous hailing on land, sea, and air points toward a simultaneously *impossible* understanding, or reading experience, of those three locales as stanzas, or stanzas as locales.

To talk about a sequential apprehension that incites an incomprehension of simultaneity is, of course, to invoke Kant's mathematical sublime (sec. 26, 107–14). To make Kant's sublime a figure for the aporia of reading itself, of sequential ("syntagmatic") apprehension outpacing simultaneous ("paradigmatic") comprehension of a text, is precisely one of the claims that de Man makes in his seminal reading of the third *Critique* (*Aesthetic*, 77–79). One can see Shelley enacting a version of this dynamic, where the radical contradictions of both the phenomenal and linguistic meet, although in Shelley's case the focus is not so much on sequential apprehension as on the implications generated by the scandal of mind that would be the impossible assertion of an (in-)comprehensible simultaneity. Shelley's formulation would thus in effect reverse the momentum of Kant's formulation, dramatizing instead the outpacing of sequential comprehension by a vertiginously *simultaneous apprehension*. This dynamic occurs not only in the "Ode" but also in other less-attended-to works such as "The Cloud," which even more so than the "Ode" uses the temporal and spatial aporias of climate change to create explicitly an ecological poetics of the sublime. Given, however, the manner in which the "Ode" is embedded so keenly within its own meta-commentary as the emblematic post-revolution Romantic lyric, we can understand its own poetic sublimity through yet another coordinate, one easily gleaned by understanding its sublime project as the reflexive result of an incredible apprehension that is emphatically *global* in nature.

The first three stanzas' challenge of simultaneity thus demands a reordering not only of linear sequential time, but of space as merely a collection of discrete localities whose sequential appearance erases all evidence, and all awareness, of each other. A global apprehension that is the impossible attempt to sense all such localities, and their dizzying interaction among a set of temporal and social planes—this is exactly what Fredric Jameson designates as the "postmodern sublime," our contemporary endeavor to represent in some fashion the radically complex workings of late twentieth and early twenty-first century global late capitalism (*Postmodernism*, 34–35).[19] The sublime, then, can also be the aporetic registering of *history*, a dynamic, moreover, that has its own precedents before our and Jameson's specific time. Thus, Georg Lukács gives his own famous Modernist-era formulation of this predicament in *The Historical Novel*, one that is especially apposite for Shelley's poem's particular moment:

> It was the French Revolution, the revolutionary wars and the rise and fall of Napoleon, which for the first time made history a *mass experience*, and moreover on a European scale. During the decades between 1789 and 1814 each nation of Europe underwent more upheavals than they had previously experienced in centuries. And the quick succession of these upheavals gives them a qualitatively distinct character, it makes their historical character far more visible than would be the case in isolated, individual instances: the masses no longer have the impression of a "natural occurrence. . . ."
>
> The enormous quantitative expansion of war plays a qualitatively new role, bringing with it an extraordinary broadening of horizons. Whereas the wars fought by the mercenary armies of absolutism consisted mostly of tiny manoeuvres around fortresses, etc., now the whole of Europe becomes a war arena. French peasants fight first in Egypt, then in Italy, again in Russia. . . . What previously was experienced by isolated and mostly adventurous-minded individuals, namely an acquaintance with Europe or at least parts of it, becomes in this period the mass experience of hundreds of thousands, of millions. (*Historical*, 23–24)[20]

Lukács's Hegelian Marxist account is not the only historical attempt to explain the rise of historicism during the Romantic era, of course.[21] For our purposes, however, the power of Lukács's *récit* lies not only in its ability to place the globalizing impulse of Shelley's 1819 poem within a larger network of historical action but also in the uncanny *formal* resemblance between the "Ode" and Lukács's story of (post-)revolutionary war and mass conscription. Lukács's story of European massification only hints through its immense scale at the multiple dissonances of the sublime, secure as the analysis is within the intelligibility of its own Hegelian Marxist framework; yet this analysis shares with the "Ode" the same sense of a momentous temporal simultaneity erupting into the plane of its narrative. In Lukács sequentiality also presents itself as a series of shocks, a "quick succession of upheavals" whose very speed of occurrence generates simultaneity, the possibility of mass historical experience. Like the wind, revolutionary war, with its "enormous quantitative expansion," literally makes new space ("Europe"), generating "an extraordinary broadening of horizons."[22] War travels and extends itself exponentially, dispersing and dislocating on a grand scale, lifting its actors out of the discrete temporal and spatial intelligibilities of " 'natural occurrence,' " what for the conscripted French peasants would literally be the agrarian temporality of seasonal local life. Lukács in effect lyricizes the sequential events of 1789–1814, representing them through a Shelleyan velocity that demands a syncretic articulation—the "mass experience of . . . millions."[23] Paradoxically, for both the "Ode" and Lukács's account, this endeavor at spatialized, global apprehension is exactly what allows the sweep of linear history to emerge out of cyclic, or seasonal, time; if history cannot exist without time and space, it's precisely the complication of those phenomenal categories, their exposure as unstable figures, readily wrecked and reorganized by war or wind, that enables the troping of history to rise into view.

We can now thus revisit, and differentiate our reading from, Wasserman's famous description of the processes of the West wind: "For the wind not only is 'moving everywhere' but also acts everywhere according to the same law, so that, however its media differ, its effect remains constant" (240). The wind does indeed move everywhere; this is less, however, the intelligible expression of a consistent set of relations coming out of the same law and more about the event of *relation* itself, of which the figures of cause and effect would be one category, along with such spatial ones as height and depth, closed and free, and nearness and horizon. *Media* is not the phenomenal means of sameness but the formal coordination of the wind's movement, whose very temporal and spatial dissonances call forth the sweeping possibility of some globally sublime simultaneity. Wasserman is correct in intuiting some aboriginal design operating in Shelley's poem, but this is less about any metaphysically sound genetic troping than about the generating force of a *non-phenomenal media*—the "radical formalism" of de Manian materiality—employed in this chapter as the lyrical instantiation of a sublime telecommunications event, the necessary formal shaping of anything we might want to call mass history. Paraphrasing de Man from his own extensive meditation on Kant and materiality, history is indeed not time; more to the point, history is not phenomenal, although it is necessarily beholden to figures of time and space, even as the play, and destitution, of those figures allows history to emerge.[24] The historical sublime is thus not an ancillary, hysterical extension of sound historical knowledge; it is, rather, the historical itself, insofar as the sublime's outpacing of the empirical senses is precisely the non-phenomenal calculation of an impossible simultaneity that generates historical identity. When in stanza 3 the "Ode" presents the reflected moss and flowers and how "the sense faints picturing them," this is not simply the radical blockage of cognition and perception; it is also the opportunity of a historical apprehension, punctuating and also outpacing the unstable sensory mirroring—the "quivering" of "sleep[ing] old palaces and towers"—of a past antiquity (lines 33 and 36).[25]

Such a scenario might seem increasingly to leave Lukács's account, secure within the causes and effects of its own dialectical materialist imperatives, behind. This is true, although one might understand Lukács's own point about the revolutionary need for grand narratives ("propaganda") to explain massification to those being conscripted as actually recognizing the need to preempt associating historical experience with contingency (23). Still, the "Ode" does contrast with Lukács's story in terms of how the poem, in its inscription of a Deleuzian becoming and de Manian materiality, first and foremost dramatizes its own historical vision as being generated out of the formal dynamics of its lyrical utterance. If, then, the meta-commentary of the "Ode" makes it historically impossible to read the poem outside (post-)revolutionary desire, the ontology of its vision of radical historical transformation is less along the lines of Lukács's narrative sweep and more akin to Alain Badiou's vision of the "supernumerary" Jacobin project, the catachrestic-like insertion of a new singular truth, seemingly independent of historical precedent and previous historical knowledge, and thus in a fundamental way, even with retroactive interpretation, radically on the side of the unpredictable and unexplainable.[26] (This view of an unaccountable genetic eruption would thus complement Chandler's reading of the "Ode" as allegorizing the *difficulty* of representing historical cause and effect.) Similarly, for all the virtuosity the "Ode" displays in its mastery of the *terza rima* sonnet form, and for all its reliance on classical and Enlightenment philosophy, as well as past literary traditions (Milton's own famous expressions of sublime space, for instance), the emergence of historical thought in Shelley's poem emblematizes one conventional—indeed, staid—sense of the high Romantic lyric, as the imposition of an utterly new poetic invention. Such resemblances not only recover the now seemingly dated association of the creativity of high Romantic imagination with radical, insurgent thought; they also add a new unstable dimension to any apparently intelligible relation that one might make out of the "Ode" and Lukács's account—to any simple relation between poem and historical explanation, form and signification, or text and context. *A history without context*—that is what Shelley's wind inspires.

> The more passionately thought denies its conditionality for the sake of the unconditional, the more unconsciously, and so calamitously, it is delivered up to the world.
>
> —Theodor Adorno, *Minima Moralia: Reflections from Damaged Life*

The "Ode" consists of more than three stanzas, however, and it is the question of the crucial link, or gap, between stanzas 3 and 4 that reinvents the problem of sequentiality, simultaneity, and history in the poem before our very eyes, in mid-breath, as it were. Readers have traditionally conceived of the question of stanzas 3 and 4 as the wager of whether the regenerating imagery of the wind in the first three stanzas will now be repeated once more in terms of the poet's own rebirth. Reformulated as the question of the historical sublime, however, the question becomes less about hope for individual and collective renewal and more about the problem of global historical knowledge nevertheless being, ultimately, the attribute of individual, alienated subjectivity.

As is well known, the difference in the rhyming couplets brings attention to the disparity between the first three stanzas and stanza 4; yet, the form of Shelley's poem as a dramatic lyric can also support the idea of a successful transition of the narrative of regeneration between these stanzas (Tetreault, 210–13).[27] *Narrative*, however, is a complicated proposition in this lyric poem. (This observation would thus be diametrically opposed to Wasserman's sense of the wind as a first principle, whose story of simultaneous renewal is in fact the very structure of the poem that manages—indeed, masters—the sequential unfolding of the "Ode.") Indeed, the pressing question is whether to read the first three stanzas as being narrated by the poet of stanza 4, or, in some fundamental way, *not being narrated by anyone at all*. This might seem an odd proposition, considering the generic presence of the speaker addressing the wind throughout the poem. But the apostrophes to the wind in the first three stanzas don't so much secure the presence of the speaker as highlight the action of what is being addressed; the poet remains less an imperial point of view and more the opportunity for a sublime denotative apprehension ("Destroyer and Preserver!") that outpaces the constraints of the subject's inevitably isolated perspective, straining past perceptual comprehension toward something like objective historical knowledge. Indeed, far from upending objectivity, the sublime in this instance is the assertion of its closest, most asymptotic double, an apprehension of history unmoored from, and thus independent of, the subject and its limited senses.

This is thus in part the familiar story of the death of lyric subjectivity, but it is also as much about what might replace the subject, at least in terms of the subject's isolated perspective. This goal is certainly the desire of the poetic "I" of stanza 4, to be lifted out of its own limited phenomenal existence. To have this wish, however, also unavoidably contaminates what the "I" desires to be lifted into; the very intelligibility of a historical apprehension outpacing subjectivity inserts the subject as a radical blockage of this action, with the voice of lyrical sublimity inevitably failing to outrace itself. The poet's own awareness of this dilemma in stanza 4 is made clear by the stanza's much-discussed phrase, "only less free / Than thou, O Uncontrollable!" (line 47). Traditionally understood as a dilemma that then needs to be explained away—why would the poet be happy to unite with the wind while remaining "only less free" than the wind?—the lines do indeed constitute a problem, one that stanza 4 actually foregrounds, the fundamental non-adequation between wind and poet, historical denotation and subjective perception, that the break between stanzas 3 and 4 also vigorously dramatizes.

The poet's desire thus revolves around an encounter with, rather than a solution to, this radical non-adequation, something that stanza 4 can only narrativize as varying levels of agreeability, rather than of any true change in kind, of this fundamental situation. The oftentimes-used comparison of stanza 4 with the Wordsworthian past figure of "Tintern Abbey" clarifies this predicament. If, as chapter 1 argued, Wordsworth's poem is structured around a plot of maturation away from youthful sensation to an intellectual and imaginative sobriety, stanza 4 of the "Ode" eschews this narrative possibility. Indeed, Shelley's poet's present is characterized by an excess of bodily sensation, emblematized by the "thorns of life" upon which he "bleeds" (line 54). It might be tempting to see such adolescent effusiveness, oftentimes excoriated from a Modernist perspective, as a direct repudiation of Wordsworth's "sober pleasures"; regardless, the key point of comparison is not even so much with Shelley's "boyhood" self but with the moment of sublime historical apprehension in stanza 3, with "sense" fainting "to picture" the reflected ruins' moss and flowers (line 48). In its singular form, "sense" makes this moment as much a failure of cognition as one of perception; the main point nevertheless remains the outpacing of the physical senses—sublimity as a vertiginous sobriety—that is forcefully contrasted with the grimly weighted acuity of the senses felt by the poet in stanza 4.

The problem of the subject and its senses is also marked in stanza 4 by the contorted semantics of the "vision" that the young Shelley "scarce[ly]" had (line 51).[28] Two different scenarios compete for the meaning of that word. In one, the young poet is so close to the wind that "outstrip[ping]" the wind's "skiey speed" hardly seems a fantasy, with "vision" exploiting the association of visuality with illusion. In the other, the young poet, like the past figure in "Tintern Abbey," is so devoid of reflexivity that he is barely able to realize the conception of outpacing the wind, with "vision" now drawing upon its role as a figure for both desire and mental abstraction. Arguably, neither scenario is that satisfactory: the first appears to be more narratively coherent, although the pejorative use of "vision" almost seems to anticipate the very Arnoldian and Modernist critique of Shelley's writing as unjustifiable poetic dreaminess; building the narrative upon the *outpacing* of the wind also seems to imply a narcissistic rendering of the whole plot, already reifying the problem of subjectivity isolating the speaker in the present.

The second presents a more indeterminate scenario, a non-reflexivity that might reference the sensory immaturity of the past subject of "Tintern Abbey" but that could also imply the more complicated dialectic of non-reflexivity and plentitude akin to the child in Wordsworth's "Intimations" ode. The unpacked, indeterminate nature of this scenario is further stymied, rather than clarified, by the again pejorative sense of "vision" as mental abstraction. The young poet *could* be marked by his non-subjectivity, his distance from a present self so reified and weighed down by the necessary abstractions of his alienated desires. Yet its very convoluted elaboration gives the second option a poetic clumsiness that makes it seem other than a serious, genuine account. In both scenarios, the complete sacrifice of "vision" to either illusion or mental entrapment also seems to stunt a term that could just as well signify sublime apprehension, rather than simply the prison house of embodied perception and abstract cognition.

There is thus something fundamentally unsatisfying—*unreadable*—about the "vision" in stanza 4. The word, then, might best be understood as a catachrestic intrusion, a formal hindrance that draws attention to the ultimately ungainly, simulated nature of the troping of the difference between the poet's childhood and present existence. The power of this stanza, then, does not lie in its intelligible rendering of a time when the younger Shelley was somehow literally more in tune with the simultaneity of what we have called the historical sublime; rather, the stanza works as a temporalizing retelling—an allegory—of the fundamental problem of the wind as objective knowledge, its inability to free itself from the weight of the subject that utters it. To extend this further, we can say that the poet himself, subjectivity per se, is an inevitable simulation, or symptom, of the lyric utterance, an unavoidable impediment to the lyric's relation to the world, insofar as the world cannot appear outside the form of the lyric as (overheard) conversation. Jonathan Culler's claim twenty years ago about the central role of the figure of voice in lyric studies is thus still relevant here.[29] The problem is not so much the death of lyric voice as its reanimation, a radically intransigent prosopopoeia that inserts itself into the evaluation of any utterance, any "vision" of the world. The sign of this reanimating intrusion in the "Ode" is the painfully embodied, physically sensing "I" of stanzas 4 and 5, although this does not make the poem's rendition of this problem ultimately a phenomenal one; the dilemma is more exactly the radically formal inability of any objective event to articulate itself fully; the inability, for example, of objective *need* to exist independently of subjective *desire*.[30] More to the point, the subject, or poet, becomes in this instance the term by which we designate precisely what objective reality, a world without subjective support, cannot overcome. Rather than a limiting horizon, textuality, the articulation of the world, cannot become what it objectively is because of its own formal impediment, what the "Ode" tropes as the poet of stanzas 4 and 5.

To resurrect dialectically the subject out of its negativity, as Žižek might, is beside the point in the "Ode" (*Tarrying*, 14). Equally so would be traditional readings of Shelley's poem that see its wager in terms of the poet's survival or redemption. The poet is not in danger in the last portion of the "Ode"; *the wind is*, insofar as we define the wind as an independent event or force beyond the poet's invocation. Indeed, the more desperately the poet hails the wind and its powers in the poem's conclusions, defining the wind by its I-Thou relation with the speaker, the more the wind becomes anchored to the poet's interpellative desire.[31] The question becomes, however, whether this was structurally ever *not* the case—whether, especially in relation to the first three stanzas, the poet has ever *not* been, in Chandler's suggestive playing off of Shelley's pun, history's lyre (525). We can formulate this problem more precisely by thinking through the connection, or gap, between stanzas 3 and 4 as once again the question of sequentiality and simultaneity.

Sequentially, the poet's thoughts in the last two stanzas follow a poetic realization of mediatized simultaneity, a historical sublime that the poet urgently wants to encounter. In that sense, a gap or temporal lag is indeed registered between stanzas 3 and 4, which nevertheless secures in the poem's later portion the wind's autonomy from the poet, who needs the wind to be a separate identity in order to confer onto him its unalienated existence. Yet, conceived as one lyric moment, with the mental gyrations of the poet in the last two stanzas occurring *during* the wind's temporal and spatial becomings in the earlier stanzas, the "Ode" presents us with a more complex set of options. The poet's thoughts could be part of a larger set of occurrences, which the poem presents him intuiting and desiring to encounter further; in this scenario, there *is* a historical sublime that the speaker wishes to channel and make intelligible. Yet the very sublimity of the first three stanzas could just as well simply be the imagination of the poet; the wind's travels, like Lucy's orbiting through the universe, could all be occurring within the mental action of the speaker, the true focus of the poem. The sublime as a register of objective denotation would suddenly appear to have always been circumscribed by plodding, subjective cognition; history as mass experience would already be a reification of the subject's abstracting powers. Simultaneity would itself be an illusory figure for the retroactive hypostatizations of a subject constantly projecting freedom and possibility beyond, or before, itself. That such a projection is itself a fiction, like the tropes of inside and outside that enable the further figure of a subject's mental action, would not lessen the formal problem: historical *consciousness* as in fact *an impediment* to history, the historical sublime as simply one more imagining of the subject, becoming in the "Ode" the only option open to the poetic utterance. If the various agents in *Prometheus Unbound* (Asia and Prometheus himself) define their praxis through some accessing of historical knowledge; if, as we have argued, the catachresis of Enlightenment subjectivity in the third *Critique* is simultaneously the imposition of historical periodicity—the "Ode" presents the subject as the alienated weight that no simultaneity of relations can simply lift out of itself.

> The very corn which is now so beautiful, as if it had only (taken)
> to ripening yesterday, is for the market; So, why shod I be
> delicate.
>
> —John Keats, Letter to J. H. Reynolds, July 11, 1819

The poet's predicament in the "Ode" is not so much an expression of Shelley's bad faith as an unflinching portrayal of a fundamental dilemma, however. A consideration of Shelley's poet as the sensory embodiment of this quandary is also something more than a simple revisiting of Wasserman's seminal pronouncements on the problem of the Romantic subject in, and beyond, Shelley.[32] We can best clarify our own formulation of these distinctions, and of what the "Ode" further dramatizes, by contrasting Shelley's poem with high Romanticism's other most famous post-revolution lyric, Keats's "To Autumn."

These lyrics are two of the most visible (a certain tradition would say most perfect) poetic works in the high Romantic canon, both produced in the *annus mirabilis*—and *annus terribilis*—of 1819. Both poems use autumn to trope the relationship between seasonal change and history. And yet both seem to resist being categorized together. This is true in even our most recent, most emphatic rendering of second-generation Romantic historicity, Chandler's foundational study *England in 1819*, where each poem is presented as a key contribution of its author to the reflexively "hot chronology" of this dizzying year in British history (3, 425–31, 525–54). Yet *England* does not juxtapose them together. This by no means implies a lapse in a study defined by the depth of its textual, material, and historical connections; rather, it confirms how, despite all their apparent similarities, the "Ode" and "To Autumn" seem intuitively to reside in separate poetic realms. Indeed, a conventional vocabulary of mood, tone, and theme can already help us list the poems' differences. If the "Ode" desperately attempts to poetize temporal change, "To Autumn" appears to luxuriate in an ever-encroaching stasis that the betwixt and between nature of the fall season helps amplify; if Shelley tropes temporal change through the structure of a proleptic rebirth, Keats envisions stasis as death, and his poem as, in Chandler's apt wording, a "thanatopsis," a viewing of this always singular, although always pervasive, event (430).[33] If the "Ode" strains after an apprehension, a velocity, beyond the physical senses, "To Autumn" moves in a completely opposite direction, creating through its imagery and diction the Keatsian sensorium for which the poet is so well known. One might see this as an opportunity to express the event of Keatsian sensation in once again Deleuzian terms, with the indeterminacies of autumnal death as Keats's own attempt to trope something akin to the molecular operation of Deleuzian becoming. I, however, want to go precisely in another direction, to see "To Autumn" as in fact a meditation on the procedures of molar abstraction—of, in particular, commodity reification.

This argument is clarified by the starkly different roles of the narrating subject in the two poems. While the poet forcefully inserts himself into the last portion of the "Ode," the opposite occurs in "To Autumn," with subjectivity of a sort being projected onto only the personified figure of autumn and perhaps the poem's bees and gnats; as many commentators of Keats's poem have noticed, the poetic "I" does not appear at all in the work, not even during, in James O'Rourke's elegant phrasing, the "imminent vanishing" of the piece's conclusion.[34] This absence of the narrator occurs in other lyrics by Keats, most notably in "Ode on a Grecian Urn" and "Ode on Melancholy," although when contrasted with the self-referential strategies of the last portion of Shelley's "Ode," the lack of the "I" in "To Autumn" is especially striking. Given the generic constraints of the lyric, it might seem an oxymoron to speak of a lyric ode narrated in the second person, although narratologists oftentimes consider the possibility of this narrative experiment in prose. Still, the lyric ode is an address, which assumes not only an addressee but an addresser, a poetic situation that Shelley's "Ode" elevates to the key component of its overriding problem of historical representation. But what if we don't simply see the "impersonality" that "To Autumn" achieves as either bad faith or fiction, but as a *cue* for one particular way to read the poem (Hartman, 146)? What occurs then?

First and foremost, the poem becomes radically depopulated in an odd but powerful way, a predicament made all the more tensely compelling by the work's lush imagery and language. There are certainly anthropomorphizing gestures in the work, such as the spectral personification of autumn with its scythe in stanza 2, the "maturing sun" and greedy bees in stanza 1, and the "mourn[ing]" gnats of stanza 3 (lines 2, 27).[35] Yet the human subject, as either intrusive poet or active figure in the poetic landscape, is missing from "To Autumn." This absence might speak to the English transfiguration of the "Eastern" poetic tradition that Hartman argues the poem accomplishes (126), or to the non-human nature that O'Rourke, using de Man, sees in Keats's piece, a nature that emphatically unmoors itself from the demands and perspectives of human consciousness in stanza 3 (152).[36] But something else is also operating in the poem. Two further points about "To Autumn" make this clear.

First, there is the contrasting way that "To Autumn" and the "Ode" trope *heaviness.* In Shelley's poem, heaviness is concentrated almost exclusively in the somatic existence of the alienated poet, "chained and bowed" by a "heavy weight of hours" (line 55); unable to be lifted by the wind, the poet is in effect a stone, more impervious to the wind's vibrations than the "oozy woods" of the deep Atlantic (line 39), which in comparison becomes one of the "pellucid spaces" that C. S. Lewis saw Shelley's poetry speeding through, and thus even more ethereal and light than the poet himself.[37] In Keats's work, however, heaviness is disassociated from any one bodily subject position and superimposed on the world itself. This claim would thus be a counter to O'Rourke's suggestion in the last stanza of de Manian images of levitation that speak to the alterity of nature floating beyond the ken of the human mind (152). Contrary to such an impulse, stanzas 1 and 2 are full of images that trade in heaviness of various sensory kinds, from the "drows'd" opiated state of autumn, surrounded by the "fume of poppies" and the thick "oozings" of the cider in stanza 2, to the heavily weighted fruit and vegetables of stanza 1, "gourds" and "shells" that sun and autumn "swell" and "plump," as well as the vines and apple tree that the elements also "load" and "bend" with ripening produce (lines 3–5, 7, 17, 22). In contrast to the "aery surge" of the "Ode," the very atmosphere of "To Autumn" seems still, thick, and ductile, laden with solar warmth and the buzzing of the bees.

If the "Ode" contrasts a sensory-laden, alienated subject with an objective historical sublime, "To Autumn" does away with the subject while retaining in its objective rendering of the world all the phenomenal heaviness of subjective existence. Such a scenario allows the faunal noises of the conclusion of stanza 3 to be read not simply as de Manian signs of nature's levitation, but as yet another set of examples of sensory events disarticulated from an intervening subject's imperial perception. As such, they "fill the air," as Hartman notes, in his own different but comparable formulation of the dynamics in "To Autumn" (132). Keats's poem thus hypothesizes not only an ode but also a world of sensation, without a human subject. One might again want to see this predicament as something akin to a free-floating form of Deleuzian sensation without organs, or as a prestidigitation on Keats's part that implicitly encases the world of "To Autumn" in a non-intrusive but nevertheless omnipresent poetic subjectivity. Indeed, both the Deleuzian and more conventional phenomenal reading can already be seen operating in New Critical statements about "To Autumn" as a poem with hardly any meaning, made up of close to pure style, or sensation.[38] Yet another option also exists: the very ductile thickness of autumn's world is employed to render exactly what the a-perceptual, sublime comprehension of the "Ode" also tries to approximate, an objectivity independent of the subject's buttressing effects. The air and everything else in "To Autumn" are characterized by a physical density that stands in for an ontological concreteness independent of the subject's own perceptual powers.

That is only part of the issue, however. For the second point about the poem is, paradoxically, how its vision of an objective world explicitly involves a recording of human activity. What that activity is, however, is precisely the question "To Autumn" asks, as quite literally, there are no human beings doing anything anywhere in the poem. *Harvest*, a theme especially associated with Helen Vendler's well-known, scrupulous reading of the ode, might very well be the answer to this query, as well as the referent for the personified autumn as dominant metaphor (257, 282).[39] Yet *harvest* in Chandler's reading of the thanatopic character of the poem could just as well mean *death*, as autumn's scythe also briskly indicates; the question remains whether these meanings can be pushed further in any one direction. One obvious further possibility, also associated with Vendler, would be *labor*, except for the fact that all we see is either the consequences of labor—overabundant, overripening fruit, the "granary floor" and "last oozings" of the cider press—or labor *in media res*, with autumn narcotized and asleep, scythe laid down in midswing (284, lines 14, 22). Autumn's napping state could just as well signify that very small respite we call *life* before autumn finishes its swing, although the point remains that labor as an activity is notably missing throughout the poem. Indeed, as O'Rourke has noted, the exception to this lack would be the bees of stanza 1. As O'Rourke observes, the association of bees with "organized labor" goes back to antiquity; coupled with the equally long-standing perception of bees' non-reflexivity over their finite nature, their productivity becomes the sign of a "perfectly functioning ideological machine" (173–74).[40] Yet Keats's stanza concludes by focusing on neither simply their labor nor their temporal cluelessness, but on, once again, what they have in overabundance produced: "Until [the bees] think warm days will never cease, / For summer has o'er brimmed their clammy cells" (lines 10–11).

The bees' non-reflexivity, then, extends beyond their obliviousness to summer's end; it also expresses itself through their non-consumption of the honey overflowing their stores, honey that in the bees' eternal summer imaginary they will never eat. The bees are ruled by a product that they make but do not use; their ideological lives are organized by commodities that have more value than they themselves, that direct their labor and supplant their intention. The honey, the overripe fruit, the stored grain, and the oozing cider exist in and for themselves; they have taken over the ontological density, the (in this case) phenomenal sensation abdicated by the missing human subject of "To Autumn." Signs of a process emphatically estranged from first nature, they are also in their poetically rendered autonomy keenly non-human. To reformulate O'Rourke's reading, they are signs of a radical *second* nature that has emphatically disarticulated itself from the intention of its producers.[41] Such an inhuman second nature could also easily include the reifications of past poetic traditions and pagan memory that Hartman and Chandler in different ways see the poem reflexively producing (*Fate*, 124–46; *England*, 431). Human activity in "To Autumn" is thus not simply harvesting, or labor, or even *consumption*, but a process that has surpassed human intention, *commodification*.[42] As Elizabeth Jones succinctly describes Keats's poem, "'To Autumn' lacks the labor that attends the interrogative mode; it represents a moment of static perfection existing between production and consumption."[43] This might readily be death insofar as this "moment" is the result of a process that involves the death-in-life of the bees; it is also death-in-life as that extended "static" instant before the final swing of the scythe that allows for an existence of things before any final consumption or production, of a "ripeness to the core" that goes nowhere beyond its own moment of continuation (line 6).

"To Autumn" thus outlines a specifically historical narrative, one in which the victors *are* the spoils. While such an account can only appear in the wake of Marjorie Levinson's path-breaking study of Keats's romances, it need not depend on the same historical coordinates as Levinson's claim about the Cockney class anxieties permeating the poet's *oeuvre*.[44] Indeed, particular debates over the historical character of "To Autumn" more readily reference the poem's immediate creation, starting with Jerome McGann's seminal reading of "To Autumn" as recoiling from the nightmare of history that was the Peterloo Massacre of 1819. Since then, a number of studies have challenged that view and reconsidered Keats not only as a socially engaged writer but also as someone literally part of the demonstrations that occurred after the Massacre.[45] If we were to connect Peterloo to "To Autumn," then, it would be to read the poem not as an expression of political escapism, but as a terribly steely diagnosis of England's rapidly developing history, which the state violence of Peterloo only punctuates, where the political desires of the nation's workers give way to the depopulated landscape of their products, and, in Marx's formulation, the "definite social relation between men" assumes the "fantastic form of a relation between things" (*Capital*, 165). The key presence throughout Keats's poem, autumn, *is* that relation, binding fruit, honey, wheat, and cider together. Autumn is thus also a process—neither simply a seasonal nor even an existential but a grimly historical one, in which the "products of labor become commodities, sensuous things which are at the same time supra-sensible or social" (165). "To Autumn" is at once a ghost town and an idealized community of objects whose intensely physical existence speaks to an ontology of sensation that is itself a sign of the encroaching horizon of commodity reification. The objective reality poetized here is also the reality of objects existing in a ductile present where their past human production and future consumption seem as transient and fading as the sounds of gnats and swallows in the "soft-dying day" (line 25).

If we have trouble coordinating the poem's analysis with the undeniable pleasure it finds in its masterful rendition of this state, we are simply experiencing in distilled fashion one of the basic fates of daily life for many since Keats in capitalist modernity. Qualifying Levinson, we would also be encountering the historically specific challenges of a Cockney School habitus—a wry acknowledgment of the pleasures and entrapments of consumer life, radically indeterminate in its class registers and subversive effects—that so distressed English militants of an earlier generation such as William Hazlitt.[46] The indeterminacy of such a tone might also be one way "To Autumn" outwits the reified nature of its objective vision: reformulating O'Rourke once again, the poem's elusive tone becomes a sign not of any deep ecology but of a deep history, the result of a critical omniscience emphatically unmoored from the distractions of human intent or desire, beholden only to the accuracy of its (ultimately) non-human truth. In that sense, "To Autumn" is indeed a post-revolution poem, although not in any clearly reactionary way; rather, its vision has ironically subsumed the "songs of spring"—revolution, the labor agitations of Peterloo—into a more long-term diagnostic of commodification as the grimly fundamental *récit* of modernity (line 23).

This is also at least in part why the lyric moment in "To Autumn" does not ply in the aporias of speed and temporality that the "Ode" does. Through a different set of strategies and precepts, "To Autumn" also achieves something very close to the simultaneity of the lyric utterance. It does so, however, through a sense of stasis, the nether existence of commodity reification, the nonhuman intention of a "ripeness to the core" cut off from past production and future consumption, that binds the poem's community of images into one state. The poem's pacing—the opposite of Shelleyan speed—certainly has something to do with the stateliness of its Horatian rhythms, but that pacing is less in the service of any unproblematic human mediation and more the entropic recognition of a set of alien (apparently unmade, uneaten) things. Its lyric utterance is of a thanatopsis of the market, a death-in-life that closes down as much as possible the difference between the act of its viewing and the substance of what it beholds.

> The answer of the oracle is prediction of an unalterable future;
> the warning of the *Nabi* implies the indeterminism and
> determining power of the hour.
>
> —Martin Buber, *Mamre: Essays in Religion*

If "To Autumn" thus answers the question of its post-revolutionary status in the affirmative, that is precisely what the "Ode" holds in suspense. Shelley's poem's anticipatory invocation of a revolutionary rebirth out of England's post-Waterloo betrayals becomes precisely what blocks that rebirth; for all its lyric speed, the very structure of the poem's request means that it cannot coincide with the realization of its invocation; the subject's desire for spring keeps that season proleptic, in abeyance. But this also means that in some fundamental way revolution is still kept alive as a possibility. This situation thus replays the very predicament of the poet in the "Ode," who desires a connection to a sublime historical apprehension whose objective status might still in some basic way be beholden to his own alienated subjectivity. That the precise relation between the first three and last two stanzas of the "Ode" remains forcefully unclear makes the simultaneity of the poem's utterance less about the success of its expression and more about the event of its lyric as an impasse.

As a lyric impasse, the "Ode" focuses intensely on the question of what it truly means to apprehend the simultaneity of history, as the first three stanzas apparently limn. For history cannot simply remain in the realm of potentiality, but must also take on the contours and shape of a particular account. The fantastic proposition of an objective apprehension inevitably takes on a more distinct, more particular shape. This is one wager, and risk, of historical thought, its entanglement with a vatic mode of expression, that Shelley along with Blake, the two Romantic poets of futurity, dramatize so well.[47] (Indeed, this distinction of Shelley's also helps explain the particular results of comparing the poet's childhood in the "Ode" with similar tropes in Wordsworth, the poet of *Nachträglichkeit* and the past.) Thus, for Lukács the mass experience of history after Napoleon is firmly embedded within a stage of dialectical materialism's own forward-pressing narrative. But how, in reference to not only Lukács but *also* Shelley, might this particular narrative be further delineated?[48]

There is in fact a bifurcation of this narrative in these famous lines of stanza 5:

Drive my dead thoughts over the universe
Like withered leaves to quicken a new birth!
And, by the incantation of this verse,

Scatter, as from an unextinguished hearth
Ashes and sparks, my words among mankind! (lines 63–67)

Conventionally understood, the "withered leaves" of stanza 5 are figuratively transformed into the "ashes and sparks" of incendiary revolutionary thought that might still help instigate such an event in the world. For Chandler, this figuration is a performative act, a self-generating tropology of "ashes and sparks" that signals the poem's "development of an alternative to the organic or 'cultural' model of social regeneration" (552)—Promethean revolution instead of seasonal, cyclic change. Chandler does not specifically say this, but such a reading would reflexively place the "incantation of this verse"—Shelley's poem's invocation of itself—on the side of the Promethean spark, transforming the reifications of "dead thought" into something besides their present form, the "withered leaves" of print textuality. Chandler does masterfully limn the aporias of cause and effect that make the "Ode" a Promethean anticipation of Marx's own statement about the difficulties of revolutionary history in *The Eighteenth Brumaire*, and this problematic can also be brought to bear on the meta-"incantation" of the "Ode." For it is not too difficult to push the hypostatized textuality of "dead thought" and "withered leaves" to glimpse a reification that is, more specifically, the book as commodity form. The question then becomes whether the "Ode" as incantation really does foresee its Promethean liberation from itself, the commodity form, or whether it actually records a tropology of "lightning" and "spark"—of revolution—that is already folding into another historical event, the story of onrushing commoditization that "To Autumn" tells.

Andrew Franta has recently argued that the stanzas' scattering leaves are actually the recipients of Shelley's writings, spread across the world.[49] Whether as books or as readers, the "driv[ing]" of the leaves can indicate a mass experience different from both Lukács's and Prometheus's. Following Franta, we can see in the trope of dispersal the reflexive recording of the historical rise of mass audiences and reading publics. Reformulating Franta, the catachresis of media erupting in the first three stanzas would then take on a concrete historical form in the poem's conclusion, as the economic and technological underpinnings of mass reading that would spread the leaves of Shelley's writings to the world. A revolution might be occurring in the "Ode," but it might be more akin to Raymond Williams's "long revolution" of literacy, reading publics, and media systems than to the apparently abrupt vision of Jacobin social transformation that Badiou sings in his own account.[50] The significance of the leaves might be not so much their revolutionary transfiguration as their necessary existence as commodities aimed at a literary public that is at once invariably a reading market. The history that the "Ode" predicts might be the revolution(s) of a yet-to-be nineteenth century, or the already inexorable encroachment of global commodification that leads to the "long twentieth century" of capitalism outlined by Giovanni Arrighi.[51] These predictions might indeed at some further level be part of a simultaneity still unfolding—the *twenty-first*-century revolutions of a *still yet-to-be* long twentieth century—or they might emphatically be discontinuous, the very indeterminacy of this question being the pathos and poignancy of the lyrical impasse of the "Ode," cathected in the parataxis between its third and fourth stanzas, a gap as immeasurable and unavoidable as the one that we saw so famously separating the stanzas of Wordsworth's "A Slumber." In that gap the poem finds the intractable dilemma of a poet whose alienation is the necessary distance between himself and a realization of history that he might actually be, paradoxically, *too* responsible for; this problematic is then replayed in terms of an "incantation" ultimately as unknowable in its utterance as the instructions of Hamlet's father's ghost—unknowable as either the definitive song of Promethean revolution or the traversing melody of a global telecommunications market. In its rendering of its own particular *Neuzeit*, the "Ode" insists on inhabiting a space always on the verge, always within the indecision, of the historical moment, precisely because in the "Ode," unlike "To Autumn," history never stops. The meta-"incantation" of the "Ode" is caught in its own *mise en abyme*, singing that its song is not the song that it sings, emitting the undecidability of incantation as either oral performance or written text, revolutionary spark or commodified withered leaf, hailing our future, or a different one, entirely.[52] In its very indeterminate articulation the "Ode" becomes a vatic expression of the *unpredictability* of Badiou's insurgent Jacobin eruption into history, the contingent but necessary aporia of a historical design that we, like Klee's "Angelus Novus," are rushing, speeding toward.[53]

The final lesson of the "Ode" and "To Autumn" is thus one about reading history. Keats's poem gains its power from its evocation of a present of commodity reification that is also at once a projection of stasis into a future dusk always betwixt and between, always the moment after the making, and before the end, of its existence. Shelley's work energetically strains toward a future fiercely entangled in the indeterminacies of a present that might be in the throes of commodification, or at the beginning of a radical social transformation that would make the poem a pre-revolutionary, rather than post-revolutionary, work. Both writings in different ways use the senses to demarcate or limn the immanence of what they represent; those distinct usages—a sublime apprehension where "sense fails" and a sensorium evacuated of subjective existence—also mark a convergence of the same problematic, of historical representation as a necessary entanglement, however amplified or attenuated, of present and future perspectives.[54] As the reflected ruins in "Baiae's bay" demonstrate, the invention of history necessarily involves an encounter with the past (line 32). But the "Ode" and "To Autumn" also remind us how, in the historical aporia of Romantic modernity, that invention also means a critique of the present that is always prophetic, and a prophecy of the future that is always, critically, about the present. For readers in the wake of these writers, and Romanticism, history always becomes a wager.

CHAPTER EIGHT

# No Satisfaction

## High Theory, Cultural Studies, and *Don Juan*

If, as I argued earlier, Romanticism can be understood as much through the figure of sobriety as that of sensation, studies of eighteenth- and nineteenth-century Britain as a time of rising, if not rampant, consumption appear to complicate such a claim.[1] Wordsworth's cry against "getting and spending" aside, Romanticism seems very much a period caught within the spell of the Lamia-like commodity product (Gill, 270; line 2). The active consumption of the commodity-as-sensation, and sensation-as-commodity, seems a major component of the narrative of Romantic modernity. Like Wordsworth, a number of writers evince their anxieties about this predicament, and thus a longing for some type of sober rectitude against the forces of this new economy. Still, the recognition of the rise of this economy now underwrites in many ways our material (in the Marxist sense) understanding of Romantic culture, and how that culture should be approached and studied.

There are several critical stories connected to this attention to Romantic consumption, such as recent considerations of Romanticism through the experience of women as both consumers and sellers in the literary and non-literary marketplace. I'd especially like to focus, however, on another related aspect of this predicament: how issues of consumption are also associated with a certain methodology, the analysis of material culture familiarly known as cultural studies. The rise of commodity consumption during Romanticism invites the study of Romanticism *as* Romantic culture, a situation made even more intriguing when one considers Romanticism's long-involved relationship with another mode of inquiry, one routinely positioned against cultural studies in the present-day academy, namely, high theory.

Back in the day, high theory was, of course, just *theory*; it became high theory precisely in opposition to cultural studies. By themselves, both high theory and cultural studies are arguably terms that date themselves institutionally. Yet together, they continue to retain a particularly strong intellectual relevance precisely because of the choices they present to us in our approach to scholarly labor, to understanding the world through *either* philosophy *or* culture, or conceiving of what we study as *either* literature *or* culture, for example.[2] If these words all seem to echo key categories of particular concern, or of distinct becoming, in Romanticism, that is one of the main points of this chapter. The debate between high theory and cultural studies is one whose vocabulary is in many ways Romantic.

There are many ways one could investigate this vocabulary, including returning to two figures that have already been discussed in this book, Kant and Rousseau. I'd like, however, to consider this predicament by way of several moments in Lord Byron's magisterial poem *Don Juan*, a work that has already been rightly and ably studied for its interest in various forms of consumption. Indeed, Byron has been a central figure not only in the exploration of Romantic consumerism and commodification but also in Romantic diet studies, a recent field that in many ways already demonstrates the Romantic character of the high theory / cultural studies debate, as well as a number of approaches to thinking beyond that debate's impasse.[3] This chapter follows in the wake of such works and other necessary precedents of scholarship on Byron and (or *as*) the market, such as Jerome Christensen's seminal study *Lord Byron's Strength*. I consider, however, such scenarios as backdrops that throw into relief the way that canto 1 of *Don Juan* actually refuses consumer satisfaction by avoiding the graphic representation of the kiss between Juan and Julia, instead giving its readers the questionable pleasure of philosophy–as–high theory. Whereas in earlier chapters theory has been shown to have its own complex relation to the dialectic between sobriety and sensation, high theory in *Don Juan* is best understood, at first at least, as the referent for a site in complicated tension with culture and the study of commodity sensation. This tension, encapsulated by the poem's ambivalence toward the graphic corporeality of Juan and Julia's kiss, makes Byron's work something besides simply an abdication of critical sobriety and embrace of consumer pleasure, regardless of how much the narrative records the sensual appeal of the commodity form.

Still, as much as Christensen's book and other studies might focus on Byron and the market, it would be a mistake to see them as all somehow simply eschewing theory; Christensen's work can especially be seen as one culminating attempt in Romantic studies to forge a study beholden to both theories of the sign and arguments about material culture. This chapter then takes as its occasion the odd predicament in which strong works like Christensen's exist simultaneously alongside constantly recurring divisions in modes of inquiry and methodology, a situation in many ways emblematized by the high theory versus cultural studies split. Certainly, one could talk about such academic phenomena in terms of institutional and non-institutional histories, politics, and, truth be told, individual intellectual dispositions. This chapter will focus, however, on seeing how Juan's and Julia's non-kiss frames this scenario in a way that its importance lies not simply in its content, much less its external referents, but in its formal structure of interruption, where the narrativization of culture and what exceeds it (philosophy, say) exist together through a permanent parabasis. Before exploring this further, however, I want to consider more fully diet, culture, and consumption in several key moments of Byron's poem.

As Denise Gigante has noted, Byron himself was not that keen on eating lavishly (117–18). But, as she and others have also observed, *Don Juan* is full of, among other things, food.[4] Banquets play a key role in the poem's narrative, as do, of course, the more problematic forms of nourishment that present themselves to the starving surviving crew of canto 2, Juan's spaniel and his poor tutor Pedrillo. Much can be, and has been, said about this scene of cannibalism in the canto; my focus will be on one question that eating Pedrillo raises, one that, arguably, simply magnifies a question already inherent in the eating of Juan's dog: what is the nature of food?[5] The what of this question is inextricably linked, of course, to the question of how—how we prepare what we eat, how we make food *into* food—which in turn makes this line of inquiry an anthropological one: what is the nature of the being that eats something prepared in such and such a way? In *Don Juan* presentations of food and drink display themselves as metonyms for cultural practice. They are signs of how Byron's poem is a cultural study.

As readers of Claude Lévi-Strauss know, food is in fact a key ingredient in determining the boundaries between culture and nature with a capital *N*.[6] To speak of food as a signifier is of course to acknowledge already the practice of some cultural language, somehow already on the other side of food as an aboriginal essence to be incorporated for some atavistic, non-signifying, biological need. The oftentimes-remarked connection between poor Pedrillo's slow bleeding and rapid cannibalization and the Eucharist can be understood as a parody of this very tension, of the collision between one highly elaborate sign system explaining the meaning of incorporation and one drawn-out instance of digestion as an ineluctable, unreflexive event of the real, imaged not simply by the ravenous sailors' appetite but also by the two sharks who eradicate all bodily evidence of the tutor's interiority, Pedrillo's "entrails and the brains" (2.77).[7]

The aftermath of Pedrillo's cannibalization seems, however, to depict a universe that decides in favor of the law over the real, as those who eat him go mad and die hideously. From the retrospective view of a later stanza this consequence is explained readily enough by how the crew "wash[ed] down Pedrillo with salt water" (1.102). Earlier, the poem is more ambivalent, suggesting that drinking seawater is actually *caused* by the madness brought on by a particularly avid indulgence in eating Pedrillo:

> For they, who were most ravenous in the act,
> Went raging mad—Lord! how they did blaspheme!
> And foam and roll, with strange convulsions rack'd.
> Drinking salt-water like a mountain-stream,
> Tearing, and grinning, howling, screeching, swearing,
> And with hyena-laughter, died despairing. (2.79)

Eating Pedrillo is indeed a kind of transubstantiation, but one that leads to the non-human instead of the divine. This could be a moment of ethical recognition by the text, although one as fugitive as the Byronic strength that Christensen maps out throughout Byron's corpus in Christensen's decisive work on the poet, especially since those in the boat who treat their appetites less "sadly" fare no better in the end—aside from Juan, of course (2.80). Or perhaps the scene acts out an especially grisly dream scenario between a celebrity poet and the ravenous appetites of an undisciplined, oftentimes-plagiarizing mass audience. We can concentrate, however, on yet another version of this scene's depiction of ethical and social consequence: the primal instantiation of the *real of the law*, of the law of eating as culture and the culture of eating as law.

What is the nature of food? Canto 2 answers: not Pedrillo, neither raw nor blessed. One of the more strange details of Pedrillo's cannibalization is how the urge to eat another crew member continues even after the effects of Pedrillo's digestion are witnessed, and how that urge slowly winds down somewhat inexplicably, as it's overtaken by a series of contingent events—the STDs of the next most ample candidate, the desultory catching of some sea birds. The urge to eat another human leaves the crew as the life force is uniformly evacuated from the entire boat. I describe this as "inexplicable" insofar as eating another human for survival, especially someone not bled to death like Pedrillo, could in fact be narrativized as a rational act, as much as the putatively rational, cosmic structure of cause and effect (eat Pedrillo and go mad) apparently used by the poem. In that sense, going mad after eating someone is actually what's irrational, the real of the law by which its unreasoning, unreflective internalization enables invocations of the Lord and expressions of "blaspheme" to make sense. (From that perspective the wretched cannibals and not Juan are the appropriate figures of comparison with Coleridge's own shipwrecked, self-interpellating ideological subject, the Mariner.) The crew eats Pedrillo, but not all of him. His remains are themselves transformed into totemic injunctions against improper eating, even as the fact that some still continue to nibble at him ("at times a little supper made" [2.82]) turns what's left over of Pedrillo into totems of the law's own law of bad faith. Dialectically, the taste of that very bad conscience becomes what the remaining noshing survivors try to clean away by "washing Pedrillo down with salt water" (2.102); they are driven mad by abjectly respecting, rather than criminally trespassing, the law.

Juan doesn't participate in the acting out of this dynamic, passively caught as he is between raging hunger and repulsion at eating his tutor. After being shipwrecked, however, he plays a central role in the creation myth of culture that cantos 2 and 3 construct. Rescued by Haidée and her servant, sequestered in a cave away from nature's hostile elements, he enacts with Haidée, "Nature's bride," the birth of society via the entwined tropes of erotic viewing, gustatory appetite, and food making (2.202). Eating and eros are in fact combined through the trick of narrative deferral, as Haidée's loving viewing of Juan is embedded within the more prosaic story of preparing breakfast for him, a long-drawn-out, teasing experience that ends with him having to eat both slowly and in small portions because of his emaciated condition. Such foreplay gives the cave scene an unmistakable eros; *as* such, the episode has many archetypical echoes besides Plato's cave. One would be the way that we can read Juan's shipwrecked story as an eroticized Robinsonade, with his castaway status becoming an opportunity for him to reinvent civilization with Haidée. Even more germane would be Rousseau's explanation for human society, law, and language, the gathering of water at a natural well that occasions a number of erotic glances as well as the prohibition against incest.[8] Together in the cave's own simulated state of nature, Juan and Haidée likewise play the part of two young lovers at the beginning of time, whose relationship is also formed around tensions between licit and illicit structures of desire, although in this case those of exogamy rather than of endogamy. As in Rousseau, their eros also leads to the birth of language as Juan and Haidée learn to communicate. Enacting Maslow's hierarchy of needs, Juan and Haidée make the world together on a full stomach.

Their passage from brute nature to culture is not only archetypical but also literal, as they move out of the cave and into Haidée's island house while her pirate father is away plying his trade. In doing so, they immerse themselves in a world of human making that ranges from the plunder that the father has gathered to the song that the poet entertains them with as they hold court. Appropriately enough, one of the central images for this passage into civilization is the carnivalesque feast that Haidée throws for Juan in canto 3, one whose description emphatically makes clear that Juan is now in the land of the cooked instead of the raw:

> The dinner made about a hundred dishes;
>   Lamb and pistachio nuts—in short, all meats,
> And saffron soups, and sweetbreads; and the fishes
>   Were of the finest that e'er flounced in nets,
> Drest to a Sybarite's most pamper'd wishes. (3.62)

The fish are indeed "drest," insofar as their preparation involves their appearance as much as their taste. This is just one among many details acknowledging the self-reflexively graphic nature of the banquet's presentation. The feast is indistinguishable from the visual or, as Marx might say more capaciously, sensual appearance of all the objects involved that make up the banquet, not only the food and spices but also the entertaining dancers, the cups of china, and the Persian tapestry. Garnered from all over the globe, they are goods in the most literal sense that modernity understands that term. The transition from the cave to the house can therefore not simply be understood as the passage from nature to culture, but also as the affirmation and magnification of commodified life during the poem's own time of the English Regency. The shift in Juan's and Haidée's locale brings together civilization and commodification as the same event.

That Byron's description of the furniture and furnishings of Lambro's house comes from Miss Tully's *Narrative of a Ten Year's Residence in Tripoli in Africa* (1816) does not so much root canto 3 in some authentic elsewhere as simply iterate, much like the Orientalist trappings of the feast, the range of the commodified imaginary on display in this scene. Juan's and Haidée's feast is thus both an expression of and commentary on what Christensen famously terms "Byronism," the wide, far-flung fact of assimilating, commodified life that early nineteenth-century, commercial England produces, an event that the social phenomenon of Byron spearheads, participates in, and resists, and which begins in many ways with the simulacra productions of the poet's own Oriental tales (4–19). The commodification of writing itself is candidly on display in canto 3, with the narrator's meta-reception of the poet's song about Greek independence, which begins first as a meditation on the relation between literature and political action but soon turns into a biting review of the moralistic postures of the Lake School. The poet's song is in fact already a replay of the poem's description of the tapestry that decorates the room:

The upper border, richly wrought, display'd,
  Embroider'd delicately o'er with blue,
Soft Persian sentences, in lilac letters,
From poets, or the moralists their betters. (3.64)

Sensually objectified as "soft Persian sentences, in lilac letters," the tapestry's writings of poets and moralists exist on display, as commodities of visual gratification that have an independent life separate from their literal messages of mortality for the hedonist. As such apodictic "monitors," the writings are likened by the next stanza to those that appeared on the walls of the haunted king Belshazzar, about whom Byron wrote two poems (3.65). They *could in fact be* Byron's poems, existing as consumer objects bought from the marketplace. Hanging as backdrop along with a litany of other objects at the feast, they exist not even as the sensation of commodity meaning. Rather, they are the overcoming of the sensation of meaning by the sensation, or sensuality, of the commodity.

The items in Haidée's house are produced by her father, Lambro, although not exactly. He is a pirate and slave trader, and thus the merchandise he brings home wryly reflects both the expropriated and circulating nature of commodities in a capitalist system. The list of goods that he brings back to the island rivals that of the feast in their depiction of a world defined by conspicuous consumption. The Orientalist luxury of the goods, something reiterated and magnified as Juan's travels away from Europe progress, speaks to both the material sources of such British consumption and the affective way such conspicuous consumption, anticipating Thorstein Veblen, knows itself.[9] Somewhat incongruously, Lambro himself is portrayed as having a sober, restrained nature, a being "moderate in all his habits, and content / with temperance in pleasure" (3.53). As such, he resembles nothing less than the typical petite bourgeois commercial middle man, whose business is, literally, piracy on the high seas.

As has oftentimes been remarked, *Don Juan* is a poem about desire, from that of the characters and the narrator, and of perhaps the text itself, to that of the poem's imagined audience, who, as the narrator says at the end of canto 1, will determine whether any more of the work will be written. The capriciousness of desire is thus imaged not only in Juan's couplings (especially in terms of who will bed him in the later cantos) and in the narrator's own apparent meanderings, but also in the market desire claimed to be one of the founding reasons for the poem's ongoing existence. Why read, or write, *Don Juan*? Why read, or write, period?[10] One might see these questions as reiterating from another angle the "what" and "how" that we asked of Pedrillo. Why eat Pedrillo? Why eat? The quick answer would be hunger, but the fact that Pedrillo doesn't get eaten entirely, and that he himself attempts to give his death a religious understanding, points to how eating and not eating are matters not entirely based on need.

More precisely, then, desire or want as the other of need would be one of the central themes that *Don Juan* plays with; more specifically still, as the banquet scene in canto 3 demonstrates, the dynamic between need and desire in the poem is oftentimes expressed through the prism of the underlying tension that constitutes the commodity form, the question of use value versus exchange value.[11] A commodity is a commodity precisely because it has a value besides the satisfaction of a use or need—if, as many have asked, such categories ever really existed in their pure, non-market form. The banquet in canto 3, with foods, objects, and people so graphically "drest," speaks to a world rapidly superseding the ostensible reality of such categories, the use value of things that resolutely satisfy the simple, recognizable need, or appetite, in us.

As Robert Miles has noted, the visual dimension of appearance most powerfully evokes the simultaneously fascinating and superficial character of the commodity object, a phenomenon that a number of eighteenth- and nineteenth-century texts knowingly evoke.[12] It is also, of course, a key component in the relationships that a number of characters in the poem have with Juan. Haidée is neither the first nor last individual to look longingly upon Juan; she is also not the only person to play dress-up with him, as he's made ready to wear in both the harem and Catherine the Great's court. Strictly speaking, in terms of the human species, Juan's visual objectification is also disengaged from use value, insofar as the visual desire for Juan really doesn't seem to have anything to do with the need for biological reproduction, a disarticulation made all the more glaring by its discontinuity from the vivid accounts in canto 1 of family and racial bloodlines. (By the time of the mock Eucharist of Pedrillo, of course, blood also exists as something else altogether, a savory drink.) Within this context, it is telling that the one child who appears for more than an instant in the poem is Leila, Juan's adopted ward. Likewise, the deaths of Haidée and her unborn "second principle of life" cut off rather violently the possibility of any narrative involving her and Juan as a family unit (4.70). Indeed, the tragedy of her fate, done up through her lengthy, wan wasting away, seems very much to free Juan and the desire he cathects emphatically from any such family plot.[13] By refusing to eat, of course, Haidée also demonstrates how the end of consumption literally means death—

"Food she refused and raiment; no pretence / Avail'd for either" (4.68). But Haidée's fate also limns the equation underwriting her experience of Juan in Lambro's emporium of goods: as such, to love Juan is not to produce his heir. The scene, as Richard C. Sha succinctly notes, "emphasizes waste and pleasure rather than procreation" (280).

The unmooring of subjectivity from bloodlines is precisely one tenet of what Christensen has called Byronic strength, a force realized by the inability of any past, aristocratic world to validate any aspect of the modern one. But we can also apply Rey Chow's reading of Freud to this predicament, as well as Sha's conception of the historically non-functionalist character of sexuality in Romanticism itself. Desire in *Don Juan* is not only capricious but also, like sexuality in both Freud and Romantic science, perverse, insofar as it eschews the purpose, the use value, of biological reproduction.[14] Desire in Byron's work, especially for Juan, doesn't seem to be conceived in terms of the reproductive exigencies of Foucaultian biopolitics. Instead, it is by and large characterized by the very same visual allure and separation from use value that constitutes the commodity object, a scopic attraction incisively portrayed in Ford Madox Brown's 1873 portrait of Haidée and Zoe first coming upon the unconscious Juan (fig. 8.1). One can, of course, read a number of different, and perhaps conflicting, sexual energies into the painting's complex dynamic of viewing and identification; to *not* read Haidée's and Zoe's entrancement by Juan in terms of the biological need to reproduce is to glimpse, however, one readily identifiable narrative of market allure, pleasure disconnected from utility or need and incited by the at once passive and beautiful thing. That the two women are in this instance the viewers would simply reinforce the painting's iconic rendering of one version of the gendered roles assumed to be available in the viewing of the market object—the necessarily "female" scopic consumption of, as it were, Juan *and Don Juan*. (In Zoe's outstretched hand checking for life in Juan—checking to see what kind of thing he really is—we can also reexperience Marx's idea of the sensual commodity as precisely the haptic combination of the visual and tactile, in this case by a servant handling the goods. As telling, Haidée stands by peering, hands folded uncannily where a purse might be.) The way that Brown's depiction of Juan also seems to bypass the mediating looks of Haidée and Zoe, exceeding any simple, heterosexualized *mise en scène*, would then be a visual insurgency disrupting the very iconic authority that interpellates the creatures who love, buy, or admire Juan as, in some inevitable way, women.[15]

*As* a work of art, Brown's painting also asks us, of course, to consider whether Haidée and Zoe are simply women in the marketplace, or readers of Byron, or

*Figure 8.1.* "Finding of Don Juan by Haidée" by Ford Madox Brown, 1873. Courtesy of Birmingham Museums and Art Gallery.

also viewers in a museum gallery—an institution very much in place by Brown's, if not Byron's, time. One might, in other words, ask why Freudian sexuality and Byronic desire aren't simply perverse but also aesthetic, in Kant's sense of a purposive non-purpose—a point that both Chow and Sha explicitly make (*Sentimental*, 123; *Perverse*, 1–2). That both the aesthetic object and commodity form shun at some level the concept of need is indeed a problematic that thinkers have confronted in different ways, with Horkheimer and Adorno, for example, asserting the unavoidably instrumental character not of use but of exchange value (157–58).[16] We will return to this issue later in the chapter. For now, I want simply to continue the thought experiment of conceiving *Don Juan* as an example of what today we understand by the term *cultural studies*, a formulation that implicitly or explicitly factors into much of the long line of Byronic scholarship.

I thus refer not only to the rich body of recent work that has overtly focused on Byronic consumption and commodification but also to the long-held critical sense of Byron as a young Whig and satirist (and thus topical historicist), who has always stood outside Wordsworthian definitions of Romanticism, be they elevated expressions of Abramsian-inspired imagination or the aporetic signatures of the Yale School. One way to state this opposition, one that Byron's writings themselves arguably thematize, is to call it the choice between the Lake School idealist and the Satanic materialist, with *idealist* and *materialist* having in many ways the traditional philosophical connotations that my earlier chapters actually problematized. Or, to use another opposition, if in the last chapter Shelley's lyricism can be read as trying to register the unrepresentable world or moment of Deleuzian becoming, in Byron we have always already fallen into the calcified world of physical objects and things—*lots* of them.[17]

To consider the thick meaning of objects (a pair of shoes by a bed, for example) is, as Clifford Geertz might argue, the anthropological study of culture.[18] As the social resonances of *materialist* and the "drest" nature of food and Juan imply, however, a study of objects in modernity (which can be seen as either reaching its apotheosis or a new instantiation in Byron) readily slides into a contemplation about commodities and commodification. This predicament very much resembles the dynamic underlying *cultural studies*, a field term that today obviously has a number of definitions and histories—a fact that has been part of its institutional problem in the United States, at least.[19] Nevertheless, the definition I've attempted to extract from *Don Juan*, which overlays the questions of eating Pedrillo with the passage from the cave to Lambro's house, seems to me one that speaks to much of what motivates—indeed, defines—scholarship in cultural studies today. *Don Juan* is a proto-work of cultural studies insofar as its reflexive narrative of desired objects undertakes an anthropological study of capital. The existence of those objects in both physical *and* social terms anticipates two of the main genealogies behind the study of material culture, the anthropological and Marxist modes of thought.[20]

Let me conclude this section with two instances that further delineate life under, or within, modern capital in *Don Juan*: the way cuckoldry and adultery work, specifically in canto 1, and the banquet at Lady Adeline's English estate in canto 15. Just as Lambro's pirate profession nicely conveys the situation of the capitalist entrepreneur, the aristocratic overlay of canto 1 says as much about the middle class's existence as that of the nobility's. Certainly, the havoc that Juan appears to wreak in the household of Don Alfonso can indicate a Byronic satire on the limitations of the sexual economy of a feudal aristocracy that depends equally on the stability of entailed land and the regulated traffic of women. Alfonso, of course, participates in the exposure of that economy's contradictions by having possibly fathered Juan through his implied affair with Juan's mother, Donna Inez. The incestuousness of aristocratic bloodlines *and* the hypocrisy of upper- and middle-class English morality are obvious targets here. But the mathematical incongruity of Alfonso's position as both adulterer and cuckold also speaks to another predicament, insofar as *Don Juan* exploits long-held conventions of satire that vividly use adultery and cuckoldry to divide the male population into winners and losers, possessors and dispossessed.[21]

The math of such conventions carries a special charge when understood through the modern world of commodified Regency desire that one can map out in *Don Juan*. The emblematic nature of the legend of Don Juan as the quintessential male heterosexual lover links together a syllogistic set of assumptions that become the hermeneutic sediment through which we can read canto 1 and the rest of Byron's poem: all men want to be Don Juan, which means that they want to have as many women as Don Juan; all men thus want to be adulterers; and, therefore, all men could in fact be, or are, adulterers. Faulty or not, banal or not, this syllogistic formulation underwrites the basic movement of canto 1, insofar as one could have as easily said that all men do not want to be cuckolded; all men do not want to be Don Alfonso. But Don Alfonso *is also* Don Juan, insofar as Don Alfonso could also have been an adulterer with Donna Inez, since their alleged affair might very well have occurred when Inez was married to Don Jóse (1.66). Like all men, Don Alfonso aspires to be Don Juan; like all men, then, Don Alfonso will be cuckolded. If all men cheat, their wives and lovers must cheat on them.

The fantasy of Don Juan, then, is that he is not Don Alfonso: he commits adultery but is not cuckolded; he cheats, but no one cheats on him. He wins, but does not lose. He expropriates, but is not expropriated. Juan's implicitly cuckold-proof status articulates what the positive, buoying effect of Adam Smith's and others' representations of capitalist self-interest cannot. Smith might argue, of course, that it's Juan's and the text's lack of sympathy for Alfonso—their inability to imagine Juan in Alfonso's position—that allows for the non-regulated possibility of mass cuckoldry in the first place. Nevertheless, Juan appears to succeed in a system that by definition marks the masses for success *and* loss, or loss altogether, even as the masses identify with the one figure separate from that system, who cannot be dispossessed, who cannot be cuckolded. "Hero" of a strict economy involving adulterers and cuckolds, resurrected by Byron's narrator for modern times, he is the Don Juan of capitalism, the avatar of masculine self-acquisition, the capitalist lover who stands outside the system that he makes go, through the system's emulation of him (1.1). That one could certainly talk of the different ways that Juan becomes dispossessed as the cantos progress simply speaks to the poem's own wry knowledge of the imaginary status of any winner in a system of expropriation, regardless of whether he escapes being a cuckold. (That Juan himself is something of a non-entity, especially in the early cantos, further delineates Don Juan's capitalist avatar function as *the* imaginary.) Likewise, one could point out that there are many other sexual economies that one can read into the articulation of desire in *Don Juan*. Indeed, insofar as the syllogism of cuckoldry can only envision male agency—a man taking another man's women—the syllogism is itself the very tautological fantasy underwriting its denotative claim. Yet the mathematical relation between Don Juan and Don Alfonso, as Alfonso as Juan and Juan *not* as Alfonso, retains an emblematic quality that speaks not only to the power of the adulterer/cuckold convention but to the appropriateness of using that convention to begin a story that is, among other things, about the aporias of market desire. In that sense, Don Alfonso sees in Juan's pair of shoes, left outside Julia's bed, not only the ribald, feudal sign of his own ignorant cuckolded state but also his forlorn fate in a world of dead magical objects, commodities, which in their prosaic casual presence constantly scream out to us the invisible yet ever-widening complex process by which Alfonso, and everyone else, loses out.

That not everyone is beaten under market capitalism is at once a basic truth of the system and its greatest fantasy. Canto 15's sumptuous feast at Lady Adeline's, populated by the explicit winners (and social climbers) of British high society, makes this clear with a moment of ambiguous syntax followed by a set of explicit, punning connections:

Amidst this tumult of fish, flesh, and fowl
    And vegetables, all in masquerade,
The guests were placed according to their roll,
    But various as the meats display'd.
Don Juan sat next to an "á l'Espagnole"—
    No damsel, but a dish as hath been said;
But so far like a lady, that t'was drest
Superbly and contained a world of zest. (15.74)

"All in masquerade" could either be the guests' fleshy food or the guests themselves, explicitly "various as the meats displayed."[22] Both are the transmuted, hypostatized *things* of capitalism, intrinsically always "drest," positioned in a world, where commodities are routinely animated and people objectified by both's sensual appearance. Metaphorically associated with the feast's meats, the guests are also metonymically turned into the banquet's spread by the cartoon-like pun on "roll." Conversely, the dish is literally the lady, as each, like everything on and around Lady Adeline's table, promises a Mediterranean "world of zest"—as such, they are all enticing advertisements for the luxury of capital, Janus doubles of Juan's forlorn shoes in Julia's bedroom.[23] If the shoes constitute the unavoidable sign of capitalist expropriation, the world of zest is the promised satisfaction of capitalist accumulation, the delight of an enhanced and expanded interiority, consuming and being consumed. But that, of course, is the rub. What gaping maw, what insatiable systemic appetite, could circumscribe everything gathered on and around Adeline's table? The real of unreflective appetite in canto 2 thus returns as the equally cannibalistic real of capitalist desire in canto 15, both underwriting and obstructing any symbolic management of this and any other feast. The teleological distance between cantos 2 and 15, between Pedrillo and "l'Espagnole," the raw and the cooked, aboriginal culture and capitalist society, disappears in the eating lesson that both moments of Byron's poem, among others, dramatize. Appetite remains, although now it resides in the exteriorized insatiability, the hyper-need, of the market. Ontologically always drest, always in masquerade, Juan and *Don Juan*, *we*, the species, are a consumable good.[24]

"Bread and Circuses" is the well-known phrase that Patrick Brantlinger has made synonymous with the supposedly distracting power of commodity culture in its mass form.[25] Brantlinger, of course, gets this formulation from the Roman writer Juvenal, who mocked how the Roman elites entertained, and thereby managed, their lower classes. In canto 1 of *Don Juan*, however, Juvenal is cast out with the rest of the hoi polloi, famously excised by Donna Ines and Juan's tutors, along with all the rest of the proto-pornographers, political satirists, and atheists that constitute the best of Latin literature, and all of whom literally return as the repressed in the tutors' notorious appendix. Getting rid of the writings of Sappho and others incites a censoring logic that takes on its own life, so that getting rid of the body also means paradoxically getting rid of those who might have railed against the sensations of the body, its indulgence in bread and circuses, in their own way. Decrying culture as sensation—what *Don Juan* identifies specifically as the culture of the commodity—becomes through the banished Juvenal the cry of that very culture, which in turn becomes a supplementary appendix that overwhelms any elite cultural attempt to contain that expression.

For our purposes, Juvenal's fate in *Don Juan* is especially instructive in two ways. First, his relegation to the appendix concisely emblematizes the risk that people critically examining mass culture's technologies of pleasures run: that they, to their detriment, might be identified too closely with what they study.[26] Taking seriously the pleasures of the commodity form, not simply seeing within such an object the bleakness of false consciousness, cultural studies seems to be constantly balancing itself against being conflated with what it examines.[27] *Don Juan* also evinces this dynamic; the ruthlessness of its eating lessons aside, Byron's poem is not what one would call ascetic. Lush in language and lavish in what it spreads on its many tables, the poem's reflexive take on market consumption can't really be described as only, if ever, occurring in a disinterested tenor, a tone that the text's routinely engrossed narrator constantly seems to resist. In that sense, the narrative pleasure that builds toward Juan's and Julia's first kiss, and the commercial anticipation of its graphic disclosure, is exactly the reflexive form of the poem's study of this dynamic. That pleasure and the mode of knowing that pleasure, cultural studies and its object of study, are both entwined in this narrativizing process.

Second, as Juvenal's association with Sappho also emphasizes, the question of the masses' desire is radically connected to the question of the body, its representations and actions.[28] *Don Juan* is, of course, heavily invested in the topos of somatic pleasure, in registers that range from the romantic and sublime to the lewd and obscene. One might want to enforce strictly the divisions between the vulgar and otherworldly in Byron's use of eros, although unsettling those divisions seems to be as much a constant impetus in his poem as ratifying them.[29] This and the last section of the chapter will indeed consider the question of the pornographic in *Don Juan*. However, the more relevant distinction underlying what follows will be whether the final horizon of the libidinal drive, in and beyond *Don Juan*, is without a doubt the commodity form.

We might thus observe that, for a work that so vigorously seems to endorse how radically impossible life, or reading, is without the sensual body, whether it be eaten, pampered, or sold, or made the agency of such events, *Don Juan* also has its own key moments of sober restraint, where the libidinal consummation of graphic, commodity eros is intriguingly denied. I especially refer to how Juan never quite gets to kiss Julia on the lips in any literally depicted way, even as, in the early cantos, the narrative twice especially builds up to this first expression of passion, once with Juan and Julia, and once with Juan and Haidée.

The latter pair, of course, do get to kiss, during Haidée's premonition of death in Lambro's house, and earlier on the beach, for several stanzas, in a moment of exquisite, ethereal sensation that seems to bend both time and space for the couple. Indeed, Christopher Nyrop cites their beach kiss as exemplary of "the kiss of love" in his classical philological study of this particular act; both he and Daniel Cottom also associate kissing with the beginning of civilization, which certainly dovetails with our own reading of Juan and Haidée's eros beginning culture anew.[30] Given also how much Juan and Haidée's story is simultaneously one of commodified desire, it seems appropriate that their kissing should be literally presented, signaling the poem's reflexive inception of culture, or originary moment of cultural study, as we have limned those terms.

And yet the graphic nature of Juan and Haidée's kissing is much less vivid than earlier moments in English literature, such as the Restoration lewdness of William Wycherly's *The Country Wife* (1675), when Mrs. Pinchwife describes being kissed by another character: "Why, he put the tip of his tongue between my lips, and so mousled me."[31] Certainly, this impulse away from the gross body could speak to the dialectic between body and spirit that for some time has been identified in Byron's work, as well as to Cottom's point about the kiss of civilization being an "an act in which we must imagine that slime is sublimated: that something base is turned into something higher" (181).[32] But it's also worth observing how Juan and Haidée's kisses are, oddly enough, *singular* moments in *Don Juan*; their kissing is in fact the exception to the rule in the poem, a fact that brings the less than fully flagrant nature of Juan and Haidée's kissing in line with how the non-kiss of Juan and Julia emblematizes the problematic of graphic display, the collision between the figurative and the literal, in Byron's poem.[33]

Bodies touch and are looked upon lovingly in Byron's epic work, and they even commingle in chaste sleep and bawdy subterfuge; but the initial graphic consummation of eros in *Don Juan*, typified before anything else by the kiss, oftentimes occurs elsewhere, or "else when," in the plot. As my references to Wycherley, Nyrop, and Cottom imply, such lacunae do conceivably place *Don Juan* in a much larger narrative about the graphic representation of amorous, romantic, and lewd passion in British literary texts, the generic codes and conventions that signal consummation up to, during, and beyond this point in British literary history for a variety of print media. The well-known pirating of *Don Juan* by London's radical publishing underground brings another level of inquiry to this subject, by inviting us to consider the continuity among Byron's poem, its knockoffs, and the seditious and pornographic material sold by the likes of William Benbow, John Ducombe, and William Dugdale.[34] We are in effect placed in the same position as Juan's tutors, who must find continuity in an array of heterogeneous, although overlapping, writings. (Indeed, isn't canto 1's appendix in some searching way a prescient allegory about how external social forces create out of such diverse material the very category of *literature*?) Yet that very connection between Byron's poetry and such underground publications, so historically existent, also brings us back to the relative absence of the kiss in *Don Juan*, insofar as the outrageous bravo of Byron's poem can be said to be proto-pornographic in pretty much only a non-literal sense: decidedly Satanic as it might be in so many ways, *Don Juan* in one manner isn't very graphic at all.[35]

Thus, as important as the material histories of erotic representation in British literature might be, the *inner* logic of Byron's poem speaks to the question of the kiss in an especially crucial and emphatic fashion. Indeed, the Planck-like operation of the kiss, which in canto 1 suddenly veers off into the immensity of the text's narrative distance at the very moment when the poem can come no closer to the kiss's realization, and the characters' lips no nearer together, seems a highly fitting emblem for the capriciousness of Byronic desire in the poem, whose influence pervades the text at a number of levels, but whose presence can never be quite categorically defined at any one point. The absence of the kiss thus speaks directly to the character of both traditional readings of the Byronic persona and Christensen's classically postmodern rendition of Byronic strength; like the signifier *Byron*, the kiss, for all its multifarious effects, oftentimes seems withheld, in reserve, or concealed, literally or figuratively out of sight. As important, the particular circumstances by which canto 1 evades the kiss tellingly complicate in striking fashion the very model of *Don Juan* as proto-cultural study that this chapter has thus far tried to describe.

The poem's most famous reflexive instance of a non-kiss appears in the pivotal scene between Juan and Julia, where the latter's mental and emotional gyrations signify the couple's slow, Zeno-like progression toward erotic consummation:

And Julia sate with Juan, half embraced
    And half retiring from the glowing arm,
Which trembled like the bosom where t'was placed;
    Yet still she must have thought there was no harm,
Or else tw'ere easy to withdraw her waist;
    But then the situation had its charm,
And then-God knows what next—I can't go on;
I'm almost sorry that I e're begun. (1.115)

Two stanzas later there is a resolution of sorts, when Julia, "whispering 'I will ne'er consent'—consented" (1.117). But, of course, "consent" could refer to both the lovers' kiss (and so much more) *and* the act, or moment, *before* the kiss. "Consent" is the moment of the kiss *and* the figurative mark of the unavoidable delay before that moment, the allegory, in the strictly de Manian sense, of desire's consummation, and thus of the temporally impossible moment of consummation's literal happenstance.[36] In consenting, Julia at once kisses, although only by figure, and *prepares* to kiss, an act that does not in fact happen, in any literal way; Julia both kisses ("consents") and consents to a kiss that then doesn't occur in terms of what the poem actually displays—a predicament that temporally freezes Juan and Julia right before their kiss; consenting at the end of the stanza, they become, like Keats's famous "Grecian Urn" lovers, perpetually on the verge of, and thus always separated from, the satisfaction of their desire. *To kiss*, of course, is itself simply a figure for this consummation, which no amount of further graphic description can adequately capture or confirm. (When, either metonymically or metaphorically, is a kiss over?) Canto 1 emphasizes this inadequacy by not even giving us the kiss, by instead narrativizing our distance from any such temporal event by abruptly interrupting the scene and replacing it instead for sixteen stanzas with the narrator's musings on the pleasure principle, a reflexive meditation that occurs in some sort of *fabula* relation to the *syuzhet* of "several months" between Julia's "consent" and the canto's next episode in Julia's bedroom (1.121). The sixteen stanzas are thus at once a diversion from the kiss *and* its metonymic extension: *as* Byron's narrator muses, the lovers kiss. The narrator keeps "Julia and Don Juan still / In sight" during the stanzas' disquisition, a figuration of proximity that highlights the very temporal and literal conundrums ("still" and "sight") about representing desire that the non-kiss has unleashed (1.121).

The content of those musings also metaphorically connects the stanzas to the lovers' kiss, although, because of their literal diversion away from Julia's "consent," the stanzas equally stress the incompletion of this metaphoric drive. Still, as the lovers kiss elsewhere and else when, the narrator meditates on what is sweetest of all, "first and passionate love" (1.127). As the narrator's thoughts progress, it becomes clear that this is the aboriginal love that will also incite Juan and Haidée's own creation of society and consumer advancement; "first and passionate love," first individualized and then made collective through its association with Promethean fire (1.127), becomes nothing less than what Fredric Jameson has called the libidinal force driving human history, conceived here as the *technē* of human production, in both its revolutionary and nightmare forms (*Political*, 67–74, 281–99):

This is the patent-age of new inventions
    For killing bodies, and for saving souls,
All propagated with the best intentions;
    Sir Humphrey Davy's lantern, by which coals
Are safely mined for in the mode he mentions,

Timbuctoo travels, voyages to the Poles,
Are ways to benefit mankind, as true,
Perhaps, as shooting them at Waterloo. (1.132)

The non-kiss between Juan and Julia thus becomes the inciting spark of this libidinal force, much like the Althusserian "absent cause" that for Jameson structurally underwrites the narrative form of human social history (*Reading*, 186–89; *Political*, 25–38). The kiss is both ubiquitous and non-existent, expressed in the sixteen stanzas by the eros of human invention and the fact of syphilis, but also absent as a full presence, signaled, papered over, and deferred by Julia's consent and the narrator's thoughts on pleasure. Like Juan and Haidée, whose love becomes the story of the first human couple venturing beyond the cave into society and conspicuous consumption, Julia's (and Juan's) "consent," their entry into what Peter Manning has called "an ambiguous sophistication" (232), becomes the originating moment of intersubjectivity for the narrator's sixteen stanzas' worth of thoughts on collective human progress.

Qualifying our earlier claim about *Don Juan* and biopolitics, we can then see the intersubjective libido of the non-kiss as ratifying what Giorgio Agamben, following Aristotle, identifies as the passage from mere biological life (*zoē*) to the "way of living proper to an individual or group" (*bios*).[37] For Agamben, of course, the human life of *bios* is about the interconnection between law and violence and the rise of sovereign power through the "state of exception" (1–29). For Byron, however, the figure for this passage to human life is undeniably eros, the Promethean "first and passionate love" shaping and driving collective social desire. (This is not to say, of course, that social law does not play a part in the stories of Juan and each of his first two lovers, or that either narrative eschews any relation between the drive of pleasure and the structure of the law.) We can thus recuperate Jerome McGann's famous choice for the title of his early humanist study of Byron to denote once more human life in *Don Juan*, again incited by the lovers' embrace, although this time as the social adventure of *bios* defined against the mere event of *zoē*: "In short, it is the use of our own eyes, / With one or two small senses added, just / To hint that flesh is form'd of fiery dust" (2.212). Flesh in terms of its finite biological drives might simply be *zoē*, but human flesh as human social being is the "fiery dust" of *bios*.

"Fiery dust," however, is not the culmination of Juan and Julia's non-kiss, but the narrative consequence of Juan and Haidée's actually depicted embrace on the beach. "Fiery dust" results in fact from the narrator's attempt to explain why there is a Juan and Haidée after there has been a Juan and Julia; how one's "first and passionate love" can be superseded by the other's Edenic "first love" (2.189). The answer is less a consideration of any ontological paradox and more a musing quite in line with the commodity-saturated thematics of the Haidée and Lambro cantos. Specifically, for the narrator, the "inconstancy" that allows aboriginal love to shift from one object to another is the "perception of the beautiful" that "hint[s] that flesh is form'd of fiery dust" (2.211, 2.212). Given how these concluding stanzas in canto 2 signal Juan and Haidée's move from the cave to Lambro's house of goods, it is difficult not to see "inconstancy" also describing the exigencies of consumer desire, where consumer satisfaction, the consumption of the commodity object, leads to an always *first* encounter with *yet another* object of desire. (That in this scenario Juan's consumer inconstancy falls upon Julia and then Haidée simply reaffirms one of the two key roles women are conventionally believed to be given in the consumer economy, with Haidée's and Zoe's scopic, market desire for Juan representing the other possibility.) The narrator's description of the "Platonic" character of this "perception of the beautiful / A fine extension of the faculties" can therefore be understood as the idealized, or mystified, nature of the commodity object, beguilingly accessed through its sensual form, by the "use of our own eyes / With one or two small senses added" (2.212). The eros of "fiery dust" thus encapsulates the tension of a critical inquiry that is caught between two different articulations: the problematic of human history as the narrativization of *bios*, the proper way to live, and as the account of "fiery dust" as one more example of human life as the glittering spectacle of commodity reification.

The "perception of the beautiful" could also, of course, speak to another way the divide between the human and the non-human is calculated, that of the aesthetic. We can thus now return to our earlier consideration of how the non-functionality of both the commodity form and the aesthetic object makes them, in the Freudian sense, perverse. Both could be signified by the aboriginal eros structuring the Julia and Haidée stories, insofar as the pleasure of first love is also separated from any purpose or use value. Instead of leading to biological reproduction, the eros in these narratives configures pleasure for pleasure's sake alone. Indeed, following Linda Williams, we could note how the perversity of that eros could *already* be encapsulated in the kiss *by itself*, an erotic act whose oral pleasures do not need to lead to anything else, much less procreation.[38] From this perspective, the pre-lapsarian references in Haidée's narrative make her and Juan less literally the first parents and more readily a couple experiencing the radically singular, and therefore stringently impractical, character of their new love. Admittedly, however, canto 1's association of pleasure with Promethean fire does make first love instrumental, insofar as it initiates the history of human invention, creating commodities such as Sir Humphrey Davy's lantern, objects as intimately associated with social production as market consumption. Yet the narrator's culminating thoughts on this history, coming after the canto on Davy's lantern and the twin actions of "killing bodies and saving souls," unsettle the functionalist drive of this account:

> Few mortals know what end they be at,
> But whether glory, power, or love, or treasure,
> The path is through perplexing ways, and when
> The goal is gained, we die you know—and then—
>
> What then?—I do not know, no more do you—
> And so good night. (1.133–34)

Within the context of our argument, the polymorphous perversity of the lewd spatial pun on "end" merely reiterates the non-functionalist teleological perversity of pleasure underwriting this passage, if not Byron's entire poem (*Complete*, 678).[39] Either as *petit mort* or as individual or collective death, Thanatos overtakes Eros, and the poem has no answer for what the purpose of its history of invention, collective or personal, ultimately is; the poem has no counter for when its kiss is over. Pleasure incites a drive that conceivably subsumes the collective narrative of the human species, whose final value or end eludes the canto's narrator, who can only come up with a clichéd, properly metered response that immediately segues back into the plot of Juan, Julia, and Alfonso. Such a deep history, like deep ecology, unmoors itself from any (human) end, much like the radical Kantian aesthetics first deployed (or glimpsed) by Horkheimer and Adorno in their specific interrogation of the commodity form.[40] If, however, the non-use of the history of invention seems to operate at another level aside from the uselessness of commodity sensation, the question of the ends of pleasure as the very drive behind this history is also emphatically suspended. *Drive*, whether it be of *zoē* or *bios*, goes nowhere, causes nothing, besides itself. The narrator can decry pleasure's entanglements with the law ("'Tis pity . . . that / Pleasure's a sin, and sometimes sin's a pleasure" [1.133]) but can advance no further to offer a final point for that pleasure, or law. Pleasure, first love, as either commodity sensation, aesthetic perception, *or* the libidinal shape of history, cannot quite account for itself.

At this point, however, we might begin to feel the strain of using *aesthetics* as the term that most completely names the terrain of the problem that we have argued *Don Juan* inscribes. We could indeed do worse than to name the reflexive attempt either to master, think through, express, or outwit this demand for first love's accounting as the task of *philosophy*, a term that certainly overlaps with aesthetics but also imbricates other *récits* such as Agamben's grim tale of the move from biological life to the sovereign state. The problem of this move, distinction, or cut, generally understood as the one between nature and the *anthropos*, whether it actually exists as human being or something phantasmic and entirely else, and whether there is any real value that we can possibly assign it—to understand this as one of the main inquiries of philosophy seems intuitively correct. Appropriately enough, philosophy by name occurs in several places in *Don Juan*; tellingly, the narrator invokes the term at crucial moments in the stories of both Julia and Haidée. These moments coincide with the events of the non-kiss and kiss in cantos 1 and 2. With Juan and Haidée's kiss, philosophy appears as the policing principle that reprimands first love's roving "inconstancy," although philosophy is then subsumed by "inconstancy's" excuse, the Platonic, ideal irresistibility of love's object(s) of desire. With Juan and Julia, philosophy also materializes as pleasure's adversary; because of the narrative structure of the non-kiss, its appearance in canto 1 is especially apposite in terms of both philosophy's own undertaking and what philosophy interrupts.

I refer to the famous appearance of Plato right after the Zeno-like progression in stanza 115 toward Juan and Julia's erotic embrace:

> Oh Plato! Plato! you have paved the way,
> With your confounded fantasies, to more
> Immoral conduct by the fancied sway
> Your system feigns o'er the controlless core
> Of human hearts, than all the long array
> Of poets and romancers:—You're a bore,
> A charlatan, a coxcomb—and have been,
> At best, no better than a go-between. (1.116)

McGann and others have established the normative way to read these lines as emblematizing the poem's wrestling with the traditional division between body and spirit, with Byron's speaker attacking the hypocritical, repressive "fantasies" of Platonic love that actually lead to erotic consummation. Yet, while perhaps not repressive, the stanza's *own* formulation of this philosophical predicament (of whether the ideal can exist without the material) is itself an interruption of the graphic portrayal of Juan and Julia's first passionate kiss. Coming just before the stanza of Julia's "consent," the invocation of Plato cuts off, diverts us from, not only Juan's and Julia's own breathless pleasure in each other, but also the (commodified) pleasure of pleasure's own objectification through its vivid depiction. Of course, one could conceive of this break as itself part of the dynamics of commodity serialization, the deferral and thus consequent incitement of consumer desire. While this is true, the abrupt transferal of the question of "first and passionate love" to the realm of (mock) philosophical discussion is jarring enough to be read as an extended disruption, one that intimates that we have left behind in some basic way the commodified drive toward graphic pleasure that the poem has scripted up to the couple's non-kiss. Indeed, the ambiguous relation of this overlay between commercialized cliffhanger and philosophical intervention emblematizes in its own way the question structuring this entire chapter, of how really different these two narratives are as histories of the libidinal drive's dissatisfaction.

If, then, *Don Juan* elsewhere seems to be a study of objects and how they come to be or mean, of cultural goods and commodity forms, stanza 116 abruptly interrupts that inquiry through its own philosophical quarrel with Plato. A traditional formulation of this moment might call it the ironic assertion of the ideal against the ideal, on behalf of the material. We might indeed say that an argument for the body is made at the expense of the body, as long as we understand the mode of that imposition to be (the) spirit (of philosophy) not so much as any ontologically assured being, and more so as an alterity that marks the departure of both objectification and the study of objectification from their own reality, the subtending world of bodies and things.[41]

To call this moment of the non-kiss an alterity is to stress its narrative structure of interruption over, or *as* in fact, its content, as a *formal* ineluctability that would then fly away not only from the graphic world of objects but also from any normative claim of philosophy's truth. As such, this moment of the non-kiss inscribes the departure of what we today would more precisely call high theory from the anthropological study of market pleasure, cultural studies. Several points can be made about this event in *Don Juan*.

First, as we have seen, such an intervention does not mean that philosophy-as-theory simply realizes itself over what it has interrupted, insofar as the speaker's sixteen stanzas of meditation on pleasure might resonate with consumer deferral, stay entangled with questions about the glittering invention of consumable things, and also never reach any real conclusion about either the narrative's or pleasure's own drives. As noticeable an example of Romantic sobriety as this episode might be, it is also a complex one—there is no simple, sober moment of philosophy triumphantly rejecting the graphic kiss for philosophy's own higher purpose. Indeed, the body does seem to return at the end of the stanza, with the lewd pun of positioning Plato as a "go-between" (*Complete*, 706); the effect of the pun is radically indeterminate, however, with the body's existence in only a punning state installing a gap between the linguistic and the graphic that blunts both modes of representation. If the climactic positioning of "go-between" in the stanza replaces Juan and Julia's non-kiss as the place of consumer satisfaction, that very process of substitution and verbal play reiterates the interrupting force of the philosophic argument against Plato that the stanza first incites. The paronomasia acts not only as an extension of but also as a prophylactic against the literally graphic.

Indeed, "go-between" ultimately doesn't refer to a particular set or type of bodies, or even a particular act, given the various options different bodies between one another may generate.[42] "Go-between" ultimately signifies a formal relation—*the fact* of that relation, of figuration as, in the case of this stanza, the mediation of desire. Whether, as the narrator implies, this is merely an ancillary identity, or whether Juan and Julia actually need to have Plato between them to come together, or whether, of course, both conditions are true—these are questions that again repeat the fundamental intrusion of stanza 116 into the description of Juan and Julia's kiss, that still intractably exist in some form as a break or interruption of the scene's narrative drive. "Go-between"—like, in a sense, Plato himself—is the imposition of the figure of relation, whose very presence both establishes and disrupts the possibility of a seamless mediation, of exactly what the concluding pun's content and literal location in the stanza appear to enact.

Second, it would likewise be a mistake to assume that the process of objectification interrupted by the tirade against Plato does not carry its own phantasmic qualities, something that canto 2 showcases with its own invocation of Plato to delineate the commodity form of "fiery dust." In that further sense, the interruption of, or departure from, the kiss is also not absolute, insofar as the phantasm of high theory never completely leaves the objects of cultural study behind: whether the phantasm of the *anthropos* does in some way exceed the sensual attractions of the commodity form is precisely the problematic that both high theory and cultural studies share. The kiss, including Juan's and Haidée's, will always be, like every event, interrupted, regardless of philosophy's intervention, which means that philosophy will always be there. The interruption of the non-kiss is thus also an *illusion*, insofar as elsewhere, and else when, Juan and Julia are constantly kissing during the speaker's thoughts on "first and passionate love," incessantly interrupting and inciting the libidinal drive of history-as-invention.

Third, then, the question becomes less whether philosophy's obstruction of the kiss neatly divides one from the other and more how such an interruption might be redistributed among both sides of the divide: how such dispersal might work toward, in Rei Terada's words, "a philosophy of culture and a culturally historical philosophy."[43] In that sense, the formal structure of the interruption has the final say on its content, the relation between the material and the ideal, kiss and philosophy, cultural studies and high theory. Parabasis, the intrusion of the narrative aside, Schlegel's definition for irony and arguably the narrative mode of much of Byron's poem, might very well be the one crucial form by which high theory and cultural studies know each other, and themselves.[44]

Since literary criticism's fall into history in the early 1980s, the horizon for many scholars working in the academy has been to create readings that incorporate both historical and formalist (re: post-structuralist) procedures, in order, in other words, to read form and history together. Romanticism, as the very question of history's shape, or sensation, has been one especially auspicious object of study for such an endeavor. And still, just within the field of Romantic studies, certain bifurcations continue to appear, between history and language, or between history and theory, or, within theory itself, between cultural studies and high theory. These categories are certainly never simply symmetric. They are also never neat and always porous—like Romanticism's own historical shape, they remain spectral but, as important, intransigent in a way that equally speaks to their non-identity with themselves and to their antagonism with one another. Perhaps, then, *we can* read these oppositions together, *but not* in terms of a Romantic synthesis. As in the non-kiss of Juan and Julia, their relationship is the event of a parabasis, which means that our own intellectual apprehensions of Romanticism might be inevitably, against whatever intention we might have, paratactic in nature. We might certainly want to historicize the form of this relation, as much as one might want to do so for any synthesizing, or even hypotactic, method. Of, course, such an effort likewise demands a return to the Romantic question of the relation between history and its oppositions (to and within itself), of which the interrupted, ongoing desire of *Don Juan* provides one response. In Byron's poem, the coming to be of the *anthropos*, of history itself, is an interrupting aside, whose different representations can likewise only be realized in the same manner. In the early cantos, at least, the understanding of this moment of parataxis is itself discontinuous, structured by parabasis. The opposition between high theory and cultural studies becomes then the latest marker for this formal interruption, from which, arguably, much of what we call knowledge in the humanities is generated. Like Romanticism, unmotivated as a kiss, *and the story* of that kiss, there will never be enough thought, which means that there will never be enough interruption.

If our reading of the early cantos subsumes the aesthetic under philosophy-as-theory, the opposition between *high* theory and cultural studies curiously rearticulates theory as an operation configured much like a normative sense of aesthetics based on the division between the high and the low, the elite and the masses. This leads to the tempting but nevertheless unstable position of supporting a mode of critique radically associated with figuration by literalizing literature as an identity securely opposed to culture, the image, and the commodified object—the world of, in other words, cultural studies.[45] An incalculable effect, literature as the sensation of meaning, or, conversely, as de Man put it, as "the place where [the] negative knowledge about the reliability of linguistic utterance is made available," is mobilized to bind the borders that putatively separate literature and language from culture and from the physical sensation of the commodity object (*Resistance*, 10).[46] There are, of course, pertinent institutional reasons for such oppositions to appear, especially in a time of ongoing, reduced resources for the humanities. Still, theorizing such a predicament can only benefit from remembering the twin movements of literariness, of theory not simply supporting the edifice of literature but also actively involving itself in literature's destitution as a positively, and thus ironically, objectified identity.

I want to conclude this chapter by considering a moment that abuts asymmetrically upon this situation, the non-kiss that concludes canto 16. I refer to stanza 123's dramatic revealing of Lady Fitz-Fulke as the ghostly Black Friar, a scene that really now can't be read without some consideration of Christensen's tour-de-force interpretation of the episode. Fitz-Fulke's appearance culminates a progression that very much resonates with our analysis of canto 1, insofar as it too narrativizes pleasure in a teleological form, suspensefully progressing toward a culminating moment. Even more so than Juan and Julia's "first and passionate love," canto 16's movement is securely embedded within market exigencies, as Juan's readerly pleasure, like Austen's character Catherine Moreland's, forms around the playing out of a quintessential gothic plot, Juan spotting late at night in Lady Adeline's estate what must be the spectral figure of the Black Friar. Whether or not one subscribes wholeheartedly to Christensen's claim that the "social function of the gothic" is to divert us away from realizing that we are already in the "hell" of bourgeois culture that *Don Juan* relates, the gothic certainly cathects commodity pleasure in a readily identifiable mass commercial form (340, 344). As Christensen also observes, the entire narrative leading up to the revelation of the Friar is riddled by parabasis, to the point that the answer to who is interrupting whom (Juan, the narrator, or someone, or something, else) is radically confused (342). The final intervention as resolution makes things no less clear:

Back fell the sable frock and dreary cowl,
    And they revealed—alas! that e're they should!

In full, voluptuous, but *not o'ergrown* bulk,
The phantom of her frolic Grace—Fitz-Fulke! (16.123)

Christensen famously reads into the name of the lady a startling pun, whose non-heteronormative associations incite a tangle of meanings (a knot "*o'ergrown*") that produces before Juan's apprehensive eyes the gothic figure of "Gordonism," Byron as a mother's son before his "entitlement" as a strong Romantic author (339–51). As important for us is one of Christensen's preliminary observations, how it's radically unclear where "Fitz-Fulke!" comes from and who, or what, speaks her name (341). We can then observe how "Fitz-Fulke!" could be both a continuation of the plot and a narrative interruption of that plot. *As* a continuation of the plot, its exclamation could also be the plot's interruption. It could, as a nominalization, *be* the plot of Byron's poem, if not of Byron the author function altogether; as a non-biologically reproductive act of pleasure, it could be the perfect emblem for the normatively perverse non-purpose of desire in the poem.[47] Yet it could also in fact be another option for, and thus another version of, Plato as "go-between"; "Fitz-Fulke!" could thus be philosophy, and therefore a repetition of what interrupts Juan and Julia, although now even less tethered to any secure axis of the high versus the low, or sobriety versus pleasure. Like cultural studies, philosophy would then find itself entwined with what it studies, the fleshy, non-purposive drive of the *anthropos*.

Paratactic *and* hypotactic, "Fitz-Fulke!" is the cut that connects—a formal predicament that could also dovetail with Christensen's (non-)Oedipalized reading of (non-)aristocratic property. A paradoxically necessary parabasis, "Fitz-Fulke!" could name a person, a sexual practice, or an injunction. It thus functions as a hyper-non-kiss; it cuts off the commodified, formulaic pleasures of the gothic plot, leading into the hungover, radically ambiguous morning after of fragmentary canto 17. But it also could be a kiss of sorts, a violently erotic consummation of *something*, although again canto 17's language and fragmentary shape leave the identity of that event emphatically suspended. "Fitz-Fulke!" is a paronomasia structured by parabasis, a pun whose ironic reverberations never cease, continually leaving its meanings to interrupt one another. The history of invention coming after Juan and Julia's non-kiss thus does not quite come into intelligible, linear shape after "Fitz-Fulke!" Rather, the fragmentary form of canto 17 is the uncanny aftereffect of "Fitz-Fulke!"; *Don Juan* ends, in a sense, with this exclamation, with the fitful ripple of canto 17 carrying through the opaque afterlife of this interruption.

What accounts for this intrusion, however, and does it somehow exceed the horizon of the commodity form as calculable object and subject of study, and as modernity's sole vehicle of pleasure? When is the paronomastic poetic and when does it become pornographic—when does a figure become an image, and what account of history are we registering with such parsing?[48] These are certainly some of the questions that high theory, in its own self-representations against cultural studies, tries to answer. While, however, the complex, structural, and semantic knot of this interruption seems to evince "Fitz-Fulke!" as indeed the sensation, or imposition, of something we might want to call literariness, Byron's own tropology, codified by the non-kiss of philosophy in canto 1, also appears to invite us to think of this event as something besides the *high* of high theory. We might then finally ask, what might the operation of *low* theory look like, and what oppositions, if any, would it demand? And, given that this is Byron, after all, how might such an operation unsettle our own derivations, oftentimes gendered and method exacting, of Romanticism, high and low?

CHAPTER NINE

# Gothic Thought and Surviving Romanticism in *Zofloya* and *Jane Eyre*

In part III of this book we first considered the relation between Shelleyan Romantic prophecy and what earlier chapters called the non-phenomenal sensation of meaning; we then explored how Byronic representations of commodity culture constitute one place where the exigencies of Romanticism and physical sensation are expressed. The present chapter returns us to a consideration of the sensation of meaning, to ask in particular whether this sensation possibly, or inevitably, exists as *false* meaning—as an inauthentic, idolatrous event, or, in a word, ideology. The force of this question is heightened, of course, by how much present Romanticist scholarship has over the years understood Romanticism itself as an ideological phenomenon.[1] Arguably, the question of ideology has organized either positively or negatively much of the work done in Romantic—and, indeed, literary—studies for the last several decades. I say negatively as well as positively, since as much as readers have attempted to expose in various codified forms the ideological nature of literary works, others have attempted as forcefully to demonstrate the limited nature of ideological critique, the inability of any ideological hermeneutic to have the final say on the textual and historical energies of the literary and cultural documents being read. The present work's encounters with Hazlitt, Kant, Michaels, de Man, and Žižek all in different ways attest to this tension over ideology's powers.

Indeed, it might seem that these encounters have increasingly complicated the efficacy of ideology as a theoretical concept. If in chapter 1 Hazlitt's interpretive sobriety anticipated the critical suspicions of both ideological and deconstructive readings of Romanticism, chapter 2's understanding of Kantian genius adamantly distinguished between deconstruction's imposition of period identity and the assertion of truth underpinning the recognition of Romantic ideology. Even though we eschewed Michaels's claim about our post-ideological, post-historical world, our arguments with both his and Žižek's attempted exorcisms of ghosts appeared to confirm chapter 2's distinction. Yet the world that ghosts inhabit—the gothic—does not let go of truth so easily. Indeed, it would not be an exaggeration to say that the gothic is obsessed with the truth—of ghosts, of madness, of the supernatural, and of evil—which is to say that the gothic is obsessed with truth's other, the idolatrous realm of ideology.

As chapter 6 asserted, Romanticism and the gothic are intimately connected. While, then, the relation between Romanticism and ideology has organized a body of primary texts and critical readings with which Romanticists are all perhaps overly familiar, the connection between gothic writing and ideology provides us with a fresh way into considering the sensation of meaning as an ideological, or idolatrous, Romantic event. Specifically, two unlikely paired novels, Charlotte Dacre's *Zofloya; or, The Moor* (1806) and Charlotte Brontë's *Jane Eyre* (1847), place the gothic question of idolatry within the arc of apocalyptic and post-apocalyptic revolutionary survival, within two different visions of the impossible task of living in, and through, the nightmares of history. In *Jane Eyre*, moreover, the paradoxes of survival constitute the radically ambivalent response we have to Jane's fate, which in the history of the novel's reading becomes the calculable bifurcation of arguments for and against her ideological containment. Yet the gothic sensation of meaning in *Jane Eyre* also demonstrates that the question of modeling our reading habits on categories besides the idolatrous and non-idolatrous is a more complicated one than either proponents or opponents of ideological critique might think. As with chapter 2's reading of Kant, the category of the constative will be of key concern, although this time approached through the epistemological demands placed on the sensation of meaning by gothic's imagery and plots—through how the gothic translates the non-phenomenal sensation of meaning into the perceptual quandary of idolatry.

If, as chapters 4 and 5 argued, Romantic writers such as Wordsworth at times exhibit a gothic fascination with the sensation of meaning, what might the gothic itself tell us about the various dynamics and consequences of that fascination? We can in fact compare the situation of Wordsworth's narrator in "A Slumber" to a famous scene in a well-known, putatively late Romantic, late gothic work, one that also involves a speaker who reencounters a lost female intimate in a realm at first similar to the rocks, stones, and trees in "A Slumber":

> In every cloud, in every tree—filling the air and night, and caught by glimpses in every object by day—I am surrounded with her image! The most ordinary

> faces of men and women—my own features—mock me with a resemblance. The entire world is a dreadful collection of memoranda that she did exist, and that I have lost her![2]

Wordsworth's Lucy, of course, is securely within the earth, below the speaker, before either his thoughts or the poem's actions dizzyingly lift her into planetary orbit, famously disrupting the spatial coordinates of above and below that an interred body implies. In this passage from *Wuthering Heights*, however, Heathcliff opines how Catherine has immediately been disseminated into the vertigo and constant present of everywhere, into the sky and fauna of nature and then also among the demotic, social world of human visages. Also in contrast to Wordsworth, there seems to be no ambiguity about the affective tone of this encounter: Heathcliff is tormented, mocked, by the sensation of Catherine still somehow in this world, even as such "memoranda" also emphatically convey that he has irrevocably "lost her." Raymond Williams's startling reading of this passage focuses on exactly how Catherine comes to be both intractably lost and present in this scene:

> "Image," "resemblance": that is the displacement, the mourned loss. What [Heathcliff] feels is so ordinary that we need no special terms for it. It is that finding of reality in the being of another which is the necessary human identity: the identity of the human beyond the creature; the identity of relationship out of which all life comes. Deprived of this reality there is indeed only image and resemblance. . . . A necessary experience of what it is to be human—of that life desire, that relationship which is given—is frustrated, displaced, lost in those specific difficulties; but is then in a profoundly convincing way—just because it is necessary—echoed, reflected back, from where it now exists only in spirit: the image of the necessary, seen moving beyond that composed, that rearranged life; the reality of need, of the human need, haunting, appearing to, a limited scaled-down world.[3]

I call Williams's reading "startling" because its Marxist humanist language nevertheless works toward carrying out a political reading of the sign. The poverty of both "image and resemblance" in securing a non-alienated intersubjective existence for Heathcliff—and, by extension, all his compatriots in northern England experiencing the corrosive, destabilizing effects of early nineteenth-century capitalist modernity—constitutes the very alienation that Heathcliff suffers as an atomized, wounded human subject. Williams also holds out the spectral nature of the image as conveying something restorative beyond the horizon of this "limited scaled-down world," something beyond the historical contingency of the new set of capitalist relations that Terry Eagleton famously describes crashing down upon both the Grange and Heights.[4] Yet the power of Williams's diagnosis comes in part from a certain undecidability in emphasis, on either the tangibility of the displaced "reality of need" or the elusive nature of that displacement, something only existing "in spirit," as an echo and a haunting. Without doing much violence to Williams's language, one can see his reading registering in Heathcliff's vocabulary of image and resemblance *either* the future signs of a world beyond the minatory social relations of *Wuthering Heights or* the unavoidably simulated nature of this wished-for world. If Williams's allegiance explicitly lies with the former, the force of the passage still arises out of the implicit presence of the latter in his formulation. Williams's phrase "the image of the necessary" can then be understood not simply in terms of human affective need but also as the aboriginal assertion of a dialectically determinate history; yet as an "image" circulating among both the natural and social worlds, the "necessary" might just be that, a simulacrum whose inauthentic existence actually delineates the capitalist (post) modernity that Emily Brontë's characters come to inhabit.

Resemblance, then, carries a certain charge in Williams's reading of this scene in *Wuthering Heights*, one that overlaps with but also complicates what occurs in Wordsworth's meditations on resemblance in nature. The Heathcliff passage exhibits a gothic sensibility not only fascinated by the possibility of beholding meaning in a world given to us by our senses, but also alert to, indeed oppressed by, resemblance's estrangement from itself, by the inherent self-distance involved in any identity generated by the twinning of sensation as both phenomenal experience and evasive linguistic event. As Jerrold E. Hogle has extensively argued, the simulacrum, one way to signify the inauthentic imagery of such sensation, structures the gothic since its inception in the eighteenth century, starting in such places as *The Castle of Otranto* with Walpole's ghostly contraptions of giant armor ("*Frankenstein*," 176–210). Of course, Hogle's point is to show how the gothic simulacrum disrupts any easy opposition between the authentic and inauthentic, as well as between the ludic and oppressive, that might underwrite a critical evaluation of the gothic's affective and ontological status. Yet this is precisely where a certain interplay between the meaning of the gothic and the question of the ideological emerges, where the latter can be seen as gaining its pointedness and alacrity precisely through the gothic encounter with a world perhaps sublimely full, or prosaically devoid, of design. In the gothic, something finds its shape in the perceived distance (perhaps also conceived as impossible to overcome) between the sensation of resemblance and what truly is; that emerging figure, which carries with it the language of truth, falsity, and value, we today call the ideological. In the gothic, the possibility of epistemological misprision, the consequence of such an ominous gap, becomes the alibi for the question of ideology's relation to the constative, at once bracing and substituting for, and thus deferring, that inquiry. In this scenario, the sensation of meaning finds itself bound to a language of both physical perception and constative discovery. The possibility of perceiving something falsely both validates and stands in for the existence of truth.

Even more so than in *Wuthering Heights*, this dynamic is vigorously thematized in explicit, reflexive fashion by another Brontë's famous novel. Others have also sensed this distinction, insofar as the Brontë text gathering the most critical attention the past several decades has arguably been sister Charlotte's *Jane Eyre*, a text that especially seems to invite pointed consideration of its ideological containment by a variety of nineteenth-century historical forces, from those of British capitalism, patriarchy, and imperialism to the English novel itself as an active social institution. Indeed, Charlotte's own comments about the raw nature of Emily's literary powers mark that very same distinction, where the active volatility of *Wuthering Heights* can be contrasted to the stricter adherence of *Jane Eyre* to the dialectical interplay among the novel's yearnings and its claustrophobic and agoraphobic impulses, a structure then especially conducive to questions of ideological control and restraint, either in their more overtly Marxist or more New Historical, Foucaultian forms.[5] If Jane appears to be an exemplary case of what Amanda Anderson has called an "aggrandized form of agency," much of Jane's representative power comes from the open question of ideology's role in shaping that agency.[6]

*Jane Eyre* has a number of obvious gothic traits. But the novel specifically explores the relation between the gothic and ideological and reflexively formulates its own discourse of ideology through its acute investigation into the idolatrous possibilities of secular love. If Heathcliff is tortured by the resemblance of trees, sky, and faces to Catherine, the (world-historical) need she represents is questioned neither by him nor Williams; that in itself is markedly different from Jane's own volatile epistemological disposition toward Rochester and St. John throughout much of Charlotte's novel. Whether love exists between Jane and either of these other characters, and whether such love is something besides idolatry—these are the very questions of the gothic romance that Jane constantly asks herself and that generate much of the gothic excess of affect that runs through the text's plot. To read *Jane Eyre* through the tools of an ideological critique is thus, in a sense, to try to do one better than Jane, to question her desire and its sociohistoric conditions better than she does herself.

It is, then, not simply a question of noting how much Jane's first person narrative holds an especially cathected place in the creation of modern female subjectivity in the English novel, but also seeing how that narrative utilizes its own vocabulary of proto-ideology to record and achieve that subjectivity. Arguably more so than *Wuthering Heights*, with its commitment to the gothic vertigo of a titular place anachronistically and affectively beyond the control of changing nineteenth-century English modernity, *Jane Eyre* allegorizes the very mechanisms of ideological containment, of uncanny domesticity, by which it has been particularly read in the latter half of the twentieth and the first part of the twenty-first century. Specifically, as much as the Heathcliff passage describes the gothic anxieties that resemblance and image can produce, *Jane Eyre* especially demonstrates how those trepidations reflect upon the relation between ideology and epistemological lapse.

Before fleshing out this relation, we need to consider one further point about our reading of the Heathcliff passage, how it putatively comes from a late Romantic, late gothic text. This assertion is commonplace among ways to designate the work produced by all the Brontë sisters; equally familiar is the assertion of its infelicity. The question for us, however, is how such genealogical debates affect our sense of the proto-ideological inquiry in *Jane Eyre*.

Responses to this question have varied, not only in their theses but also in their formulations of how Romanticism, the gothic, and social possibility—the prospect of the non-ideological—connect in Charlotte's work. In many well-known scenarios—in Virginia Woolf's famous critique of Charlotte and in the searching, historicizing academic scholarship on nineteenth-century fiction in the 1980s and early 1990s—Romanticism and the gothic, sometimes together and sometimes not, are envisioned as either contained or irrepressible features of the text, with both their regulation and activity signs of either the novel's collusion with or resistance to various ideological horizons.[7] Especially apposite for us, however, is the injunction by Cora Kaplan and others to take seriously the charge of "moral Jacobinism" that was leveled at the novel by a contemporaneous reviewer, along with the famous indictment of another such reader, Elizabeth Rigby, of the book's seditiousness.[8] Kaplan, writing in response to Woolf, sees the gothic intrusion of "Grace Poole's" manic laugh in the text as punctuating the fleeting expression of a revolutionary Romanticism that cannot help connect, no matter how inchoately, "political rebellion and gender rebellion" (174). My interest, however, lies not in simply identifying the revolutionary elements in Charlotte's text, but also in noting a certain dissonance among such features that paradoxically enables a more precise historical rendering of the gothic moments of the work.

Accomplishing this does first mean considering how Romanticism as a revolutionary, and counterrevolutionary, topos maps onto the novel. Recently reflecting on his thirty-year-old study of the Brontës, Eagleton provides a highly suggestive template for narrativizing that topos:

> The Brontës, I suppose, could be described as late Romantic writers, which is more than just a comment on chronology. They emerged as authors towards the end of the great Romantic epoch around the turn of the nineteenth century, and towards the beginning of industrial capitalist England. As such, they were transitional figures, flourishing as they did in the overlap between an era of high Romantic, revolutionary drama, and the birth of a new, crisis-racked form of industrial society. It was a society which had its origin in the factories and cotton mills of the Brontës' own region (the north of England), but was eventually to spread itself across the planet.
>
> The sisters, then, were writing at the source of global industrial society. (xi)

For Eagleton, the Brontës are "transitional figures" whose late Romanticism is a hybrid sign of a larger historical formation, a long nineteenth century involving the mutation of social antagonisms and relations first exploding in the great revolutions of the Romantic period and later consolidating in the Victorian era into what would soon be recognized as "global industrial society." One could qualify or perhaps even dispute Eagleton's characterization of this historical identity; what interests me, however, is his explicit distinguishing of two parts to this event, brought together in the "transitional" late Romantic nature of the Brontës, and the terms by which the two parts might reflexively designate themselves and this larger identity. Using Eagleton, let us call the first part *revolution* and the other *global industrial society*. Revolution and its other, counterrevolution, would designate the first phase of this identity, the *Romantic* in late Romantic. Global industrial society would designate the second phase, the "beginning of industrial capitalist England" both marked by and supplanting the *late* in that same term.

Of course, rebellion and revolution do not simply go away during the second phase, as the English Chartist movement and France in 1848 amply illustrate. Likewise, it is not as if the shaping of global industrial society waited patiently until after the earlier Romantic moment of revolution; the rise and acceleration of such a society could in fact be understood as articulating itself exactly through such prior revolutionary, and reactionary, events. Yet Eagleton's in many ways standard narrative gains its analytical power from the sense that at some intransigent level revolution was indeed what was occurring in the first phase of this historic identity, and that the creation of a "new, crisis-racked form of industrial society" was fundamentally what happens in the second stage. This power is certainly about the persuasive force of particular historical narratives, such as the post-revolutionary, nineteenth-century alliance between the English middle class and landed gentry against the working class. But it is also about how such narratives are themselves caught up in the collision of different discursive fields (*revolution* and *global industrial society*) that works itself out in a complex rendering of historical representation and subsumption, as well as retroactive and vatic projection. This condition does not simply describe, moreover, the nature of our own present historical viewing; rather, this predicament also constitutes the reflexive languages of the viewed event itself and the self-referential articulations of its rendition—what we in fact today designate by such codes as the arc from revolution to industrialization and the Romantic to the Victorian, or the Brontës as "late Romantic" transitional figures and the Romantic character of Charlotte's early Victorian text.

Indeed, *Jane Eyre* can be read as working out this collision in all its dissonance through its self-conscious, gothic thematizing of the proto-ideological. We can gain a better perspective on this dynamic by first comparing *Jane Eyre* to a text that unproblematically belongs, chronologically at least, to the earlier nexus of Romanticism, gothic, and revolution, Charlotte Dacre's *Zofloya*. Dacre's work is important precisely to the degree that it revolves around the quintessential gothic problem of seeing past the illusory to the truth and configuring that issue in terms of historically specific ideological actions.

Admittedly, anxiety over epistemological deception defines the gothic so thoroughly that the specific question of the ideological could conceivably be folded into this larger problematic. Daniel Cottom has in fact suggestively argued for locating the origins of the gothic in Descartes's *Meditations*, in especially the philosopher's famous suspicion about the "evil genius" controlling and tormenting the Cartesian ego.[9] More typically, one could point out the anti-Catholic iconoclasm structuring much of the eighteenth- and early nineteenth-century gothic's interest in the menacing monasteries and nunneries of an imagined medieval Italian landscape, as well as the standard definition of the female gothic as a narrative formulaically about a heroine working her way through the temptation of perceiving the supernaturally irrational where the rational actually exists. This is where Eagleton's topos is instructive, however, insofar as it reminds us of other more immediate historical transcodings through which the question of gothic perception might make itself known. I refer to a certain revolutionary—or, more precisely, reactionary—language about the dangers of idolatry operating in Dacre's thought experiment on the origins of feminine evil. Specifically, the malign nature of the novel's main character, Victoria, is delineated by an Edmund Burkean, counterrevolutionary language that equates epistemological mystification with both cognitive failing and ethical turpitude.

As has been observed since its scholarly recovery in the 1990s, *Zofloya* stands out among the generation of gothic romances produced in the 1800s and early 1810s as a text overflowing with a variety of transgressive energies.[10] Indeed, one might be tempted to see in it and *Jane Eyre* an allegory of the relation of Romanticism to Victorian culture, with the former's more atavistic, more explicit rendering of its themes—anxiety over and fascination with the sexualized and racialized body, the relationship of female assertion and a sadomasochistic plotting—sublimated by the latter into the more realistic conventions of the Victorian novel. That and other points of comparison—the stupefaction readers expressed over the gender of the creator of the sensationalized material in *Zofloya* versus the mounting suspicions readers had about Currer Bell—make Dacre's novel seem a hyperbolic, cartoonlike precursor to Charlotte's text, one exemplar of the gothic dream material from which *Jane Eyre* fashions its own waking, conscious sense of reality. As has also been noted, the explicitness of the material in *Zofloya*, along with its singular manipulation of gothic formulas, makes it something of an anomalous example of the commercial gothic, transgressing traditional distinctions between the male and female gothic. More like M. G. Lewis's *The Monk* than Radcliffe's *The Mysteries of Udolpho*, Dacre's novel vigorously problematizes settled notions of the literary history of English women's writing, with its heroine having "more in common with the heroines of the Marquis de Sade or . . . Lewis than with those of . . . Radcliffe, Charlotte Smith, or Jane Austen."[11]

One standard yet by no means exclusive distinction between the male and female gothic involves the latter's epistemological association with the "explained supernatural": while the male gothic trades in the graphic exhibition of its monstrous, oftentimes-supernatural worldview, its female counterpart exploits the suspense involved in having its heroine ultimately discern between the false and actual *syuzhets* structuring the narrative progress of the plot.[12] Contrary to this tendency in the female gothic of explaining away supernatural occurrences, *Zofloya* appears to luxuriate in the overt display of adulterous and violent desires, organized by a demonic presence. Like Ambrosio in *The Monk*, Victoria discovers that a satanic messenger, the North African servant Zofloya, has manipulated those desires. Dacre's antiheroine therefore in many ways resembles the central male protagonist of this classic male gothic, to which *Zofloya* oftentimes refers. Indeed, Victoria's odd morphing into a Zofloya look-alike toward the end of the book could mean something else besides the fairly obvious psychosexual identification with, and projection of, racialized, phallic alterity; it could also be explained as a wry acknowledgment by the novel of the gendered character of generic pressures, which literally begin to mold Victoria into a bodily form better suited for the desires and actions of a male gothic protagonist.

That being said, it also becomes highly difficult *not* to compare Victoria's epistemological deception of herself and others with the perceptual errors tempting the protagonist of the explained supernatural in a female gothic. Women like Victoria do exist, of course, in Radcliffe novels; they do so, however, as secondary characters, like Madame Laurentini in *Mysteries*, as examples of what *not* to do in a Radcliffe plot, of women who have given into the irrational, the illusory, and the promiscuous. What, then, to make of a central female character in a Romantic-era gothic story, who fails to get things right, who incorrectly perceives the workings of the outer world, and thus of her own mind?

Radcliffe's works have especially oftentimes been understood in terms of a larger narrative struggle over the character of modernity, of negotiating the best impulses of the Enlightenment in order to create a world of (feminine) reason that has banished the irrational and the superstitious; their medieval settings constitute the medium through which this enlightened vision of the present might be achieved. But by using the conventions of the male supernatural gothic, Dacre's *Zofloya* ensures that no rational modernity can be an option in the text; the supernatural presides over the world, and reason is powerless to banish it. If reason's point is to exorcise, surpass, or supplant superstition, and superstition doesn't really exist because the supernatural is real, then reason doesn't really factor into the narrative dynamic, historical or otherwise, that *Zofloya* creates.[13] (Indeed, the morally innocent characters in Dacre's novel appear to derive their goodness from the stock values of the feudal imaginary that they chronologically live in, fifteenth-century Italy. One of the fascinating features of Radcliffe thus becomes how her characters can mediate between a similar imaginary and one where they can be conceived as modern—enlightened—beings.) The pressing question for us, then, is what the foreclosure of the option of a rational modernity might mean for a gothic novel coming out in 1806.

The inquiry is connected to another question *Zofloya* asks: what is the origin of feminine evil? Gothics oftentimes have a stock answer, a natural feminine weakness that tautologically equates evil and femininity with the darkness of natural division, aggressive sexuality, and death. At first glance, Victoria's character might seem very much to support this conventional understanding, with the additional subversive twist of exploiting such (super)natural evil in order to create an actively strong, feminine agency. Yet the novel's transgressive energies are also involved in a complicated interplay, one avidly studied in the eighteenth century, between natural tendency and social influence. The hyperbolic character of Victoria's graphic crimes, coupled with her gender, reinvigorates the question of her upbringing, a well-recognized convention in the gothic plot, with a singular pertinence. Indeed, part of the fascinating ungainliness of Dacre's novel lies in the tension between the wild nature of Victoria's crimes and the text's early, almost clinical, scholarly consideration of a girl gone wrong. As David Brookshire notes, the appeal of the novel's opening lines to a historian's allegiance to the tracing of cause and effect in human behavior could have been at home in either La Mettrie's *L'Homme Machine* or Holbach's *Système de la Nature*.[14] How, aside from satanic malfeasance, does Victoria get to the point of drugging her sexual prey and imprisoning and stabbing her sexual rival? The very emphatic nature of her agency, heightened by her exaggerated, lurid embrace of deviance and violence, makes the rendition of how she was reared all the more a point of focus.

Of course, Victoria is actually characterized by the lack of a responsible upbringing, as her mother abandons her and her brother after an adulterous affair, and the mother's lover poisons her father. The question of nurture is, however, linked to the issue of nature, since the mother Laurina's one flaw, the "error" by which she is seduced, is vanity, the key primal fault shared by Victoria and a number of other characters, both male and female, in the text (57). In a parody of Mary Wollstonecraft, the absence of a proper parental education leads Victoria to an unregulated life of the passions; this is, however, less a seduction away from Victoria's innate reason (as it is conventionally understood with Wollstonecraft) and more about the undisciplined encouragement of her native vanity.[15] In that sense, Victoria's slide toward evil could just as well be a testimony to the educational philosophies of Wollstonecraft's simultaneous nemesis and inspiration in *A Vindication of the Rights of Woman*, Jean-Jacques Rousseau, with Victoria an example of what occurs when the warnings of the tutor in *Emile* go unheeded and the ostentatious vanities of the young female are not discouraged by the adults around her.[16]

Yet *Zofloya* also has fun with the caricature of Rousseau as generic Enlightenment thinker through the person of Victoria's lover and husband, Il Comte Berenza, who is first introduced as a "liberal philosopher" who comes to Victoria's home to "analyze its inhabitants, and to discover . . . whether the mischief they had caused . . . arose from a selfish depravity of heart, or was induced by the force of inevitable circumstances: [he visits Victoria's home] to investigate character, and to increase his knowledge of the human heart" (58).[17] Indeed, Berenza imagines a relation to the much younger Victoria that is in fact a patriarchal attempt at Rousseauist, Enlightenment pedagogy, relying "upon the power he believed himself to possess over the human mind for modeling her afterwards, so as perfectly to assimilate to his wishes. Her wild and imperious character he would have essayed to render noble, firm, and dignified, her *fierté* he would have softened, and her boldness checked" (59).

Dacre at this point already indicates the misbegotten vision of this "misguided philosopher," who mistakes Victoria's beauty and vivaciousness for her inner character, "so unconscious is the heart of man of the springs of its own movements" (59), a joking reference if not specifically to Rousseau's watchmaking heritage then to the mechanist strains in Enlightenment thought. Blind to the vanity underpinning his own "philosophic mind," Berenza turns out to be no match for Victoria, who ends up poisoning him because of her lust for his brother, all the while deceiving him in terms of her professed love and loyalty to him (59). A good portion of the book is actually devoted to the emotional seduction of Berenza by Victoria, who, in order to marry the Comte, needs to convince him of both her love and the success of his philosophic teachings: "She saw only that it would be necessary and politic to answer his sincere and honorable love at least with the *appearance* equally ardent and sincere. . . . Artifice on her side, and natural self-love on his, would easily make him attribute [her behavior] to the effects of a violent and concealed love: thus would . . . the hesitations of Berenza [be] at an end" (98). The passage in which Berenza finally succumbs to Victoria's deception is particularly telling:

> His ideas underwent a wonderful, but natural revolution . . . his heart now throbbed with excessive tenderness, and now ached with compunctious pangs, that he could ever have deemed unworthy of his honorable love the creature before him, shining superior in a glory emanating from *herself*!—the creature to whom he now thought himself inferior! So complete and powerful a dominion had the act of Victoria obtained over his mind, that his *proud* and dignified attachment, softened into a doting and idolatrous love. (137)

Given Berenza's pitiful fate, this "revolution" turns out to be neither "wonderful" nor "natural"; it *is*, however, a revolution, as it marks a radical change in the hierarchy of class and gender underwriting the relationship between Victoria and Berenza. Up to this point Berenza has resisted making Victoria his wife, even though she is his mistress, because of the dishonor that Victoria's mother had brought to her family. Love, or the contrived illusion of love, becomes the means by which Victoria resolves this social conflict in her favor. The passage describes Berenza's love, moreover, not as an enlightened moment of the Radcliffean sublime, but as a surfeit of bodily and emotional sensation: "excessive tenderness" and "ach[ing] with compunctious pangs." Its high-pitched excess a sign of its constative infelicity, Berenza's epistemological condition is explicitly described as a "doting and idolatrous" one, with Victoria's "dominion" over him signaling the upending change in both his mental state and the material relations of power between the couple.

Victoria's strength, then, is explicitly associated with her ability to deceive others, a talent fantastically literalized by the seductive potion that she gives Hernriquez, Berenza's brother, in order to convince him that she is his virginal love, Lila. As conventional as this association of feminine sexuality and perceptual manipulation is, so too is the fate of Victoria, who finds herself the ultimate victim of such deceptive practices, falling under the spell of Zofloya and then literally tumbling to her death for her sins. Yet Dacre gives this familiar plotting of a wayward, self-deceiving feminine mind a further resonance early on in the initial encounter between Berenza and Victoria, when the book describes her increasingly aberrant disposition in terms of how "her ideas wildly wandered, and to every circumstance and situation she gave rather the vivid colouring of her own heated imagination, than that of the truth" (59). This quote could describe the woeful mind of a young girl exposed to too many romances, gothic tales, and other forms of sensational literature, something that many writers, including Wollstonecraft, bemoaned.[18] But in *A Vindication* Wollstonecraft primarily targets someone else as the exemplar of the solipsistic, sensationalized mind, in a famous phrasing that Dacre's own language echoes: "[Rousseau] debauched his imagination, and reflecting on the sensations to which fancy gave force, he traced them in the most glowing colours, and sunk them deep into his soul" (91).[19]

This description of Rousseau, as the talisman of a masturbatory, fictive, and rampant imagination, was a familiar one across the English political spectrum, to both Wollstonecraft and her reactionary opponents. Together, Berenza and Victoria thus depict two complimentary, pejorative views of a figure well known to the early nineteenth-century English public, the Rousseauist Enlightenment philosopher whose own vanity dangerously blinds him to the limits and dangers of his philosophical vision, and that same subject as the hypocritical master of epistemological (self-)deception and undisciplined, self-indulgent desire, whose appetites lead to his own destruction and that of all those around him. Such a figure is ultimately marked by his or her own ruinous self-deception, as Victoria ends up in the same idolatrous position with Zofloya as Berenza does with her. That the last part of Dacre's novel actively problematizes its earlier thought experiment involving Victoria's education, with her brother charging that a "mother's example" could never have simply left Victoria's malign character "virtuous," makes the novel's depiction of putatively failed Enlightenment thought all the more accurate (247). Contrary to Berenza's own pedagogical beliefs, the "depravity" of Victoria, whose "base mind was naturally evil," is not something that can be cured by societal intervention; such a belief is, as *Zofloya* exuberantly demonstrates, a fatal vanity for all concerned (247).

A sentimentalist philosophy arrogant in its ability to understand and change the world; a figure of increasingly unrestrained desire adept at manipulating reality for her own promiscuous purposes; a revolution of mind and social relations described in terms of heightened sensation and idolatry—these constitute the British reactionary topos of not only a dangerously failed Enlightenment but also the outcome of that failure, the ostensive catastrophe of the French Revolution. As such, the key figure for much of the discourse on evil in *Zofloya* is not the radical Wollstonecraft but the counterrevolutionary Burke, who most famously codified the anti-Jacobin attack on France in his *Reflections*, explicitly connecting the epistemological fallacies of the Enlightenment to the ethical depravity, the "monstrous fiction" of the Revolution (124). As W. J. T. Mitchell has shown, the modern understanding of ideology, which includes Marx's own, is as much—if not more—related to Burke's iconoclasm as it is to Napoleon's original expression of the term (*Iconology*, 135, 143–49).[20] To this attack upon the misbegotten senses we might add other points of connection between counterrevolutionary tropology and Victoria's story: the way she turns into a gender-bending, manlike figure and how she explicitly says that she is escaping from a "tyrant" (her ward, Signora di Modena), only to be called the same thing later in the novel (83).[21] This is not to say that there are no other discourses subtending the evils of idolatry in Dacre's book: Milton, Bunyan, and, indeed, Wollstonecraft all figure in how *Zofloya* imagines its sensationalized narrative. But, conversely, the specific formulation of evil as an epistemological problem, of perceiving or sensing the world incorrectly, is more than simply a sign of the characters' aristocratic decadence; it is also, paradoxically, the mark of their revolutionary deviance.

What, then, to make of this anti-Jacobin discourse of idolatry in Dacre's book? Such a finding might certainly complicate the association of *Zofloya* with the Jacobin traits of a horror gothic such as Lewis's *The Monk*—the latter's critique of institutionalized feudal power and its belief in how much circumstances make the individual, for instance (Kelly, 55–56). The Tory flavor of at least part of Dacre's life could support such a complication, although other portions might ultimately problematize any one-to-one connection between Dacre's biography and the political meaning of the text. Similarly, several critics argue strongly on behalf of the finally inchoate nature of the novel's attempt to explain Victoria's evil, a case that could very well complicate any attempt to read *Zofloya* simply through one historical transcoding (Kelly, 106; Craciun, 16; and Miles, 18). Nevertheless, the Burkean anti-Jacobin topos of the novel does allow us to read into Dacre's work a dynamic that is at once more precise in its historical expression and, paradoxically, less clear in its political affiliations.[22]

Above all, Adriana Craciun is correct in claiming that the novel's punishment of Victoria doesn't really dilute the palpable pleasure associated with her transgressive, criminal actions (13–28). This obviously expands our notion of female agency in the gothic (and, indeed, early nineteenth-century England), but it also has another implication, insofar as that agency relies solely on Victoria's evil nature, her idolatry—her perceptual, and thus ethical, distance from anything that we might want to call the truth. Victoria's subjectivity is most vividly enabled both when she manipulates the world of appearances around her and, paradoxically, when she self-deludingly succumbs to Zofloya and his satanic designs. (Indeed, the two actions are not at all separate in the book.) This observation is by no means an attempt to temper the force of Victoria's agency by pointing out its masochistic resonances; rather, it's to reaffirm how powerful that agency really is, to note how it dominates the novel and becomes the only real form of subjectivity in the text's universe, while *still* seeing how it comes *solely from the side of the ideological*—how, for *Zofloya*, there really is no other side *besides* idolatry, a situation that Craciun's claim about the novel's disinterest in its own moralizing, punitive procedures bears out. Insofar as we vividly remember Victoria's iniquitous behavior more than the actions of any other character, it could be argued that *Zofloya* does indeed throw its lot in with the revolutionary Jacobin subject, in all her self-deluding, criminal, sensationalized failure.[23]

The significance of this dynamic can be further understood by returning to our comparison of Dacre and Radcliffe. One long-standing take of the author of *Mysteries* is that, as a deeply conservative writer, she solves the problem of mediating the Enlightenment present through the feudal past by actually discarding the former for the latter. As David Durant succinctly puts it, "Radcliffe remains a fine spokesman for the gothic simply because her themes were as escapist as her genre. This is not to say that her novels ignore contemporary life, but that they reject it."[24] The modernity of the French Revolution, with its upheaval of social hierarchies, is exactly what Radcliffe's books try to forestall. Critics such as Robert

Miles have since argued forcefully against this view of a counterrevolutionary Radcliffe.[25] Yet one observation of Durant's remains especially suggestive for Dacre: "[Radcliffe's] gothic underworld pictures an era so threatening in its newness that it seemed uninhabitable; her conclusions depict an ideal which finds its happiness in resolutely turning its back on modern life" (530). We might debate with Durant whether newness is indeed signified by the irrational "gothic underworld" or a rational Enlightenment modernity, or both. What is clear, however, is that if *Zofloya* cannot establish a rational modernity, a non-supernatural present, its reaction to Radcliffe's feudal, pastoral past is neither nostalgic nor compensatory; by the time Victoria and Zofloya rampage through Italy, and he throws her down to her hellish damnation, it is *this* past feudal world that has been made uninhabitable. The force of the text's rendering of the historical past is not unlike a scorched earth aesthetic. The novel's violent treatment of its characters is thus utilized for a specific effect: Dacre's novel limns a historical aporia quite appropriate for a work appearing in 1806, just as counterrevolutionary forces embarked on successfully making the word *Jacobin* an unspeakable, and unimaginable, word in the public lexicon. Caught between a feudal past that its protagonist has ravaged and a more immediate, revolutionary past that has apparently ended in catastrophe, *Zofloya* is emphatically blocked in its inkling of what the future might bring: there is no other side beyond ideology that might be temporally narrativized; there is no future on the other side of our debauched present. Demystification, or what we might want to designate as the future's truth, can only be imaged by the vertigo of Victoria's yawning drop. Conversely, there is also no more of the same, since the same, the world of Radcliffe's feudal order, is gone forever. (For Craciun, this vanquishing would also include the novel's excoriation of patriarchal marriage, what we have read as the failed revolutionary means by which Victoria attempts to become Berenza's equal [15].) There is only the transgressive energy of the idolatrous moment, the paradoxical agency of an exuberant self-annihilation, Victoria's triumphant "vivisection of virtue."[26]

It may seem a stretch to describe Victoria as some sort of Jacobin Nietzschean, until we admit how seriously we might entertain that phrase for particular works of Blake and, perhaps, Shelley and Byron.[27] The gothic account of history in *Zofloya*, the "newness" of *its* "gothic underworld," thus resembles nothing less than the high Romantic apocalypse, with Victoria's fall into hell less the certitude of any moral or empirical position and more the radical breaking up of plot in the face of history's aporia, the impossible moment after the (failed) revolutionary attempt. In its own exploitation of the male gothic's graphic pleasures, *Zofloya* makes this moment more untenable than what has traditionally attracted us to the high Romantic apocalypse of verse; yet the novel also renders this moment violently necessary for the possibility of female—indeed, any—agency. Still, when Victoria falls, and her eyes finally open to the machinations of Zofloya, it's not at all clear that there's anything to see: no sight outside ideology, no relief from the supernatural, no sensation that might indicate, or really be, the revolutionary day after.

Such a reading gives us the perspective by which a comparison of *Zofloya* and *Jane Eyre*, two texts so seemingly different in literary reputation and the complexity of their generic codings, can be especially pertinent. *Zofloya* becomes not only the atavistic, hyperbolic precursor to Charlotte's novel's own obsessions, but also its temporal differend, insofar as *Jane Eyre* can be read as in fact narrativizing the impossible revolutionary day after. If *Zofloya* is about apocalypse, *Jane Eyre* is about survival, something that very much coincides with the way that Charlotte's text acts like a *Bildungsroman*. *Jane Eyre* is thus post-revolutionary both in the way that Eagleton identifies its author as a transitional figure, as a text that, quite simply, comes after *Zofloya*, and in the sense that the fate of her heroine is itself post-apocalyptic, all about the creation of an enduring, domestic subjectivity. Like Victoria, Jane holds out for something more than the role of a mistress; unlike Victoria, she not only wins the position of wife but seemingly attains her desire, living on with her wounded and repentant (but not poisoned!) husband. After her own gothic travails, Jane flourishes (apparently). Deceptions are revealed, sacrifices are made, and lives are lost, but Jane stubbornly creates a world singularly defined by its hospitality toward herself and her chosen loved ones.

This transmutation of sensationalized material by Jane and in *Jane Eyre* certainly has a traceable historical reality, as Heather Glenn has suggestively shown by recovering our sense of the literary annuals and popular romances that Charlotte had as a resource for her novel's affect and tone (105–43). My interest, however, lies more formally in the ideological resonances that this transformation emits, or more precisely, in what this attempted domestication has to say about ideology itself.

We might be tempted, then, to see the forward-looking, gothic insurgency of the combined gender and political rebellion that Kaplan identifies in *Jane Eyre* as actually a reworking of the residue dream material of the past revolutionary apocalypse that *Zofloya*, in its own over-the-top manner, tries to articulate. The material's ephemeral nature, signified by "Grace Poole's" manic laugh immediately disappearing in the winds, would then refer not so much to any fragile claim about the revolutionary future as to a past trauma almost immediately made a questionable memory after its first fleeting sensation. We might wonder, however, whether such a view reifies too emphatically the sequential distinction between *revolution* and *global industrial society* structuring Eagleton's narrative of the Brontës' historical moment. Indeed, as Sally Shuttleworth asserts, Charlotte's own second preface to the book defiantly defends the iconoclastic, searching tone of her novel as a "radical, political act of unveiling"; as Shuttleworth also notes, a later letter to W. S. Williams meditates on this defense and the preface's eulogy of Thackeray by explicitly referencing the revolutionary energies of 1848, *not* 1789.[28] This connection is complicated, however, by the *negative* use of the 1848 revolution in Charlotte's *criticism* of her earlier writing: "I did not like it. I wrote it when I was a little enthusiastic, like you, of the French Revolution."[29] Charlotte's letter represents her preface as imagining the momentum of her novel as a forward-moving one that coincides with the revolutionary history making of her own present, and not of the past; yet that history is also made into the past, by her admission that she herself has gotten beyond that moment when she "was a little enthusiastic" of the events in 1848 France. By no means an absolute, empirical ascertaining of any ultimate biographical turn in Charlotte's ambivalent relation to the political realm, the letter's remark functions more as an emblematic troping of a predicament that revolutionary history oftentimes finds itself inhabiting, the allegorizing, or narrativizing, of one of its temporal conundrums, where the utterance of revolution can somehow also mean, sometimes more phantomlike and other times more emphatically, revolution's end, the event of revolution as also post-revolutionary, or counterrevolutionary, disengagement.

For Shuttleworth, Charlotte's criticism of her preface signals the author's deep concern that the forces of radical social transformation be managed through an early Victorian scientific, economic, and philosophical model for "control[ling the] circulation of energy" (150). As persuasive as this claim is, my focus lies more on how Charlotte's remarks clear a space for the complicated mapping of ideology's historical self-referencing in *Jane Eyre*, by expressing the way revolution structures the question of the novel's own attempts at demystification in a fundamentally *partial* way. We might consider, then, the novel's own famous, explicit use of the language of idolatry in order to crystallize Jane's basic dilemma at Thornfield:

> My future husband was becoming to me my whole world; and more than the world; almost my hope of heaven. He stood between me and every thought of religion, as an eclipse intervenes between man and the broad sun. I could not, in those days, see God or His creature: of whom I had made an idol.[30]

Like Berenza's, Jane's love is an idolatry. Unlike the implicit association in Berenza of the enlightened, and therefore blind, philosopher, Jane's idolatry works more as an "eclipse" intervening between her and religious truth, a formulation also at odds with the more conventional way the blinding light of idolatry works in her juvenilia and other writings. Seemingly more straightforward than these other instances of idolatry, Jane's idolatry still blocks her vision of . . . what, exactly? The conventional answer would be an authentic Christian love soberly grounded in religious understanding instead of solely worldly desire, a distinction based on one usage of the term *idolatry* that was, as Glenn notes, widespread in nineteenth-century literature.[31] What the religious might mean, however, is precisely the question we are asking. To press this further, we might also notice how Rochester as an intervening eclipse blocks Jane's vision not only of the sun but of Rochester himself. Rochester as an idol eclipses our sight of Rochester as "His creature"; as Jane's "hope of heaven," Rochester's very intrusion makes him somehow not there.

In terms of the plot, not seeing Rochester can mean simply not knowing him as fully as Jane ought to, as Bertha's still-wedded husband. (Unlike Berenza's, Jane's idolatrous love is thus not simply a sign of her narrative's gothic frisson but also, paradoxically, the means by which Jane is prevented from realizing that she *is in* a gothic story.) Yet, given the different ways that the discourse of revolution still swirls ambivalently around Charlotte's novel, the ways that Jane both positively and negatively displays herself as a neo-Jacobin, it's also not too difficult to see her idolization of Rochester as echoing the fatal epistemological temptation that characterizes the revolutionary event in *Zofloya.* Of course, a one-to-one encoding of Jane's idolatry within the Burkean template, as vivid or exacting as what occurs in Dacre's novel, is difficult to do; that, however, is the very point.[32] Reading *Zofloya* and *Jane Eyre* side by side, remembering the ways both Charlotte's text and readers allude to the novel's engagement with social conflict, it becomes hard not to sense in *Jane Eyre* the ideological shape of idolatry, the way her love resembles this epistemological problem as it comes to be understood in modernity, and as it's already rehearsed in *Zofloya.* Yet it becomes equally tough trying to conceive of this resemblance as simply a repetition. Jane's statement about her idolatrous love, then, presses against itself; the passage signals yet another social conflict different from the terms used to denote the very ones that still make up and resonate in the passage, the meaning of idolatry from religious thought, popular romances, *and* (anti-)Jacobin discourse. The text actually elaborates on this other conflict earlier, when the book makes clear that it's not simply Jane confronting Rochester with so much "earnest religious energy" (310)—rather, their love is mutually idolatrous, something that Rochester feverishly demonstrates with his fetishized dressing up of Jane as their relationship intensifies:

> With anxiety I watched his eyes rove over the gay stores; he fixed on a rich silk of the most brilliant amethyst dye, and superb pink satin. . . . With infinite difficulty, for he was stubborn as a stone, I persuaded him to make an exchange in favour of a sober black satin and pearl-gray silk. "It might pass for the present," he said; "but he would yet see me glittering like a parterre." (296)

Rochester's fetishization of Jane takes on an increasingly ominous, gothic tone, cathected in the expensive veil he buys her, a "delicacy and richness of the fabric" that soon emits an excess of meanings that delineate the diverse psychological and historical narratives bearing down on the book's wedding plot (309). Yet as violently archetypical and uncanny as the imagery of the veil becomes, the question of Jane's bridal outfit is part of a social conflict first played out explicitly in these scenes of modern shopping. Rochester's own idolatrous relation to Jane, his desire to see her become a spectacle, literally "glittering like a parterre," is very much conveyed through the sensual power of the commodity fetish.

Jane knows this, of course, as her protests against Rochester's conspicuous consumption, her desire to retain a modicum of financial independence with her governess pay after the marriage, and her tart remarks about Céline Varens make clear.[33] Buying things for Jane comes very close to buying Jane. But even more to the point, buying Jane and loving her might be the same thing. Jane senses the degree to which, in her world, intersubjectivity follows the money form—how the epistemological character of social relations, epitomized by Rochester's "rov[ing]," shopping eye, is that of the commodity's, a predicament that turns people into a taxonomy of things, women like Jane "dressed like a doll" and African slaves toiling in the West Indies (297).[34] (Thus, Jane's memory of desperately loving her little "faded graven image," the little doll she slept with alone in the Reeds' house, uncannily anticipates the relation among things that the commodity form underwrites in her adult life [61].) That Jane's own relation to Rochester is unavoidably about the economic is also the case; despite her explicit protests against any interest in his wealth, the text manipulates events in order to ensure that we understand the possibility of Jane succumbing to her "love and idol" as one and the same as becoming his mistress, with his reciprocating love, and thus he himself, fundamentally defined by the money relation.

Noting the economic character of Jane's struggles with Rochester might seem a familiar claim; indeed, the connection between idolatry and material wealth is prefigured early in the novel through the hypocritical figure of Mr. Brocklehurst, the head of Lowood. My point, however, is more about the novel's intimation of the commodity form as influencing the ontological and epistemological character of social relationships at their most intimate, and thus ostensibly most real, in Jane's world. Love's idolatry, then, both refers to and hides from itself, the abstraction of the commodity form as the way in which people know each other most vividly and completely. Loving Rochester as an idol means loving him too much, too intensely; it means speaking to him with too much misplaced "earnest religious energy." That excess also becomes a change in kind; it becomes idolatrous as the love of a thing that eclipses a subjectivity marked now only by what has taken its place. Jane's eclipse, then, is not so straightforward as we earlier intimated; rather, it marks an odd positioning of the loved object with regard to the senses, so that the object itself disappears, leaving only its darkened silhouette. The eclipse's own sensory confusion thus leads us to an epistemological and ontological place similar to the simulacrum images of Catherine that besiege the despairing Heathcliffe, signs of an increasingly abstract social alienation, of fetishized, totemic veils and people as "glittering" things.

Jane's imagery also adamantly insists on a sun that, if not impeded, might light this world's loving relations in a correct way. Rochester as an idol blocks not only himself but the possibility of a regenerate world somehow beyond the grasp of commodity relations—what, according to Williams, Heathcliffe can only abjectly sense through the alienating images resembling Catherine. That the viability of this world in many ways structures the conflict between Jane and Rochester is made clear not only by her rejection of his offer of an idolatrous love but also by the earlier terms through which Rochester feverishly envisions their future: "but he would *yet* see me glittering like a parterre" (my emphasis). Indeed, the entire latter part of the novel—from Jane's individual actions to all the apparently contingent circumstances of the plot—is mobilized to create an alternate future to Rochester's, in which love is precisely *not* structured by the spectacle of commodification, with the fate of Rochester's sight emphatically disarticulating him from the scopophilia of his earlier consumer desire.[35] The God eclipsed by the idol Rochester thus also stands for this future world, a modernity not beholden to the golden calf of the commodity form.

Whether Jane's and Rochester's downward mobility, cushioned by Jane's own inheritance, actually allows for this beatific modernity—*Jane Eyre* problematizes this issue early on, in an overt manner. Thus, the radically ambivalent questions that structure the novel's explicit renderings of religion—what to make of Helen Burns and St. John, whether there is a truly non-idolatrous, religious stance beyond the institutionalized Evangelical rote and dogma of Lowood—can be reinscribed as the novel's own questioning of the success of its machinations in inducing a non-alienated future. Such radical ambivalence sends the novel into a series of narrative torques—such as, for example, the way that Jane presciently declares that she will become a missionary to escape Rochester's pashalike demand for the opulent quality of their life together, only to have the literalization of that option become the last temptation standing in the way of her now supposedly *non*-idolatrous love. Such twists act out this radical ambivalence over escaping the commodity form, the *formally* convoluted character of which all the great ideological readings of Charlotte's text from the 1980s intuit and express in their own ways.

Idolatrous love in *Jane Eyre* thus constitutes something akin to what Slavoj Žižek calls a "parallax view"—a predicament that occurs when different aspects of an identity, or event, can only be viewed separately, instead of together.[36] To say then that *Jane Eyre* is not about *revolution* but instead *global industrial society*, that its discourse on idolatry is not about revolutionary, or counterrevolutionary, ideology but instead about the commodification of subjectivity, is to say, paradoxically, that Charlotte's text *is* about revolution and ideology. To align *Zofloya* and *Jane Eyre*, then, with the move from revolution to alienated commodification is to replay one way of resolving the parallax view, of temporalizing it into the intelligibility of historical sequentiality. There is thus the odd way that the linear order of this narrative retains its semantic force, even as we can radically qualify it: 1789 and 1848 do indeed haunt, proleptically and retrospectively, *Jane Eyre*; conversely, Victoria in *Zofloya* could very well be acting like a girl under the malign influence of a commodified art form, a genre whose simulacrum-like entities can be explained, as Hogle argues, through the gothic's intimate connection to a rising, commodified mass culture (176–210). The synchronic existence of revolution and commodification in both *Jane Eyre* and *Zofloya* is itself, however, simply one distinct moment of the parallax view that, in its own realization, eclipses the diachronic sweep of Eagleton's narrative; conversely, that synchronic view can be eclipsed in turn by the diachronic narrative. History itself thus becomes its own idol, not so much obstructing the sun of a critical intelligence that would show us things as they really are, but as an intrusion actively blocking portions of its own presence. This diagnosis of a parallax view is not simply the result of our own critical reading; it is also the inchoate registering that the language of idolatry in *Jane Eyre* emits, as a bundle of historical significations never certain, because history never stops, of what narrative it's in: the *medias res* of revolution, the end of revolution as the rise of commodified society; a revolution tied or not tied to class struggle, or to the rise of global capitalism; a Romanticism either contained by or exceeding the long eighteenth and nineteenth centuries. If the apocalyptic imagination in *Zofloya* cannot imagine the post-revolutionary future, *Jane Eyre* senses too many futures, too many desires for and anxieties about the day after and, with the novel successfully realizing its domestic *Gemeinschaft* for its living survivors, the day after that.

> There is one fault, too, in *Jane Eyre* . . . too much of artifice.
>
> —Anonymous, *The Spectator*, November 6, 1847

As Shuttleworth and Hermione Lee have amply demonstrated, *Jane Eyre* is a text replete with the hermeneutic drama of "lurid hieroglyphs," with Jane again and again encountering sensations of meaning that she cannot quite absolutely fathom.[37] Radically unlike the Wordsworth of "A Slumber" and "There Was a Boy," and even more than the Heathcliff beset by images of Catherine, Jane discovers the object of her interpretive focus to be not nature but society. Even when rummaging through Beckwith's volume of birds or peering into the distant horizon from her room in Lowood, Jane seems to be plumbing for some basic truth about the vast social networks of human relations surrounding her. An archetypical instance of this dynamic would be the young Jane trying to parse the significance of the stone tablet recording the founding of Lowood, replete with scriptural verse. The scene is itself an allegory about ideology, insofar as the words from Matthew refer to the Lord's light shining upon our good works, a light that in Lowood's case actually blinds its true believers to the school's institutionalized greed and mendacity. The young Jane ponders the words of the religious tablet turned graven idol, feeling "that an explanation belonged to them, [although she remains] . . . unable fully to penetrate their import" (81). She devotes special attention to the term "Institution" but makes little headway before the vast, ongoing history of expropriated relations codified and organized in that term, within which she stands enmeshed.

As Lee notes, this attempted reading of the social immediately gives way to the introduction of Helen Burns and the transference of Jane's hermeneutic drive to the intensity of the private, intersubjective relationship (236). The goal, however, remains the same: to understand at its most founding the truth of social relations. This attempt, both magnified and distilled, underwrites the stakes of Jane's and Rochester's desired transmutation of their idolatrous love. Nancy Armstrong has famously read the self-questioning of Jane's desire as helping to create a female sexuality both inherently mysterious and ahistorical, the bourgeois ideological subject par excellence (186–202, 205–13). One might argue, however, that Jane's self-questioning is actually less about the self and more about what the self faces, the question of love as, in the Shelleyan sense, the possibility of reality as unalienated social connection.

Paradoxically, this movement away from the self means once again comprehending the book's struggle with idolatry in ideological terms, since understanding what we love also means questioning to what degree love might distort our perceptual powers. As Adela Pinch has suggested, love becomes an epistemological problem about our ability to understand the outer world; thus, love as an authentic form of human existence might be what Jane wants to attain, but in going back to Rochester love as idolatry might instead be her fate.[38] Jane must not outwit reason so much as love. If Rochester as an idol means the possibility of him and Jane as commodified, non-human things whose exchange value conditions a complicated, mutual response of "glittering" predatory, and submissive, sensation, Jane's decision to go back to him rests on the question of perceiving the world correctly, on doing away with the possible idol within, not simply outside, her mind. She must discern whether her love is itself an ideological event.

In doing so, Jane must also judge whether there is actually something ideological about St. John's offer. This is not simply a presentist projection on Jane's perceptual dilemma: whether in some manner Jane intuits the nightmare of colonial history behind St. John's proposal of Christian missionary self-sacrifice, something she certainly cannot quite articulate when faced with Bertha Mason, but which might register with her at Moor House in some ominously, shadowy way as the engraved term "Institution" does at Lowood, we can still understand St. John's worldview as an ideological one, in terms that are already congruent with the text's self-contorting religious discourse. For St. John's argument is not simply that missionary work is the highest, most noble calling, but that, in some fundamental, existential way, it is the correct vocation for Jane, that she in some sense has already chosen this destiny, and it her. To accept this as true, if it is not, would be to transform this calling into idolatry; to succumb to this false destiny would be to accept something made ideological by that very self-deceiving, untrue credence.

What to make of Rochester and St. John, then? This question also trades in the formulaic dilemmas of the romance and gothic, of course. Indeed, Charlotte's novel seems to resemble most the female gothic as the heightened emotion of this epistemological question bears down on Jane in climactic fashion, only to be transformed, as in the female gothic, into the healing, secure feelings of the domestic plot after Jane perceives the world correctly and chooses accordingly.[39] St. John himself seems to personify the iconoclast run amok, someone so intent on outwitting the "love of the senses" that almost ensnares him through Rosamond that he seems as oblivious as Jane to the erotic sublimation characterizing the intensity of the conflict between them (418). Arguably, Durant's term of the "gothic underworld" could just as well apply to the welter of violent affect underwriting Jane's relationship with St. John as it could to her relation with Rochester. Like the narrative of a Radcliffe heroine, the gothic in *Jane Eyre* thus operates as a self-consuming artifact, gathering itself up as Jane contemplates marrying St. John, and dispersing after she decides to go back to the now-penitent Rochester. His long-distance cry to her, just as "marriage to St. John . . . was fast becoming the Possible," works then as the very moment of ideological demystification, of epistemological certitude, that enables her and the text to narrativize a future space of emotional sobriety beyond idolatry, emblematized by Rochester's Miltonic, Samson-like blinding, and designated by the authentic melding of secular love and religious experience (443–44).

Of course, this space of the revolutionary day after, insofar as it apparently exists beyond the novel's earlier social struggles, invites precisely the analyses of ideological containment that have characterized readings of the book since the 1980s. Unlike *Zofloya*—and *Samson Agonistes*, for that matter—*Jane Eyre* imagines human life after the apocalypse of ideological demystification. As a number of readers have demonstrated, however, it becomes inordinately difficult not to see Jane's ascertaining of the truth as in fact the keenest form of mystification, or Rochester's call as the most vivid form of Althusserian interpellation, subjecting Jane to a countless number of histories that transform her freedom into something as relentlessly delimiting as Weber's iron cage. One can argue with this view of Jane's ideological confinement, citing how, for example, she triumphs in some fundamental way over Rochester's wounded patriarchal body. Yet more important is how the text's gothic energies also represent a critical awareness of Jane's ideological condition. Far from simply exorcizing or creating ideology, Rochester's unearthly cry generates a critical dissonance, instantiating a new plotting where the gothic and the domestic, *das Unheimliche* and *das Heimliche*, merge irresistibly together.

The burning of Thornfield and the immolation of Bertha, Rochester's ruined body, the dynamics of mastery and enabling between Jane and Rochester, the very religious language used to make Jane's fraught story and desires akin to something like the normative—all such material can be read as the signs of an ending still alive to the forces that have haunted the text from its very inception.[40] In this scenario, at least, the gothic complicates the clarity of the ideological reading of

Jane's containment by intimating how the novel recognizes that very predicament, with the gothic frisson of the last chapters a reflexive sign of the book's own sense of historical and psychological irresolution, despite the contrary mechanisms by which the narrative also adamantly insists on a life, mind, and society distinctly beyond the idolatrous.[41]

*Jane Eyre* thus does not quite banish the "gothic underworld" as resolutely as Radcliffe's female gothics; indeed, the superstitious does not simply give way to reason, regardless of the "rational" explanation for the occurrences at Thornfield. Thus, Jane's moment of enlightenment occurs through Rochester's call, an impossible event that turns out, fantastically enough, to be empirically true. Jane herself immediately asserts the non-idolatrous character of Rochester's cry: " 'Down superstition! . . . This is not thy deception, nor thy witchcraft: it is the work of nature' " (445). We might wonder, however, if Jane's policing claim delimits the natural too easily in the scene: we might argue, then, that, as with the male horror gothic, superstition has been replaced by the *super*natural, which consequently grounds Jane's insight in the religious authenticity of her and Rochester's secular love. *Jane Eyre* thus upends its own resemblance to the explained supernatural by relying on the supernatural character of Rochester's cry. That the religious, natural, and supernatural together potentially create a scandal of mind that actually veers *toward* idolatry and madness—something Coleridge's Mariner knew intimately—speaks to what Charlotte's novel risks in depending so much on Rochester's call, a predicament that intimates another way to consider the scene besides describing it through the generic shortcomings of feverish romance or "gothic claptrap" (Armstrong, 197).[42]

The novel's apparent succumbing to the need for a literal, empirical account of Rochester's cry registers the complex, conflicted way that Jane's senses are foregrounded as essential actors in this moment of demystification:

> My heart beat fast and thick; I heard its throb. Suddenly it stood still to an inexpressible feeling that thrilled it through, and passed at once to my head and extremities. The feeling was not like an electric shock, but it was as quite as sharp, as strange, as startling: it acted on my senses as if their utmost activity hitherto had been but torpor, from which they were now summoned and forced to wake. They rose expectant: eye and ear waited while the flesh quivered on my bones.
>
> "What have you heard? What do you see?" asked St. John. I saw nothing, but I heard a voice somewhere cry—
>
> "Jane! Jane! Jane!"—nothing more.

> "Oh God! what is it?" I gasped.
>
> I might have said, "Where is it?" for it did not seem in the room, not in the house, nor in the garden; it did not come out of the air, nor from under the earth, nor from overhead. I had heard it—where, or whence, for ever impossible to know! And it was a voice of a human being—a known, loved, well-remembered voice—that of Edward Fairfax Rochester; and it spoke in pain and woe, wildly, eerily, urgently. (444–45)

Several things occur at once in the passage. Jane's moment of demystification transpires, appropriately enough, through a rearrangement of her perception. She falls out of idolatry by having her senses shocked into a new realization as they're "summoned and forced to wake." As important is the reorganization of her senses, the way the "expectant" eye, the avatar of misled sense, mystified by constant sensory overload (oftentimes of the "glittering" type), gives way to a more embodied apprehension of the constative, with the aural power of the Protestant ear coming to the fore. The double meaning of "Oh God!" as an exclamation but also as an address ("Oh God! what is it?") reinforces the impression of Jane repeating a long Christian standing pose of being called out of idolatrous, untrue behavior.

There is also, as Jane's recollection intervenes, a play on the change from "what is it?" to "Where is it?" a move from discerning content to locating form, from "what does this mean?" to "where does this meaning come from?" "What does this mean?" however, does not quite fully exhaust the full force of "what is it?" which could also express stupefaction over the very nature of the event itself, before any question of the semantic meaning of what Jane hears. This ambiguity speaks to the actually problematic role that Jane's senses play in the first part of the passage, as they ostensibly structure Jane's realization of the authentic, intelligible truth of Rochester's call. In fact, Jane's initial reaction, at once embodied but also radically dislocating, threatens to overwhelm the possibility of any meaning, false or true, whatsoever: "an inexpressible feeling . . . thrilled . . . through [my heart]. . . . The feeling was not like an electric shock, but it was as quite as sharp, as strange, as startling." Jane's feeling is at once so strange and powerful that it comes close to signifying only that uncanny, unreadable intensity. Indeed, what this feeling is exactly is never made quite clear, a confusing predicament that St. John's panicked questions ("What have you heard? What do you see?") only amplify. Whether Jane's "inexpressible" thrill is the active premonition to Rochester's cry, the reaction to the cry, or even the cry itself—the text actively resists any resolute answer to this question. Jane's uncanny sensation not only disarticulates the phenomenal from the semantic but radically scrambles the cause-and-effect nature of their relation.

The disconnection both underwrites and exacerbates the indeterminate nature of Jane's response, "what is it?" She could be answering the caller of "Jane!"; she could be asking what "Jane!" means; she could also be asking what the phenomenal nature of the cry of "Jane!" is; and she could also finally be asking what she herself is experiencing at the moment of the cry. That these possibilities can all blend into one another speaks to how the confusion of her response pulls the phenomenal and semantic apart in several directions even while insisting on their fundamental connection together. At this moment, Jane's predicament is less the triumphant moment of critical demystification, less the rendering of enlightened Habermasian communication, and more the vertiginous sensation of meaning that our previous chapters have outlined—what Hamlet endures when facing the specter of his father, or what Rousseau instigates when he mouths "Marion!" as a performative act that outpaces the ethical narrative within which his cry occurs. The shape or substance of "Jane!" "Marion!" or fatherly ghost, whose semantic and sensory nature is radically unclear, blocks cognition of what even to ask—"what is it?" becomes "what am I asking?" which becomes an *ad infinitum* replay of itself, the very hermeneutic *mise en abym*e that arguably structures Hamlet's actions throughout most, if not all, of Shakespeare's play.

This infinite, indeterminate replay does not appear to be Jane's fate, however. Yet, for this moment to have the ontological intelligibility and closure of a demystifying event, the "it" of "what is it?" has to be emphatically transformed into the truth of Rochester's own speech act. Rochester's own account two chapters later appears to confirm the transformation, as does the apparent ghostly conversation between Jane and Rochester that immediately follows the cry of "Jane!" But such empirical validation is actually ancillary to Jane's realization of the voice as Rochester's, a recognition that occurs immediately after the movement from "what is it?' to "Where is it?" Jane does describe the voice as "well-remembered," which implies that she identifies in the cry her memory of Rochester's own speech. But the movement of the passage before this description actually intimates that the "well-remembered" quality of Rochester's voice might also come after its recognition, insofar as Jane's words vividly deracinate the cry from any embodied, perceptual coordinate: "For it did not seem in the room, not in the house, nor in the garden; it did not come out of the air, nor from under the earth, nor from overhead. I had heard it—where, or whence, for ever impossible to know!" Jane hears the voice and knows it as a voice, distinguishing it from a sound that merely resembles a human cry; she does so, however, in a manner that doesn't actually involve the aural as a somatic, perceptual event. The senses have actually been left behind at the very moment that the cry, nowhere and everywhere, inside and outside Jane, instantiates the truth of Jane's relation to Rochester, and to the world. The novel's arguably clumsy, consequent appeals to the empirical validity of "Jane!" are actually compensatory, signifying instead how much empirical sensation *is no longer* the context for Jane's recognition of the cry.

A certain generic idealism about Jane and Rochester's romance relationship might be at work here. But the tropology of ideology that we've extricated from both *Zofloya* and *Jane Eyre* also allows for another reading. Jane *should* make her recognition of Rochester's cry a moment of *a-perceptual* truth, because ideology *is not really about the senses.* The tropology of ideology that we have read in both *Zofloya* and *Jane Eyre* is precisely that, a tropology. The physical sensation that Berenza feels when mystified by his love for Victoria; the French Revolutionaries blinded by Enlightenment reason; the eclipsing of Jane's sight by Rochester as an idol—these are *figures* of sensory error that *stand in* for the ideological moment. Ideology is not about physical perception, insofar as one's senses need not be blunted, tricked, or deceived for one to be ideologically mystified. Thus, contrary to what we at times have seemed to be saying, *ideology is neither empirical nor epistemological.* Ideology, like the sensation of meaning, is neither simply nor primarily a phenomenal event. If, as de Man argues, ideology is the error of confusing the phenomenal with the linguistic, the phenomenal characterization of ideology will itself be ideological (*Resistance*, 11).

Thus, even if our relation to the commodity object is entwined in some fundamental way with the literal, sensual makeup of such a thing, our ideological understanding of this relation is still not fundamentally about the phenomenal. What the gothic epistemologies of *Zofloya* and *Jane Eyre* demonstrate, however, is just how difficult it is to figure idolatry and ideology as anything besides sensory deception.[43] It becomes even more onerous, then, to figure the constative character of ideological demystification, the truth that appears after ideology's dismissal, as something besides the phenomenal correction of a sensory mistake.[44] The gothic dilemma of deception and truth demonstrates how the epistemological provides ideological critique with the alibi of the constative, where the answer to the problem of ideology becomes a matter of correcting perceptual confusion, or laxity. The scene of Rochester's cry begins to follow that script with the "inexpressible feeling" that awakens Jane's senses from their torpor. But in its a-perceptual transformation of Rochester's voice, the novel leads us elsewhere.

We might call that place the theological, but only if we entertain the fully aporetic semantic force of that term. Rochester's voice appears, "where, or whence, for ever impossible to know," as the catachrestic imposition of truth—the truth of, and as, love—that underwrites Jane's apprehension of her world from that point to novel's end. The call's intrusion marks the figuring of truth that ideological critique leads us toward. What, then, does *Jane Eyre* say lies beyond, or after, ideology as the figuring of epistemological deception? In a word, more figure. This involves the catachresis of truth as the figuring of the non-ideological, as well as in this particular case the prosopopoeia that figures Rochester's cry as human truth. This dynamic also refers to the entire narrativization of the attempt to do ideological critique. The spatial coordinates of a beyond, within, or outside ideological containment; the temporal ones of a present of and a future after ideological mystification; the very relation by which sense as semantic meaning and sense as phenomenon signify and resist one another—such relations are ultimately figures, the tropology by which the action of ideological critique becomes intelligible. The replacement of the perceptual by the ideological and (non-)ideological—engaging with ideology instead of its proxy—is itself a figurative event.

Ideology is an emphatically formal (de Man might say material) proposition in a manner much more radical than Jameson's own dialectic between the ideology of form and the form of ideology, which attempts nevertheless to grasp the constative nature of the historical real (*Political*, 74–102). It is thus appropriate that *Jane Eyre* figures the imposition of Rochester as the truth that appears before such coordinates, "where, or whence, for ever impossible to know." We can thus also see the cry's consequent, compensatory empirical verification as being generated by that initial imposition, with newly revitalized figures of time and space, the realist encodings of memory and distance, orientating the last chapters' confirmation of its truths around the event of the cry. It is also appropriate that St. John's own exclamation concludes *Jane Eyre* with a reinstantiation of apocalypse that both marks and acknowledges the hyperbolic knowledge behind any such temporal, spatial, or embodied troping: "'*Come,* Lord Jesus!'" (477; my emphasis). The radical ambivalence that readers might have to St. John's religious speech act, embracing his death—and, by extension, the religious dimensions of Charlotte's entire text—marks the cognitive dissonance the novel reaches by following through the contorted logic of its own drive beyond mystification: the impossible day after the apocalypse, Jane's life beyond and after idolatry, rushes itself headlong into apocalypse, into a nullity of space and time that can only be troped by a space and motion marked by their allegorical incompleteness. In a novel that so powerfully maneuvers itself toward the emphatic closure of Jane's story, St. John's cry acts as a caesura, the break to any grounding belief in the ongoing as a conclusive end; in life—Jane's happy life—as the simple ideological overcoming of what went before it.

The failure of Jane to escape ideology, then, does not mean, as many ideological readings of *Jane Eyre* imply, that we can. But it also does not mean that we can do away with either ideology or ideological demystification in any simple, absolute manner. As exhausted as the field of ideological critique might seem, the possibility remains that, as Charlotte's novel demonstrates, the problem might not be that there has been too much talk about a politics of ideology, but that there hasn't been enough. If, for example, what lies on the other side of ideology is not truth but figure, the question becomes whether the parallax view of Žižek and others is able to maintain a constative hierarchy in which what cannot be seen in its entirety is best registered by the view of either revolution or commodification, or of, in Jodi Dean's formulation for today, the parallax view between "class struggle" and "communicative capitalism."[45] Given the ability of figure to generate not only truth but more figure, we might wonder instead whether the parallax view, registered in its own way, as Shuttelworth shows, in the host of inchoate sensations composing Jane's body (148), is more precisely the sensing of *social antagonism* per se, the formal impossibility of the social that works itself out in a number of complicated narratives of history, so many of which *Jane Eyre* forcefully indexes.[46] Regardless, the choice itself reemphasizes what should already be clear: figure can have literal effects.

Figure, as the interstice between the before and after of idolatry, can also tell time, quite literally. This dynamic points toward one obvious and important characteristic of Charlotte's novel, as a narrative structured by Jane's recollection of events. The before and after of Rochester's call is itself a creation of Jane's present narrative voice. Considered through not only the revolutionary but also the many other possible arcs of *Zofloya* to *Jane Eyre*—through their gothic plots as a tremulous sounding of history's variegated nightmares—Jane's recollection is the aporetic rendering of a survival, the impossible recording of living past historical catastrophe to its resolution, of moving outside or beyond ideology.[47] As this is the impossible task that Romanticism from a number of different conflicting positions tries to express, *Jane Eyre* models a surviving Romanticism within its inscription as an early Victorian, realist novel. At the same time, insofar as a chronological Romanticism stands for the very sensation of historical trauma as radical change, *Jane Eyre* and its remaining, wounded characters also survive Romanticism and live on to the impossible day after. That others in the novel obviously *do not* speaks to the ethical impossibility of survival that from another parallax view narrates the unavoidable ideological shape of anyone able to live a happy life in history. In depicting such a predicament, *Jane Eyre* also disconcertingly asks us to wonder who the ultimately more radical Nietzschean is: the female protagonist of the supernatural gothic or of the domestic ending—dead Victoria or living Jane.

CHAPTER TEN

# Coming Attractions

## *Lamia* and Cinematic Sensation

> The spectacle is not a collection of images, but a social relation among people, mediated by images.
>
> —Guy Debord, *Society of the Spectacle*

> The visual is *essentially* pornographic, which is to say that it has its end in rapt, mindless fascination. . . . Pornographic films are thus only the potentiation of films in general, which ask us to stare at the world as though it were a naked body.
>
> —Fredric Jameson, *Signatures of the Visible*

In their mordantly clever 1991 steampunk novel *The Difference Engine*, William Gibson and Bruce Sterling depict an alternate Victorian reality marked by technology (steam computers) and historical events (an independent Manhattan island following the Civil War draft riots) that superimpose the *what if* of science fiction onto 1855 Great Britain and the world. The book also suggests a different relation between English Romantic and Victorian culture in the guise of various Romantic personages whose destinies take a skewed turn in this reality, most notably the elderly British prime minister Lord Byron, infamous for his betrayal of the Radical turned Revolutionary movement, and his daughter Ada, mathematical genius and computer hacker, or "clacker." Appearing for several pages is also John Keats, a "little fellow with clever blue eyes" and "long graying hair" who has quit "versifying" and entered the profession of "kinotropy," entertaining London through shows based on a steam-powered technology of moving images.[1] As small and fanciful as it is, the Keats cameo is also a provocative one, for two reasons. First, Keats's appearance wittily resonates with one of the key ideas motivating film history today, the connection between early and pre-cinema. Second,

Gibson and Sterling quite rightly make this point through the person of John Keats, the British Romantic poet whose 1819 poem *Lamia* allegorizes the conflicted social and epistemological principles of visuality implicit in pre- and early cinema as historic institutions of modernity.

Keats and his poem occupy this position because of the overlapping meanings in studies of pre-cinema and the poet (and, indeed, Romanticism) of one key term running throughout the present book: *sensation*. As is well known, Tom Gunning and others have argued for a new understanding of cinematic history, in which demonstrations of early film are in continuity with other nineteenth-century American, British, and European forms of mass entertainment and public recreation, the spectacle of carnivals, circuses, exhibitions, peep shows, and urban amusements that come to characterize the advent of capitalist modernity. Early cinema is thus an extension of pre-cinema, rather than a separate social and artistic formation; in Gunning's famous phrase, the display and viewing of early film constitute a "cinema of attractions" whose power lies more in technological wonderment over this new medium of the visual than in any glimpse of the future movie-going pleasures of narration and character identification associated with classical cinema.[2] Like other forms of pre-cinema entertainment, the cinema of attractions is more properly an appeal to the senses; film is a form of sensation that, as a part of the mass entertainment of the nineteenth-century public, is sensational, and sensationalized.

This chapter's focus on the pre-cinema thus returns us to a treatment of sensation different from our prior linguistic study of the sensation of meaning, insofar as here sensation's social dimensions emphatically coincide with the workings of the phenomenal world. This is as much an issue of the particular poet being read as the mode of inquiry being used; indeed, in this instance, the two are not easily separated. As we previously argued, whereas the Shelley of "Ode to a West Wind" seems obsessed with realizing a vatic historicity beyond the physical senses, the Keats of "To Autumn" evinces a diagnostic of history enmeshed in the dense viscosity of sensory experience. We can extend this characterization of the latter poet beyond this one poem, insofar as traditional literary criticism, in an aesthetic manner that at first seems quite different from the sociohistorical valence of pre-cinema studies, has long associated Keats with a poetics of the senses—of sensation as the sensual.[3] If Romanticism has long been characterized by the philosophically traditional division between the material and the ideal, and if that distinction seems in a Romantic work to be tipped in favor of (non–de Manian) material and phenomenal experience, a discussion of Keats is oftentimes close at hand. This is not to foreclose a study of Keats that might follow our earlier explorations of how in Romanticism various sensations of meaning estrange themselves from the perceptual. But this does recognize the gravitational pull in Keats studies toward a consideration of sensation as sensory event. Indeed, it is not too much of a stretch to say that Keats is the best argument for an aesthetics of sensation understood in this manner, both thematic and expressive, in English literature. But, of course, that very same characterization has long been used by a critical sobriety to dismiss Keats, and Romantic poetry, as bad literature—or as something besides literature altogether. As with so many critiques of Romanticism, this view can be traced back to the writings of that very same era, in this case to the 1818 review of Keats's youthful *Endymion* and his branding by *Blackwood's Magazine* as a member of Leigh Hunt's "Cockney School." From the perspective of *Blackwood's* and, among others, Byron, Keats's sensuality was the sensation of overly sentimental, flowery writing, the vulgar exhibition of, in Byron's memorable phrase, "a sort of mental masturbation—frigging [Keats's] *Imagination*."[4]

Since Marjorie Levinson we have been reminded that this estimation was neither simply aesthetic nor sexual, but also laden with class implications explicitly condensed in the pejorative social usage by John Lockhart, the *Blackwood's* reviewer, of "Cockney." For Levinson the meaning of this interpellation is a reflexive, petty bourgeois class anxiety that colors Keats's oeuvre in rich, complex ways. James K. Chandler has suggested otherwise, that "cockney sensationalism" might very well "have to be understood in some kind of tension with, and some kind of alternative to, that regnant bourgeois domain."[5] Whether Levinson or Chandler is correct about the class register of Keats's work, their discussion stresses how, as a poetry of sensation, Keats's writing occupies an especially volatile position in his era's sense of mass and elite culture—categories that historically begin to take on their modern, or postmodern, meaning at that very moment of time. Implicit in the opprobrium of *Blackwood's* and others is that Keats's writing is not real poetry and, thus, not real literature. It is sensation as entertainment; sensation not as an elite aesthetic principle but as one diversion among many for a growing, increasingly commercial, mass public. It is sensation in the social sense of the pre-cinema.

It is also like the pre-cinema in its relation to *visual* sensation, an implicit point of Byron's remark about Keats's stylistic onanism—insofar as its folly lies in both its exhibitionist nature and the underlying association of masturbatory fantasy with the virtual nature of the image, a link made in the writings of a number of eighteenth-century and Romantic writers, including Blake, Wollstonecraft, and Rousseau.[6] One detail of Lockhart's review emphasizes the social character of this visual condition. Derisive of Keats's criticism of Pope and Boileau, Lockhart notes how they, unlike the Cockneys, never chose to "exert their faculties in laborious affected descriptions of flowers in window-pots, or cascades heard at Vauxhall."[7] As much as Lockhart's reference to flowers in window-pots would have signified petty bourgeois life, his allusion to Vauxhall Gardens would have done so even more. The site of spectacles, shows, and entertainment in London throughout most of the seventeenth, eighteenth, and nineteenth century, Vauxhall in Keats's and Lockhart's time was increasingly associated with recreation for the middle class, as well as a more diversified mass public. While any cascade heard there would, of course, have been artificial, Lockhart's dig could very well have been even more pointed, since one of the most famous (and ridiculed) attractions at Vauxhall was the "tin cascade," which created the illusion of a mill's moving water through sheets of tin.[8] As such the tin cascade was a symbol of visual attraction in its crudest, most hokey, social marketability. To have been poetically inspired by, to have "heard," the tin cascade would have meant enacting the most painful social and perceptive error, an accusation of cultural maladroitness that Lockhart levels at Keats and his comrades through the inappropriate mixing of poetry and commercialized visual sensation.

The tin cascade was a staple of Vauxhall for many years, going back to the eighteenth century, where it appears in both Burney and Smollett. As Richard Altick's monumental *Shows of London* demonstrates, it and other attractions at Vauxhall were only few of the many exhibitions, fairs, spectacles, and sideshows that characterized the London of both Keats's time and the later Victorian era, so much so that Edward Bulwer wrote in 1831 about "that love of shows, / Which stamps [the English] as the 'Staring Nation.'"[9] Crowds came together to see hot air balloons, fireworks, zoo animals, mechanical automatons, wax figures, medical curiosities, scientific displays, ancient relics, Orientalist memorabilia, and various non-European examples of the *noble savage*. As Laurent Mannoni's equally imposing *The Great Art of Light and Shadow* relates, the pre-cinema was very much part of this increasingly complex and robust economy of public, mass viewing. Chief among the pre-cinema of this time was the phantasmagoria, an especially vivid form of the magic lantern show that involved the illusory movement of images through their shrinking and enlargement, and the panorama, an immensely huge circular painting that formed its own virtual landscape reality (and about which Wordsworth wrote in book 7 of *The Prelude*). As Mannoni adumbrates about the magic lantern and other optical illusions, "In the eighteenth and nineteenth centuries only a blind person would have been unaware of their charms and effects" (103).[10]

To situate Keats and his poetry within this social milieu is to extend but also to modify our sense of Romanticism's relation to the image. W. J. T. Mitchell and William Galperin have both argued for the forceful presence of the visual in Romantic writing, how the image aroused in Romantics conflicted feelings of investment and resistance even as its power and character became dominant tropes in a number of writers' works.[11] A concern with the visual and plastic arts is also obviously the case with Keats, a circumstance that a long tradition of scholarship centered on "Ode on a Grecian Urn" as ekphrastic poetry upholds. My thesis differs from this tradition in Keats studies in two ways. First, such criticism tends to see the image in Keats as a static, frozen entity, opposed to the flowing temporality of the written word. While art writing from the Hunt circle certainly supports this view, I believe that a more capacious dialectic exists in Keats between the still and the *moving* image.[12] Keatsian sensation also connects the Romantic image to the pre-cinema's promise of visual motion. This kinetic promise in Romanticism is neither simply a formal nor technical matter, but more crucially a social issue, which leads to my second point, that the aesthetic, psychological, and philosophical stasis associated with the Keatsian image is itself based on a historical reification: the notion that Keats's imaginative forum for viewing is the socially and economically secure modern museum, where his sculpted and painted figures, silent and still, reside. Hence, we are reminded of Philip Fisher's strangely appropriate remark about the "Grecian Urn" as a museum with one work inside; the canniness of this observation must, however, be qualified, insofar as museum displays still very much belonged in early nineteenth-century Great Britain to the larger, more socially combustible realm of amusement exhibition.[13]

As Altick explains, it was not until the 1860s that the "age of exhibitions was succeeded by the age of public museums" (509).[14] In Keats's time the display of objects today associated with either the art gallery or museum—objects from antiquity and paintings—was often done in the showman's hall. Indeed, after the destruction of Church relics during the seventeenth century, the non-aristocratic public viewing of art depended heavily on such venues. Even upper-class viewings of paintings, such as the 1787 Royal Academy exhibition at Somerset House, eschewed any notion of the solitary collector or museumgoer contemplating the isolated art object—the social and visual energies of Martini's engraving of the exhibition (fig. 10.1), with numerous paintings stacked on top of one another and the aristocratic crowd engaged in conversation (tellingly, Joshua Reynolds is equipped with an ear trumpet), are anything but that.[15] Cruikshank's 1835 etching of another Royal Academy exhibit, "All Cockney-land" (fig. 10.2), depicts the "middle-classification" of these same motifs, with one noticeable difference being

*Figure 10.1.* The Royal Academy exhibition at Somerset House, 1787. Engraving by Pierre Antione Martini after J. H. Ramberg. Courtesy of the Trustees of the British Museum.

*Figure 10.2.* "All Cockney-land" at the Royal Academy. Etching by George Cruikshank (*Comic Almanack*, 1835). Courtesy of the Trustees of the British Museum.

the upward gazes and open mouths of Cruikshank's central figures, as opposed to the generally downward aristocratic glances of those at Somerset House. In that light perhaps Keats's greatest poetic, and ideological, achievement as a "Cockney" was the level attention that the poet trained on what he wrote.

Regardless, such depictions connect artworks and their images to a social kinesthesia that traditional notions of Keats and art foreclose. At the same time, he and his friends certainly had the opportunity to attend collective viewings where people did not converse so avidly, but where the object displayed was also an optical trick or apparently moving image. One well-known commercial venue begun in the 1820s, the Cosmorama, displayed examples of still art and a sophisticated version of the peep show simultaneously (fig. 10.3). Keats, of course, died in 1821; nevertheless, the multimedia Cosmorama demonstrates the interpenetrating economies of commercial and aesthetic display that he and his circle of London friends knew. As a decidedly cosmopolitan group of writers and artists, the Hunt coterie was very much active in this volatile world of public exhibition, in all its forms. While we remember the painter Benjamin Haydon for trying to

*Figure 10.3.* The Cosmorama: interior and plan. The two right-hand views depict the optical arrangement of the Cosmorama from above and horizontally (*La Belle assemblée*, 1 December 1821). Courtesy of Bodleian Libraries, University of Oxford: *John Johnson Collection, Dioramas 3 (6a).*

ensure that the Elgin Marbles would be displayed somewhere devoid of "squalor and peril," we have pretty much forgotten Leigh Hunt's later attempts to reform the conditions at the Regent's Park Zoo.[16] Still, of perhaps all of Keats's close friends, Haydon most vividly embodied the connection between London elite and popular visual culture. While grumbling about how England's "leading historical painters should be obliged to exhibit their works like wild beasts, and advertise them like quack doctors," Haydon himself did not shy away from entrepreneurial showmanship.[17] The 1820 exhibition of a number of his canvases, including his huge *Christ's Triumphal Entry into Jerusalem*, was very much a sensational happening, with both Keats and Hazlitt attending; it was done in William Bullock's famous Egyptian Hall, a forum for a number of commercial attractions, including Napoleon's carriage. The link in Haydon between art and show was also aesthetic technique. As an avid devotee of the *cult of the immense*, Haydon championed a pictorial vision that in many ways drew stylistic comparisons between his paintings and the gigantic objects of the panorama (and later diorama) shows.

Keats's own letters refer to both the panorama and the phantasmagoria.[18] Perhaps even more germane to my thesis, Jeffrey Cox has suggestively argued for the active presence of commercial exhibition in Keats's greatest contribution to elite aesthetic culture—how the "fair attitude" of the "Attic shape" in "Ode on a Grecian Urn" refers to Emma Hamilton, "wife of the one-time owner of the Portland Vase, Sir William Hamilton, and mistress of Admiral Nelson" (169).[19] The daughter of a blacksmith, Hamilton got her start working in the world of attractions, such as James Grahams's "Temple of Health" and its "Celestial Bed," which claimed to cure the reproductive and sexual problems of couples renting it for the night. After marrying Lord Hamilton, she became famous for what were literally her fair attitudes—her poses within a blackout box as a number of characters from Greek antiquity. To think of such public exhibition as one representational model for Keats's urn is to associate the erotic and visual qualities of Keats's classicism with a suddenly more dynamic, topical, and commercial realm. No longer simply the result of an "abstract Romantic classicism," the "Grecian Urn" becomes a much more complex negotiation between the imaginary space of the museum and that of Hamilton's "arty strip show" (Cox, 150, 168–72).[20]

As a performance, Hamilton's display of attitudes also indicates the complex relation of the world of shows to theater. In sharp contrast to Gunning's description of early cinema, David Bordwell has famously argued that classical cinema derives its geneaology from the pleasures of narrative and character identification associated with the "well-made play."[21] Yet, against Bordwell, we need to remember the degree to which theater itself overlapped with the sensation of nineteenth-century English exhibition and shows. Within this imbrication there were a number of cultural productions that would fall between both categories, such as Hamilton's attitudes, various pantomimes, monodramas, and tableaux vivants. Moreover, the tension between narrative and sensation also existed *within* theater. When in 1802 Wordsworth soberly condemned the numbing of human spirit by the escalating sensations of urban life, the overly mediatized "rapid communication of intelligence" and "craving for extraordinary incident" that reduced the minds of city inhabitants to a "savage torpor," his example, for which his poetry was the antidote, was the gothic hit of "sickly and stupid German tragedies" that reigned over London at that time (599).[22] (In Wordsworth, of course, a love of sensation found its most pure expression in the ultimate expression of modernity's error, the French Revolution.) Indeed, during the teens and twenties there was much sentiment that visual spectacle had taken over the production of London theater, a criticism that was made well into the Victorian era.

Sensation, then, could exist within a genre or medium as well as appear exterior to a certain art form. It named the set of social relations that a cultural production actively existed within, as well as the types of publics and audiences that the cultural work reflected, imagined, and produced. It also marked the degree to which such relations were antagonistic, adversarial as well as dynamic in terms of what was being defined, represented, and enforced.

To situate Keats's work within this world of mass exhibition is not to collapse all these genres, media, and publics together—far from it. There is, of course, a material limit to the resemblance between the reception and consumption of print culture and those of exhibits and shows. (Likewise, simply assuming that Keats actually had a mass readership, in terms of both size and diversity, is complicated at best.) Also, obviously, the public experience of certain media was historically longer and more involved than others. Scholars such as Jon Klancher and Iain McCalman have demonstrated how within just print culture alone a number of distinct audiences grew around such disparate print forms as poetry collections, novels, middle-class journals, radical and reform newspapers, and pornography.[23] Within and beyond print culture, the vitality of this social world can only be sensed by appreciating the variety of publics exploding at this time. The point would be, however, to recover this very sense of explosive growth, a dynamic that allows for a much more diffuse set of boundaries among all these various publics.

Keats has in fact from early on in the twentieth century been the object of exemplary interdisciplinary work that would link his poetry to a number of cultural experiences, from the aesthetics of pictorial art to that of theater (of which Keats was an avid follower). But the tendency has been, even in this post–New Historicist age, more "extra"-disciplinary than interdisciplinary; there is usually an underlying assumption of the historically secure, intrinsically stable nature of the cultural work (literature and the fine arts, for example) being brought together—if not in social reality then at least in Keats's mind. Even to consider the presence of the pre-cinema in Keats, however, is to conceive of his emphatic relation to a much more socially combustible arena in which a number of cultural activities collided and overlapped, even as tremendous energy was expended to define one against the other.

The habit in Keats studies of reifying such activities as sharply distinct identities points to a process already actively taking place *and* being interrogated in the poet's work. Keats is the English poet of mediated cultural experience par excellence, a characterization that would also include, as the poem "On First Looking into Chapman's Homer" suggests, his experience of literature.[24] As such, his work powerfully demonstrates how these mediations come to be separated and recognized as autonomous modes of activity. He remains an especially apt gauge for the intensely complex British Romantic construction of elite, mass, and private cultural experience. In and beyond Keats the use of sensation, as both opprobrium and self-advertisement, becomes one especially vivid way that these hegemonic articulations are troped. In turn, the sensational (or, in Keats's case, masturbatory) image becomes a reflexive sign of the virtual nature of those identities striving for social distinction—of, indeed, distinction itself.

At the same time, the voyeuristic consumption of the sensational image paradoxically implies the opposite of reflexivity: an overwhelming, mindless immediacy. It seems more than historically fortuitous that early nineteenth-century England also witnessed a noticeable growth in pornography, something Lockhart implicitly accuses Keats of by opining about the "prurient and vulgar lines" of a love poem that Keats wrote for his brother George to give to Mary Frogely (McCalman, 215). For Lockhart the pruriency seems to come from not only an improper physicality titillatingly described but also a gross, non-ethereal immediacy. As Bulwer's epithet the "Staring Nation" implies, the London world of shows also seemed especially to draw upon the pornographic power of visual sensation in this larger sense of a powerful, nonreflective immediacy, a trait that Jameson's characterization of film also cites (*Signatures*, 1).

Arguably, Romanticism provides us with many of the moralistic, class, and ideological codes used to express both social anxiety over and attraction to such forceful, unreflective immediacy—as chapter 1 showed, for instance, the Romantic sobriety of Wordsworth's "Tintern Abbey" flies away from a pornographic relation of mindless sensation with nature while also recounting a tale of spiritual maturation and changing political affiliation. We can see a similar logic against pornographic immediacy in the sober, moral outcry of Keats's detractors against his and others' "cockney sensationalism." However, as chapter 7's reading of "To Autumn" indicated, Keats by no means internalizes the aesthetic or political character of Wordsworth's sobriety. As Geraldine Friedman's reading of Keats's *Hyperion* suggests, the story of progress and redemption from the senses never inspired, or oppressed, Keats in the same way that it did the older poet (9, 91–112). From a different angle, if chapter 8's Byron problematizes the immediacy of pornographic punning that supposedly underlies the graphic depiction of eros in *Don Juan*, Keats appears to embrace the possibility of this kind of immediacy, with all its fraught class significations, even more straightforwardly and emphatically. He especially anticipates a filmic potentiality that today has realized itself exponentially by how much special effects dominate Hollywood and video and Web images proliferate throughout the globe.[25]

Keats did so, however, in a milieu where individuals both attacked and defended specific attempts of supposedly elite culture as or against the charge of pornographic sensation. Interestingly, entrepreneurs behind London's commercial attractions also represented their spectacles as something *besides* sensational immediacy. The discursive internalization of this dialectic between sensation and its "other" runs through many of the disparate modes of cultural activities during this time. If literature had a complex, ambivalent relation to sensation, so did sensation itself. London exhibitions, including those of the pre-cinema, most forcefully expressed this ambivalence through the tension between their twin missions of entertainment and education. The panorama, for example, was generally considered much more of an elevated cultural experience, full of historical and world information, than the spooky phantasmagoria.[26] Yet those behind the phantasmagoria also insisted on representing their show in educational terms. Indeed, the projected images of the phantasmagoria, especially in late eighteenth- and early nineteenth-century France, were oftentimes recently deceased historical personages such as Benjamin Franklin, Voltaire, and leaders of the French Revolution. Likewise, the showmen of the phantasmagoria would claim that their spectacles served the science, rather than the magic, of image making. Yet equally insistent by others was the opposite view, that the showmen produced "illusions of pure charlatanism" and fantasy.[27] As much as the images of the phantasmagoria were from topical history, they were very much ghosts; indeed, the implicit uncanniness of their conjuration was emphasized by the other staple of images of the phantasmagoria, truly frightening phantasms and creatures from the world of the supernatural and myth. In England the subject matter and scary presentation of the phantasmagoria (which means in Greek "[With] ghosts I speak") were especially associated with the gothic craze of Radcliffe's novels and Wordsworth's "sickly" German dramas.

These oppositions—between sensation and thought, show and fine art, entertainment and education, pornographic and proper viewing, and magic and science—also structured the more properly "commercialized Classicism" drawn upon equally by elite and mass culture. Many exhibits like Graham's "Temple of Health" employed motifs from Greek mythology; many—noticeably those of the pre-cinema—took their names from the Greek language: the Eidophusikon, Cosmorama, Eidoprotean, panorama, and phantasmagoria, for example. As the etymology of *phantasmagoria* literally indicates, the meaning of such Greekness could easily mix with the popular mass entertainment of the gothic. Greek antiquity could stand for the modernity of science as well as (along with Egyptomania) the gnostic knowledge or Orientalist magic of the past. Its replicated or imagined physical spaces could be the site of either higher learning or popular diversion. And its eros could be embodied by either aesthetic desire or commercialized libido. Its display could be aesthetic experience or entertainment *as* aesthetic experience. Greek antiquity provided a "surface of inscription" for all these heterogeneous social and epistemological energies.[28] It's not too much of a stretch to take Laclau's textual term and say that the literal form of this interstice in Keats's time was the surface of *projection* of the phantasmagoria and other optical shows. The images projected onto such a screen underscored the intrinsically virtual nature of cultural desire and knowledge for the mass audience, the a priori mediation of culture that was also the paradoxically raw material of Keats's poetic career.

But, as any serious reader of Keats knows, the virtual is not simply something to be dismissed. Neither is that the case with the spectacle of London's shows. To begin to understand the full meanings of social exhibition in Keats is to link these two worlds together. Indeed, Keatsian sensation can be seen as occupying that strange indeterminate point when genre *becomes* a medium—when, as a genre of literature, the poetry of sensation is contrasted with high literature and deemed non-literary, consequently finding, as non-literature, its sociocultural meaning in the same realm as the media of the pre-cinema. To consider Keats's literary work also as a form of pre-cinema sensation is to remember keenly the degree to which the struggle over such distinctions and their enforcement was a product of the Romantic era. It is also to ask how much a poem by Keats might reflexively thematize the question of sensation *as* a social issue, a "social relation" in the manner of Debord's emphatic definition of the spectacle.

The pre-cinema suggests a new way to understand the staging of action in *The Eve of St. Agnes* and the overload of sensation in "To Autumn"; it could perhaps explain the revolving figures in "Ode on Indolence" through the mediality of a *lanterne vive* or another revolving optical toy, while imparting perpetual motion to the "mad pursuit" of the "Ode on a Grecian Urn" through the same device.[29] But all such formulations depend on the social argument found in another of Keats's works, one especially engaging in its sustained allegory of Keatsian sensation as the reception of the pre-cinema by a public, mass audience.

> I am certain there is that sort of fire in it which must take hold of people in some way—give them either pleasant or unpleasant sensation. What they want is a sensation of some sort.
>
> —John Keats on *Lamia*, Letter to George and Georgiana Keats, September 18, 1819

Its classical setting understood within the broader field of commercialized Grecian attractions, and its visual appeal especially understood through the magic lantern phantasmagoria, *Lamia* actually projects itself forward, toward a set of problems that the social history of cinema and technology of film will refine, clarify, and make their own. In doing so, *Lamia* comments not only on the history of the visual but also on the very nature of such a history, on how cinematic history might actually begin before the apparent object of its narrative, film technology, appears.

In particular, the thematic rendering of visuality and sensation in *Lamia* implies a disjuncture between itself and the pure unreflective immediacy of sensation, a reflexive dilemma at the constitutive heart of Keats's poetry. As much as the aural and formal qualities of Keats's work might engender a sensual immediacy, or as much as the textuality of his writing seems to strive, at another level, toward something like, after Deleuze and Guattari, a sensation without organs, the very anticipation of such goals within Keats's work ensures their failure—a situation that "Ode to a Nightingale" most famously narrativizes. A certain reflexivity characterizes the social and epistemological sensation of Keats's work, which *Lamia* is able to use proleptically to delineate a predicament that spans not only pre- and early cinema, but also classical and post-cinema as well. As a knowing example of Cockney sensation, *Lamia* demonstrates how visuality becomes the preeminent recourse for negotiating *between* sensation and *its abstraction* in modernity, a task that, until the past decade's video and digital explosion, has been most vividly associated with film.[30]

The abstraction of meaning and narrative from sensation is very much the critical pleasure connected with classical narrative cinema, what, according to Bordwell, distinguishes this stage of film production and viewing from early and pre-cinema. But this action also replays the social tensions between thought and sensation, art and show, science and magic, and education and entertainment that structure mass and elite cultural experience in early nineteenth-century England. By reflexively thematizing the dialectic between sensation and its abstraction, *Lamia* places that dynamic within the poem's own critical horizon, instead of vice versa. In doing so, Keats's poem proleptically reworks Gunning's seminal term for early cinema by foregrounding two meanings implicit in the idea of *attraction*, sensation as the locus for both desire and bodily motion. *Lamia* anticipates a negotiation between Lacanian and neo-Habermasian concepts of visuality as markers for social, public, and somatic desire. Specifically, Keats's poem poetizes the relation between such desire and the ocular mystery of mass culture's commodity form. Simultaneously, *Lamia* also propounds a specifically cinematic notion of the image, insofar as it plays off of the dynamic between still and moving corporeality. Much as Jonathan Auerbach has argued that narrative, through the moving body, actually exists in the early cinema of attractions, so too does Keats's work instill within its dialectic between sensation and abstraction the concept of visuality as the story of kinetic embodiment, of cinema as the active imaging, or imagination, of the body (798–820).

The body most looked upon in Keats's poem is Lamia's. Much like the optic dynamics involving urn and "Ode on a Grecian Urn," the "diegetic" viewing of Lamia coincides with the audience's experience of *Lamia*, the poem. Unlike Keats's ode, this exchange is not simply fetishized as the look of a solitary observer. Instead, the poem indicates the social, plural nature of the reception of *Lamia* and Lamia. As Chandler has observed about the poem, the "critical response to the creature named in the title seems to destroy her/it—the poem stages within its narrative an account of its own reception by a reviewing public" ("Hallam," 531). While that critical response might first and foremost be associated with the icy stare of Apollonius, the moment of (re)viewing takes place within the public forum of Lamia and Lycius's wedding and also involves the visual participation of Lycius and a number of onlookers. Within a more biographical vein, Susan Wolfson has specified the audience involved in Lamia's viewing: the reading public that Keats felt compelled to serve, also reflexively characterized by the "herd" of wedding guests, who "each . . . with busy brain, / Arriving at the portal, gaz'd amain, / And enter'd marveling" (Stillinger, 342–59; 2:150–51).[31] Whether Keats really did resent a public intent on a "sensation of sort," it does seem that *Lamia* allegorizes the mass reception of that attraction, a sensation embodied by the poem's titular character.

For both Chandler and Wolfson the scopic nature of public reception in the poem stands for a specifically literary form of activity; seeing Lamia means reading *Lamia*. But if that scopic nature is taken literally, if we take seriously the proposition of Lamia as visual sensation, a more complicated sense of the public emerges, one that would connect Lamia's literary sensation to that of the world of London's shows and pre-cinema. Certainly, the enclosed, charmed space of Lamia's home is the site of the most explicit moment of public viewing, the wedding. (And this housing of mass viewing, the mixing of interior space and publicness, certainly does express the social dynamic and architecture of many London shows.) But an earlier passage is also pertinent in developing the sense of public viewing in Keats's poem, the description of Corinth when Lamia and Lycius enter the city gates together:

As men talk in a dream, so Corinth all,
Throughout her palaces imperial,
And all her populous streets and temples lewd,
Mutter'd, like tempest in the distance brew'd,
To the wide-spreaded night above her towers.
Men, women, rich and poor, in the cool hours,
Shuffled their sandals o'er the pavement white,
Companion'd or alone; while many a light
Flared, here and there, from wealthy festivals,
And threw their moving shadows on the walls,
Or found them cluster'd in the corniced shade
Of some arch'd temple door, or dusky colonade. (1:350–61)

Ostensibly more real than the (super)natural setting of the lovers' initial meeting, Corinth is likened to being in a dream state. Levinson has suggestively explained this dreaminess as emblematic of Corinth as the social manifestation of the commodity form, a predicament that plays off of Corinth's historical reputation in antiquity as a site of both intense commerce and the "temples lewd" of prostitution (255–79).[32] We can also add to that the description in Burton's *Anatomy of Melancholy*, Keats's inspiration for the poem, of Lamia taking Lycius to her house in the "suburbs of Corinth."[33] Living in Hampstead and elsewhere, decidedly cosmopolitan but denigrated as either middle-class or lower, Keats and his Cockney colleagues were members of London's new suburban urbanity. More social ambience than simply geographic location, *suburban* describes Keats's material relation to London, something that the poem's opening lines on Corinth also suggestively register in their particular detailing of the commercial world.

The market life of Corinth that Levinson persuasively extracts from *Lamia* is actually somewhat hidden in these lines, its anxieties reflexively displaced by the image of a "tempest in the distance" brewing, but also its daily enterprises supplanted by those of the "wide-spreaded night." In such "cool hours" commerce is predominantly designated by entertainment and pleasure, activities that the relationship between Lamia and Lycius also very much combines. We might also venture to say that such entertainment is oftentimes visual, another key component of the lovers' relation. In that sense the commodified sexual favors of the "temples lewd" could refer as much to the eros of housed exhibitionism and voyeurism as to any true bodily contact. Similarly, the "wealthy" in "wealthy festivals" need not so much name the customers of these events as denote the commercial character of such attractions. Indeed, Corinth's crowds, made up of "men, women, rich and poor," are explicitly diverse in the manner of a mass audience. In its mixture of anonymity, recreation, public heterogeneity, and libidinal promise, nighttime Corinth resembles the social ambient of a Vauxhall or a Couvent des Capucines, the site of the phantasmagoria and other attractions in late eighteenth- and early nineteenth-century Paris.[34] The flaring "lights" of the festivals might very well then be the center of such attractions, which would imply another way to understand the shadows cast by the strolling crowd. Like such lights, the "moving shadows" thrown on walls throughout Corinth are those of the festivals, the moving projections of the phantasmagoria and other magic lantern shows. Their breaking out of the showmen's hall to cluster also around cornice, temple door, and colonnade would then proleptically allegorize a social condition with which we, and Debord, are very familiar: a world of spectacle, where human relations—economic, sexual, and ideological—are mediated by the omnipresent moving image. Indeed, both readings of the shadows mutually support each other, insofar as such projected images *are* the mass public's shadows; they are our desire literally embodied, or mediated, on a screen and given back to us, the fitting substance of the articulated "mutter[ings]" of urban capital in, or as, a dream.

Within and beyond Corinth the center of visual attention is Lamia. Indeed, one way to order the notoriously wayward narrative of Keats's poem would be to consider the story a series of staged visual encounters with the titular character, a set of looks that then organizes all the other viewing occurring throughout the work. Hermes sees Lamia the creature; Lycius sees Lamia the natural woman; Corinth and the wedding guests see Lamia the social woman; and Apollonius (possibly along with Lycius) sees Lamia the creature. Much of the interpretive energy generated by Keats's work comes from adjudicating among all these different visions of Lamia. Hermes, for example, sees (and hears) a creature who claims to have been a woman, while Apollonius sees a creature with no real prior history, as she really is and always will be, Lamia as *das Ding an sich*. Keats's readers have tracked such interpretive choices back to the central question of whether to see Lamia as a creature or a woman, which in turn becomes the putatively more basic, and ontological, choice of whether she *is* a creature or a woman.

This formulation, often assumed, is somewhat odd, given the fact that the creature is also gendered as a female. So the more precise ontological choice should be between Lamia as a creature and Lamia as a human. The reconception of this question as between creature and woman might then signify one rare instance in literature when woman, rather than man, signifies humanity. But as the feminine is distributed evenly among all the stages of viewing Lamia, as there is not only a "natural" woman outside Corinth (so natural that Lycius can only think that he is seeing a god) but also a female snake and a socialized woman (Lamia the bride), it becomes clear that *woman* does not signify human in any ontological sense. As Judith Butler and others have argued, the status of *woman* is not an ontological one.[35] Neither is it for *man*, of course; it is *woman*, however, that bears the brunt of this Apolloniusian insight, a truth that, as the patriarchal sage insists, must be monstrous and therefore exorcized.

Apollonius's visual knowledge of Lamia is then supremely contradictory, insofar as he supposedly sees her as she really is, the thing-in-itself, but as such sees her as the truth of non-identity. To understand the full meaning of this antinomy means considering another possibility regarding Lamia's existence, that she is first and foremost an image. She is, more precisely, the epistemological question of visual sensation, of the reflected or projected image. No vision of Lamia, not that of Hermes, Lycius, the wedding guests, or Apollonius, has more ontological density than the others. As the replication of a series of conflicting images, Lamia constantly exists in a state of distortion, a radical version of the anamorphic principle found in different ways in Renaissance optical toys and the anamorphic lens of modern movie technology. Playing off of Bruce Clarke's canny depiction of Lamia as the metamorphosis of metaphor, or metaphor for metamorphosis, we might say instead that Lamia is the anamorphosis of image, or image for anamorphosis.[36]

As in Clarke's meditation on Lamia's mutability, anamorphosis is intrinsically linked (in Lamia's case, perhaps, fatally) to the anthropomorphic. As Clarke writes, "We have foresworn but not undone our animistic impulses: we have simply thrust them into sexual and economic relations, and then looked for gods in eros and capital" (561). For Clarke the return to animism in *Lamia* takes place through figure; for W. J. T. Mitchell, however, the site of animism is best understood through the power, the attraction, of the image.[37] To make Clarke's observation about the animation of our sexual and economic relations one about the animated, moving image is to conceive of Lamia's world as Debord's, where the metaphysics of the image cannot be understood separately from its social character. The opening of Keats's poem, which catalogues the movement from an English faerie land to an ancient Greek world of myth, "before the faery broods / Drove Nymph and Satyr from the prosperous woods" (1:1–2), might then be understood as the juxtaposition of two different sets of animistic beings who embody Clarke's, and Debord's, social relations. This was the literal case for such creatures, who together made up one specific staple of projections for the phantasmagoria and other magic lantern shows. Within the context of the commercialized antiquity central to London's exhibitions, Greek mythological and English faerie characters were oftentimes part of the same commodified culture of supernatural visual entertainment. As *Lamia* suggests, they literally are the images, the phantasms of our desire, defined by political struggle and history. As such, they mirror the phantasmagoria's other collection of favorite images. The magic lantern's Benjamin Franklin and Robespierre were historical, political figures who appeared as phantoms in the phantasmagoria seance; the dryads and elves in *Lamia* are phantoms who engage in history and politics. Oberon's "bright diadem" and "Sceptre" could then be taken reflexively, not simply as images of power, but as those of the social power that images wield, embody, and realize (1:3, 4).

The social optics of *Lamia* are therefore not simply those of the theater. Certainly, as scholars have done with other pieces of Romantic literature, one could profitably discuss the spectacle of Lamia's changing self-display through the performative dynamics of staged theater and related genres.[38] But just as the question of gender is diverted by assuming the option of conceiving of Lamia as a "real" woman, so too is the question of animism by assuming that Lamia has a real body. Lamia is cinematic in a fundamental way that ties together classical, early, and much of pre-film history. Theater gives us images of social desire through the kinetic display of bodies; in contrast, film embodies that desire through the kinetic image. In *Lamia* and the cinema, the image precedes corporeality.[39]

As a *moving* image, Lamia is also involved in a somatic animation vividly different from the static pictorialism of the fine arts. Through movement the image realizes an animistic state that expresses not only social desire but biological life itself. Late eighteenth- and early nineteenth-century pre-cinema was very much aware of these associations. Indeed, one of the first advertisements of the phantasmagoria in France also featured a display of galvanism, whose application, it was claimed, gave "temporary movements to bodies whose life [had] departed."[40] The dream of the living dead thing, the (re)animated object, is the dream of much Romantic literature, from Wordsworth's "A Slumber" to Kleist's *Marionettentheater* to Shelley's *Frankenstein*. It is also the dream of the living image, the attraction of much pre-cinema as well as the charm of Keats's sensational creature.

Fittingly, Hermes and the reader become aware of Lamia's desire and kinetic potential at the same time. Her first words combine the two sides to her identity in a cry for transformative reanimation: "When from this wreathed tomb shall I awake! / When move in a sweet body fit for life, / And love, and pleasure and the ruddy strife / Of hearts and lips!" (1:38–41). Hermes finds Lamia in snake form, "palpitating . . . / Bright, and cirque-couchant" (1:45–46). Coiled in this manner, Lamia is literally wound tight; not quite still, she seems already to contain great energy, to be on the verge of apparent motion. The next well-known lines describe her in detail:

> She was a gordian shape of dazzling hue,
> Vermillion-spotted, golden, green, and blue;
> Striped like a zebra, freckled like a pard,
> Eyed like a peacock, and all crimson barr'd;
> And full of silver moons, that, as she breathed,
> Dissolv'd, or brighter shone, or interwreathed
> Their lustres with the gloomier tapestries—
> So rainbow-sided, touch'd with miseries,
> She seem'd, at once, some penanced lady elf,
> Some demon's mistress, or the demon's self. (1:47–56)

It is difficult not to read these lines meta-poetically, as Keats either cynically or defiantly giving the public "sensation of sort" in its most gaudily overwhelming visual form. The passage's perceptual and conceptual confusion, its breathtaking clash of color and design, would then stand for a Cockney sensationalism brazenly resplendent in all its hyperbolic class colors. The splendid gaucheness of such psychedelic intensity would then also account for the jarringly abrupt move toward interpreting the image's identity in the passage's last lines ("some penanced lady elf, / Some demon's mistress, or the demon's self"), a seemingly incongruous literary mixing of the supernatural, gothic, and antiquity that actually reiterates the blended commercial product of the phantasmagoria and other lantern shows. Aside from its social resonance, the passage's frenetic description also characterizes an image resistant to any static or frozen mode of being. Hermes and the reader look at Lamia and cannot quite see or capture her; apparently framed by the poem's narrative eye, she does not visually remain at rest.[41] Such kinetic quality also speaks to the failure of the image to rise emphatically out of the sensation of its description. The passage tries to do so through a series of similes that attempt to anchor Lamia's riotous visual qualities in a set of known animals ("zebra," "pard," and "peacock"). The conceptual result, however, is a hybrid zoo whose exotic exhibition fails to secure Lamia's image in any mentally synthetic manner. A hyperbolic version of the zoo displays that Hunt would try to reform, Lamia remains a menagerie of different optic effects. As such, she also depicts the wide array of public visual sensation of Keats's London milieu.

Lamia's description much more resembles the atomistic, paratactic dynamism of Coleridgean fancy than any version of high Romantic organic imagination that traditional readings habitually assume she represents. Likewise, the attempt to abstract from Lamia's visual presentation her identity as lady elf, demon's mistress, or demon clumsily falls short of its goal. Even as Keats's poem instills a reflexive structure in the scopic experience of Lamia's visual immediacy, her initial description paradoxically asserts that, at some basic level, she remains a visual sensation allergic to further conceptual hypostatization. Conversely, each portion of the poem's anamorphic sequence, each image of Lamia, is a dialectical attempt to challenge this constitutive opacity. The poem's first depiction of this sequence, Lamia's change from serpent being, emblematizes how anamorphosis, desire, and visual kinetics converge in a flash of "phosphor and hot sparks" further signified by the somatic pain of transformation (1:152). Not coincidentally, the two other moments of the anamorphic sequence, Lycius and Apollonius in different ways forcing Lamia to become the creature that they want, are also troped as forms of psychic, and then existential, pain.

Tellingly, when Hermes first comes upon Lamia, she is also associated with two specific forms of light: "full of silver moons . . . as she breathed," she is "rainbow-sided" (1:51, 54), descriptions later reinforced by the much more addressed lines about Lamia as the "awful rainbow, once in heaven" undone by "Philosophy" (2:231, 234). Lamia is the product of another source of light besides herself. She can be viewed, like the moon, because of the silvery reflection of light. Likewise, as a rainbow her colors are the refraction of light; they are the projection of light through one medium onto another—in the case of a rainbow, through rain onto the air; in the phantasmagoria, through glass lenses onto a wall, sheet, screen, or even smoke.[42] If Lamia seems more than a still object, full of kinetic energy, she is also an image, constitutively an effect of either reflected or refracted light.

As Paul Endo has observed, "The ear is a prominent opening for Lamia's magic—her singing enchants Lycius on a number of occasions, and music is the sole 'supportess' of her palace—but it is the eye that she exploits most skillfully."[43] Endo's remark about the two senses could also extend to a familiar dynamic present in both theater and pre-, early, and classical cinema. Arguably, sound and image differ in their illusory properties only by degree. Sound can pretend that it is another sound: cymbals can be thunder, a recorded voice can be a live speaker, and extra-diegetic music can actually be diegetic. Through acoustic imitation sound can also ratify the psychic and physical illusion of space that the cinematic image especially presents. But, more radically, through its vibratory character sound can actively, like the image, present itself as another sense, most immediately that of a tactile presence. Through vibration sound can validate the illusion of motion and break the silence of the still, frozen object. In the cinema, visual and audio sensations create the intelligibility of material sensuality, something that Lycius, staring at and listening to Lamia, very much buys. That being said, paraphrasing Endo, it is the eye that the cinema exploits most skillfully. Insofar as we must argue for the self-evident role of sound in the cinema, *Lamia* seems cinematic precisely to the degree that it recounts how sight appears most able to apprehend reality, and most likely to be in error.[44] Supported by sound, sight signals the very phenomenon of sensory effect. The fact that the visual is a signal, however, also implies that it can be wrong, a predicament that Lycius at the end of the poem must face. Visuality, as many readers of *Lamia* have noted, is the very principle behind the coherent distinction between illusion and reality in Keats's poem. The epistemology of *Lamia* is the epistemology of the image.

One might object that understanding Lamia as an image occludes one crucial detail, the degree to which Lamia *herself* looks upon Lycius with desire. Even one noticeable description of Lamia's putative interiority is configured around her longing, telepathic vision of Lycius in Corinth ("She saw the young Corinthian Lycius / Charioting foremost in the envious race" [1:16–17]). By participating in the relay of scopic desire, Lamia appears to be more than an image; she seems to gain the agency of an observer instead of simply remaining the observed. While this dynamic certainly has its own interpretive power, there is a radically different way to understand Lamia's specific scopic abilities, one that uncouples Lamia's look from any simple condition of intentional subjectivity or unproblematic agency.

Lamia's look might instead be that of the Lacanian *gaze,* which is *not*, as is commonly assumed, about the subject's scopic desire; the gaze, as Slavoj Žižek explains, is "not on the side of the looking . . . subject but on the side of what the subject sees."[45] Keats literalizes this condition in Lamia through his physical description of her human eyes in her snake form. Both highlighted and dislocated from the human face ("what could such eyes do there [on a serpent's head] . . . ?" [1:61]), Lamia's eyes contain something besides the absolute, subjective intelligence of what she wants; literally rendered for us to see, they become partial *objects* in the Lacanian and Freudian sense, both blocking and enticing our comprehension of her desire. Through the poem's objectification of her eyes, Lamia embodies the gaze, insofar as we do not so much inhabit the gaze as see the gaze looking, or not looking, at us. The gaze is more exactly this point of us not being seen; the looked-upon gaze is therefore always mysterious, at some level always the sign of desire's unknowability, the degree to which desire always exceeds the Lacanian symbolic. The gaze is a stain or screen, the image of the impossibility of knowing what desire wants.

Aside from her eyes, Lamia in her snake form also has a human mouth. She is all eyes, all mouth, and, literally, as a serpent, all throat; she is all desire, while exceeding our knowledge of that desire. Mouth and throat together also make *voice*, which along with the gaze is another prominent member of Lacan's list of partial objects that externalize for the subject the *objet petit a*, the object cause of desire. As such, Lamia's features resonate with those of another mythological being who was actually showcased in the turn-of-the-century phantasmagoria: the Medusa, whose moving eyes and tongue visually foreground the gaze and voice (much like the later-in-the-century image of fig. 10.4). Lamia's human seduction of Lycius depends on her gaze and voice precisely to the degree that whatever meaning her eyes and words convey to him is less important than the fact that she *is* looking at and speaking to him, that she is leveling her mysterious gaze and voice at him. Similarly, the Medusa is an exemplary reflection of the frightening power of the phantasmagoria not simply because of what her mouth might have said or what the audience thought her eyes communicated, but because her features embody the phantasmagoria's ability to give living desire, condensed in gaze and voice, to nothingness—to an object world "on the side of what the subject sees and hears" (Žižek, 91).[46] Their mythological sexual meaning distilled by the sensational media of Keats's poetry and the phantasmagoria show, Lamia and Medusa act as complementary components of the same monstrous optics, mutual mirrorings of woman's double bind as the allure and balefulness of desire's mysterious gaze.[47] Indeed, as *Lamia* illustrates, the patriarchal economy's terroristic response to the aporia of the *objet petit a* falls on woman; in Keats's poem the double binds of this predicament are the same for Lamia as an image of woman and as a feminized image. The questions that Mitchell has asked of the image are the same that Keats's work asks of Lamia. What does she want? What does her gaze signify? In that sense, Lamia *is* Galperin's Romantic "return of the visible": "the 'familiar thing that has undergone repression' (to borrow from Freud), something that is no more forgotten than it is necessarily anterior."[48]

Lamia, then, gazes at Lycius; she is the image of gazing, or the gazing image. As Joan Copjec elucidates, "For everything that is displayed to the subject, the question is asked, 'What is being concealed from me?' The point at which something appears to be *in*visible, this point at which something appears to be missing from representation, some meaning left unrevealed, is the point of the Lacanian gaze. It marks the *absence* of the signified."[49] As Endo says, in a somewhat differ-

*Figure 10.4.* The Head of Medusa, an animated slide for the phantasmagoria, ca. 1830–40. Courtesy of Laurent Mannoni and *Cinémathèque française, collections d'appareils.*

ent context, Lamia also "accedes to her role [of being viewed] while holding a little in reserve—in other words, a *secret*" (120). This is actually true in a radically constitutive manner commensurate with Copjec's argument; Lycius and the reader see displayed in Lamia's gaze something *in*visible. More prosaically put, what she sees in Lycius is never clear to us, or him. Does she want to become human to love him, or does loving him make her truly human? As Levinson argues, Lamia's desire is not even simply her own, insofar as her deal with Hermes regarding the nymph illustrates her collusion with a commodified libidinal economy from the start. But it is even more complicated than that, since, *as* the commodified image of Cockney sensationalism, she embodies the innately mysterious desire, the mystifying desirability, of the objectified commodity form. From such a perspective, Lamia becomes the *objet petit a* of a desire equally specific and vertiginous in its historicity, the commanding eros of a still-nascent but feverishly expanding capitalist mass culture.

If that culture's commodified image does indeed embody social desire, that desire's ultimate mystery installs within the social body a certain opaque density, the self-estrangement of the social optative that the commodity form historically evinces. Similarly, the resistance of the *objet petit a* to knowable desire does not necessarily have to be conceived in terms of something that exists in space before, after, or beyond that desire. More exactly, as Slavoj Žižek outlines, the *objet petit a* can also be a certain constitutive distortion within space itself, the Lamia-like sinuous curve that "causes us to make a bend precisely when we want to get at the object" (*Enjoy*, 48–49). The imagination of somatic desire in *Lamia* allegorizes the complex interplay between these two versions of the optative. When Hermes searches for the nymph, her invisibility can stand for an immaterial, undefinable desire as yet to come into being, as yet to be given knowable, bodily form—the condition that Lamia the image tellingly grants. (We only have Lamia's word and the narrator's rumor of her that the nymph was once visible before that moment.) But if we take the nymph to be, in Copjec's phrase, *in*visible, then the nymph as *objet petit a* is *already* embodied in the glens where she supposedly hides; her visual nothingness *is something*, the opacity of the symbolic in relation to itself.[50] She is hidden in the same way that Lamia the image has a radical secret; she is the secret that makes the desire of Lamia's own gaze *in*visible. These contrasting accounts depict the tensions between a linear and more synchronic understanding of the coming-to-be of desire in the commodified image.

Ultimately, *Lamia* seems unwilling to give a historically full, genetic account of commodified desire's opacity.[51] The poem deflects such symbolic mastery by, as in the Hermes episode, its juxtaposition of a linear sense of desire's becoming with a more synchronic one. The idea of going back to a less mystified origin is given little credence by the poem, as the cul-de-sac of deciding Lamia's true ontological origins indicates—whatever Lamia's own explanation for her situation, the power of the work comes more from its sense of mythic repetition, the narration of a constitutive state of desire that Lamia exemplifies. Yet that same eschewing of the simply linear ensures the poem's understanding of desire as always socially material. If the poem solely existed within a diachronic mode, its move from country to urban venue could be understood simply as the transformation of the lovers' natural desire into a socially commodified one. Lycius's sadism toward Lamia would then be explained, as Endo has suggested (118), as one consequence of the narrativization necessary for the social reification of his initial scopic desire, his later intent to have others see her publicly as his bride: "Let my foes choke, and my friends shout afar, / While through the thronged streets your bridal car / Wheels round its dazzling spokes" (2:62–64).[52] But, as Levinson has pointed out, Lamia's rural habitat is already marked by exchange and commodification, social activities emblematized by how the optative secret of the glens is carved out and congealed within the nymph's corporeal form. The moment is emblematic precisely because the glens are not part of a pure, untouched nature; they themselves already embody the secret of the nymph. In *Lamia* nature is already the process of hypostatization. The move from nature to city, from an unmediated, natural optics to a social one, is the poem's fundamental myth, its linear repetition of a socially material constant. In its reflexive disenchantment of that myth, *Lamia* portrays desire as always embodied socially; it is always radically mediated, as much as Keats's own irreducible, virtual sense of cultural experience. It is also unavoidably anamorphic, always opaque. *Lamia* describes the image as at once social and *in*visible, a simultaneity analogous to the there-not-quite-there phantom materiality of the projections of the phantasmagoria. As Žižek might add, the opacity of such an image is also, dialectically, the very object cause of desire (*Sublime*, 65). The mystifying allure of Lamia is her, and our, mystery, our alien body and commodity form.

Another name for this opacity is sensation, the unreflective immediacy of Lamia's sensory image. To know Lamia as a living being; to know her as something besides sensation; to extricate from commercialized sensation aesthetic elevation, scientific edification, or public instruction—all these are endeavors to realize social desire in a lucid, knowable form, to see in the exhibited image the constative clarity of what we want. The failure to abstract from optic sensation the narrative of social desire is also the pornographic success of visuality as a pure, mindless attraction. If in Keats's time sensation named the set of social relations that a cultural work occupied, in *Lamia* those social relations are characterized as ultimately opaque. But, conversely, as a commodity visual sensation is already estranged from itself; it and its non-knowledge cannot simply be "pure." Likewise, the very duplicitous charm of the moving image, its representation of tactile presence, also makes the image at some unavoidable level an *abstraction* of sensation. The image is both sensation and abstraction, a predicament whose tensions are negotiated and, paradoxically, exacerbated by the literalized kinetics of the image's animism.

As Gunning observes, the moving image in the magic lantern is an illusion that the human eye can, with enough scrutiny, discern; in contrast, motion in film and later optic devices of the nineteenth century is something that the eye cannot physiologically see as a deception.[53] Still, the exploration of visual sensation and its abstraction in *Lamia* suggests the shared social character of the dream of bodily movement in pre-, early, and later cinema. Cinematic narrative always exists in sensation as the potential lucid embodiment of social desire through the animistic image, or moving figure—even if, as Jonathan Auerbach suggests of many early short films, the narrative arises out of pointless running and chasing.[54]

Conversely, cinematic sensation always exists in narrative as the limit of that intelligibility, the kinetic diversion away from absolute comprehension of what seems to move before us. Insofar as this dialectic informs the pre-cinema—insofar as it informs Keats's *oeuvre*—they are already cinematic. But the dreaming of this dialectic in Keats's time is also specifically the dream of mass and elite audiences, public viewing, and the commodity form. The working out of this dialectic between sensation and abstraction in both its diachronic and synchronic modes is the interstice between cinematic history and capitalist modernity. Revising an earlier formulation, we should say that—in Keats, at least—the galvanic, biological reanimation of the Romantic and cinematic dead object *is* social desire, animism as publicity, a mass public's act.

> If one concludes that imitators and masters of illusion will later be presented as charlatans and thaumaturges—species of the genus *pharmakeus*—then once again ontological knowledge becomes a pharmaceutical force opposed to another pharmaceutical force.
>
> —Jacques Derrida, "Plato's Pharmacy"

Apollonius's and Lycius's triangulated relationship with Lamia condenses much of these dynamics. We might first understand Lycius's relations to Lamia and to Apollonius as simply contrasting sensation with education, and Apollonius's actions as attempts to exorcize sensation from a Habermasian public sphere of bodily disinterest. But, as Levinson implies, and as the Greek overlay of the story allows, Apollonius and Lycius's teacher-student relation mixes pedagogy with libido, power, and affect; Apollonius's desire to teach Lycius visually what Lamia is could also be about teaching the young Corinthian who he is in relation to his stern master—a relation that Lycius replicates earlier in his sadistic treatment of Lamia.[55] For Apollonius public education might already be colored by drives usually associated with the non-reflection of sensation. Similarly, as his name implies, Lycius is associated with the lyceum, the site of higher learning. But the Lyceum in Keats's time is also the one located in London's Strand district, a famous hall for many of the city's exhibitions and shows. Lycius himself embodies the contradictions between elite and mass culture and between pedagogy and entertainment; by forcibly socializing Lamia as his public bride, he also connects these contradictions to one between private and mass viewing. As important, these contradictions are equally about Lycius's relation to Apollonius as they are about the student and Lamia.

But if Apollonius's and Lycius's (initially) separate visions of Lamia mediate their conflicted relation to one another, the coherence of that mediation is further complicated by an aspect of the sophist's identity that converges with the history of the phantasmagoria. One of the most influential practioners of this sophisticated magic lantern show was Étienne-Gaspard Robertson, "who opened his 'Fantasmagorie' in Paris in 1798" (Mannoni, 147). A physicist and chemist, Robertson first conceived of the phantasmagoria in explicitly educational terms:

> The *Bureau Central* has authorized me to give a class in Phantasmagoria, a science which deals with all the physical methods which have been misused in all ages and by all peoples to create belief in the resurrection and apparition of the dead. The Government protects this establishment: it has recognized the need to encourage the physicist-philosopher, whose works and morality tend to destroy the enchanted world which only owes its existence to the wand of fanaticism.[56]

Robertson's vision squares with much of the self-representations of individuals involved in the phantasmagoria, and it fits Apollonius as well; in his stare we see the disenchanting instruction of the magic lantern's "physicist-philosopher." He is the Apollonian sun to Lamia's moon—both the source of her projected light and the searching rational inquiry that shows her to be simply an image and nothing more. Robertson's deliberate rhetoric against "fanaticism" and his reference to France's revolutionary government also constitute something besides a coincidence. They point to the same identity for Apollonius that Paul Philodor, the likely inventor of the phantasmagoria, also advertised, when, using the "philosophical ideas of the Enlightenment and Revolution," he "claimed to be debunking popular credulity towards sorcerers, prophets, visionaries, exorcists and other charlatans (including priests, monks, and popes)" (Mannoni, 143). The physicist-philosopher's science of images is also the dream of a science of ideology, a term whose own complicated history likewise begins in revolutionary and Napoleonic France.[57] Conflating perceptual deception with ideological mystification in the way that the previous chapter examined, Apollonius unmasks Lamia as an image, denuding her of motion and turning her the "deadly white" of a projection curtain or screen; he shows her to be an idol of the mind, her visual sensation and visual abstraction of tactile matter the signs of her ideological untruth (2:276).

But, of course, a dream of a science is still a dream, which is very much Lamia's realm. Likewise, Mannoni notes how Philodor's Revolutionary iconoclasm "exploited the public's taste for the occult" and, even more unambiguously, a committee investigating Robertson's patented right to the name Fantasmagorie described his practice as the making of optical illusions "which, without advancing by a single step or making any progress in the pursuit of the sciences, serve[d] only to capture the admiration and above all the money of the Public, to whom [he and his rival were] careful not to explain the causes."[58] As critiques of ideology from both the left and the right have opined since the Revolution, the ideological scientist might be the biggest charlatan of all. The "physicist-philosopher" is also a priest, a vocation that Robertson trained for in his youth. Apollonius's scopic possession of Lamia the image is a science marked by jealousy, suspicion, guarded authority, and its own optics of mystification, a condition literalized in the phantasmagoria by its back projection, which hid the lantern from the audience's view. Himself irreducibly defined by such optics, Apollonius, like the priest and capitalist London showman, can also never absolutely know himself, his science, or his desire.

Many have noticed the resemblance between Apollonius and Lamia; more precisely, the two antagonists mirror each other but are not the same.[59] Lamia begins in the poem as a snake with human eyes, while Apollonius has a petrifying, serpentine stare ("lashless eyelids stretch / Around his demon eyes!") and a human form (2:288–89). This and other traits (his vampiric intrusion into the lovers' domicile) make him a male version of Geraldine from Coleridge's *Christabel*, a famously incomplete piece of gothic sensation that shares many of the obsessions and themes of Keats's poem. Yet Apollonius's monstrousness both converges with and exceeds Lamia's, as well as Geraldine's and Medusa's, two more explicit possessors of the female evil eye. Like them, he is a monster in both the Lacanian and Derridean sense, insofar as his desire also remains ultimately opaque, (terrifyingly) unknowable in any (phallic) representation. He might look at Lamia in a certain way to regain Lycius, but he might do so also to kill the young student. With his scopic control he might be either exorcizing or possessing Lamia. He might kill Lycius in order to possess Lamia; he might possess Lamia in order to kill Lycius. We cannot tell if he looks upon Lamia as a teacher, physicist, ideological critic, magician, huckster, or pornographer. He himself might very well just be another image, a parody of Apollo or one of the "Theosophers" also called up by the phantasmagoria's seance. But he is also a monster simply in his ability to make Lamia pay for being an image—for the opacity of social desire, and social relations, embodied in both of them. His patriarchal stare might really be either Lamia's feminine gaze or Medusa's castrating evil eye, but it is also the terroristic enforcement of the difference between them and him. Apollonius and Lamia might be the same, but their stories are not, which is what constitutes, and what counts in, social antagonism.

Whether Lycius ultimately sees Lamia the way that Apollonius does is, of course, an open question. This quandary is even more prosaic than wondering what it might mean to see Lamia as a snake. The predicament is generated by how the last lines of Keats's poem energetically confuse their pronouns. Burton's *Anatomy* would suggest that "'A serpent!' echoed he" refers to Apollonius repeating himself (2:305); as Mark Jones observes, however, "he" could just as well refer to Lycius finally seeing Lamia through Apollonius's eyes, an epistemological event that then arguably incites her disappearance and his death (see n. 38). Similarly, the descriptive action of Lycius's death, which coincides with the end of the poem, is by no means clear:

> And Lycius' arms were empty of delight,
> As were his limbs of life, from that same night.
> On the high couch he lay!—his friends came round—
> Supported him—no pulse, or breath they found,
> And, in its marriage robe, the heavy body wound. (2:307–11)

In his death Lycius might now be the "it" of the "heavy body," now finally as inanimate as the image he loved. Or "it" might refer to Lamia the creature, either living or dead, now wound or coiled in the marriage robe after Lamia's human form has "vanished." This indeterminancy could speak to an Apolloniusian perspective in which the non-human is always a type of death. But if the heavy body is Lycius, the marriage robe wrapped by that form could also be Lamia's. More precisely, the robe could *be* Lamia, the screen or sheet upon which the optic illusion of her tactile form and inner self was projected. The robe is literally one side to Lamia, the reflexively physical, social, *and* semiotic material remainder left over by her abrupt, emphatic vanishing, the disenchantment of visual sensation by *Lamia* that dialectically informs the increasingly visual mediality of early nineteenth-century England.

But is disenchantment only Apolloniusian, and is it simply fatal? Chandler, in his own discussion of the poetry of sensation, quotes from Oskar Negt and Alexander Kluge's proletariat complication of Habermas's narrative of one public sphere, what occurs when a laborer's fantasy meets alienated reality: "As fantasies move further away from the reality of the production process, the goal that drives them on becomes less sensitive. Therefore, all escapist forms of fantasy production tend, once they have reached a certain distance from reality, to turn around and face up to real situations."[60] Obsessed with the compulsions of the commodity form, the Corinthian circuit of exchange, commerce, and consumption, *Lamia* seems less sanguine about the possibility of facing the "reality" of the production process.[61] Nevertheless, by its very animistic nature, the commodity form advertizes its inanimate status, the unavoidable moment when its fantasy confronts something besides itself. This might not be reality (as Žižek might say, that *was* the fantasy), but it might also not be biological death (*Sublime*, 30–49). Lamia's vanishing could also be the end of a show, the conclusion to an attraction or sensation when the mass audience gets up from their seats when lights replace the darkness. It could be the series of disjunctures inherent in our optic mediations of the world, what we know today as much by the push of a button or click of a mouse. If, at the end of the poem, as many suggest, Lamia returns to the country and Apollonius to his study to await another cycle of their (apparently) eternal story, we might ask, regardless of the narrator's explicit claims, whether Lycius, the public subject of proto-, not simply pre-, cinema, also awakens from his nerveless state and exits the exhibition hall, to await once more the consequences of Hermes's stolen light, the chance to see desire in nothing, the *in*visible in the image, the always social self in projected, kinetic form. We are all Keats's heirs in that we experience culture, both high and low, as equally constituted by different degrees of virtuality. We all, like Lycius, inhabit the fatal moment of inter-medial discontinuity, the consciously physical and mental limit of any one social representation, of any one resolution to the captivating, worrisome dialectic between visual sensation and its abstraction. Whether that parataxis is a moment of freedom or quotidian repetition, whether it suggests the possibility of oppositional practice or the symptom of co-optation—these are alternatives perhaps indeterminate as the meanings of death. But, as *Lamia* sensationally anticipates, this discontinuity is more than ever our public life.

# The Embarrassment of Romanticism

> Is not Romanticism itself a fossil formation in the history of culture, not only because of its obsession with lost worlds, ruins, archaism, childhood, and idealistic notions of feeling and imagination, but because it is itself a lost world, swept away by the floods of modernity it attempted to criticize? And is not Romanticism therefore itself a totem object, a figure of collective identification for a tribe of cultural historians called Romanticists, and beyond that, for a structure of feeling more generally available to anyone who identifies himself as a "romantic"?
>
> —W. J. T. Mitchell, *What Do Pictures Want?*

In his 1974 study of Keats and the affect of embarrassment, Christopher Ricks extends his meditation to the activity of public and private reading both in and beyond Keats's letters:

> Keats sets such store by the attempt to imagine a writer or a reader because doing so will release reading and writing from the inevitable anxieties of solitude—narcissism, solipsism, lonely indulgent fantasizing. It is for such reasons that many of us set such store by the public discussion of literature. To write about literature, argue about it, teach it: these, though they bring other anxieties, are valued because they can help to restore a vital balance of private and public in our relation with literature. (195–96)

By pointing out how Keats imagines a necessarily public dimension to literary knowledge, Ricks links the poet to the modern institutionalization of literary studies. That sense of the mediated character of the literary in Keats also underwrites how in different ways Levinson, Pfau, and others, including myself, have read in Keats a poetics of the pastiche. Implicit in our recognition of the mediated nature of literary knowledge in Keats is the possibility that of all the Romantic poets Keats might provide the best template for the predicament of reading in our current historical moment, especially within, but also outside, the academy. Ricks's thoughts comment on this dynamic in a complicated way. For even as he claims that the study of literature bracingly offsets the embarrassingly solipsistic "indulgent fantasizing" of private reading, he also notes that such public study occasions its own "anxieties," with the balance between private and public so "delicate . . . it is easily upset into uneasiness" (196). Referring in particular to the activity of the library, Ricks identifies a "disconcerting and embarrassing aspect of reading in public: a lot of people doing separately and publicly what it seems natural to do on one's own and privately, and thus having neither the truly public sense of literature nor the truly private" (196).

Taking Ricks's anecdote of the library as an example of the mediated, institutionalized study of literature during this and the previous century, we can suggest several things. First, this hybrid space of the public and private seems to obstruct as much as enable any genuine experience of the literary in either a "truly public" or "truly private" form. Second, the reason for this obstruction has to do with the non-literary pleasures that seem to attend to this hybrid space, a sociability based on, for Ricks, a mixture of "embarrassment and erotic anxiety" (196), best expressed in a poem by Merrill Moore that Ricks quotes:

> Men and women go there and sit and read
> But they squirm and rove, survey each other
> Not as sister, quite, and not as brother,
> But more with nervous desire or anxious dread.
>
> ("Eyes in Libraries"; lines 11–14)

Third, then, one term that encompasses both the embarrassing distraction of this public yet subterfuge eros and the equally diverting indulgence of private, fantasized reading is *sensation* as both an embodied and disembodied event, a collection of sights, sounds, and wayward feelings formally defined by their non-identification with literature. Yet, as Ricks's own association of solipsism with private reading implies, the authentic experience of literature in either its "truly public" or "truly private" mode might be a *fiction*. A pre-lapsarian world that could neatly divide itself between literary experience and the subaltern realm of sensation might never have existed; such a division would then only appear in retrospect, from the fallen perspective of Moore's mediating library. The unnatural state of the library, *das Unheimliche*, actually becomes the "natural" state of reading. The "delicate" balance that Ricks seeks is in fact the phantom sign of the messy blending of the private and public, the non-mediated and mediated, the sober and sensational, that the (post-)modern—or *Romantic*—engagement with literature always activates. In its radical form, this balance becomes the less deluded although perhaps even more intransigent series of disciplinary and methodological scissions that signifies the formal parataxis underlying knowledge in the humanities, which we examined in Byron's proleptic *Don Juan*. More to the point, the possibility arises, as Byron's poem also paradoxically shows, that the attractions of the literary cannot be separated from the distractions of non-literary sensation; we might attend to the library *because* of such distractions, *define* reading by its unavoidable relation to the subterfuge glances and noises that Moore describes. Likewise, we might read alone exactly *for* the privative, for our own narcissistic, lonely versions of Moore's "nervous desire" and "anxious dread." Because of such public and private distractions, reading might always be the mediated double of its purer, fictional self. Reading might indeed be its own allegory, its own mediation and alterity—its own sensation.

The academic study of literature can then also be understood as quite literally, and quite especially, an institutionalized allegory of reading. Certainly, outsiders observing the rites and conventions of our profession would have no trouble agreeing to this description, although the further point is to see within such apparently arcane, or techno-bureaucratic, practices an intensely distilled version of the predicament of literary reading in general—an allegory of the allegory, as it were. As such, the academic study of literature doesn't find itself necessarily protected from the distractions of either noisy library or solipsistic mind; rather, the opposite is true. While it might then appear, because of straitened resources and the reorganization of knowledge under global capitalism, that the field of literary studies is reaching a crisis point, the modern history of the discipline can be narrated as a series of crises about its purity since its inception during the late nineteenth century.[1] This is not to diminish the problems that we and our students face today; it is simply to clarify more thoroughly the historical contours of the discipline's dilemma, and how much that historicity inheres in the aporetic logic of literature's own identity, and non-identity. We can then observe how Ricks's and Moore's library has been overtaken by a new archival model, that of the Web, and how this latest medium lays out a new public/private space, topos, surface, or grid, within and upon which reading's entanglement with "nervous desire," "anxious dread," and a host of other affects and sensations is acted out. One might wonder whether such a dynamic will mutate reading into an altogether unrecognizable form or, as Jerome Christensen argues by connecting new media users and Romantic addicts, intensify an aspect of reading that already operated in earlier literary print practices (*End*, 177–206). Or, in contrast to Christensen's compulsively focused user, future cultural players might increasingly define reading as a cognitive and epistemological experience structured emphatically by distraction, akin to Benjamin's utopian vision of the non-auratic, cinematic moment (*Illuminations*, 240–41). One can only wonder how self-representations of intellectual and philosophical reading will respond to such developments.[2]

More immediately pertinent, the problems that belie Ricks's "delicate" balance can be found operating in not only emerging but also residual, or still dominant, forms of intellectual labor. The published scholarly book already finds itself unavoidably caught in the messy blending that Ricks's balancing act tries to surmount. How can such an event avoid the embarrassment of a private allegory made public? How can the purported constative effect of such public, and (in the Habermasian sense) publicized, readings escape the idiosyncratic, eclectic, even masturbatory dimensions of what, in effect, is our solitary, hermeneutic behavior, especially when such singularity also characterizes the force of our strongest readings? And how, conversely, can such singularity, our "truly private" experience of the literary, avoid the myriad sensations of Moore's anxious library, professional and personal, that run through the geometries of context and text that we try to manage when we attempt to read literature or produce literary history? It isn't difficult to imagine this dynamic structuring a host of examples that make up the professional study of literature, in and outside the classroom. There is something embarrassing about professing the literary, about how we invariably make the case for the literary with performative, charismatic, *and* functionalist gestures that in actuality intensify the aporia of literary value that has been literature's fate since its inception, or apogee, during the Romantic era. That current debates between literary and cultural studies might be one way the volatility of this condition becomes intelligible, and that such debates themselves occur in a moment when value calcifies daily into the hegemonic fact of global techno-instrumentality, speaks to how this embarrassment (or "mood," in Pfau's strong use of the term) is something else besides the limited narcissism of individual personality.

Neither Keats nor the poet's interest in embarrassment, we should note, embarrasses Ricks. But Ricks writes in response to people who were, and are, embarrassed. I want to suggest how their embarrassment can today mean something more than simply a discomfort over Keats. Ricks's formulation of one scholarly debate in Romanticism, over the aesthetic value of Keats's writerly indulgences, his Cockney adolescent appetite for, in Carlyle's memorable term, "sweets," can be extended to include not only an embarrassment over Romanticism, what in a variety of ways this book has tracked, but also an embarrassment over Romanticism as a metonym for literature per se.[3] This discomfiture can signify more than the fear of the literary as the overly sentimental, emotional, and self-indulgent; it can also mean more than the particular anxieties of professional Romanticists who feel the pressure to validate their specific historical field against new disciplinary reorganizations and interests. Such awkwardness can also specifically mark how the study of not only Romanticism but *all* national literatures increasingly feels like an embarrassment, a purposeless sweet, within Bill Readings's "university in ruins," the place of higher education in a world of transnational, techno-administrative capitalism (*University*, 1–20).[4] Readings's analysis is not the only one we have of literature's diminishing academic cultural capital, of course, but its basic diagnosis of literature departments dealing with new demands, or a new language, of corporate instrumentality is one that should sound familiar to many of us involved in academic labor. It's not much of an exaggeration to say that everyone within the discipline of literature today has their own narrative to tell—embattled, defiant, theorizing, pragmatic, or cynical—of this most recent allegory of reading. At the start of the second decade of the twenty-first century, the profession of the literary is invariably a complex reflection on literature's embarrassment—on, either positively or negatively, literature's functions and, whether welcomed or feared, literature's disappearance.

Embarrassment goes well with sobriety, unless one perhaps lingers too long or too avidly with the embarrassing.[5] Referencing our coda's epigraph, we might then say that the only thing more embarrassing than a Romantic fossil would be one that stubbornly persists not only as a totem *into* modernity but also as a sign *of* that event. Extending Mitchell's observation, we might add that the structure of feeling that he identifies as Romantic, an affect reflexively about the persistence of putatively discontinued narratives and desires, is ineluctably in part embarrassment.[6] This book could thus be considered one meditation on what embarrassed Romanticism, and how Romanticism embarrassed, from its late eighteenth- and early nineteenth-century inception to its ongoing presence in critical debates of the present day. In this study, out of such different and sometimes conflicting embarrassments, out of so many varied attempts to impose sobriety onto the event of reading, not only have certain familiar notions of the literary arisen, but also the very intelligibility of historical narrative, as well as the historicities of Romantic revolution and commodification themselves. This is neither a pure nor absolute nor complete story of generation, but it is one that clarifies many of the conflicting investments that we have had in Romanticism for the past two centuries.

The *récit* is complicated at least in part because of the differing roles that both sensation and literature have played in the story's tropology. A rejection of sensation has meant straightforwardly a dismissal of the overly sensory, or sensual, which has clarified in various narratives both ideological positions and distinctions of taste. But we have also studied Romantic sensations of meaning that in their literariness also disarticulate themselves from the phenomenal and sensory as any final markers for constative and cognitive resolution; in such cases, sobriety involves an attempt to preempt or control the manner in which a sensation of meaning disavows the sensory limitations that physical materiality imposes on figural resemblance. The obstacles to the latter form of sobriety consequently also inform our examination of how Romantic, gothic, and ideological discourses entwine. In complex ways, both the sensory and the sensation of meaning have either embarrassed or invigorated the authors featured in this work, with arguably the Wordsworth and Shelley of this study being the two most complicated instances of this dynamic.

The discursive operations of Romantic sobriety thus provide a tropological resource for understanding literature's present predicament during the global reorganization of knowledge in and beyond the humanities. If we have associated the literary with the sensation of meaning, we have also seen literature distinguish itself in a variety of ways from the alterity of sensation per se, in the Wordsworth of "Tintern Abbey," Knapp and Michaels's polemic on interpretation, the reviewers of Keats, and Ricks's estimation of the inhabitants of Moore's library. Romantic sobriety, its (self-)embarrassment, provides a discursive rehearsal for our present institutional dilemma, the embarrassment of literature in an era of global information retrieval.

Many of the consequences of this present situation, as well as the choices thrust upon us as a collective profession and as individuals, will be self-evident soon enough, if they are not already, one suspects. Let me conclude with several points that abut against this situation in asymmetric, but pertinent, fashion. One takes seriously the way that sensation can be *formally* deployed as literature's other, insofar as in Romanticism sensation is slotted into the necessary role of literature's non-identity in various origin myths of literature's becoming. The necessity of that structure speaks to a necessarily formal self-scission constitutive of literature, how the literary always carries its own non-identity within itself, insofar as *within* and *without* are simply spatial tropes. While the literary as a positive identity can separate itself from what it is not, the sensation of Ricks's solitary dreaming and public distraction, the volatility of Ricks's "delicate" balance shows how that positivity becomes invariably characterized by its friability. The movement of the literary will always be a double one, not only the performative denotation of literature *as* literature but also the equally vehement signification of the literary as something inevitably beside itself. The resemblances involved in a sensation of meaning cannot be easily managed; the literary cannot simply cordon itself off.

If Romanticism has always been structured by its own legitimation crisis, so has literature, a predicament whose present form we know today mostly because of the meta-commentary of, and on, Romanticism. We should know this fact about literature's aboriginally insecure nature by now, and the fact that we do not, that we only come to this insight through the phantom *Nachträglichkeit* of our various readings, says something about the stuff of literature's, and Romanticism's, historicity, which strains but can never cohere fully into the story of progress that such terms create and try to inhabit. This is why allegories of readings are not information retrievals, although that is also why they are not actual readings, genuine moments of cognition and phenomenal access. Reading is *not* itself, which is one reason why the argument for the study of literature in a time of diminishing resources is such a difficult one to make—which is not to say that we should avoid making the argument, of course. But the larger point is that this is precisely literature's power, the value of its non-value. Like Romanticism, the force of the literary also comes from its reflexive engagement with this very aporia. If Romanticism exemplifies the reflexive problem of history's identity and non-identity, literature dramatizes a similarly necessary contradiction involving the heteronomy of value and non-value. Both Romanticism and literature are scandals of thought, which is why they are embarrassments, and also why they generate within and beyond themselves so many different calls, from so many ideological and aesthetic positions, for their sober management.

To forget the spectral (non-)quality of the literary while we make our institutional arguments for literature's place in the global techno-administrative world of ideas would be just that, a form of amnesia. It would mean forgoing or sacrificing those very areas that especially worry the boundaries of literature's domain, and which could actually ally with literature during its present troubles—the study of the image, for example.[7] But first and foremost, it would mean evading the impossible demand that the literary puts on us with its scandal of thought. If literature is first and foremost a *figure* for an alternative to the techno-administrative instrumentality daily encroaching upon us globally and locally, it is no coincidence that the present sense of crisis in literary studies seems to have the ontological weight of a teleological narrative, as grim as that *récit* may be. But *as* a figure, literature imposes on us something akin to the visor effect of the Marx in Derrida's ghost theory, a spur, demand, or call for something we can neither avoid nor completely fathom, the value of (non-)value, Kant's absurdist *nihil negativum*, a shape or spirit whose very sensation obstructs its cognitive and semantic realization at the very moment of its articulation. It is in this radically unthinkable sense that Shelley's elusive figuration in "A Defense of Poetry" can be reconceived, so that his description of poetry's "unapprehended inspiration" of the future as the mirroring of a shadow becomes the sign not of an insurmountable problem but of an ongoing, incalculable resource or strength.[8] The reference to Derrida's *Specters* is also no coincidence since it enjoins in hyperbolic fashion the (post-) apocalypse of literature to the radical form of history, constituted by the multitude of pre- and post-apocalypses, and pre- and post-revolutions, crashing down on us this very moment. Indeed, literature's commitment to history's exceptional form might be literature's finest Romantic embarrassment, the way reading voluntarily breaks out of Ricks's library to search for ever-noisier, ever-more-distracted, public stagings of its allegories of the libidinal shape of history's desire. And yet it might be in the most nonsensical staging of that relation to the world, of literature beside itself as a Kantian "nothing without a concept," that we glimpse the other of commodity eros, an alterity to capital's iron-willed, instrumental presence (Dalzell, 97). And what if that glimpse, or blink, was indeed the moment of dialectical history's *Darstellung*? How narcissistic, how embarrassing, how sobering, how *Romantic* would that be?

## *Introduction* · *The Sensation of Romanticism*

1. For two recent works on the senses in which Romanticism plays a central role, see Susan Stewart, *Poetry and the Fate of the Senses* (Chicago: U of Chicago P, 2002); and Catherine Gallagher, *The Body Economic: Life, Death, and Sensation in Political Economy and the Victorian Novel* (Princeton: Princeton UP, 2005). The difference between Stewart's arguably transhistorical study of poetry from antiquity to the present day and Gallagher's decidedly historical argument about the intersection of British literary and economic discourse in the eighteenth and nineteenth centuries demonstrates the range of approaches people have taken in studying sensation and Romanticism together. Both works share, however, a founding belief in sensory experience *as* experience, as an embodied physical event, a phenomenal conception that the present study's own figural emphasis explicitly complicates. For a recent historical study of the ways that Romantic understanding of the empirical senses intersects with Romantic aesthetics, see Noel Jackson's compelling *Science and Sensation in Romantic Poetry* (Cambridge: Cambridge UP, 2008). For an account of the relation between empirical thought on the senses and eighteenth-century sensibility, see G. J. Barker-Benfield, *The Culture of Sensibility: Sex and Society in Eighteenth-Century Britain* (Chicago: U of Chicago P, 1992). For three works that consider the social and epistemological question of sensibility and the attendant one of emotion in Romanticism, see C. B. Jones, *Radical Sensibility* (London: Routledge, 1992); Adela Pinch, *Strange Fits of Passion: Epistemologies of Emotion from Hume to Austen* (Stanford: Stanford UP, 1996); and Thomas Pfau, *Romantic Moods: Paranoia, Trauma, and Melancholy, 1790–1840* (Baltimore: Johns Hopkins UP, 2005). For a summary of work on the history of the senses about, beyond, and in the eighteenth and nineteenth centuries, see Jackson, 64–72; see also Alain Corbin, *Time, Desire, and Horror: Towards a History of the Senses*, trans. Jean Birrell (Cambridge: Polity P, 1995).

2. As Hans Ulrich Gumbrecht succinctly adumbrates, in Western philosophy "sense making" largely "hinges upon the epistemological dominance of the Subject/Object paradigm" ("Martin Heidegger and His Japanese Interlocutors: About a Limit of Western Metaphysics," *Diacritics* 30.4 [2000]: 83); the notion of a sensation of

meaning developed especially in chaps. 4 and 5 of this study will attempt to complicate that formulation, while chap. 7 will examine one instance of its figurative intransigence. For perhaps the most technically extensive and scrupulous consideration of the relation between sense and meaning, see Gottlob Frege's distinction between sense and denotation, "On *Sinn* and *Bedetung*," in *The Frege Reader*, ed. Michael Beaney (Oxford: Blackwell, 1997) 151–71.

3. For a listing of some of the many works that have considered the relation between Romanticism and history, see James K. Chandler, *England in 1819: The Politics of Literary Culture and the Case of Romantic Historicism* (Chicago: U of Chicago P, 1998) 33; Chandler's seminal study can be seen as a reflexive summation, and transcendence, of many of the historicizing impulses motivating Romantic studies since the 1980s. For my own engagement with portions of Chandler's thought, see chap. 7.

4. For a previous attempt to triangulate de Manian thought, Marxism, and Romanticism, see Forrest Pyle, *The Ideology of Imagination: Subject and Society in the Discourse of Romanticism* (Stanford: Stanford UP, 1995). Pyle's elegant study especially uses Althusser's theory of ideology to formulate these connections; the present study employs a more varied, but hopefully no less fruitful, set of writings from the Marxist tradition in its interrogation of these relations.

5. Consider, for example, Brian Massumi's opening statement in a recent work: "When I think of my body and ask what it does to earn that name, two things stand out. It *moves*. It *feels*. In fact, it does both at the same time. It moves as it feels, and it feels itself moving. Can we think of a body without this: an intrinsic connection between movement and sensation whereby each immediately summons the other?" (*Parables for the Virtual: Movement, Affect, and Sensation* [Durham: Duke UP, 2002] 1). This dynamic physicality is arguably a key attraction in Deleuzian thought, no matter how indeterminate or volatized it becomes in his and others' formulations; as such, Deleuzian sensation at least in this key instance diverges from the non-phenomenal disposition that informs large portions of the notion of sensation developed in this book. See also chap. 7, n. 13, and Deleuze and Felix Guattari's *A Thousand Plateaus: Capitalism and Schizophrenia* (Minneapolis: U of Minnesota P, 1987).

6. I'm thinking of how Romanticism becomes subsumed under the more pressing historical question of Modernism in Lukács and Modernism and postmodernism in Jameson. For Lukács, see his *The Historical Novel*, trans. Hannah Mitchell and Stanley Mitchell (Lincoln and London: U of Nebraska P, 1962); and *The Meaning of Contemporary Realism*, trans. John Mander and Necke Mander (London: Merlin P, 1963). For Jameson, see his *The Political Unconscious: Narrative as a Socially Symbolic Act* (Ithaca: Cornell UP, 1981).

7. Jerome J. McGann, *The Romantic Ideology: A Critical Investigation* (Chicago: U of Chicago P, 1983); Marjorie Levinson, *Keats's Life of Allegory: The Origins of a Style* (Oxford: Blackwell, 1985); and Jerome Christensen, *Lord Byron's Strength: Romantic Writing and Commercial Society* (Baltimore: Johns Hopkins UP, 1993).

8. M. H. Abrams, "English Romanticism: The Spirit of the Age," in *Romanticism Reconsidered: Selected Papers from the English Institute*, ed. Northrop Frye (New York: Columbia UP, 1963) 26–72. That Abrams's essay is itself a self-interested reformula-

tion of William Hazlitt's famous 1825 work speaks to how long and intensely the term *revolution* has reflexively been part of the Romantic imaginary.

9. This is not to say of course that Levinson's study somehow enacts the same belief in nineteenth-century Communist revolution that Marx expresses, but that the critical force of her hermeneutic comes from a sense of class antagonism and market forces that reproduces the power of the Marxist analysis, although one obviously coupled with the strategies of post-structuralism. In contrast, Christensen's study of Byronic commercial culture exploits but also more explicitly troubles the ontologies of Marxist categories of dialectical history, something that becomes even more clear in the conceptual shape of his later work, *Romanticism at the End of History* (Baltimore: Johns Hopkins UP, 2000).

10. "Wordsworth's greatest gift to literary history, and his greatest contribution to an understanding *of* history, is that he was never sure that he knew what to say, or how to say it. His failure of resolution and independence which, however conscious it was, was in every important sense deliberate and is as such open to careful intellectual and theoretical articulation, aligns him with those readers of the twenty-first century who are engaged in trying to understand the dynamics of their own society as that society becomes, increasingly after 1989 and again after 9/11, more and more obliged to confront the possibility that the very mechanisms with which it purports to alleviate its concerns are themselves significantly implicated in their continued and urgent existence" (David Simpson, *Wordsworth, Commodification, and Social Concerns* [Cambridge: Cambridge UP, 2009] 234).

11. Slavoj Žižek, *The Parallax View* (Cambridge, MA: MIT P, 2006) 4–13.

12. Jürgen Habermas, *The Theory of Communicative Action, Vol. 1: Reason and the Rationalization of Society*, trans. Thomas McCarthy (Boston: Beacon P, 1984) 341–42, 357–60. See also chap. 7, n. 2.

13. See Chandler, 67–74; Jackson, 64–91.

14. See, for example, David Simpson's *Subject to History: Ideology, Class, Gender* (Ithaca: Cornell UP, 1991) 1–33, 163–90, as well as his "Is Literary History the History of Everything? The Case for 'Antiquarian History,'" *SubStance* 28 (1999): 5–16.

15. Paul de Man, *The Rhetoric of Romanticism* (New York: Columbia UP, 1984) viii.

16. See, for example, n. 2 in chap. 1. Orrin N. C. Wang, *Fantastic Modernity: Dialectical Readings in Romanticism and Theory* (Baltimore: Johns Hopkins UP, 1996).

## *Chapter 1 · Romantic Sobriety*

1. Jürgen Habermas, *The Philosophical Discourse of Modernity: Twelve Lectures*, trans. Frederick G. Lawrence (Cambridge, MA: MIT P, 1990) 1–22.

2. Northrop Frye, "The Drunken Boat: The Revolutionary Element in Romanticism," in Frye, 14–15. Frye takes the term *vehicular form* from Blake (14). For recent work on Romanticism and addiction, see Alina Clej, *A Genealogy of the Modern Self: Thomas De Quincey and the Intoxication of Writing* (Stanford: Stanford UP, 1995); Margaret Russett, *De Quincey's Romanticism: Canonical Minority and the Forms of Transmission* (Cambridge: Cambridge UP, 1997); Josephine McDonagh, "Opium and

the Imperial Imagination," in *Reviewing Romanticism*, ed. Philip W. Martin and Robin Jarvis (New York: St. Martin's, 1992) 116–33; Barry Milligan, *Pleasures and Pains: Opium and the Orient in Nineteenth-Century British Culture* (Charlottesville: U of Virginia P, 1995); and Sue Vice, Matthew Campbell, and Tim Armstrong, eds., *Beyond the Pleasure Dome: Writing and Addiction from the Romantics* (Sheffield: Sheffield Academic P, 1994). For an important earlier treatment, see M. H. Abrams, *The Milk of Paradise: The Effect of Opium Visions on the Works of De Quincey, Crabbe, Francis Thompson, and Coleridge* (New York: Octagon, 1971). While the testing case for this study is a British Wordsworthian high Romanticism, it should be noted that the dialectic between intoxication, or addiction, and sobriety impacts on other Romantic national traditions. Witness, for example, Nietzsche's distinction between Dionysus and Apollo in *Die Geburt der Tragödie*, vol. 3 of *Werke: Kritische Gesamtausgabe*, ed. Giorgio Colli and Mazzino Montinari (Berlin: de Gruyter, 1972) 5–152; Hölderlin's "heilignüchterne[s] Wasser" in his poem "Hälfte des Lebens" in vol. 1 of *Sämtliche Gedichte*, ed. Detlev Lüders (Bad Homburg: Athenäum, 1970) 300; and Hegel's references to Bacchus and Bacchanalian revelry in *Phänomenologie des Geistes*, vol. 2 of *Werke*, ed. Johannes Schulze (Berlin: Duncker und Humblot, 1832) 37, 82, 538, 543–44. See also Rodolphe Gasché, "The Sober Absolute: On Benjamin and the Early Romantics," in *Walter Benjamin and Romanticism*, ed. Beatrice Hanssen and Andrew Benjamin (New York: Continuum, 2002) 51–68; and David L. Clark's essay on the figure of addiction in German philosophy, "Heidegger's Craving: Being-on-Schelling," *Diacritics* 27 (1997): 8–33.

3. See Norman Longmate, *The Waterdrinkers: A History of Temperance* (London: Hamilton, 1968); Brian Harrison, *Drink and the Victorians: The Temperance Question in England, 1815–1872*, 2nd ed. (Staffordshire: Keele UP, 1994); and Roy Porter, "The Drinking Man's Disease: The 'Pre-History' of Alcoholism in Georgian Britain," *British Journal of Addiction* 80 (1995): 385–96. Porter acknowledges the traditional view of locating in late Georgian medicine the new perception of alcoholism as a medical illness; he argues against this historical distinction, however, by asserting that this view of alcoholism already existed in the early eighteenth century, a fact that would bind eighteenth- and nineteenth-century views on drink together (390–91). See, however, n. 22. Sobriety, of course, also appears in other discourses early on in the eighteenth century; consider, for example, some of the titles of the Irish archbishop Edward Synge: "Religion Tried by the Test of Sober and Impartial Reason"; "Sober Thoughts for the Cure of Melancholy, Especially that which is Religious"; and "Two Tracts; the One, Directions to a Sober Christian for the Offering Up to the Lord's Prayer to God in His Private Devotions; the Other, Sober Thoughts on the Doctrine of Predestination" (*The Works of Edward Synge, Late Lord Archbishop of Tuam in Ireland* [London: Thomas Trye, 1744]). I am grateful to Richard C. Sha for this reference.

4. Clifford Siskin, *The Work of Writing: Literature and Social Change in Britain, 1700–1830* (Baltimore: Johns Hopkins UP, 1998) 107, 129. Siskin focuses, of course, on the Romantic conception of creative writing at work and on the relation of that vocation to the rise of the professional classes. In this sense his is a New Historicist engage-

ment with an earlier sociological and materialist scholarship that stressed the relation of sober industry to a Protestant work ethic, to the working classes, or to both. See Max Weber, *The Protestant Ethic and the Spirit of Capitalism*, trans. Talcott Parsons (New York: Scribner, 1958); and E. P. Thompson, *The Making of the English Working Class* (New York: Vintage, 1966) 57–59. But see also n. 16 and chap. 8, n. 1. The nexus of these relations could also be applied beyond the working and professional classes; in this light George III, with his change in reputation from modest Farmer George to the Mad King, becomes the quintessential Romantic subject. For a discussion of his conscious remaking of the image of the monarch, see Linda Colley, *Britons: Forging the Nation, 1707–1837* (New Haven: Yale UP, 1992) 209–10.

5. *The Ruined Cottage*, in *William Wordsworth*, ed. Stephen Gill (Oxford: Oxford UP, 1984) 34.

6. For a discussion of many of these issues in terms of sensational literature, see Karen Swann, "Suffering and Sensation in *The Ruined Cottage*," *PMLA* 106 (1991): 83–95. For an analysis of Wordsworth's poem in terms of commodity reification, see Simpson, *Wordsworth*, 22–53.

7. Andrew Elfenbein, *Byron and the Victorians* (Cambridge: Cambridge UP, 1995) 89.

8. T. E. Hulme, *Speculations: Essays on Humanism and the Philosophy of Art* (London: Routledge and Kegan Paul, 1936) 127.

9. William Wordsworth, "Preface to *Lyrical Ballads, with Pastoral and Other Poems*," in Gill, 599.

10. I am indebted to Michael Macovski for this insight. For a discussion of Wordsworth's ghostly figures in relation to commodity reification, see Simpson, 1–16; see also my introduction.

11. Geoffrey H. Hartman, *Wordsworth's Poetry, 1787–1814* (New Haven: Yale UP, 1964) 33–69. Of course, Hartman's famous study is itself structured around a perceived act of sobriety on Wordsworth's part, in which his poetry narrativizes the domestication of the more vertiginous aspects of his imagination by the steady hand of nature (210–11).

12. The work that most fully reads "Tintern Abbey" through this political apostasy is Marjorie Levinson, *Wordsworth's Great Period Poems: Four Essays* (Cambridge: Cambridge UP, 1986) 14–57. See also James K. Chandler, *Wordsworth's Second Nature: A Study of the Poetry and Politics* (Chicago: U of Chicago P, 1984); Alan Liu, *Wordsworth: The Sense of History* (Stanford: Stanford UP, 1989); Jerome McGann's *The Romantic Ideology*; and David Simpson, *Wordsworth's Historical Imagination: The Poetry of Displacement* (New York: Methuen, 1987). See also Jerome Christensen, "Once an Apostate, Always an Apostate," *Studies in Romanticism* 21 (1982): 461–74.

13. Irving Babbitt, *Rousseau and Romanticism* (Boston: Houghton Mifflin, 1919) 379; Samuel Taylor Coleridge, *Biographia Literaria*, ed. James Engell and W. Jackson Bate, vol. 7 of *The Collected Works* (Princeton: Princeton UP, 1982) 189–90.

14. Alan Richardson, *Literature, Education, and Romanticism: Reading as Social Practice, 1780–1832* (Cambridge: Cambridge UP, 1994) 6. Richardson focuses on the differences between educating children and educating youths. See also Julie A. Carlson,

"Forever Young: Master Betty and the Queer Stage of Youth in English Romanticism," *South Atlantic Quarterly* 95 (1996): 596–98. Carlson identifies youth with unfinished development but also associates it with the first-generation Romantics, who especially found its theatrical staging a site, and a defense, of their earlier revolutionary enthusiasm. See also most recently Richard C. Sha's smart and provocative reading of *Don Juan* as allowing Byron to use puberty to "question the value of maturity and conventional masculinity," with the poem primarily about the founding powers of the "youthful body . . . as full of perverse potentiality . . . a paradoxical ground of latency" (*Perverse Romanticism: Aesthetics and Sexuality in Britain, 1750–1832* [Baltimore: Johns Hopkins UP, 2009] 241–42).

15. Geraldine Friedman, *The Insistence of History: Revolution in Burke, Wordsworth, Keats, and Baudelaire* (Stanford: Stanford UP, 1996) 9. One could qualify this view with Helen Vendler's claim about "Keats's characteristic sobriety," ostensively gotten from Milton's *L'Allegro*, which underwrites her own well-known narrative about the poet's maturation during the writing of the Great Odes, and which is exemplified by the "rejection of 'Bacchus and his pards'" during "Ode to a Nightingale" (*The Odes of John Keats* [Cambridge, MA: Harvard UP, 1983] 250). Yet one might also observe how this "characteristic sobriety" is folded into the larger movement of "Nightingale" toward a variety of imagined sensations based on the poetic thought experiment of the senses' nullification; thus, sensory deprivation becomes the occasion for poetic sensation. Similarly, the end point for Vendler of Keats's putative poetic maturation is "To Autumn," a work whose lyrical sense of perfection has oftentimes been understood to be a triumph of sensation over semantic meaning. For a reading of Keats's poem that focuses on its relation to physical sensation, see chap. 7; see also the analysis of Keats's relation to pre-cinematic sensation in chap. 10.

16. Blake to William Hayley, 23 October 1804, in *The Complete Poetry and Prose*, ed. David V. Erdman (New York: Doubleday, 1988) 757. One might also argue that Blake, unlike Wordsworth, complicates any simple consolidation of childhood and error with the twin states of innocence and experience; see Richardson's suggestion that Blake's view of childhood should be understood through a "dialectical triad" (20). For the perception of Blake's later works as in fact depoliticized, see Marilyn Butler, *Romantics, Rebels, and Reactionaries: English Literature and Its Background, 1760–1830* (Oxford: Oxford UP, 1981) 51. But consider also Jon Mee's association of Blake with the radical antinomian energy of Protestant "enthusiasm" in *Dangerous Enthusiasms: William Blake and the Culture of Radicalism in the 1790s* (Oxford: Oxford UP, 1992). Indeed, Mee's later argument that Romanticism can be understood as an attempt to regulate this radical enthusiasm is another compelling formulation of the sobering impulses in Romantic writing; see his *Romanticism, Enthusiasm, and Regulation: Poetics and the Policing of Culture in the Romantic Period* (Oxford: Oxford UP, 2003). See also, however, this chapter's discussion of the trope of sobriety in the Protestant-influenced radical and reform movement.

17. Shelley to William Godwin, 16 January 1812, in *Letters*, ed. Frederick L. Jones, 2 vols. (Oxford: Clarendon, 1964) 1:231. I am indebted to Neil Fraistat for pointing this letter out to me.

18. William Godwin, *Enquiry Concerning Political Justice and Its Influence on Modern Morals and Happiness* (New York: Penguin, 1985) 252. I am grateful to Richard C. Sha for this reference.

19. Louis de Saint-Just, *Rapport sur la police générale, la justice, le commerce, la législation et les crimes des factions* (Paris: Imp. nat., n.d.), cited in Mona Ozouf, *Festivals and the French Revolution*, trans. Alan Sheridan (Cambridge, MA: Harvard UP, 1988) 282.

20. David Simpson, *Romanticism, Nationalism, and the Revolt against Theory* (Chicago: U of Chicago P, 1993) 40–43, 64–83. But see also n. 21.

21. Samuel Bamford, cited in Thompson, 679. A counterpoint to such Reform strategy would be not only the anti-Jacobin narrative of sobriety but also the sobriety in dress and manners of the Anglo-European ruling classes after the French Revolution, a response to the "sartorial and political disaster" of the procession of the Estates General in 1789, when "the representatives of the Third Estate, dressed in somber black, had been cheered; but the traditionally lavish costumes of the nobility and clergy had met with jeers or silent disgust" (Colley, 187). I am indebted to Daniela Garofalo for this reference. For an in-depth study of radical and Reform culture, see Kevin Gilmartin, *Print Politics: The Press and Radical Opposition in Early Nineteenth-Century England* (Cambridge: Cambridge UP, 1996).

22. H.O. 40.4, Rules of the Bath Union Society for Parliamentary Reform, January 1817, cited in Thompson, 740. Thompson argues, in fact, that "the Temperance Movement can be traced to this post-war campaign of abstinence" (740). This Reformist and Radical rhetoric can be ironically juxtaposed with Edmund Burke's own admonition to the English poor: "Patience, labor, sobriety, and frugality, should be recommended to them; all else is downright fraud" (quoted in Roy Porter, *English Society in the Eighteenth Century* [Hammondsworth, Middlesex: Penguin, 1982] 111).

23. See also n. 28.

24. Mary Wollstonecraft, *A Vindication of the Rights of Woman: An Authoritative Text, Backgrounds, Criticism*, ed. Carol H. Poston (New York: Norton, 1975) 110.

25. For an extended analysis of this passage along these lines, see Wang. For a detailed discussion of the relation between passion and epistemology on Great Britain during the eighteenth and nineteenth centuries, see Pinch.

26. The *locus classicus* for scholarship on civic republicanism is J. G. A. Pocock, *The Machiavellian Moment: Florentine Political Thought and the Atlantic Republican Tradition* (Princeton: Princeton UP, 1975). See also Pocock, *Politics, Language, and Time: Essays on Political Thought and History* (New York: Atheneum, 1971); and Pocock, *Virtue, Commerce, and History: Essays on Political Thought and History, Chiefly in the Eighteenth Century* (Cambridge; Cambridge UP, 1985). For one post-1980s application of the concepts of civic republicanism and the long eighteenth century to Romanticism, see Robert J. Griffin, *Wordsworth's Pope: A Study in Literary Historiography* (Cambridge: Cambridge UP, 1995) 8–23. It would be a mistake, however, to assume that there has been no overlapping between the 1980s Romanticist focus on Jacobin politics and studies of civic republicanism; see Griffin's point about the presence of Pocock in the works of James K. Chandler, David Simpson, and John Barrell (9).

27. *The Complete Works of William Hazlitt*, ed. P. P. Howe, 21 vols. (London: Dent and Sins, 1930–34) 5:161–62. For a discussion of this passage's relation to the concept of modernity, see Wang, 184–85.

28. We should be mindful, however, of the mediations necessary for such articulations. Percy's friend Leigh Hunt, for example, was annoyed at being confused with the working-class Reformer and antitax agitator Henry Hunt and, along with his brother John, kept the *Examiner* "aloof from the plebeian movement" (Thompson, 675). It should also be noted how the rhetoric of a progressive sobriety rests not only on a bifurcation between Jacobin and anti-Jacobin politics but also on one that grounds the sobriety of the working class: "The struggle of the reformers was one for enlightenment, order, sobriety, in their own ranks; so much so that Windham, in 1802, was able to declare with some colour that the Methodists *and* the Jacobins were leagued together to destroy the amusements of the people" (Thompson, 59; my emphasis).

29. For a seminal discussion of the "stability of metaphor," see de Man's treatment of Rousseau's *Second Discourse* in *Allegories of Reading: Figural Language in Rousseau, Nietzsche, Rilke, and Proust* (New Haven: Yale UP, 1979) 135–59.

30. "To William Wordsworth," in *Samuel Taylor Coleridge*, ed. H. J. Jackson (Oxford: Oxford UP, 1985) 126.

31. It has long been debated whether Kant or Schelling has a stronger presence in the *Biographia*; my narrative representation takes as its point of departure Engell and Bate's argument regarding the centrality of Kant for any discussion of German thought in Coleridge's work (cxxv–cxxvi).

32. The very point of overdetermination is to make secondary whether Coleridge knew about Kant's fastidious reputation; he certainly may have, however, as there were brief biographies of Kant in England from quite early on, and Coleridge probably knew them. Moreover, Coleridge would certainly have known of Kant's references to immoderate consumption and ethical ascetics (see Kant, "On Stupefying Oneself by Excessive Use of Food or Drink" and "Ethical Ascetics," in *The Metaphysics of Morals*, ed. and trans. Mary Gregor [Cambridge: Cambridge UP, 1991] 222–24, 273–74).

33. For a sustained argument regarding Kant's Enlightenment and French revolutionary associations and the adverse reaction that Wordsworth might have had to Coleridge's interest in the philosopher, see Chandler, 251–57. For the British and European association of Kant with Jacobinism, see Simpson, *Romanticism*, 94–99; and René Wellek, *Immanuel Kant in England, 1793–1838* (Princeton: Princeton UP, 1931) 13–15. As Chandler notes (257), the *Biographia* demonstrates Coleridge's own awareness of these issues in the passage where his praise of Kant is also a reflexive disaffiliation from "those who have taken their notion of IMMANUEL KANT from Reviewers and Frenchmen" (153). See also, however, Peter Thorslev's distinction between the reason of German idealism and the reason of French Enlightenment abstraction in "German Romantic Idealism," in *The Cambridge Companion to British Romanticism*, ed. Stuart Curran (Cambridge: Cambridge UP, 1993) 74–94.

34. See Wellek, 88–89; and G. N. G. Orsini, *Coleridge and German Idealism: A Study in the History of Philosophy with Unpublished Materials from Coleridge's Manu-*

*scripts* (Carbondale: Southern Illinois UP, 1969). See also Mary Anne Perkins, *Coleridge's Philosophy: The Logos as Unifying Principle* (Oxford: Clarendon, 1994) 239–40. Coleridge also, however, uses a rhetoric of Stoic philosophy to affiliate himself with Kant and to distinguish himself from other philosophical traditions; thus, he uses as an opprobrium Epicurus, who can refer both to a philosophical position of receptivity (Wellek, 18) and to thinkers such as Helvétius, Paley, and Priestley, practitioners of the Jacobin-associated, Enlightenment error that is the familiar target of his more explicit moments of conservative sober rhetoric (Orsini, 157). But see also Kant's own philosophical balancing of Stoic and Epicurean principles in "Ethical Ascetics," 273. Finally, James Engell uses the language of addiction to assert how Coleridge feared that metaphysics was leading him from Christianity to pantheism (*The Creative Imagination: Enlightenment to Romanticism* [Cambridge, MA: Harvard UP, 1981] 361–62). Thus, Coleridge's engagement with metaphysics both exploits a language of sobriety and is generated by varying, asymmetrical moments of that discourse.

35. Coleridge is referring to the distinction between reason and understanding (*Aids to Reflection*, ed. John Beer, vol. 9 of *The Collected Works of Samuel Taylor Coleridge* [Princeton: Princeton UP, 1993] 215). I am indebted to David Perkins for this and the observation about Coleridge's lyricism.

36. Karl Marx and Friedrich Engels, *The Marx-Engels Reader*, ed. Robert C. Tucker (New York: Norton, 1978) 476.

## *Chapter 2 · Kant All Lit Up*

1. For an extended discussion that very much parallels my own on this point, see Marc Redfield, *The Politics of Romanticism: Aesthetics, Nationalism, Gender* (Stanford: Stanford UP, 2003) 29–34.

2. For extended accounts of the history of Romantic studies into the 1990s, see Jon Klancher, "Romantic Criticism and the Meanings of the French Revolution," *Studies in Romanticism* 28 (1989): 463–91; Jon Klancher, "English Romanticism and Cultural Production," in *The New Historicism*, ed. H. Aram Veeser (London: Routledge, 1989) 77–88; Herbert Lindenberger, *The History in Literature: On Value, Genre, Institutions* (New York: Columbia UP, 1990) 23–43; and Wang, 4–11.

3. See also the example of Cynthia Chase, *Decomposing Figures: Rhetorical Readings in the Romantic Tradition* (Baltimore: Johns Hopkins UP, 1986) 1–10.

4. A notable exception to this trend in Romanticist historicist scholarship would be James K. Chandler's commanding *England in 1819*, which argues for the singular influence of British Romantic historical thought. Interestingly, Chandler's paradigms are buttressed by engagements with thinkers usually associated with the concept of the long eighteenth century, such as J. G. A. Pocock (101–2).

While this chapter focuses on the relation between Romanticism and the long eighteenth century, its argument should in many ways also be applicable to the possible reorganization of Romanticism into the long nineteenth century—indeed, this will be one of the main claims that I make. For one analysis voicing concerns about the recent collusion between Romanticism and the nineteenth century, see Tilottama

Rajan, "'The Prose of the World': Romanticism, the Nineteenth Century, and the Reorganization of Knowledge," *Modern Language Quarterly* 67 (2006): 479–504.

5. One might also object to delimiting the historicist work of the 1980s through the operations of an ideological critique. But see Wang, 71–82, for the argument that revisionist, ideological critique best characterizes 1980s Romanticist historicist work, as opposed to the more imprecise nomenclature of 1980s Foucaultian-inspired New Historicism.

One might finally point out the appearance in the last decade or so of a new generation of Romanticist scholarship implicitly or explicitly inspired by deconstruction. Whether such institutional soundings ever achieve the status of a true overturning in critical thought—for or against deconstruction, or Romanticism for that matter—is in one way the question explored by this chapter.

6. *Romanticism: A Critical Reader*, ed. Duncan Wu (Oxford: Blackwell, 1995). While the collection does have one contribution by Tilottama Rajan that engages explicitly with deconstruction, the absence of any scholarship directly related to the Yale School is striking. I am grateful to Steve Newman for this observation.

7. See, for example, "The Romantic Century: A Forum," ed. Susan Wolfson, *European Romantic Review* 11 (2000): 1–45; and William Galperin and Susan Wolfson, "The Romantic Century," *Romantic Circles* (April 2000) www.rc.umd.edu/reference/misc/confarchive/crisis/crisisa.html. See also n. 10.

8. See also Klancher, "Romantic Criticism."

9. For an extended consideration of the diminished role of the Revolution in Romantic studies, see chap. 6.

10. For one example of expanding Romanticism's period boundaries, see the *Oxford Companion to the Romantic Age, 1776–1832*, gen. ed. Iain McCalman (Oxford: Oxford UP, 1999). See also n. 7.

11. For a critique of the normative assumptions behind this equivalence, see Wang, 71–82.

12. The argument regarding the Revolution's closure is, of course, associated with the work of the French historian François Furet; see his *Interpreting the French Revolution*, trans. Elborg Foster (Cambridge: Cambridge UP, 1981). For an emphatic rejoinder to this view, see Simpson, *Romanticism*. See also chap. 6.

13. Looming over this issue is, of course, Romanticism's relation to Marxism, *the* theoretical discourse that attempts to supplant the historicist's perception of nominalist non-periodicity with a troping of history's particular identity and value. Extending Redfield's comments, we might then consider the different disciplinary representations of McGann's book and Frederic Jameson's *The Political Unconscious*, a work very much about the Modern, and aesthetic, ideology. While Jameson's text does engage with Marxist theory in a more wide-ranging manner than McGann's, Redfield's point suggests another reason why *The Romantic Ideology* has always been more about Romanticism than Marxism while *The Political Unconscious* has always been more about Marxism than Modernism. As the disciplinary embodiment of history's figurative dimension, Romanticism enables the quest in Marxism for historical value and

meaning, while simultaneously instilling an unavoidable sense of tropic drift within the project.

14. This dimension to Romanticism has always existed, of course, even before the early 1980s ideological critique by McGann and others. See Wang, 26–36.

15. For the most thoroughgoing attempt to historicize this proposition, see Chandler.

16. The mordant history of Western empire certainly demonstrates that fact. See, for example, the role of Enlightenment in Alan Bewell, *Romanticism and Colonial Disease* (Baltimore: Johns Hopkins UP, 1999). Studies on the meaning of Enlightenment are legion, but, aside from Kant's own thoughts on the subject, all in some way orbit around Max Horkheimer and Theodor Adorno, *Dialectic of Enlightenment*, trans. John Cumming (New York: Continuum, 1989). See also Michel Foucault, "What Is Enlightenment?" in *The Foucault Reader*, ed. Paul Rabinow (New York: Pantheon, 1984) 32–50; and Clifford Siskin and Bill Warner, eds., *This is Enlightenment* (Chicago, U of Chicago P, 2010). See also n. 21.

17. For three short accounts of that structure, see Ted Cohen and Paul Guyer, "Introduction," in *Essays in Kant's Aesthetics*, ed. Ted Cohen and Paul Guyer (Chicago: U of Chicago P, 1982) 1–17; Eva Schaper, "Taste, Sublimity, and Genius: The Aesthetics of Nature and Art," in *The Cambridge Companion to Kant*, ed. Paul Guyer (Cambridge: Cambridge UP, 1992) 367–93; and Howard Caygill, *A Kant Dictionary* (Cambridge, MA: Blackwell, 1996) 139–43.

18. Immanuel Kant, *Critique of Judgment*, trans. Werner S. Pluhar (Indianapolis: Hackett, 1987) 99.

19. But see also n. 27.

20. *Subreption* is the specific term that Kant uses in his discussion of the sublime to describe the act of reification, whereby "respect for the object is substituted for respect for the idea of humanity within ourselves as subjects" (sec. 27, 114). For an engaging argument as to how subreption actually structures the judgments of both the beautiful and the sublime, and, indeed, Kant's very rhetoric, see Marc Redfield, *Phantom Formations: Aesthetic Ideology and the* Bildungsroman (Ithaca: Cornell UP, 1996) 12–22. For an example of Kantian beauty in the service of a radical critique of the metaphysical, see Jacques Derrida's reading of pure and ideal beauty in *The Truth of Painting*, trans. Geoffrey Bennington and Ian McLeod (Chicago: U of Chicago P, 1987) 82–118. For two deconstructive approaches that focus on the Kantian sublime, see Derrida, *Truth*, 119–47; and Paul de Man, *Aesthetic Ideology* (Minneapolis: U of Minnesota P, 1996) 119–28. For two previous deconstructive readings of genius and the third *Critique*, see Jacques Derrida, "Economimesis," *Diacritics* 11.2 (1981): 3–25; and Richard Klein's response to Derrida in "Kant's Sunshine," *Diacritics* 11.2 (1981): 26–41. The ways that I intersect with and diverge from Derrida and Klein, especially on sec. 49, should become clear as this reading progresses.

21. It could be said that sec. 50 does away with the problem of conception and aesthetics altogether by further separating the acts of genius and imagination from those of taste and judgment to the point that the two sets of activities, while affecting

one another, remain completely different. There is a strain in this separation, however, to where the division acts less like part of a constative system and more like a trope employed to describe a much more complicated situation. The strain appears not only in the continued problematic presence of what genius is supposed to explain (the non-conceptual conception of beautiful art) but also in the odd way that taste, the province of the non-conceptual judgment of beauty, becomes *more reflexive* than genius. Secs. 47 and 48 demonstrate this self-consciousness by associating taste with the "diligence and learning" of mechanical art and genius with fine, or beautiful, art. Furthermore, in sec. 50, taste is specifically made more reflexive than genius, insofar as taste's reflection upon the products of genius modifies, indeed disciplines, the imaginative process: "Taste, like the power of judgment in general, consists in disciplining (or training) genius. It severely clips its wings, and makes it civilized, or polished; but at the same time it gives its guidance as to how far and over what it may spread while still remaining purposive" (sec. 50, 188). Genius is placed in the position of a savage nature at odds with Kant's earlier formula of genius as the mediation of nature giving rule to art, while, conversely, taste is made a civilizing force paradoxically defined by its intimate relation to a purposiveness earlier allied with nature. Thus, far from simply disappearing, the contradictions between human design and natural purposiveness crystallized in the problem that genius addresses are here distributed evenly along both sides of the distinction between taste and genius. For a discussion of the resonances of European empire within tropes of nature and civilization in the *Critique*, see Henry Schwarz, "Aesthetic Imperialism: Literature and the Conquest of India," *Modern Language Quarterly* 61 (2001): 563–86.

22. See John H. Zammito, *The Genesis of Kant's* Critique of Judgment (Chicago: U of Chicago P, 1992) 131–47, for the view that Kant is actually arguing with Herder that the self-conscious studiousness of mechanical art is as important as, if not more so than, the genius of fine art. This thesis implies a certain circumscription in Kant of his more radical lines of inquiry, such as the notion of a pure or free beauty that Derrida explores. Regardless of whether a more philosophically moderate intent can be extrapolated from the *Critique*, my essay asserts a textual dynamic in Kant's work that nevertheless puts into play the more volatile effects of his words on genius within and beyond the putative attempts of the *Critique* to limit or segregate them. See also n. 21.

23. See Cohen and Guyer, 8–9; and Schaper, 379–80. See also Lyotard's assertion of the "violence" of moral universality's and aesthetic universalization's differend in the *Critique* in *Lessons on the Analytic of the Sublime* (Stanford: Stanford UP, 1994) 234–39.

24. I am, of course, thinking of Adorno here; see his magisterial *Aesthetic Theory*, ed. and trans. Robert Hullot-Kentor (Minneapolis: U of Minnesota Press, 1997). For one exemplary elucidation of the relation between Kant and Adorno, see Robert Kaufman, "Red Kant, or the Persistence of the Third *Critique* in Adorno and Jameson," *Critical Inquiry* 26 (2000): 682–724. There is, arguably, overlap between the catachrestic sense of genius in Kant and the more properly dialectical "aconceptual" generative quality of "construction" in Adorno that Kaufman perceptively identifies as

a Kantian moment in Adorno's *Aesthetic Theory*. The question remains, however, whether Adorno's generation of critical reflection from aporia is a moment of truth. If that is the case, one could say that the movement of this generation is teleological, making aporia a necessary condition *toward* truth. In contrast, this chapter's reading of the *Critique* involves a genetic dynamic, whereby truth and falsehood are effects of the catachrestic nature of genius. But of course, this occasions (yet) another question: is the relation between these teleological and genetic movements dialectical or deconstructive? Indeed, as I bluntly ask at the start of part III, is the relation between the dialectic and deconstruction dialectical or deconstructive?

25. Conversely, insofar as genius purports to carry out nature's rule, one could say that it is a catachresis that knows itself through a "synecdochic transference." See J. Hillis Miller, "Introduction," in Charles Dickens, *Bleak House*, ed. Norman Page (New York: Penguin, 1971) 13.

26. For the argument that genius is indeed the ability to make new sense, as opposed to nonsense, see Timothy Gould, "The Audience of Originality: Kant and Wordsworth on the Reception of Genius," in Cohen and Guyer, 179–93.

27. This distinction anticipates the terms by which Kant later solves the antinomy of taste in the later section on the "Dialectic of Aesthetic Judgment." In sec. 57 Kant associates the indemonstrable nature of the concept in the rational idea with the indeterminate concept of the supersensible substrate, insofar as that concept cannot, simply, be imagined. Thus, while an aesthetic idea reaffirms the estrangement between the aesthetic and conception, a rational idea introduces a more phantomlike sense of a concept, which becomes Kant's resolution of the antinomy of taste, that a judgment of taste is both based and not based on concepts, insofar as there are two forms of conception, the determinate concept and the indeterminate and indemonstrable concept. But in sec. 49 Kant seems to be describing the predicament of determinate concepts that are indemonstrable.

Also, in different places the *Critique* refers to "Spirit" as either a quality of the artwork or a talent of the creative human mind. This mobility could be said to replicate the tension between subject and object that runs through the *Critique* and so much of Kant's oeuvre, such as, most immediately, whether the mental judgment of a beautiful object is actually qualitatively different from the explicit focus on the sublime powers of the mind. See Zammito, 147.

28. Paul Guyer, *Kant and the Claims of Taste*, 2nd ed. (Cambridge: Cambridge UP, 1997) 355–61.

29. Guyer's translation depends on his transformation of the more neutral German "zu" into the more active preposition "of":

> Thus genius properly consists of the happy relationship, which no science can teach and no diligence learn, ***of*** discovering ideas for a given concept and further, finding the *expression* for these ideas that enables us to communicate to others, as accompanying a concept, the mental attunement that those ideas produce. (bold italics mine; 360)

J. H. Bernard's intervention changes the referent of the happy relation altogether:

> The mental powers, therefore, whose union (in a certain relation) constitutes genius are imagination and understanding. . . . Thus genius properly consists in the happy relation [between these faculties], which no science can teach and no industry can learn, by which ideas are found for a given concept. (Immanuel Kant, *Critique of Judgement*, trans. J. H. Bernard [New York: Hafner, 1951] 160)

Pluhar's translation, much like the German, preserves the ambiguity of the passage, where, literally, the "happy relation" exists only in the certainty of itself, and not its referent:

> So the mental powers whose combination (in a certain relation) constitutes *genius* are imagination and understanding. . . . Genius actually consists in the happy relation—one that no science can teach and that cannot be learned by any diligence—allowing us, first, to discover ideas for a given concept, and, second, to hit upon a way of *expressing* these ideas that enables us to communicate to others, as accompanying a concept, the mental attunement that those ideas produce. (sec. 49, 185–86)

30. A reading that insists on the integrity of Kant's aesthetic attributes as first and foremost *images* does not necessarily oppose my more linguistic analysis, however. In the terminology of W. J. T. Mitchell, Kant's reliance on a vocabulary of images in describing the workings of an aesthetic idea points to the "totemic" nature of the philosopher's project, his desire to animate (give Spirit to) the lifeless world, something very much like how the catachresis of genius and figure operates in my argument, as that which makes sense, or meaning, from nonsense. See his "Romanticism and the Life of Things," *What Do Pictures Want? The Lives and Loves of Images* (Chicago: U of Chicago P, 2005) 169–87. The other term in Mitchell's historicist binary, the fossil, provocatively parallels Paul de Man's counter-term to rhetoric, grammar, insofar as both demonstrate in their own way how the animism, or animation, of both totem and figure is the dynamism of a non-human thing. For a reading of catachresis as mechanically subtending Marx's notion of abstract labor, and of de Manian grammar as an inhuman machine, see the next chapter.

31. Jacques Derrida, "White Mythology: Metaphor in the Text of Philosophy," in *Margins of Philosophy*, trans. Alan Bass (Chicago: U of Chicago P, 1982) 218. See also, of course, the role of the sun in de Man's "Shelley Disfigured" in his *Rhetoric of Romanticism*, 93–123.

32. Klein suggestively opposes the gift of Kant's generous sun to light as theft in a poem by Baudelaire, pitting Hermes against Apollo, as it were. In distinguishing between *gift* and *theft* as two different systems of "pure giving" (39), Klein proleptically engages with Derrida's later work on gift and ethics, whose own interrogation of the (non-)exchange of the gift retroactively comments on the categories underwriting "Economimesis" and Klein's reading of it. See Derrida's *Given Time: I, Counterfeit Money*, trans. Peggy Kamuf (Chicago: U of Chicago P, 1992); and *The Gift of Death*,

trans. David Wills (Chicago: U of Chicago P, 1995). Consider also how the predicament of Kantian genius, stretched between conceptual identity and imaginative infinity, also resonates with the challenge of justice that marks the aporia between the precedent of law and the particular integrity of each specific demand for justice in Derrida's "Force of Law: The 'Mystical Foundation of Authority,'" *Deconstruction and the Possibility of Justice*, ed. D. Connell, M. Rosenfield, and D. Carlson (New York: Routledge, 1992) 3–29. It could be said that my description of Kantian genius as the catachresis of figure worries from yet another angle the same impossibility that Derrida does, which he has troped as both a vertiginous generosity and unavoidable demand of justice; see also my discussion of Derrida's take on Hamlet's ghost in chap. 6.

33. Certainly, the question of what flows from what is repeated in its own peculiar way through the issue of translation, of, for example, what flows between and among the *Critique* and its English translators. Bernard translates Wilfhof's lines ("Die Sonne quoll hervor, wie Ruh aus Tugend quillt") as "The sun arose / as calm from virtue springs" (159). "Flow" has been replaced by "springs," both of which conceivably flow, or spring, from the German *quellen*. But in either case questions of continuity, contingency, and self-integrity remain. Indeed, the structural flaw in Bernard's parallelism—if calm springs from virtue, what does the sun arise from?—more explicitly restates the question implicit in the sun flowing as light and origin in Pluhar. For a pertinent discussion of another especially violent sun springing into action, see de Man, "Shelley," 117–18.

34. For two different attempts to understand Kant's relation to the social realm, see Bill Readings's consideration of *The Conflict of the Faculties* in *The University in Ruins* (Cambridge, MA: Harvard UP, 1996) 54–61; and Hasana Sharp's treatment of the *Critique of Pure Reason* in "'We Are All Kantian,'" *Crossings* 3 (1999): 147–57.

35. Within the context of a conventional history of ideas one might point out that the content of Kant's Romanticism—his thoughts on genius—is in fact part of the English eighteenth century, insofar as his ideas were very much influenced by the discussion of the term in eighteenth-century Great Britain. But, of course, this discussion was mediated for Kant by his own dispute with Johann Herder and the *Sturm und Drang* movement. In Kant the Romantic genius exists before British Romanticism and opposes what some have seen as a source of Continental Romanticism. This close reading has attempted to explore how Kant's specific words speak to this predicament about the inherent contradictions in historical and national periodicity, a condition that at the level of figure we specify as Romanticism. For scholarship on the English genealogy of Kant's thoughts on genius, see Otto Schlapp, *Kants Lehre vom Genie* (Göttingen: Vandenhoeck and Rupprecht, 1898); James Meredith, *Kant's Critique of Aesthetic Judgement: Translated with Seven Introductory Essays, Notes, and Analytical Index* (Oxford: Clarendon, 1911); Walter Jackson Bate, *From Classic to Romantic: Premises of Taste in Eighteenth-Century England* (New York: Harper and Row, 1946); Engell; and Zammito.

36. Slavoj Žižek, *Tarrying with the Negative: Kant, Hegel, and the Critique of Ideology* (Durham: Duke UP, 1993) 14.

## *Chapter 3 · De Man, Marx, Rousseau, and the Machine*

1. Fredric Jameson, *Postmodernism, or The Cultural Logic of Late Capitalism* (Durham: Duke UP, 1991), 246.

2. In a word, Jameson's quote about an eighteenth-century noumenon which "language cannot assimilate, absorb, or process" implies a scission between the noumenal on the one side and language and the phenomenal on the other, whereas de Man will get from Kant (among others) a way to place language on the *other* side of the phenomenal, so that, arguably, Kantian materiality refers to how language cannot assimilate *itself.* In describing Kant's noumenon as the "inward experience of consciousness," de Man's immediate point refers to how the Kantian sublime is, paradoxically, "a noumenal entity [that] has to be phenomenally represented (*dargestellt*)" (74).

3. There are, of course, a number of thinkers, such as Heidegger, Adorno, and Derrida, whose writings explore these issues, and who could just as well have provided access to the topos considered here. The goal of this chapter, then, is as much to clarify the specific rhetorical and conceptual operations of the specific writings examined as to suggest a more general overlapping of deconstructive and Marxist discourse. A possible comparison with particularly timely suggestiveness might contrast the role of the machine in this piece with the references to "the external, nonsensical, 'machine'—automatism of the signifier" of Pascal and the concept of "ideological fantasy" in Slavoj Žižek's *The Sublime Object of Ideology* (London and New York: Verso, 1989) 30–33, 36–37. Along those lines, see also Jacques Derrida's remark on possible resonances among de Man, Lacan, and the Deleuzian "desiring machine" of the *Anti-Oedipus* ("Typewriter Ribbon: Limited Ink (2) ('within such limits')," in *Material Events: Paul de Man and the Afterlife of Theory*, ed. Tom Cohen, Barbara Cohen, J. Hillis Miller, and Andrzej Warminski [Minneapolis: U of Minnesota P, 2001] 308–9). See also nn. 5 and 22. I am indebted to Tilottama Rajan for the phrase "technological unconscious."

4. Paul de Man, *Allegories of Reading: Figural Language in Rousseau, Nietzsche, Rilke, and Proust* (New Haven: Yale UP, 1979) 268.

5. Perhaps unavoidably, this passage seems today pretty much joined to the historico-biographical coordinates of the young Paul de Man's writings for the collaborationist paper *Le Soir* during World War II. For two helpful—that is, complicated—leftist responses to this situation, see *Postmodernism*, 256–58; and Ernesto Laclau, "Totalitarianism and Moral Indignation," *Diacritics* 20 (1990): 88–95. See also Wang, 35–68. Moving in another direction, we might also consider the American translation of Jacques Lacan's use of the Freudian *Wiederholungzwang* as "repetition automatism" in his famous "Seminar on 'The Purloined Letter,'" *Yale French Studies* 48 (1973): 39, as well as that concept's relationship to Lacanian intersubjectivity and his assertion that the "displacement of the signifier determines the subjects in their acts, in their destiny, in their refusals, in their blindnesses, in their end and in their fate, their innate gifts and social acquisitions notwithstanding, without regard for character or sex, and that, willingly or not, everything that might be considered the stuff of psychology, kit and caboodle, will follow the path of the signifier" (60). But see also Žižek's

comment about how Lacan moves beyond the mechanical repetition of the "Seminar" in his later years (*Enjoy Your Symptom: Jacques Lacan in Hollywood* [New York: Routledge, 1992] 22–23).

6. Paul de Man, *The Resistance to Theory* (Minneapolis: U of Minnesota P, 1986) 86, 94–97, 99–102.

7. Fredric Jameson, *The Ideologies of Theory: Essays 1971–1986, Volume 1: Situations of Theory* (Minneapolis: U of Press, 1988) 121.

8. Karl Marx, *Capital: Volume 1*, trans. Ben Fowkes (London: Penguin, 1990) 163–77.

9. Karl Marx, *Economic and Philosophic Manuscripts of 1844*, trans. Martin Milligan, in Tucker, 95. By citing both this text and *Capital*, I am, of course, qualifying Althusser's argument for an epistemic break between Marx's earlier and later works. See Louis Althusser, *For Marx*, trans. Ben Brewster (London: New Left Books, 1977); and *Reading Capital*, trans. Ben Brewster (London: New Left Books, 1970).

10. Indeed, for Geoffrey Bennington, the machine in de Man necessarily means confronting the "nature of the ethical and the political," which requires more than simply conceiving a " 'position' on ethical and political issues" (*Legislations: The Politics of Deconstruction* [London: Verso, 1994] 149). For Bennington, de Man's "apparent 'neutrality' on such matters is no more and no less neutral than, for example, the question concerning technology" (149). The last section of this chapter could thus be seen as considering how Marx does not simply calculate an immediately intelligible political position for his readers but also attempts this other form of engagement as well. See chap. 6 for a consideration of how Derrida's own reading of Marx might be seen as thinking through the continuity and disparity between these very two movements.

11. See, for example, *Resistance*, 10–11; Cathy Caruth, "The Claims of Reference," *Yale Journal of Criticism* 4 (1990): 193–205; and Friedman.

12. Jean-Jacques Rousseau, *The Confessions*, trans. Christopher Kelly, vol. 5 of *The Collected Writings of Rousseau* (Hanover: UP of New England, 1995) 85.

13. The use of such terms does not necessarily imply a fundamental belief in the organic essentialness of preindustrial, capitalist society. Rather, they allude to the new questions of value, destiny, and worth associated with the vocational choices of a capitalist subject increasingly unmoored from the traditional roles and strictures of that earlier society. For an application of these issues to a twentieth-century moment of modernity, one still generated by the European history of Rousseau's eighteenth century, see Jameson, *Political*, 249–50. But see also this chapter's discussion of the interpretation of Marx's exchange value as a corrosion of traditional, organic society.

14. Jean Jacques Rousseau, *Oeuvres complètes, Les confessions, autres textes autobiographieques*, ed. Bernard Gagnebin and Marcel Raymond (Paris: Gallimard [Bibliothèque de la Pléaide], 1959) 1:1036; cited in *Allegories*, 298.

15. But see also Derrida's own reading of the machine in *Allegories*, where he actually points out how de Man says grammar and the machine are *only* "like" one another, a resemblance that exists in tension with other quotations by de Man that Derrida cites, which emphatically insist on the mechanical character of language's

performative nature ("Typewriter," 353–54). Derrida's insistence on resemblance instead of identity is motivated by the desire to assert in *Allegories* the radical formality that de Man examines in his later writings, which in this case resists transforming the mechanical condition of language into any form of positive knowledge, or insight. One might argue, however, that a literal understanding of language as a machine duplicates, rather than overcomes, the problem of a radical instrumentality that *Allegories* dramatizes. The same might be said for how this singular literalization actually opens deconstruction to history, insofar as the status of this history as a serviceable, positive form of *technē* is far from clear, a predicament that, along with the question of resemblance, we will take up in the following chapters.

16. That both these options come from Kant, and that both differ in crucial, perhaps radical ways, simply speaks to the centrality of Kant to our own inescapably theoretical moment; see also the editors' introduction in Cohen, Cohen, Miller, and Warminski ("A Materiality without Matter?" vii–xxv) and n. 16 of chap. 4. For one attempt to parse the different phases of Lacan's thoughts on the real, and which also resorts to Kant in doing so, see Tom Dalzell, "Kant's Nothings and Lacan's Empty Objects," *The Letter: Irish Journal for Lacanian Psychoanalysis* 39 (2008): 97–102.

17. Gayatri Spivak, "Scattered Speculations on the Question of Value," in *In Other Worlds: Essays in Cultural Politics* (New York: Routledge, 1988) 155–58.

18. This is not to say, of course, that Horkheimer and Adorno are nostalgic for use value in any simple fashion. See also chap. 8's discussion of the relation of the commodity form's purposeless instrumentality to other forms of non-purpose in Byron's *Don Juan*.

19. See Jean Baudrillard, *For a Critique of the Political Economy of the Sign*, trans. Charles Levin (St. Louis: Telos Press, 1981) 130–63; and *Simulations*, trans. Paul Foss, Paul Patton, and Philip Beitchman (New York: Semiotext[e], 1983).

20. For further readings about this debate, see Piero Sraffa, *Productions of Commodities by Means of Commodities* (Cambridge: Cambridge UP, 1960); Lucio Colletti, *From Rousseau to Lenin* (New York: Monthly Review Press, 1973) 87; Diane Elson, ed., *Value: The Representation of Labor in Capitalism* (Atlantic Highlands: Humanities Press, 1979); Ian Steedman, *Marx after Sraffa* (London: Verso, 1981); and Ian Steedman et al., *The Value Controversy* (London: Verso, 1981).

21. For a discussion of this passage as a proleptic allegory of the commodification of social and economic theory after 1848, see Friedman, 169–70.

22. Another, more radically Hegelian reading of this passage would consider the objective knowledge of commodities and abstract labor a retroactive effect of the reconstructed historical memory of the subject under capital. In that sense Aristotle could not have had access to this knowledge, insofar as it is the outcome of an analysis that can only come from the position of a subject secured within the historical nexus of capital and commodity exchange. Within this scenario "popular opinion" is not a second-order effect, but the index of this nexus. As such, "popular opinion" has as much ontological weight as the slavery of Aristotle's Greek society. Indeed, the relations of domination and servitude that inhere in Greek slavery, unequal labor, become under capitalism the fetishized relations among commodities and, conse-

quently, their owners. The fetishized social relations of commodities can only be calculated, however, if their "common substance" exists, that is, the "popular opinion" of equal labor—what "'in reality'" human equality actually is.

While securely imbedding abstract labor within the historical *epistēmē* of capitalism's subject, this retroactive construction of the difference between that subject and Aristotle is structured by the impossibility of answering when that difference—when capitalism, in effect—occurs. (Similarly, Žižek asserts the impossibility of asking when capitalism attains the self-realization that would dialectically lead to its end: "When can we speak of an accordance between productive forces and relations of production in the capitalist mode of production? Strict analysis leads to only one possible answer: *never*" [*Sublime*, 52].) Abstract labor is the index of a historical difference that history cannot account for; insofar as capitalism's retroactive memory structures the very parameters of that memory, the moment before that memory objectively begins becomes an impossible point in time. Abstract labor signifies capitalist (and Marxist) history as a simulation that needs no other prior history for either its existence or its historicizing force. Abstract labor is the historical insight into capital's procedures that is no less real than the waking origins of precapitalist history and heterogeneous social labor. Rather than dialectically solving the rhetorical tensions in Marx's passage on Aristotle, an interpretation based on the retroactive remembering of unequal labor, or slavery, ends up reemphasizing the robotic, catachrestic nature of the remembering subject of capitalism in relation to its own history. See also n. 3.

23. Louis Althusser, *Lenin and Philosophy and Other Essays* (New York: Monthly Review Press, 1971) 160.

## Chapter 4 · Against Theory beside Romanticism

1. Such a "turn" has to be complicated, of course, by how much that very event was theorized by New Historicism, Jamesonian Marxism, and other historicist arguments of the 1980s. The underlying thesis of this chapter, however, is that one contemporary outcome of such theorization has been the validation of the *récit* that remembers this movement as simply a change from theory to history. In Romantic studies the theorization of history in the 1980s is synonymous with McGann's ideological critique; for an account of that critique, see Wang, 70–106, as well as chaps. 2 and 6. See E. D. Hirsch, "Against Theory?" in Steven Knapp and Walter Benn Michaels, *Against Theory: Literary Studies and the New Pragmatism*, ed. W. J. T. Mitchell (Chicago: U of Chicago P, 1985) 48–52.

2. Jonathan Crewe, "Toward Uncritical Practice," in *Against*, 60.

3. In a footnote Knapp and Michaels state that the "device of contrasting intentional speech acts with marks produced by chance is a familiar one in speech-act theory." The question is whether this fact sufficiently resolves the question of meaning raised by their example—the number of chance meanings (a concept that Knapp and Michaels would dispute) that the wave poem generates, iterations all the more foregrounded by the explicit theme of contingency formulated in their note.

4. P. D. Juhl, *Interpretation: An Essay in the Philosophy of Literary Criticism* (Princeton: Princeton UP, 1980) 199–202; Percy Bysshe Shelley, *The Triumph of Life*, in *Shelley's Poetry and Prose*, ed. Donald Reiman and Neil Fraistat (New York: W. W. Norton, 2002) 496; and Michel Foucault, *The Order of Things: An Archaeology of the Human Sciences* (New York: Vintage, 1973) 387. I'm grateful to David L. Clark for the Foucault reference.

5. See Jacques Derrida, "Signature Event Context," in *Margins*, 309–30; John Searle, "Reiterating the Differences: A Reply to Derrida," *Glyph* 1 (1977) 198–208; and Jacques Derrida, "Limited Inc abc . . ." (trans. Samuel Weber), in *Glyph* 2 (1977) 162–254. The pertinent Derrida essays, along with a summary of Searle's, are all collected in *Limited Inc*, ed. Gerald Graff (Evanston, IL: Northwestern UP, 1988).

6. Peggy Kamuf, "Floating Authorship," *Diacritics* 16 (1986): 3–13.

7. I'm grateful to Ian Balfour for this observation. The title essay of de Man's book is also pertinent, of course, since one could also very productively interrogate the semantic relation between *resistance* and *against*; see Wlad Godzich's thoughts on the former in his forward to *Resistance* (xii–xiii).

8. See also, however, de Man's problematization of the literality of denomination in *Allegories*, 135–59; and Ernesto Laclau and Chantal Mouffe's deconstruction of particular elements in *Hegemony and Socialist Strategy: Towards a Radical Democratic Politics* (London: Verso, 1985), 103–4.

9. E. D. Hirsch, *Validity in Interpretation* (New Haven: Yale UP, 1967) 227–30, 238–40; Cleanth Brooks, "Irony as a Principle of Structure," in *Literary Opinion in America*, 2nd ed., ed. M. D. Zabel (New York: Harper & Brothers, 1951) 736; and F. W. Bateson, *English Poetry: A Critical Introduction* (London: Longmans Green & Co., 1950) 33, 80–81. As Deborah Elise White has pointed out to me, Knapp and Michaels's argument really does not require the wave's serialization of two separate stanzas, as one set of squiggles should be enough to make the argument about intention—a fact that confirms the overdetermined nature of "A Slumber" in the essay, as the poem's iconicity rests in part on how different readings have all traditionally stressed the divide between the poem's two stanzas. One might argue that the poem is an icon of interpretation precisely *because* of the divide.

10. As Alan Bewell notes, there is, for example, a long-standing recognition of the centrality of death in "A Slumber" and a number of other Wordsworth poems (*Wordsworth and the Enlightenment: Nature, Man, and Society in the Experimental Poetry* [New Haven: Yale UP, 1989] 188). See Bewell, 187–234, for a suggestive account of the anthropological "history of death" in Wordsworth's writings, including "A Slumber" and "There Was a Boy."

11. To talk also of some *thing*, of course, is to invoke another genealogy beside that of Knapp and Michaels's, one that involves Heidegger more than Austin. Our most immediate point of departure, in terms of its simultaneous complication of both the linguistic and ontological, would be Paul de Man's famous comparison of Lucy's becoming a "thing" to Baudelaire's falling man in "The Rhetoric of Temporality," in *Blindness and Insight: Essays in the Rhetoric of Contemporary Criticism*, 2nd ed. (Minneapolis: U of Minnesota P, 1983) 213–14, 224; see also J. Hillis Miller's reading of

Lucy-as-thing, Heidegger, and sexual difference in "On Edge: The Crossways of Contemporary Criticism," in *Romanticism and Contemporary Criticism*, ed. Morris Eaves and Michael Fischer (Ithaca: Cornell UP, 1986) 104–5. Recent developments in thing theory have tended to focus on the physical nature of this designation—see, for example, the special issue "Things," ed. Bill Brown, *Critical Inquiry* 28 (2001); and Mitchell, *What Do Pictures Want?* 111–24, 144–87. See also chap. 8, n. 17.

12. For two treatments of this trope in de Man, see Chase, 82–112; and Wang, 49–68.

13. For one discussion of the essay's place in the dialectical reading of Romanticism, see Wang, 40–46.

14. Daniel T. O'Hara, "Revisionary Madness: The Prospects of American Literary Theory at the Present Time," in *Against*, 38.

15. For a more precise formulation of the meaninglessness of "Marion" in de Man as the catachrestic discontinuity between the performative and cognitive aspects of language, rather than as simply the performance of meaninglessness, see Andrzej Warminski, " 'As the Poets Do It': On the Material Sublime," in Cohen, Cohen, Miller, and Warminski, 25–27.

16. See Derrida, "Typewriter," 281. See also especially in *Material Events* the editors' introduction ("A Materiality without Matter?" vii–xxv) and also Warminski, 8. *Materiality* is, of course, a difficult term in de Man's later writing, most significantly in his posthumous *Aesthetic Ideology*; readers will see how this and the following chapters try to contribute to an understanding of the term and how that overlaps and diverges from other approaches, such as those presented in *Material Events*. For a complimentary discussion of non-material materiality in German idealism, see Rajan's introduction to *Idealism without Absolutes: Philosophy and Romantic Culture*, ed. Tilottama Rajan and Arkady Plotnitsky (Albany: SUNY P, 2004) 1–3.

Finally, see "Shelley Disfigured," for a moment (or, arguably, an *event*, in the way that Warminski has posited) that marks a change in de Man's own use of the term, when he contrasts the "non-signifying, material properties of language" with a deeper understanding of figure as *not* being constituted by the "iconic, sensory, or if one wishes, the aesthetic moment" (114). What becomes clear is that the latter, radically disturbing sense of figure in the essay, the "madness of words" (122), rather than the sensory form of the signifier, is what *materiality* seems to expand upon in *Aesthetic Ideology*. The difference between phenomenal sensation and figuration is elaborated in a further passage relevant to our present discussion of the sensation of meaning as the resemblance of non-meaning to meaning: "The particular seduction of the figure is not necessarily that it creates the illusion of sensory pleasure, but it creates an illusion of meaning" (115). The present analysis puts force on the term "seduction" as a *compulsion*—but like seduction, without the originating presence of a human agency.

17. For a possible comparison of this notion of resemblance to the concept of semblance, the problematic condition of likeness, unlikeness, and deception used by Theodor Adorno, see his *Aesthetic Theory*, 100–107.

18. Sigmund Freud, "The 'Uncanny,' " ed. James Strachey, vol. 17 of *Complete Psychological Works* (London: Hogarth, 1955) 219–52.

19. The distinction between seeing and reading has inspired a wide array of historical thought, of course. For a succinct summary of such thought, and the argument that de Man is best understood as articulating the inevitable cul-de-sac that any claim about the relation between perception and cognition reaches, see Rei Terada, "Seeing Is Reading," in *The Legacies of Paul de Man*, ed. Marc Redfield, in *Romantic Circles Praxis* (May 2005) www.rc.umd.edu/praxis/deman/index.html. For two pertinent treatments of the issue in Romantic studies, see Chase, 32–64; and David L. Clark, "How to Do Things With Shakespeare: Illustrative Theory and Practice in Blake's *Pity*," in *The Mind in Creation: Essays on Romantic Literature in Honor of Ross G. Woodman*, ed. J. Douglas Kneale (Montreal: McGill-Queen's UP, 1992) 106–33.

20. For the seminal Yale School (or pre–Yale School) engagements with the strangeness of the poem, see Hartman, 19–22; "Wordsworth and Hölderlin," in *Rhetoric*, 51–54; and Paul de Man, *Romanticism and Contemporary Criticism: The Gauss Seminar and Other Papers* (Baltimore: Johns Hopkins UP, 1993) 74–93, 137–46. For perhaps the most theoretically literate recent reading of both "There Was a Boy" *and* "A Slumber" together, see Anne-Lise François, *Open Secrets: The Literature of Uncounted Experience* (Stanford: Stanford UP, 2008) 158–70. As the title of her work implies, François's attempt to identify the "recessive action" of these and other literary works engages with a semantic strangeness similar to what our analysis confronts, although, arguably, the destination of her remarkable readings differs from ours, as they move to a hushed denuding of consequence released from sensation, as well as compulsion and trauma (1). In that sense, François's lyrical Wordsworth might be the most quietly sober version of the poet yet.

21. "There Was a Boy," in *Lyrical Ballads*, ed. R. L. Brett and A. R. Jones (London and New York: Methuen, 1984) 134.

22. For a historicist reading that understands the mimic hootings through "the historical perspective of eighteenth-century language theory," see Bewell, 209.

23. Lionel Trilling, "Wordsworth and the Rabbis," in *The Opposing Self: Nine Essays in Criticism* (New York and London: Harcourt Brace Jovanovich, 1955) 143.

24. Compare this unmooring to how de Man claims that the poem's double use of "hanging" tropes the spatial indeterminancy of correspondence itself, a situation that poetry can only hope to ameliorate through the gentle cushioning of sky by lake (*Rhetoric*, 52–54). Consider also Simpson's suggestion of how this imagery connects the "loneliness of the living" to a "community of the lifeless" (*Wordsworth*, 166).

25. J. Mark Smith, "'Unrememberable' Sound in Wordsworth's 1799 *Prelude*," *Studies in Romanticism* 42 (2003): 502, 504. Compare to Hartman's claim that the success of nature's development of the boy's mind rests upon how unaware he is of the process, where the unintentional consequences of the boy's hooting are subsumed under the intention of a personified nature (19). To what degree, then, can Hartman's nature be retrospectively read as the figure of a figure, the personification of the placeholder for precisely the aporia this chapter discusses?

26. Readers usually see the poem, of course, in two parts, one about the lake and one about the town. See Bewell, 211.

27. At this point one could conceivably pass further into psychoanalytic discourse,

associating the sensation of meaning not only with the uncanny but also with one understanding of Lacanian *jouissance*, as, literally, "enjoyment-in-sense" (*joui-sense*), especially insofar as one reads the poet's compulsion as a way to organize his desire. See Žižek, *Sublime*, 43–44. The point of divergence might very well be one of emphasis and detail rather than of any complete break, insofar as the psychoanalytic especially focuses on how, in a way that resonates with the resistance of de Manian materiality to figuration, *jouissance* marks what the symbolic can't assimilate, while the sensation of meaning stresses through the event of resemblance how figure is still generated by that non-assimilation, or resistance. See, however, François's argument against the implications of reading "There Was a Boy" in terms of trauma, especially as first formulated in Hartman's encounter with the work (162–68).

28. Aptly enough, the speaker might not have been able to face the tombstone because, during Wordsworth's time, a grave might only have been a mound, since stone markers would only get in the way of sheep herds crossing the lands. The poet might have literally faced the earth as the grave of the boy. I am grateful to Paul Betz for this observation. For an explicit connection between the "death-in-life imagery" of Wordsworth's poem and alienated market life, see Simpson, 222–23.

29. For a suggestive reading of some of these same issues through a Gadamer-inspired assertion of phenomenal, "lived experience," see Smith, 506. But Smith also makes a distinction between physical sensation and what he calls the "mood" of the "intervenient" established aurally in Wordsworth's poems (508). One might also see the sensation of meaning as a radically unstable, linguistic version of the problem that William Empson identifies in *The Prelude*, where Wordsworth's use of "sense" ambiguously refers to either sensory or imaginative experience (*The Structure of Complex Words* [Cambridge, MA: Harvard UP, 1989] 289–305). See also Jackson, 10, 82–83.

30. Such a document would be for Hirsch Wordsworth's explanation in the preface to *Poems in Two Volumes* (1815) of how the poem describes the boy's psychological state (see Brett and Jones, 299). The same could be said for those chapters in the *Biographia Literaria* that argue for the unmistakable style of Wordsworth, in terms of their applicability to Coleridge's 1798 letter. My point would be that such recordings are unable to cordon off or limit the more uncanny resemblances generated between various writings and the semantic effects that follow; in that sense the difference between the 1815 preface and Coleridge's letter as proof for the meaning of "There Was a Boy" (or between the *Biographia* and "Against Theory" as evidence for the meaning of Coleridge's letter) is, ultimately, not so much about kind as about degree.

31. Coleridge to William Wordsworth, 10 December 1798, ed. Earl Leslie Griggs, vol. 1 of *Collected Letters of Samuel Taylor Coleridge* (Oxford: Clarendon, 1966) 452–53. I am grateful to James McKusick for this citation.

32. The ongoing vitality of this view can be seen in Colin Jager's own recent engagement with "Against Theory," in his elegant Kantian phrasing of Wordsworth's power: "At the center of Wordsworth's literary effect, then, is his extraordinary ability to place his readers in a world brimful of a purpose that can be felt but not pinned to a particular purposive agent" (*The Book of God: Secularization and Design in the Romantic Era* [Philadelphia: U of Pennsylvania, 2007] 221). See also François's description

of key Wordsworth works as "lyrics of inconsequence" (154), as well as Brian McGrath's intriguing claim about the Wordsworthian vacillation between the extraordinary and the inconsequential in his "Wordsworth, 'Simon Lee,' and the Craving for Incidents," *Studies in Romanticism* 48 (2009): 565–82.

33. This does not mean, of course, that pragmatism is not part of a transatlantic Romantic genealogy. For a treatment of the most vivid argument for this narrative—in the writings of Harold Bloom—see Wang, 147–48. Furthermore, the very fact of the long-held association of Romanticism *with* intentionality (or, more exactly, its aporia) speaks to why "Against Theory" has to be against Romanticism. See W. K. Wimsatt and Monroe Beardsley, "The Intentional Fallacy," in W. K. Wimsatt, Jr., *The Verbal Icon: Studies in the Meaning of Poetry* (Lexington: U of Kentucky P, 1954, 1967) 6.

34. For de Man's own blunt consideration of intention without a subject, see *Resistance*, 94.

35. Consider, for example, Vala, Blake's figure for unredeemed nature in *Jerusalem*. For a treatment of animism in Keats, see Denise Gigante, "The Monster in the Rainbow: Keats and the Science of Life," *PMLA* 117 (2002): 433–48.

36. Arguably, one's reading of Kant's third *Critique* (see chap. 2) depends on one's estimation of the distance between *moral analogy* and *sensation of meaning*.

37. Or, "going mad with reason" as translated in Bernard, 116.

38. See Terada for the incisive point that seeing is *always* a figure, a placeholder for precisely our *non-knowledge* of what happens, semantically, cognitively, and phenomenally, when we see. See also Timothy Bahti's formulation of how reading also appears beyond the far side of seeing, although ultimately in the mode of a sublime impossibility, in *Ends of the Lyric: Direction and Consequence in Western Poetry* (Baltimore: Johns Hopkins UP, 1997) 33–39.

39. See Stanley Fish, *Is There a Text in This Class? The Authority of Interrogative Communities* (Cambridge, MA: Harvard UP, 1980).

40. This would also be the most productive way to recall Wimsatt and Beardsley's famous dictum, "It is not so much a historical statement as a definition to say that the intentional fallacy is a Romantic one" (6).

## *Chapter 5 · The Sensation of the Signifier*

I am grateful to Jerome Christensen for bringing Ferry's poem to my attention.

1. "This movement from questions about the ontology of the text to an insistence on the primacy of the subject makes a single argument out of what I have in my own writing treated as two separate arguments and two separate projects. . . . So, although I did not in writing it understand *Our America's* critique of identity to be in any significant way connected to the defense of intention in 'Against Theory,' the argument of the current book is not only that they are connected but that each claim entails the other" (Walter Benn Michaels, *The Shape of the Signifier: 1967 to the End of History* [Princeton: Princeton UP, 2004] 10). Unlike "Against Theory," *Our America* plays no real role in *The Shape*; Michaels thus does not address a dissonance between both books' historical arguments, insofar as *Our America* finds in American literature dur-

ing the interwar period a "nativist modernism" whose combination of culture and race provides the model for the postmodern, post-historicist identitarian politics that *The Shape* critiques. Thus, in *The Shape* Modernism is opposed to such politics, whereas in *Our America* Modernism is the historical expression of that very problem. For one suggestion of a historical arc that would consist of both a Modern (1920s) and postmodern (1960s) chapter to this dynamic, see Werner Sollers, "*Our America: Nativism, Modernism, and Pluralism*: Review," *Modern Philology* 96 (1999): 552.

2. Kamuf speaks to this issue with her witty dubbing of the authorial agency behind "Against Theory" as "KaM" (4).

3. Still, see n. 1.

4. Francis Fukuyama, "The End of History," in *The New Shape of World Politics*, ed. Fareed Zakaria (New York: Norton, 1997) 2.

5. One could also certainly argue with Michaels's view of the basically post-ideological nature of today's global conflicts. Indeed, it's difficult not to see the most recent Iraqi war as the occasion for ideology, vulgar or not, returning with a vengeance. When Michaels thus equates the War on Terror with the post-ideological, one wonders what exactly the term *War on Terror* is, or was. Or when media commentators spoke of this latest conflict in terms of civilization versus barbarism, it's hard not to see the ideological nature of such statements, either using or eschewing Michaels's definition of the term.

6. Indeed, the era before the post-historical fall of the Soviet Union would be the 1970s and early 1980s, when the time of *high theory* was precisely characterized by intense disciplinary argument within the academy. If academic study has since become balkanized, high theory actually denotes a time of universal disagreement in the humanities, including the one generated by "Against Theory," that Michaels wants once again to establish.

7. Thus, while Michaels cites Judith Butler's essay in her, Ernesto Laclau's, and Slavoj Žižek's *Contingency, Hegemony, Universality: Contemporary Dialogues on the Left* (London: Verso, 2000), in order both to acknowledge and to dispute her own postmodern grappling with the universal, he does not consider what she and the other authors of that collection are formally doing, which is actively differing from and disagreeing with one another. In narrativizing such a stringent separation between difference and disagreement, Michaels must confer onto "Against Theory" the characteristics of an institutional origin myth, bringing argument back to literary studies: "The point of 'Against Theory's' call for the end of theory . . . was to give [readers at the end of history] something to disagree about" (80).

8. Fredric Jameson, "Actually Existing Marxism," *Polygraph* 6/7 (1986): 176.

9. Examples are legion, but see Stuart Hall, "The Toad in the Garden: Thatcherism among the Theorists," in *Marxism and the Interpretation of Culture*, ed. Cary Nelson and Lawrence Grossberg (Urbana: U of Illinois P, 1988) 35–73; and Laclau and Mouffe, *Hegemony and Socialist Strategy*. See also Michaels's own argument against any transparent continuity between a class agent's interests and beliefs in his *The Gold Standard and the Logic of Naturalism* (Berkeley: U of California P, 1987) 179.

10. Compare Michaels's critique of Hardt and Negri's "poor" with Ernesto Laclau's

more pointed questioning of the unsustainable homogeneity of Hardt and Negri's idea of the "multitude" (*Empire* [Cambridge, MA: Harvard UP, 2000] 156–57, 399; and "Can Immanence Explain Social Struggle?" *Diacritics* 31 [2001]: 3–10).

11. For two sympathetic responses to *Our America* that still question Michaels's rejection of any strategic use of either race or culture, how for him those terms function only as ends instead of means, see Pricilla Wald, "*Our America: Nativism, Modernism, and Pluralism*: Review," *Modern Language Quarterly* 59 (1998): 124–29; and Bill Brown, "Identity Culture," *American Literary History* 10 (1998): 166–82. Such a line of query could certainly be applied to *The Shape* as well.

12. Conceivably, this would be a more difficult observation to make about the historical argument in *Our America*; it is precisely the theoretical argument in *The Shape* that opens Michaels's present book to this charge.

13. This is not to say that sensation and feminism are essentially connected—just that sensation, as well as the body, are made intelligible by various narratives of gender, historical and otherwise. See Redfield, *Politics*, 34–40.

14. For an extended discussion about how the aesthetic is thus not simply ideology but the site of its own self-referential impasse, see Redfield, *Phantom*, 1–37. For a vigorous argument that de Man's thought is precisely *not* about the instantiation of the subject, see Rei Terada, *Feeling in Theory: Emotion after the "Death of the Subject"* (Cambridge, MA: Harvard UP, 2001), 48–89.

15. Jonathan Culler, "'Paul de Man's War' and the Aesthetic Ideology," *Critical Inquiry* 15 (1989): 781.

16. In a Marxist materialism, of course, materiality is not about matter but the signification of social relations. For an incisive critique of the implicit idealism in such materialism, see Ernesto Laclau and Chantal Mouffe, "Post-Marxism without Apologies," in Ernesto Laclau, *New Reflections on the Revolution of Our Time* (London: Verso, 1985) 97–137. See also chap. 4, n. 16, and chap. 6.

17. A similar difference occurs in Michaels's summary of Derrida's language of the "mark" as yet another example of a physical materiality that can only be experienced, not understood, insofar as Michaels ignores how Derrida's argument about the mark with John Searle and his earlier engagement with J. L. Austin are fundamentally connected to his overlapping critique of the phenomenal character of language in Edmund Husserl. See *Margins*, 155–73, 307–30.

18. I am grateful to Jonathan Culler for this observation.

19. Michaels also looks at the essay "Form and Intent in the American New Criticism," focusing on how de Man sees the text in New Criticism as a sensory natural object (a stone) as opposed to an intentional object (a chair) (106). There does seem to be continuity between the non-teleological status of the stone and that of Kant's ocean. But, in using this as proof of de Man's early investment in a physical materiality, Michaels ignores both de Man's critique of this sensory object in New Criticism and the essay's reworking of the notion of intention in Heideggerian terms.

20. One might wonder if it is that easy, or whether the wave's action highlights what is equally unintelligible on Mars, the discovery of what looks like the *entire first stanza* of "A Slumber" on the planet's sand or rock face. See also chap. 4, n. 9.

21. "This is the difference in Smithson's terms, between the view of a quarry and the ('great artist's') 'glance' that turns the quarry into a map. Where the view is entirely dependent on where the viewer is—the view is a relation between the viewer and what he or she sees; the view is how things look to a certain person from a certain position—the text or map is its opposite. Two people in two different positions will see two different views; two readers in two different positions will read the same text" (104). Jameson's own postmodern use of "cognitive mapping" could also make us ask what the non-status of perspective is when we are viewing a map of our own subject position (*Postmodernism*, 51–54). The meaning of a map does change according to our location, if it is a map of that location.

22. One might observe the same about the very relation between maps and non-maps, or texts and objects: that discerning something as a map and not something that simply looks like a map depends on your particular perspective, on getting close or far away enough to see which it is. Conversely, to discern the resemblance between a noise and the name "Marion," we orient ourselves around the very meaning of that name. In one instance, meaning depends on perspective, while, in the other, resemblance depends on the very perspective of meaning. Michaels might counter that once you've decided that a map is a map it stays a map, no matter where you position yourself. But if you leave and return, deciding whether what you see is *that* map or something that resembles it again depends on your perspective.

23. This correlation would be more apt than the one that Michaels employs that conflates de Man's materiality with the physical world presented in David Abram's deep ecology argument, *The Spell of the Sensuous* (New York: Vintage, 1996). When Michaels thus claims that the argument for no meaning is the same as one for many meanings, he is correct, although not because of the joining of idealist skepticism and relativism. The evacuation of human meaning, what anchors calculation, is simultaneously a generation of resemblances that is *incalculable*.

24. The effects of such materiality are also associated with the performative nature of Derrida's mark, another extension of the argument about de Manian materiality made by *The Shape*. But see then Warminski's description of the materiality of Rousseau's mouthing of "Marion" as more exactly the catachrestic discontinuity between the performative and cognitive aspects of language, rather than as simply the performance of meaninglessness (Cohen, Cohen, Miller, and Warminski, 25–27).

25. See Michael Fried, *Art and Objecthood: Essays and Reviews* (Chicago: U of Chicago P, 1998). Michaels's argument should not be confused with attempts to protect textual literariness from the encroachment of cultural studies. See, for example, Tilottama Rajan, "In the Wake of Cultural Studies: Globalization, Theory, and the University," *Diacritics* 31 (2001): 67–88. For a cogent critique of the concept of culture in *Our America* from the position of cultural studies, see Loren Glass, "The End of Culture: Reviewing *Our America: Nativism, Modernism, Pluralism*," *Modern Language Studies* (1996): 1–17.

26. Framing is specifically opposed to the non-framing implication of the Derridean mark as formulated in *Limited Inc* (112). Michaels thus does not engage with Derrida's own discussion of artistic framing in *The Truth of Painting*, especially Derrida's

association of the frame with the logic of the supplement (193–200). Indeed, the question of the supplement does not inform any of Michaels's critique—including his association of "Il n'y a pas de hors texte" with deep ecology's claim that the world speaks. The absence is notable, given how Michaels's own desire to separate meaning from sensation depends on an intelligible distinction between inside and outside, as well as *not* seeing separation for what it is: a figure. In associating Derrida with the end of frames, Michaels also conflates deconstruction with the pragmatic relativist argument that contexts determine meaning. See however, Jan Mieszkowski's argument with Stanley Fish over this very point (*Labors of Imagination: Aesthetics and Political Economy from Kant to Althusser* [New York: Fordham UP, 2006] 2–4). Finally, there is the question of what is occurring when Michaels makes Fried's essay about art and framing the intention of the iconic "*1967*," a term that, by generating a host of historical semantic effects, enacts the very dynamic that Michaels's frames are supposed to resist. If this is Michaels's intention, it is also the intention of the supplement.

27. This moment exemplifies a tension in the book between the instrumental and the constative, where arguing whether something is true or false seems to be the same as arguing whether something is good or bad. In contrast, see Laclau and Mouffe's assertion that the fact of subordination by itself is not the same as social antagonism (*Hegemony*, 154).

28. "Men make their own history, but they do not make it just as they please; they do not make it under circumstances chosen by themselves, but under circumstances directly found, given and transmitted from the past" (Tucker, 595). See also n. 33. One might also consider how this problem of facing either nature or history might also be the dilemma of reading *science*—about how the argument in "Against Theory" against "intentionless meaning" reproduces the debate between the theory of evolution and the practice of creationist design (Jager, 220–27).

29. Indeed, the aphasic scientist that Michaels cites in Robinson's trilogy, who sees "shapes without the names" (*Green*, 349), is also the character most associated with the study of history (*Green Mars* [New York: Bantam, 1994] 189–92; *Blue Mars* [New York: Bantam, 1997] 481–84). He is also *not* the deep ecologist; that is another character with whom he spends much of the three books intensely debating. The appeal to a nonhuman Mars is thus part of a much larger practice of political argument that characterizes the Martian culture represented in the books. The theme of history in the trilogy, as well as Jameson's influence on Robinson, has been widely noted; see Carl Abbott, "Falling into History: The Imagined Wests of Kim Stanley Robinson in the 'Three Californias' and Mars Trilogies," *Western Historical Quarterly* 34 (2003): 27–48; and Robert Markley, "Falling into Theory: Simulation, Transformation, and Eco-Economics in Kim Stanley Robinson's Martian Trilogy," *Modern Fiction Studies* 43 (1997): 773–99.

30. Undergirding Michaels's claims, especially visible in his argument against slave reparations, is the provocative assertion that politics and historicism should be separated. The question then becomes whether Michaels actually wants to turn all social issues into ones of ethics, and how much the later Derrida's writings on ethics and justice could have impacted on such a formulation. See, for example, Derrida's

discussion of the tension between past precedence and present justice in "Force of Law," 3–29.

31. Thus, in his reading of Shoshana Felman's argument about testimony and de Man's wartime journalism, Michaels seizes upon the word "like" in her statement that reference as a form of absence returns "like a ghost," asserting that, as such, the deconstructive object of non-meaning is not, and does not need, the New Historicist ghost, which in the former functions as a supererogatory figure ("like") (141–46). See Shoshana Felman and Dori Laub, *Testimony: Crises of Witnessing in Literature, Psychoanalysis, and History* (New York: Routledge, 1992) 267. A contrasting reading would focus on "like" as the very operation of figure-as-ghost, the spectral *mise en abyme* of reference; ghosts are not simply on one side of reference but *the act* of reference. Also, whether all New Historicists would recognize themselves in the simplified model of experiential memory that Michaels extrapolates from Stephen Greenblatt is, of course, open to debate.

32. Derrida's *Specters of Marx*, with its own complex rendering of the performative injunction from *Hamlet*, immediately comes to mind as one study that would have complicated Michaels's summary. Redfield's *Phantom Formations* would be a further example of a work whose ghostly language does not assume a resolute divide between the figural and the literal. For a discussion of this predicament with regard to Derrida's own presence in Romantic studies, see chap. 6.

33. Within another context and along another coordinate, Michaels is much more nuanced about this capitulation: "The ascription of interests to a money economy (or, for that matter, to a disciplinary society) is only a figure of speech or a mistake, personification or pathetic fallacy. At the same time, however, as literary critics—and as critics in particular of [American] naturalism—we can hardly dismiss this mistake, this particular figure, as merely one among others. For according to the logic of naturalism it is only because we are fascinated by such mistakes—by natural objects that look as if they were made by humans—that we have any economy at all" (*Gold*, 178–79). In this account the personification of nature and of the bourgeois economy as well ultimately provides the grounds for distinguishing between what persons are and are not; yet such an end is also entangled with the constant "mistake" of personification, a fascination that appears more pervasive and important for human society than the distinction itself, as it is purified in Michaels's reading of his Mars example. In this passage *Gold* outlines a predicament for study, whereas *The Shape* describes a mistake that must be corrected. Indeed, the Foucaultian-inspired description of the economy in *Gold* resembles the problem of history that this chapter relates: "the desire to personify the economy is the desire to bridge the gap between our actions and the consequences of our actions by imagining a person who does not do what we do but who does what what we do does. As it happens, there is no such person" (179). The question is whether the "desire to personify" resides in "no such person" as well. That Wimsatt and Beardsley's complement to the pathetic fallacy is the *Romantic* mistake of the intentional fallacy also explains why the polemic in "Against Theory" and *The Shape* is also an argument against Romanticism.

34. See Virginia Jackson, *Dickinson's Misery: A Theory of Lyric Reading* (Princeton:

Princeton UP, 2005) 100–117, for her complementary argument about the wave poem as an a priori hypostatization of the lyric poem, as well as for her provocative reading of de Man's own lyricization of theory. If for Jackson the wave poem is about the reading of literature as the lyric, for me the wave poem is about the reading of literature as Romanticism—two formulations that are by no means mutually exclusive. See also Jager's argument about how "Against Theory" also engages with Romanticism, insofar as Knapp and Michaels are "replaying a debate [now conceived between evolutionary theory and creationism] that has its roots in a positing of divine intentionality that goes by the name of the argument from design. Even more particularly, they inherit a version of the design argument inflected through romantic-era literature; not only Wordsworth's ruminations on what it means to be conscious of intention but Barbauld's meditations on design as a distinctive set of practices" (224).

35. Such a dynamic is, of course, not simply the same as Wordsworth's own politics, both pro- and post-Girondin.

## *Chapter 6 · Ghost Theory*

1. The specific occasion for an earlier version of this chapter was the special issue "Romanticism and the Legacies of Jacques Derrida," ed. David L. Clark, *Studies in Romanticism* 46:2 (2007) pts. 1 and 2.

2. Gayatri Spivak, "Forum: The Legacy of Jacques Derrida," *PMLA* 120 (March 2005): 492. Derrida makes a similar point with the wry title of his response to critics of his *Specters of Marx: The State of the Debt, the Work of Mourning, and the New International* (New York: Routledge, 1994). I refer to his "Marx & Sons," in *Ghostly Demarcations: A Symposium on Jacques Derrida's* Specters of Marx, ed. Michael Sprinker (London: Verso, 1999) 213–69. The original French version of *Specters* was published in 1993.

3. It should be clear that, even without adding the concept of *compulsion* to this list of terms, the spectral legacy of Freud entangles itself within any such discussion. I approach this predicament more explicitly in the final section of the chapter.

4. Consider, for example, Geoffrey Hartman, "The Psycho-Aesthetics of Romantic Moonshine: Wordsworth's Profane Illumination," *The Wordsworth Circle* 37 (2006): 8–14.

5. See Michael Gamer, *Romanticism and the Gothic: Genre, Reception, and Canon Formation* (Cambridge: Cambridge UP, 2000). See also Robert Miles, *Gothic Writing 1750–1820* (Manchester: Manchester UP, 2002); E. J. Clery, *The Rise of Supernatural Fiction: 1762–1800* (Cambridge: Cambridge UP, 1995); and Anne Williams, *Art of Darkness: A Poetics of Gothic* (Chicago: U of Chicago P, 1995).

6. The most sophisticated discussion of gothic and Romantic commodification would be Jerrold E. Hogle's use of the Baudrillardian simulacrum in his "*Frankenstein* as Neo-Gothic: From the Ghost of the Counterfeit to the Monster of Abjection," in *Romanticism, History, and the Possibility of Genre: Reforming Literature 1789–1837*, ed. Tilottama Rajan and Julia Wright (Cambridge: Cambridge UP, 1998) 176–210.

7. With regard to Marxism, consider Fredric Jameson's startling admission about

use and exchange value in "Marx's Purloined Letter," in Sprinker, 46. With regard to Romanticism, consider Marc Redfield's discussion of Romanticism as the quintessential phantom event: "Romanticism occurred—when, exactly, is forever uncertain, because Romanticism altered our understanding of temporality" (*Politics*, 34).

8. For the key discussion of genre *as* a mode, see Jameson, *Political*, 101–10.

9. See Ronald Paulson, *Representations of Revolution (1789–1820)* (New Haven: Yale UP, 1983) 213–47. The gothic narratives of Romantic revolution and Romantic commodification are, of course, not necessarily separate. See Clery for a consideration of how much eighteenth-century supernatural fiction registers the historical trauma of the change from the imaginary of a feudal landed property to a paper economy.

10. Here is the passage:

> And in such way I wrought upon myself,
> Until I seemed to hear a voice that cried
> To the whole city, "Sleep no more!" To this
> Add comments of a calmer mind—from which
> I could not gather full security—
> But at the best it seemed a place of fear,
> Unfit for the repose of night,
> Defenseless as a wood where tigers roam.
> (*The 1805 Prelude*, bk. 10, 75–82)

See William Wordsworth, *The Prelude: 1799, 1805, 1850*, ed. Jonathan Wordsworth, M. H. Abrams, and Stephen Gill (New York: Norton, 1979). The allusion is to Macbeth's lines, "Methought, I heard a voice cry, 'Sleep no more! Macbeth does murther sleep,'" II. ii. 34–35, *The Riverside Shakespeare*, ed. G. Blakemore Evans (Boston: Houghton Mifflin, 1974) 1320. For Mary Jacobus this scene actually implicates Wordsworth in a theatricalized revolutionary imagination that bk. 11 of *The Prelude* rejects. See her *Romanticism, Writing, and Sexual Difference* (Oxford: Clarendon, 1989) 40–45. See also Deborah Elise White's argument about how Coleridge's identification with Hamlet plays off of a sense of Hamlet's father as the specter of Jacobinism, in "Imagination's Date: A Postscript to the *Biographia Literaria*," *European Romantic Review* 14 (2003): 467–78.

11. Edmund Burke, *Reflections on the Revolution in France* (New York: Penguin, 1986) 119.

12. See Wang, 58; W. J. T. Mitchell, "Visible Language: Blake's Wond'rous Art of Writing," in *Romantic and Contemporary Criticism*, ed. Morris Eaves and Michael Fischer (Ithaca: Cornell UP, 1986) 50; and W. J. T. Mitchell, *Iconology: Image, Text, Ideology* (Chicago: U of Chicago P, 1986) 143–49.

13. For a discussion of the related threats of the French speculators and French *philosophes*, see Pocock, *Virtue*, 193–212.

14. Quoted in Jerome Christensen, "'Like a Guilty Thing Surprised': Deconstruction, Coleridge, and the Apostasy of Criticism," *Critical Inquiry* 12 (1986): 775.

15. See Laclau, *New Reflections*. Laclau's post-structuralist and post-Marxist theory

is first most fully adumbrated in his and Chantal Mouffe's *Hegemony*. The spectral character of Burkean second nature could, of course, also be approached through the category of ideology; see Chandler, *Wordsworth's*, 216–34. See also the last section of this chapter.

16. For Christensen's own deployment of the gothic and the spectral in Byron, see his *Lord Byron's Strength*, 300–363.

17. See, for example, Aijaz Ahmad, "Reconciling Derrida: 'Specters of Marx' and Deconstructive Politics," in Sprinker, 88–109. See also Derrida's response to Ahmad in that same collection, "Marx" (213–69).

18. Stuart Hall, *The Hard Road to Renewal: Thatcherism and the Crisis of the Left* (London: Verso, 1988). This is by no means to conflate Derrida with either Laclau or Hall, or Laclau's use of hegemony with Hall's for that matter. It is, however, to note the way Laclau's and Hall's senses of hegemonic politics are both inflected with the ghostly premises of deconstruction. For Laclau's own sense of that connection, see his review of *Specters*, "The Time is Out of Joint," *Diacritics* 25 (1995): 86–96.

19. For another institutional fable also covering Romantic studies, see Wang, 4–7. For a discussion of the institutional history of deconstruction and ideological demystification in Romantic studies, see chap. 2.

20. I, of course, take this term from the title of Jerome McGann's field-defining work, *Romantic Ideology*.

21. The *locus classicus* of this engagement is arguably Paul de Man's "Shelley Disfigured"; in retrospect, the uncomfortable power of de Man's essay's interrogation of history lies in his use of a writer associated with revolutionary rather than reactionary history. For two readings of that political difficulty, see Pyle, 94–128; and Wang, 37–68.

22. See, for example, Carl Woodring, *Politics in English Romantic Poetry* (Cambridge, MA: Harvard UP, 1970). Other examples include David Erdman, *Blake, Prophet against Empire: A Poet's Interpretation of the History of His Own Times* (Princeton: Princeton UP, 1954); Kenneth Neill Cameron, *Shelley: The Golden Years* (Cambridge, MA: Harvard UP, 1974); and the pre–World War II instance of Crane Brinton, *The Political Ideas of the English Romanticists* (London: Oxford UP, 1926). For a discussion of the relation of 1980s Romanticist historicism with this earlier variety, see Wang, 78–80. A crucial, intriguing link between both historicisms would be Marilyn Butler's *Romantics, Rebels, and Reactionaries*.

23. One notable exception would be Thomas Pfau's recent *Romantic Moods*, which tracks the social affect of the Romantic era through both its revolutionary and post-revolutionary phases.

24. Benjamin's term comes from his "Theses on the Philosophy of History," in *Illuminations*, ed. Hannah Arendt (New York: Schocken, 1968), 253–54.

25. Slavoj Žižek, "The Spectre of Ideology," in *Mapping Ideology*, ed. Slavoj Žižek (London and New York: Verso, 1994) 4. In Romantic studies the handling of the issue of ideology is best measured by the distance between McGann's *Romantic Ideology* and Paul de Man's *Aesthetic Ideology*.

26. Somewhat surprisingly, Žižek does not explicitly engage with perhaps the most controversial point of Derrida's reading of the fetish in Marx, how the religious

does not simply signify the superstitious but also "informs, along with the messianic and the eschatological, be it in the necessarily undetermined, empty, abstract, and dry form that we are privileging here, that 'spirit' of emancipatory Marxism whose injunction we are affirming here, however secret and contradictory it appears" (166–67).

27. Elizabeth Wright and Edmond Wright, *The Žižek Reader* (Oxford: Blackwell, 1999) 55.

28. Evincing his own version of revolutionary and epistemological sobriety, Marx writes, "The social revolution of the nineteenth century cannot draw its poetry from the past, but only from the future. It cannot begin with itself, before it has stripped off all superstition in regard to the past. Early revolutions required world-historical recollections *in order to drug* themselves concerning their own content. In order to arrive at its content, the revolution of the nineteenth century must let the dead bury their dead" (Tucker, 597; my emphasis). But see in *Specters* Derrida's own reading of these lines, how having "the dead bury their dead" is the most fantastic proposition there is, and therefore how the *Brumaire* tries to counterconjure away a logic of historical simulacra that, regardless, "has never stopped happening to what is called Marxism" (116). See also Deborah Elise White's chapter on the *Brumaire* from her forthcoming book project, *Revolution's Date: Carlyle, Marx, Hugo* (unpublished).

29. Jameson, *Political*, 23–58. It is an open question, of course, whether Jameson's use of the Althusserian concept of the absent cause merely makes explicit a referential ontology already in Althusser's theory. See Althusser, *Reading Capital*, 186–89.

30. To explicate the way that the ideological exposure of class struggle actually leads to the "inherently incomplete, 'non-all' character of historical materialism" (28), Žižek quotes Étienne Balibar's observation that the "idea of ideology was only ever a *way ideally to complete historical materialism*, to 'fill a hole' in its representation of social totality, and thus a way to constitute historical materialism as a system of explanation complete in its kind, at least 'in principle.'" "Politics and Truth: The Vacillation of Ideology, II," in *Masses, Classes, Ideas* (New York: Routledge, 1994) 173–74. Žižek gets the concept of antagonism from Laclau and Mouffe, *Hegemony*, 122–27. While Laclau and Mouffe would not dispute Žižek's explanation of the term, it's unlikely that they would contest my characterization of antagonism as a spectral event. For their use of Derrida, see Laclau and Mouffe, 88, 111–12, 146. See also Laclau, "Time."

31. "The 'Marxist theory of ideology' would then be symptomatic of the permanent discomfort Marxism maintains with its own critical recognition of the class struggle" (Balibar, 173–74).

32. See, however, the provocative argument for a future Romantic ethics embedded within the contradictions of corporate capital in Christensen's *Romanticism at the End of History*.

33. The question of other points of social antagonism that exceed the Marxist narrative is exactly Spivak's own issue with *Specters*; see her "Ghost Writing," *Diacritics* 25 (1995): 65–84.

34. "The time is out of joint." (*Hamlet*, I. x. 188, in Evans, 1151). Epigraph for *Specters*.

## *Chapter 7 · Lyric Ritalin*

1. Earl R. Wasserman, *Shelley: A Critical Reading* (Baltimore: Johns Hopkins UP, 1971) 238–41, 245–51.

2. For one reference to the topos of blood and gold in Shelley, see McGann, 113. For a perceptive treatment of the political resonances of the topos of light and wind in Shelley, see Forrest Pyle, "'Frail Spells': Shelley and the Ironies of Exile," in *Irony and Clerisy*, ed. Deborah Elise White, *Romantic Circles Praxis Series* (August 1999) www.rc.umd.edu/praxis/irony/index.html. See also de Man's seminal remarks about light in *The Triumph of Life* in "Shelley Disfigured," 109–11, as well as the discussion of Kantian light in chap. 2. For a discussion of the social implications of the lyric's ephemeral nature, see Robert Kaufman's "Adorno's Social Lyric, and Literary Criticism Today," in *The Cambridge Companion to Adorno*, ed. Tom Huhn (Cambridge: Cambridge UP, 2004) 354–75.

3. Virginia Jackson, "Who Reads Poetry?" *PMLA* 123 (2008): 181–86.

4. Tilottama Rajan, "Romanticism and the Death of Lyric Consciousness," in *Lyric Poetry: Beyond New Criticism*, ed. Chavina Hošek and Patricia Parker (Ithaca: Cornell UP, 1985) 194–207. The dominant formulation of the Romantic lyric, which all post-humanist readings of Romanticism have attempted to revise or resist, is, of course, M. H. Abrams's "Structure and Style in the Greater Romantic Lyric," in *Romanticism and Consciousness*, ed. Harold Bloom (New York: Norton, 1970) 201–29. As will become clear, I see the "Ode" exploiting for its own purposes Abrams's definition of the lyric as involving a speaker's response to a "particularized, and usually a localized, outdoor setting," insofar as the apprehended *multiplicity* of outer scenes is the crux of the first half of Shelley's poem (201).

5. Theodor Adorno, "Lyric Poetry and Society," in *Critical Theory and Society: A Reader*, ed. Steven Eric Bronner and Douglas MacKay Kellner (London and New York: Routledge, 1989) 155–71. For two lucid adumbrations of Adorno's argument, see both Kaufman's "Adorno's Social Lyric" and also his "Lyric Commodity Critique, Benjamin Adorno Marx, Baudelaire Baudelaire Baudelaire," *PMLA* 123 (2008): 207–15. For a discussion of the ways the lyric has traditionally been understood to resist narrative, see Sarah M. Zimmerman, *Romanticism, Lyricism, and History* (Albany: SUNY P, 1999) 27, 85.

6. Chandler's elegant reading of the "Ode" in his conclusion to *England in 1819* identifies two levels of figuration in the "Ode" distinguished by their contrasting levels of intelligibility (532–41); in that sense, Chandler and I share the same tactic of exploiting the Modernist critique of the figural clarity of the "Ode" for our own aims. The ways in which his argument about the poem's troping of historical causality both diverges from and converges with my analysis will become clear as the chapter progresses. Looking at a number of British and European writers, although not Shelley, Pfau sees the Romantic lyric recording the social moods of especially two moments in Romanticism's crisis of modernity: the trauma of the Napoleonic era and the melancholy of stalled, post-Napoleonic history (*Romantic Moods*, 69–70, 227–46, 313–15). Zimmerman's interest in the historical contours of the Romantic lyric particularly

focuses on historically situating the lyric within a public mode of interaction with large reading audiences; for an erudite survey of the ways the Romantic lyric has been understood and taught, see her first chapter, 1–37.

7. "Shelley's Speed" is in fact the title of a fascinating chapter in William Keach's *Shelley's Style* (New York and London: Metheun, 1984), which considers how critics have evaluated the presence of this trait in Shelley's poetry (154–83). After a notably sensitive examination of the formal properties in Shelley's poetry that convey the notion of speed, Keach identifies the "speed of the mind" as the primary condition that Shelley's speed tries to elucidate (183). This chapter's following assertion of a sublime cognitive as well as perceptual failing in the historicity of the "Ode" might be seen as exploring what categories appear next *past* the outpacing of the "mind" in Shelley's poem.

8. See chap. 10, n. 3.

9. F. R. Leavis, *Reevaluation: Tradition and Development in English Poetry* (Westport: Greenwood, 1975) 207. As Leavis earlier writes disparagingly, "Shelley's genius was 'essentially lyrical'" (207)—the point for us is to see that as precisely the same scandal of mind that Leavis dismisses, while discovering an entirely new set of implications radiating out of this particular critique.

10. For one recent and comprehensive study of the revolutionary sublime in Shelley, see Cian Duffy, *Shelley and the Revolutionary Sublime* (Cambridge: Cambridge UP, 2005).

11. Harold Bloom, *Shelley's Mythmaking* (New Haven: Yale UP, 1959) 65–90; and Jerrold E. Hogle, *Shelley's Process: Radical Transference and the Development of His Major Works* (New York and Oxford: Oxford UP, 1985) 1–27, 205–7. Interestingly, Bloom actually has no real defense against Leavis's specific critique of the "blue surface of thine aery surge," saying simply that Leavis's "challenge enters the category of the fantastic; and no reply to it is possible, except that I would claim that no poetic figure will stand pressing past a certain point" (80). The question, of course, is whether the "Ode" is actually doing the pressing, in the service of its own fantastic history.

12. See Chandler, 533; and Paul Fry, *The Poet's Calling in the English Ode* (New Haven: Yale UP, 1980) 210.

13. For the most comprehensive argument for Lucretius's presence in Shelley's writing and thought, see Hugh Roberts, *Shelley and the Chaos of History: A New Politics of Poetry* (University Park: Penn State UP, 1997). For Roberts, any sense of history generated by the "Ode" necessarily must also focus on Lucretian "entropic decay," as well as "processual flux" (424–25, 430–31). For Deleuze's interest in Lucretius and later moments of the Epicurean tradition, see *The Logic of Sense*, trans. Mark Lester and Charles Stivale (New York: Columbia UP, 1990) 266–79; and "Spinoza and Us," *Spinoza: Practical Philosophy*, trans. Robert Hurley (San Francisco: City Light Books, 1988) 122–30. For one reference to Shelley's own interest in Spinoza, see Roberts, 85.

14. Ronald Tetreault, *The Poetry of Life: Shelley and Literary Form* (Toronto: U of Toronto P, 1987) 213–14. See also John Rudy, "Shelley's Golden Wind: Zen Harmonics in *A Defense of Poetry* and 'Ode to the West Wind,'" in *Romanticism and Buddhism*,

ed. Mark Lussier, *Romantic Circles Praxis Series* (February 2007) www.rc.umd.edu/praxis/buddhism/index.html. The idea of flux in a Shelleyan landscape is, of course, not new; see, for example, Roberts's Lucretian take on this idea (430).

15. For a recent attempt to theorize what a Deleuzian intervention into Romantic studies might mean, see the collection of essays in *Romanticism and the New Deleuze*, ed. Ron Broglio, *Romantic Circles Praxis Series* (January 2008) www.rc.umd.edu/praxis/deleuze/index.html. As the title of the volume suggests, there is more than one Deleuze that can underwrite such an intervention.

16. For the purposes of this chapter, I would thus distinguish this linguistic sense of figure from the more precise sense of the term "Figure" that Deleuze employs and distinguishes from both "figuration" and "the figurative" in his study of the paintings of Francis Bacon in *Francis Bacon: The Logic of Sensation* (Minneapolis: U of Minnesota P, 2002) 11–19, 79. This is not to say that a profitable comparison of the de Manian and Deleuzian figure/Figure does not wait to be made.

17. This question of temporality is, of course, best allegorized in de Man's "Rhetoric"; the question of the non-conceptual dimensions of the lyric underlies Adorno's "Lyric." See Kaufman's "Lyric Commodity" for a further discussion of the lyric and the non-conceptual.

18. I am grateful to Brian McGrath for pointing out the contrasting semantic actions in "cleave" to me, the ambiguity of which Shelley highlights by having the "powers" neither "cleave" onto something, nor "cleave" from something, but "cleave themselves *into* chasms" (lines 37–38; my emphasis).

19. See also Bruce Robbins, "The Sweatshop Sublime," *PMLA* 117 (2002): 84–97.

20. See Chandler's assertion of how *England in 1819* extends and complicates Lukács's paradigm by applying his theory of European military massification to post-Napoleonic Britain (41–42). One might also want to compare the lyric speed of the "Ode" with the more properly "traumatic" lyric writings of 1800–1815 that Pfau identifies, when at "the heart of that disturbance lies the recognition that no one, however peripheral to the economic and geopolitical upheavals of the Napoleonic and early capitalist era, can escape being implicated in this inchoate and threatening welter of modernity" (21).

21. Besides Chandler's *England in 1819*, see, for example, Reinhart Koselleck, *Futures Past: On the Semantics of Future Time*, trans. Keith Tribe (Cambridge, MA: MIT P, 1985) 3–20, 39–54.

22. That the liminality of this new historical space is denoted by the term "Europe" demonstrates, of course, how enclosed this space still really is. Indeed, the creation of Lukács's "Europe" could be seen as helping enable what Saree Makdisi sees as the Romantic imperialist regulation of uneven development that coordinates the temporalities of non-Western peoples with the hegemonic narrative of European history (*Romantic Imperialism: Universal Empire and the Culture of Modernity* [Cambridge: Cambridge UP, 1998]). But the simultaneity of space in the "Ode" could also be seen as the necessary creation of a synchronic template allowing for the non-hierarchized, decentered ensemble—outside and beyond "Europe"—of a number of different diachronic planes. Regarding the exclusive character of Lukács's analysis, see also Chan-

dler's similar point about the implicit gendering of Lukács's mass agents as men, not women (42).

23. This gesture should not be confused with Rajan's suggestive formulation of how Lukács "sees in Romanticism the beginning of a lyricization of narrative which culminates in the Modern novel" ("Death," 202). She is referring to his pre-Marxist *The Theory of the Novel* (Cambridge, MA: MIT P, 1971), where the diffuse, ephemeral quality of lyricism is primarily associated with the limitations of expressive, subjective interiority, the opposite of what I am arguing is occurring in this passage (112–31).

24. "History is therefore not a temporal notion, it has nothing to do with temporality, but it is the emergence of a language of power out of a language of cognition" (*Aesthetic*, 320). Might not the sublime voyage of the wind (the materiality of a "language of power") outpacing a fainting sense (a "language of cognition") be one allegory for this emergence? For a notably cautious response to de Man's statement, see Derrida, "Typewriter," 319–20. Consider also Jacques Rancière's claim that "there is history because no primeval legislator put words in harmony with things" (*The Names of History: On the Poetics of Knowledge*, trans. Hassan Melehy [Minneapolis: U of Minnesota P, 1994] 35). One might also compare this chapter's reading of Shelleyan historical space with Rancière's meditation on historicizing the Mediterranean (77–89).

25. This unstable reflection of the past ruins would thus be, with all the implications of epistemological volatility, the optical counterpart to Shelley's description of poets in "A Defense of Poetry" as the "mirrors of the gigantic shadows which futurity casts upon the present" (Reiman and Fraistat, 535).

26. Alain Baidou, *Being and Event* (New York: Continuum, 2007) 170–83. See also Peter Hallyward, *Badiou: A Subject to Truth* (Minneapolis: U of Minnesota P, 2003) xxvi–xxvii. To make this connection is neither to ignore Badiou's problematic relationships to both poetry and Deleuze (Badiou, 123–29; Hallward, 174–180) nor to overlook Badiou's hostility toward a mystified, auratic Romanticism (*Theoretical Writings*, trans. Ray Brassier and Alberto Toscano [New York: Continuum, 2004] 22–25). Given Badiou's own notion of the subject, the problem outlined in this chapter of the subject necessarily (formally) being the genesis of historical (revolutionary) truth might very well be no problem at all. Associated with what I'm arguing the first portion of the "Ode" expresses is Jerome Christensen's formulation of how the "*commission* of anachronism romantically exploits lack of accountability as the emergence of unrecognized possibility" (*Romanticism*, 11). I'm grateful to David Rettenmaier for bringing this quote to my attention.

27. See also, however, Wasserman's claim of a difference between the passive elements of the first two stanzas and the more active elements of the third stanza (248).

28. Here is the passage:

> If even
> I were as in my boyhood, and could be
>
> The comrade of thy wanderings over Heaven,
> As then, when to outstrip thy skiey speed
> Scarce seemed a vision . . .  (lines 47–51)

29. Jonathan Culler, "Changes in the Study of the Lyric," in Hosek and Parker, 50–51. For the well-known notion of the lyric as overheard conversation, see John Stuart Mill, *Essays on Poetry*, ed. F. Parvin Sharpless (Columbia: U of South Carolina P, 1976) 12; and Northrop Frye, *Anatomy of Criticism* (Princeton: Princeton UP, 1957) 249–50.

30. I am contrasting Lacanian desire with Jean Paul Sartre's thoughts on objective need in *The Critique of Dialectical Reason I: Theory of Practical Ensembles*, trans. Alan Sheridan-Smith (London: NLB, 1976) 79–83, 217. As David L. Clark has kindly reminded me, one response to this problematic might be a certain Heideggerian impatience with the German idealist tradition of even talking about subjects and objects, insofar as that action necessarily imports "a fundamental anthropology back into philosophy" (Clark, in correspondence). One might in fact see the lyric speed of the "Ode" as being fueled by a similar impatience, which attempts to outwit, or outpace, its own I-Thou rhetoric while ultimately being hemmed in by the formal structuring of such an address. Such a formal impediment might then be as necessary an imposition as the sensation of meaning's tropological sidestepping of the language of subjects and objects; in that sense, whether *any* language—Heideggerian, de Manian, *or* Keatsian—achieves the circumvention that the "Ode" tries to poetize remains, from this poem's particular perspective, emphatically unresolved.

31. Without ever abolishing the wind as a genuine ontological identity, Wasserman gestures toward this dilemma in his own language concerning the increased agency, or freedom, of the poet (247–51). The seminal application of Martin Buber's concept of the I-Thou relationship to the "Ode" remains Bloom's (73–90).

32. As Wasserman in his own terminology asserts, "In part [the concluding question of the "Ode"] is consistent with the fact that he is petitioning a higher authority than himself; but essentially it reflects the fact that there is no inherent guarantee that man will not continue to deflect the operations of the Power by his will" (251). I am also thinking of Wasserman's *locus classicus* on Romantic subjectivity, "The English Romantics: The Grounds of Knowledge," *Studies in Romanticism* 4 (1964): 17–34.

33. Along these lines, one can also contrast the way that Helen Vendler sees "To Autumn" orchestrating time and space in a smooth unfolding with how we have argued that the "Ode" creates its sense of global history out of the uneven, volatile evocation of these same phenomenal categories (244–45).

34. James O'Rourke, *Keats's Odes and Contemporary Criticism* (Gainesville: UP of Florida, 1998) 177. As O'Rourke observes about "To Autumn," "There is neither first person pronoun nor Wordsworthian deictic, no 'here' that would mark the speaker's presence" (167). Other readings that observe the non-subjectivity of "To Autumn" include Walter Jackson Bate, *John Keats* (Cambridge, MA; Harvard UP, 1963) 581; Geoffrey Hartman, *The Fate of Reading* (Chicago: U of Chicago P, 1975) 124–46; and, most recently, Jacques Khalip, *Anonymous Life: Romanticism and Dispossession* (Stanford: Stanford UP, 2009) 55–56. The poem's non-subjectivity has thus figured in Bate's humanist celebration of the piece, to Hartman's claim that "To Autumn" enacts an English or Hesperian overcoming of the Eastern consciousness associated with the Greek Hebrew traditions of the sublime poem (126), to Khalip's estimation of Keats

as a key figure in the troping of the anonymity of Romantic life (40–65). For an extended consideration of the impersonal in American and Modern literature, see Sharon Cameron, *Impersonality: Seven Essays* (Chicago: U of Chicago P, 2007).

35. John Keats, *The Poems of John Keats*, ed. Jack Stillinger (Cambridge, MA: Harvard UP, 1978) 360–61.

36. O'Rourke refers to the "images of levitation [that] . . . uncover a fundamentally new kind of relationship between nature and consciousness" that de Man formulates in his essay "The Intentional Structure of the Romantic Image" (*Rhetoric*, 14). It should be noted that I am focusing on only one stage of O'Rourke's argument, which in its entirety is perhaps one of the most complex and subtle readings of "To Autumn" in quite some time, an extended meditation of the poem's "gift," its resistance to becoming the instrumental object of both humanist readings and ideological critiques (177).

37. C. S. Lewis, *Rehabilitations and Other Essays* (Oxford: Oxford UP, 1939) 28. What I call heaviness in "To Autumn" Christopher Ricks arguably identifies as "pressure," the "ambivalence of physical sensation" in Keats's poem (*Keats and Embarrassment* [Oxford: Clarendon, 1974] 208).

38. As Allen Tate famously writes, the poem is "a very nearly perfect piece of style but has little to say" (*Essays of Four Decades* [Chicago: Swallow P, 1968] 264). See O'Rourke, 144, for a listing of other mid-twentieth-century observations similar to Tate's about the poem's sensory nature.

39. For Vendler, however, the labor of autumn and of humans has to remain distinct (257). Interestingly, Vendler's claim that the poem poetizes the radical ambiguity between necessity and desire pushes her study nearer to a dialectically materialist analysis than has been previously realized (288). One might also say the same of the relation of the following reading to her argument for the main trope in the poem, that of "plentitude" or "enumeration," insofar as commodification might be defined as the simulation of plenitude, beyond human intent (266).

40. Bees actually *can* survive winter very well, although when one combines the thanatopic character of Keats's poem with the traditional literary motif of the bees' unawareness of their mortality, it's difficult not to see "To Autumn" associating their death with the impending winter, which would add even more pathos to the single-mindedness of their activity. That bees have also emblematized the storing of scholarly memory would in this reading simply broaden the activity of commodification to the estranged products of intellectual labor, including, obviously, Keats's own. See Mary Carruthers, *The Book of Memory: A Study of Memory in Medieval Culture* (Cambridge: Cambridge UP, 1982) 38–39. I am grateful to Brian McGrath for this reference. For a survey of the tropes of honey and the viscous in Keats, see Ricks, 133–42. See also Vendler's clearly more ameliorative sense in "To Autumn" of Keats as the poet of "socially productive labor" (284). Finally, see Marshall Grossman's discussion of bees and work in both Milton and Marx in "The Fruits of One's Labor in Miltonic Practice and Marxian Theory," *ELH* 59 (1992): 77–105.

41. But see also O'Rourke's own contention that the poem goes beyond the "appropriative economy that imposes second nature everywhere" (170).

42. We might then wonder what the relation is between the poem as the story of commodity production and the poem as, in Hartman's reading, the nationalist Hesperian transformation of the Eastern ode. Might the English countryside origin of the goods in "To Autumn" be a blind for a more complete representation of British commodity production at this moment, which Hartman's generic narrative both displaces and more fully enacts? Might such a displacement gesture toward the workings of empire that involve the transmutation of foreign ("Eastern") material into nativist ("Hesperian") goods?

43. Elizabeth Jones, "Writing for the Market: Keats's Odes as Commodities," *Studies in Romanticism* 34 (1995): 362.

44. Levinson's *Keats's Life of Allegory* describes the "deadly arrest" in "To Autumn" as analogous to the formal resistance that the odes, unlike the romances, incite against a culturally materialist reading; in my account, however, such "arrest" would actually align with the poem's depiction of a world of commodities separated from the temporal activities of human use (30). For a sustained engagement with Levinson's seminal work, see chap. 10.

The more explicit precedent for my reading is Jones's highly suggestive piece. Like Levinson, Jones also links the troping of the commodity form in Keats to a biographical response to the anxieties and pressures of the literary marketplace. But Jones and I converge in our understanding of the objects in "To Autumn" as exuding a nonhuman shelf life beyond either production or consumption. See also Pfau's suggestive description of Keats's poem, with its "insistent juxtaposition of sensual plentitude and barren emotions, a pungent material world encoding a denatured psyche" (341).

45. Jerome McGann, *The Beauty of Inflections: Literary Investigations in Historical Method and Theory* (Oxford: Clarendon, 1985) 51–62. For two accounts that take issue with McGann's historicization of Keats's relation to the Peterloo Massacre, see Chandler, 426–28; and O'Rourke, 156–58. For two arguments about the oppositional politics of Keats and other members of the Cockney School, see Jeffrey N. Cox, *Poetry and Politics in the Cockney School* (Cambridge: Cambridge UP, 1998); and Nicholas Roe, *John Keats and the Culture of Dissent* (Oxford: Clarendon Press, 1997).

46. I am thinking of, for example, the fascinating account of Hazlitt's discomfort over becoming involved in the Cockney School struggle to stage Mozart in London in Gillen D'Arcy Wood's *Romanticism and Music Culture in Britain, 1770–1840* (Cambridge: Cambridge UP, 2010) 118–50. This indeterminate relation to commodification colors not only Cockney aesthetics, I would argue, but also the cultural and political positions of other Romanticists as well as theoretical debates in our own time; see chap. 8. For a skeptical treatment of the Hunt coterie's association of politics with pleasure, see Gilmartin, *Print Politics*, 195–226; for the claim that Hunt and Keats were involved in a commodified, bourgeois aesthetics of pleasure, see Ayumi Mizukoshi, *Keats, Hunt and the Aesthetics of Pleasure* (New York: Palgrave, 2001) 10–38, 171–83.

47. For a recent, subtle meditation on the vatic character of Blake's language, see Ian Balfour, *The Rhetoric of Romantic Prophecy* (Stanford: Stanford UP, 2002) 127–72. See also Bloom, 65–69, for the classic formulation of Shelley and Blake as poets-as-prophets.

48. This is not to imply, of course, that Lukács did not have his own account of commodity reification; indeed, the idea would be unintelligible without his own analysis of modern life under the commodity form. See his *History and Class Consciousness: Studies in Marxist Dialectics*, trans. Rodney Livingston (Cambridge, MA: MIT P, 1986) 83–149.

49. Andrew Franta, *Romanticism and the Rise of the Mass Public* (Cambridge: Cambridge UP, 2007) 135–36.

50. See Raymond Williams, *The Long Revolution* (New York: Columbia UP, 1961); for Williams of course, the wager of this revolution is precisely *not* its entanglement with, and enframing by, commodification.

51. Giovanni Arrighi, *The Long Twentieth Century: Money, Power, and the Origins of Our Time* (London: Verso, 1994) ix–x. More precisely, for Arrighi, Shelley and Keats would inhabit the chaotic transition between two earlier long centuries, the "Second (Dutch) Systemic Cycle of Accumulation" and the "Third (British) Systemic Cycle of Accumulation" (127–44, 159–74).

52. In his Lucretian reading of the spark imagery in both the "Ode" and the "Defense of Poetry," Roberts sees the former circumscribed by a "purely personal, almost despairing desire for revolutionary capability," while the latter is characterized by a "calm assurance that 'all high poetry' inevitably contains the 'sparks' that will unwrite the present and rewrite the future" (323). Roberts's Lucretian sense of the spark in the "Defense" as some atomistic fragment scattered in the present but proving "central to some future, perhaps radically different understanding of the [Shelleyan] text" (321) would thus converge with Franta's conception of the futurity of mass reading that Shelley envisions for his writings (*Mass*, 111–36). It could be argued that this chapter attempts to see in the "Ode" the same radical volatility of the future that Roberts finds in the "Defense"—so much so, however, that the lyrical affect of the poem's prophetic stance is the very opposite of a "calm assurance." In its vertiginous prophetic stance the "Ode" could also be seen to approximate a hyperkinetic version of what Žižek calls a "parallax view" (*Parallax*, 4–13); see also chap. 9.

53. Of course, in one future of Shelley's writings, the fate of his "leaves" has been anything but indeterminate. As Neil Fraistat has shown, the viability of Percy's poetry as a market form markedly shaped Mary Shelley's editorial conception of his *Posthumous Poems* ("Illegitimate Shelley: Radical Piracy and the Textual Edition as Cultural Performance," *PMLA* 109 [1994]: 409–23). The strength of the "Ode," then, lies in its resistance to what already has been determined, to a future reification of the poet's work that constitutes a distinct part of our own (literary) past. That that past might *not* be the future of the "Ode," or, for that matter, ours, is precisely what the dislocations of the poem pry open, and obsessively insist upon.

54. In making this contrast, I have intentionally left open the question of the sublime nature of "To Autumn"; one could very well argue that it is sublime, not by its overcoming of the physical senses, but by the cognitive vertigo it induces precisely through its embrace of a pervasive phenomenal sensation divorced from a locatable subject. My interest, however, has been not so much in the truth of either poem's sublimity as in the way the dynamics of one notion of the sublime helps clarify the

conflicted way the "Ode" relates to a vatic historicism. For some suggestive comments about the sublimity of "To Autumn," see Hartman, 127.

## *Chapter 8 · No Satisfaction*

1. Consider, for example, Colin Campbell's argument against Weber's Protestant work ethic in his *The Romantic Ethic and the Spirit of Modern Consumerism* (Oxford: Blackwell, 1987) 173–201.

2. Two studies germane to both the high theory / cultural studies question and the field of Romanticism would be Tilottama Rajan's critique of cultural studies as a mode of knowledge in collusion with the forces of techno-administrative capital ("Wake," 67–88) and the *Romantic Circles Praxis Series* volume *Philosophy and Culture*, ed. Rei Terada (June 2008) www.rc.umd.edu/praxis/philcult/index.html. For one response to an earlier version of Rajan's essay, see Orrin N. C. Wang, "The Embarrassment of Theory," *Literary Research / Recherche Littéraire* 18 (2001): 36–44. As Rajan's essay indicates, the perceived tension between theory and cultural studies seems most readily acute in the writings of (literary) theorists. See also Michael Riffaterre, "On the Complementarity of Comparative Literature and Cultural Studies," in *Comparative Literature in the Age of Multiculturalism*, ed. Charles Bernheimer (Baltimore: Johns Hopkins UP, 1994) 66–75; as well as, both in Bernheimer, Peter Brooks, "Must We Apologize?" 97–106; and Jonathan Culler, "Comparative Literature, At Last!" 117–21. The immediate context for Riffaterre's, Brooks's, and Culler's arguments is the question of the relation between cultural studies and comparative literature, the latter of which obviously has its own multitiered relation with Romantic studies. Culler has since worked out in extended fashion his argument about rearticulating the relationship between theory and literature in *The Literary in Theory* (Stanford: Stanford UP, 2007).

3. See especially *Cultures of Taste / Theories of Appetite: Eating Romanticism*, ed. Timothy Morton (New York: Palgrave, 2004); see also Denise Gigante, *Taste: A Literary History* (New Haven: Yale UP, 2005); and Joshua Wilner, *Feeding on Infinity: Readings in the Romantic Rhetoric of Internalization* (Baltimore: Johns Hopkins UP, 2000). For a study that shrewdly considers consumption in *Don Juan* as a Jamesonian allegory of a capitalist world-system, see Eric Strand, "Byron's *Don Juan* as a Global Allegory," *Studies in Romanticism* 43 (2004): 503–36.

4. See, for example, Janet Stabler, "Byron's World of Zest," in Morton, *Cultures*, 141–60.

5. For an account of all the immediate historical references to cannibalism available to Byron for canto 2, see Gigante, 118–24. For Gigante, the behavior of Juan's cannibalizing crewmates is enmeshed in the cultural symbolic of taste, making canto 2 a key example of how "*Don Juan* is a calculated outrage to taste. [Byron's] critique is directed not only at the transcendental taste that Wordsworth, Coleridge, and Southey were trying to create but also at the reigning consumer taste for food, women, and other commodities that characterized a society in which discretionary choice was

enabled by the rejection of taboo desire" (124). While very much involved in the same topos of "consumer taste" as Gigante's study, this chapter attempts to see *Don Juan* as unsettling the distance between the commodity form and its critique, a predicament that underwrites the poem's own interruption of the graphic drive of cultural studies by philosophy as theory in canto 1.

6. See Claude Lévi-Strauss, *The Raw and the Cooked: Introduction to a Science of Mythology*, trans. John and Doreen Weightman (New York: Harper, 1975).

7. Lord Byron, *Don Juan*, ed. Jerome McGann, vol. 5 of *The Complete Poetical Works* (Oxford: Clarendon, 1986). The sharks in canto 2 thus resemble Fredric Jameson's and Slavoj Žižek's overlapping understanding of the shark in Steven Spielberg's film *Jaws*, as the ravaging limit of, or on, any symbolic meaning (*Signatures of the Visible* [New York: Routledge, 1990] 26–27; *Enjoy Your Symptom*, 133–34). The connection is not simply playful, insofar as it demonstrates how this section's use of the *real* is in continuity with the discussion of the term in chap. 6, as not only the content resistant to symbolization but also the formal destitution of the symbolic's own network of meaning.

8. Jean-Jacques Rousseau, *Essay on the Origin of Languages*, trans. and ed. John T. Scott, vol. 7 of *Collected*, 314–15. The classic reading of the lovers at the well is, of course, Derrida's *Of Grammatology* (Baltimore: Johns Hopkins UP, 1976) 255–68. For a thorough consideration of the biblical, classical, and early modern references in cantos 1 and 2, see Peter Manning, *Byron and His Fictions* (Detroit: Wayne State UP, 1978) 200–219; for a discussion of Rousseau's influence on Byron, see Charles E. Robinson, *Shelley and Byron: The Snake and Eagle Wreathed in Fight* (Baltimore: Johns Hopkins UP, 1976) 8–11, 22–25.

9. See Thorstein Veblen, *The Theory of the Leisure Class* (Boston: Houghton Mifflin, 1973) 60–80. As Strand succinctly writes, "Juan wallows in luxury and wealth with Haidée in what amounts to an original consumerist paradise" (511).

10. *Don Juan* of course famously refines this formulation in canto 11, by ostensively distinguishing between the need to write ("I wrote because I felt my mind was full / And now because I feel it growing dull" [14.10]) and the desire to publish:

But "why then publish?" There are no rewards
  Of fame or profit, when the world grows weary.
I ask in turn—why do you play at cards?
  Why drink? Why read?—To make some hour less dreary.
It occupies me to turn back regards
  On what I've seen or pondered, sad or cheery;
And what I write I cast upon the stream,
To swim or sink—I have had at least my dream. (14.11)

Desire and need are in fact muddied in a way that converges nicely with consumer drives ("To make some hour less dreary") even as the ultimate horizon of the market is rejected ("There are no rewards / Of fame or profit when the world grows weary"). Manning asserts that these lines conceive of publishing as a way to "combat [Byron's] own melancholy," which would be the psycho-biographical version of this market dynamic, our constant attempt to use the commodity form to ward off the inevitable atrophying of our drives—the world that grows weary (234–35).

11. Similarly, Elizabeth Kowaleski-Wallace has suggestively discussed the rise in eighteenth-century commodity culture in terms of the opposition between need and luxury (*Consuming Subjects: Women, Shopping, and Business in the Eighteenth Century* [New York: Columbia UP, 1997] 73–78).

12. Robert Miles, "Introduction: Gothic Romance as Visual Technology," in *Gothic Technologies: Visuality in the Romantic Era*, ed. Robert Miles, *Romantic Circles Praxis Series* (December 2005) http://Romantic.arhu.umd.edu/praxis/gothic/index.html. See also Jonathan Crary, *Techniques of the Observer: On Vision and Modernity in the Nineteenth Century* (Cambridge, MA: MIT P, 1992) 42.

13. Juan's distance from such a plot is also reemphasized later in the poem, with the possibility that Juan might "with some virgin . . . [take] to regularly peopling earth" being only one among several options that the narrator muses upon when considering Juan's fate (11.89). But see also Jerome McGann's reading of Juan and Haidée's "second principle of life" as the social world created by their Edenic fall in his *Don Juan in Context* (Chicago: U of Chicago P, 1976) 152.

14. Sigmund Freud, *Three Essays on the Theory of Sexuality*, trans. and rev. James Strachey (New York: Basic, 1975) 97; quoted in Rey Chow, *Sentimental Fabulations, Contemporary Chinese Cinema* (New York: Columbia UP, 2007) 123–25; and Sha, 1–50. See also Leo Bersani, *The Freudian Body: Psychoanalysis and Art* (New York: Columbia UP, 1986) 34. The argument in Sha's *Perverse Romanticism* profitably and intriguingly parallels this chapter's own, with Sha's focus not on the commodity form but on the historical entanglement of the non-instrumental in both Romantic scientific and aesthetic discourse. His chapter on *Don Juan* thus concentrates on "situat[ing] Byron in the context of puberty and Brunonian medicine" and asserting how in the poem the "radical instability of the body makes it an insecure foundation for sexual identity and even gendered hierarchy"; Byron "thus makes the Epic epicene, lacking fixed gender characteristics or violating accepted gender roles" (14).

15. Such an insurgency could thus readily be interpreted through Sha's paradigms—by seeing Brown's Juan as beautiful, passive, and *young*, as the very image of pubescent latency containing a multiplicity of non-instrumental sexual energies or, strictly speaking, perversities.

16. See also chap. 3's discussion of how the abstract labor underwriting commodity value functions as a mechanical catachresis—a purposeless instrumentality.

17. Theories of the Romantic object, or thing, have themselves garnered much attention of late. See, for example, Judith Pascoe, *The Hummingbird Cabinet: A Rare and Curious History of Romantic Collectors* (Ithaca: Cornell UP, 2006). The physically material character of Byron's writings is also aptly signaled by Robinson's description of the poet as "fundamentally empiricist" (11). See also chap. 4, n. 11. But see also Bill Brown's suggestive distinction between objects and things ("Thing Theory," *Critical Inquiry* 28 [2001]: 1–22).

18. Clifford Geertz, *The Interpretation of Cultures* (New York: Basic, 1973) 3–30.

19. One genealogy of cultural studies in the United States that overlaps with but also diverges from my account is that of multiculturalism and identity politics; for a consideration of the politics of that genealogy, from the perspective of the tropology of a spectral intention, see chap. 5. Certainly, Byron scholarship on Orientalism and empire intersects with this aspect of cultural studies; for a recent, provocative example of such work, see Colin Jager, "Byron and Romantic Occidentalism," in *Secularism, Cosmopolitanism, and Romanticism*, ed. Colin Jager, *Romantic Circles Praxis Series* (August 2008) www.rc.umd.edu/praxis/secularism/index.html.

20. I am not claiming that Marxism and anthropology are mutually exclusive terms, or that the social and physical are neatly distinct, or that Marxism itself is not riven by different positions on consumption and the commodity form. I would still assert, however, the anthropological and Marxist as two imbricating modes of thought that are proleptically emblematized in the early cantos' origin stories of (commodity) culture. For a discussion of the tension between the social and the physical in the material, see chap. 6.

21. For an intriguing discussion of the public expression of anxieties over cuckoldry caused by the publication of the harem cantos, see Colette Colligan, "The Unruly Copies of *Don Juan*: Harems, Underground Print Culture, and the Age of Mechanical Reproduction," *Nineteenth-Century Literature* 59 (2005): 449–51.

22. This scene's reification of food and guests via their "masquerade" thus anticipates canto 11's more famously remarked-upon epistemological musing on "And, after all, what is a lie? 'Tis but / The truth in masquerade" (11.37). Indeed, the relationship between the two moments in the poem can be understood as precisely expressing the (dis-)continuity between the fact of reification and the indeterminacies, both epistemological and ethical, of error.

23. For Stabler, Byron's "world of zest" points to how his "foodiness is less to do with large-scale oppositions between mind and body or philosophy and history . . . than it is with minute adjustments of seasoning" (157). My argument, then, attempts to return Byron's topos of consumption to that very world of "large-scale oppositions"—to consider the formal dynamics of how the Byron of cultural studies, of body and history, is interrupted by the Byron of theory, of mind and philosophy.

24. The eating lesson of canto 15 could thus also be the dark other, or grim logical consequence, of the prescriptive philosophy of John Brown, who was the main influence behind Byron's physician, George Pearson (Sha, 243); one principle of Brown's medical theory was the belief that the debilitating effects of too much gustatory and other types of stimulation could in fact be ameliorated by more somatic excitement; as Sha writes, Brown theorizes a "capitalist fantasy" that suggests the "cure for high living, at least in terms of diet, [to be] more high living" (270).

25. Patrick Brantlinger, *Bread and Circuses: Theories of Mass Culture as Social Decay* (Ithaca: Cornell UP, 1983) 22–23.

26. A current permutation of this issue would be questions within and without digital studies about where that field might go, and how that direction might affect the humanities. See also Rajan, 67–88, for the claim about how cultural studies extends, rather than critiques, global techno-administrative society.

27. This has been, of course, an issue routinely debated within the field of cultural studies itself. See, for example, Judith Williamson, "The Problems of Being Popular," *New Socialist* (September 1986): 14–15; and Meghan Morris, "Banality in Cultural Studies," in *What Is Cultural Studies: A Reader*, ed. John Storey (London: Arnold, 1996) 147–67. Morris Is responding to John Fiske, "British Cultural Studies and Television," in *Channels of Discourse: Television and Contemporary Criticism*, ed. Robert C. Allen (Chapel Hill: U of North Carolina P, 1987) 254–89; reprinted in Storey, 115–46.

28. For some, of course, genealogies of the body are as or more pertinent to understanding cultural studies than the account that this chapter adumbrates. See, for example, J. Hillis Miller, "Crossroads of Philosophy and Cultural Studies: Body, Context, Performativity, Community," in Terada, "Philosophy and Culture," para. 1–15.

29. Similarly, a more strictly psychoanalytic reading might want to separate those drives of the pleasure principle from those moments of *jouissance* in Byron's text. See Jacques Lacan, *The Seminar of Jacques Lacan Book VII: The Ethics of Psychoanalysis, 1959–1960*, trans. Dennis Porter (New York: Norton, 1986) 184–85, 188. Yet again, one might also want to parse out more fully the difference between (proto-)pornography and libertine writing, the latter the preferred term for Iain McCalman's consideration of Byron's work; see his *Radical Underworld: Prophets, Revolutionaries, and Pornographers in London, 1795–1840* (Oxford: Clarendon, 1993) 211. For one attempt to historicize this distinction, see Bradford Mudge, "How to Do the History of Pornography: Romantic Sexuality and Its Field of Vision," in *Historicizing Romantic Sexuality*, ed. Richard C. Sha, *Romantic Circles Praxis Series* (January 2006) www.rc.umd.edu/praxis/sexuality/index.html.

30. Christopher Nyrop, *The Kiss and Its History*, trans. William Fredrick Harvey (London: Sand & Co., 1901) 27–29; and Daniel Cottom, *Cannibals and Philosophers: Bodies of Enlightenment* (Baltimore: Johns Hopkins UP, 2001) 180–208. For Nyrop, the move from the nose to lip kiss marks the passage from savage to civilized society (186–88). I am grateful to Jonathan Auerbach for bringing these texts to my attention.

31. William Wycherly, *The Country Wife*, IV.ii. 35–36, ed. John Dixon Hunt (New York: Norton, 1973) 81. I am grateful to Laura Rosenthal for this reference. This quote and Nyrop's chapter on "Love Kisses" (29–75) would thus qualify Edward Shorter's claim that from "the middle ages to the end of the nineteenth century there are remarkably few references to deep kissing in either literature or folklore" (*Written in the Flesh: A History of Desire* [Toronto: U of Toronto P, 2005] 123). Christopher Ricks also notices the reticence in Byron's graphic displays, especially when contrasted with the description of kissing in Keats; Ricks, however, sees Keats as a rare example of such mimetic enthusiasm, and Byron as exemplary of a line of more graphically reluctant erotic poets that includes Chaucer, Marlowe, and Dryden (68, 104–5). But we might still ask whether the punning of *Don Juan* and a conception of print literature beyond high poetry complicate the literary history that Ricks depends on for his comparison.

Elsewhere, Haidée *does* use her tongue, but in a much more circumspect punning manner, teaching Juan her language: "And words repeated after her, he took / A lesson in her tongue" (2.163). We might be tempted to see this as the difference between finding pleasure in the play of the signifier and finding it in the signified, while recognizing the non-eternal character of this distinction.

32. See, e.g., Jerome J. McGann, *Fiery Dust: Byron's Poetic Development* (Chicago: U of Chicago P, 1968) 294–99.

33. In both the Sultana's harem and Catherine the Great's court, kissing is also absent, although arguably with different resonances than in the early cantos. For the Sultana kissing revolves around the question of Juan's obsequiousness, whether he is willing to kiss her toe. Graphic consummation is transferred to the plot involving Juan and Dudú's ambiguous night together, which, curiously enough, like the non-kiss of Juan and Julia, isn't very graphic at all. In Catherine's case, eros seems already *in medias res*, far from the genetic structures of both the Julia and Haidée episodes. See the chapter's last section for the argument about how the non-kiss returns in a new variation at the end of *Don Juan*, through the exclamatory appearance of Lady "Fitz-Fulke!" I am grateful to Delores Phillips for first pointing out to me the question of the kiss in the early cantos.

34. The way that the English public first knew of *Don Juan*, mostly through pirated editions of the early cantos, has been well documented. See Hugh J. Luke, Jr., "The Publishing of *Don Juan*," *PMLA* 80 (1965): 199–209; Jerome J. McGann, "The Text, the Poem, and the Problem of Historical Method," *New Literary History* 12 (1981): 272–74; McCalman, 211; and Colligan, 435–41.

35. The famous anonymous *Quarterly Review* article about *Don Juan*, possibly written by Southey, is apposite for two reasons. First, the class anxieties of the piece, expressed through concern over the dissemination of the pirated editions to the lower classes, locate the obscene nature of Byron's work not simply in the poem but in its shifting reception by different readerships. The essay claims that the lower classes, unlike elite readers, will not be able to ignore the pornographic elements of the poem; however, the very language of the writer used to describe such obscenities ("indecencies" and "images [that] pamper a depraved imagination") makes it unclear how literally present such elements are in Byron's poem, and how much they are the result of a certain class-formed, interpretive disposition. Second, the writer also decries how some of the pirated editions come with "obscene engravings"—a predicament that could mean either that the pirated copies are amplifying a pornographic potential already in the poem *or* that the copies *need to supply* that graphic, literal imagery, because it actually *isn't* in *Don Juan*. The supplementary status of the pirated editions therefore might very well be the necessary ingredient by which we can say that anything erotically graphic actually occurs in Byron's text ([Robert Southey?], "Art VI.—Cases of Walcot V. Walker; Southey v. Shewood; Murray v. Benbow; and Lawrence v. Smith," *Quarterly Review* 27 [1822]: 127–28; quoted in Colligan, 439).

In part, this is the question of how much linguistic punning (of which *Don Juan* is lewdly full) constitutes (porno-)graphic display. For a consideration of some such punning in the early cantos, see *Fiery Dust*, 295–97, and also McGann's notes for *Don Juan* in *Complete* (678); see also the chapter's last section. Such a question does not preempt, of course, the possibility of punning and graphic display occurring in the same text, something to which the title of Wycherly's play attests. For a discussion of the sexual wordplay throughout Byron's poem, see Sha, *Perverse*, 246–84.

36. Likewise, as a simultaneous literal and figurative action, "consent" could also evince the undecidable knot between de Manian grammar and rhetoric (*Allegories*, 9–10).

37. Giorgio Agamben, *Homo Sacer: Sovereign Power and Bare Life* (Stanford: Stanford UP, 1998) 1–5. Cottom seems to be getting at something similar with his sublimation narrative and his statement about how in "Western cultural history" the "kiss . . . establishes life" (180–81).

38. Linda Williams, "Of Kisses and Ellipses: The Long Adolescence of American Movies," *Critical Inquiry* 32 (2006): 313, 319. Williams's title demonstrates a productive convergence among hers, my, and Sha's studies. I am grateful to Jonathan Auerbach for this reference.

39. See also Sha's consideration of the later pun on an "end" in canto 5 and its relation to both sexual and narrative, or serial, ambiguity (253). Sha cites Jonathan David Gross, *Byron the Erotic Liberal* (Lanham: Rowman & Littlefield, 2001) 138.

40. This correspondence is not, of course, of the exacting, jesuitical variety, insofar as it's highly problematic to insist that the aesthetic language retrieved from *Don Juan* is also fully disengaged from an agreeability of the senses.

41. See also, however, Daniel Tiffany's highly intriguing suggestion about studying culture not through such an ontologically secure topos, but through the more epistemologically obscure Leibnizean monad, in "Club Monad," in Terada, "Philosophy and Culture," para. 1–22.

42. Interestingly, Mary Ann Doane sees the resolution of Zeno's paradox by the kiss in early cinema as instantiating, among other things, the *doxa* of heterosexual sexuality (*The Emergence of Cinematic Time: Modernity, Contingency, the Archive* [Cambridge, MA: Harvard UP, 2002] 199–205). The highlighting of Zeno's paradox through Juan and Julia's interrupted kiss and the polymorphous perversity of canto 1's puns can then be seen as an earlier, alternate resolution to this particular predicament in modernity. I am indebted to Deirdre Lynch for this reference.

43. "Introduction," in "Philosophy and Culture," para. 8.

44. See de Man's well-known discussion of irony, parabasis, and Friedrich Schlegel in "Rhetoric," 218–19.

45. See, for example, the implications of Riffaterre's and Brooks's arguments for the singularly decontextualizing identity of literature as literariness (70–71, 103). Riffaterre does stress how literariness can characterize other discursive forms, such as "a work of history, of philosophy, or even law" (70), although his point is how such texts then survive as literature. In the case of both Riffaterre and Brooks, literariness never worries the literal event of literature per se.

46. Indeed, literariness in "Resistance to Theory" seems to presage the violence of de Manian materiality that is realized in the later *Aesthetic Theory*: "Literature involves the voiding, rather than the affirmation, of aesthetic categories" (*Resistance*, 10). If de Man himself could be held as a model for the argument for a literature that could withstand the claims of cultural studies, the implications of his writings still

seem to go beyond the disciplinary retrenching of borders that has occurred since the 1990s. Arguably, the cultural studies position that factually states the end of literature and the high theory position that argues with that empirical supposition are *both* acting out in different ways a much too literal reading of de Man. For a sense of the cultural studies argument that Riffaterre and Brooks are responding to, see "The Bernheimer Report, 1993: Comparative Literature at the Turn of the Century," in Bernheimer, 39–47. See also Culler's suggestion that we should "reground the literary in literature" and "go back to actual literary works" in order to understand the postmodern proliferation of the literary in other humanistic modes of knowing (*Literary*, 41–42). This heuristic argument, however, assumes that the expansion of the literary is simply or mostly the consequence of scholarly will, and not about the question of whether "*actual* literary works" exist in a manner that readily separates them from works that perform the literary in some invalid, but still recognizable, way (my emphasis). Finally, see chap. 10, n. 24, for Marjorie Levinson's formulation of the difference between the literary and literature, one that also complicates Culler's confidence in the actuality of certain literary works.

47. Christensen in fact reads the injunction to "Fitz-Fulke!" as a "homlier declassed variant of the 'Carpe Diem!' topos" that appears earlier in the poem as advice from the narrator to Juan (342; 11.86).

48. Paradoxically, as Williams's study of the Hollywood kiss shows, the graphic display of an image doesn't necessarily resolve the issues of continuity, substitution, and elision that both complicate and ground the narrative intelligibility of the represented act (288–340). As parabasis, synecdoche, or other implicit relation, Williams's cinematic kiss might very well make us further ask, when is an image *not* a figure? From his own perspective, Cottom formulates a similar problematic, noting how to "offer a kiss is implicitly to articulate the entire body, as one articulates a statement, into a series of parts and relationships systematized with a view to social and metaphysical orders" (204).

## *Chapter 9 · Gothic Thought and Surviving Romanticism in* Zofloya *and* Jane Eyre

1. For a recent critique of this form of Romanticist writing, one that explicitly understands the problem of ideology through the question of idolatry, see Simon Jarvis's nuanced *Wordsworth's Philosophic Song* (Cambridge: Cambridge UP, 2007). The divergent paths Jarvis and I take will soon become apparent; one question that we can nevertheless ask of Jarvis's subtle book has to do with his argument that we, like Wordsworth, should replace the binary between idolatry and idol breaking with the one between non-life and life. While this chapter begins, like Jarvis, with a questioning of ideology, we might still wonder how the opposition between non-life and life escapes the question of ideological value. See also the wide-ranging discussion of the nature of idolatry in Mitchell's *What Do Pictures Want?*

2. Emily Brontë, *Wuthering Heights*, ed. Linda H. Peterson (Boston: Bedford, 1992) 274.

3. Raymond Williams, *The English Novel from Dickens to Lawrence* (London: Hogarth, 1984) 68.

4. Terry Eagleton, *Myths of Power: A Marxist Study of the Brontës*, Anniversary ed. (Houndmills: Palgrave, 2005) 97–121.

5. See Charlotte Brontë, "Editor's Preface," *Wuthering Heights*, 1850 ed. Cited in Peterson, 21–24. One could, of course, argue that many of Foucault's analyses are motivated by the desire to distinguish themselves from the Marxist reading of ideology. See, for example, Leila Silvana May's vigorous critique of Nancy Armstrong's particular blending of Marx and Foucault, "The Strong-Arming of Desire: A Reconsideration of Nancy Armstrong's *Desire and Domestic Fiction*," *ELH* 68 (2001): 274. One might observe, however, that Foucault's own referencing of the term *ideology* is itself contradictory, and that, insofar as Foucault is still in some manner committed to the category of class, he is still committed in some way to ideology—which is not to assert any simple homogeneity between the Marxist and Foucaultian project.

6. Amanda Anderson, *The Powers of Distance: Cosmopolitanism and the Cultivation of Detachment* (Princeton: Princeton UP, 2001) 36–46. Anderson's explicit examples are actually Victorian women authors, such as the Brontës, rather than their characters; her point is how literary critics view these writers as figures "who seem not only to instantiate modern power but to manipulate if not inaugurate it" (42).

7. One could, for example, see the text actively participating in the evolution of the Victorian realist novel through a process not unlike ideological containment: by the domestic regulation or literal extinguishing of its more unstable, Romantic gothic elements—the Byronic, then chastened, Rochester and the mad, then immolated, Bertha Mason. Yet Virginia Woolf's famous critique of Charlotte actually focuses on the supposedly inopportune intrusion of the gothic laugh of "Grace Poole" into Jane's most explicit, proto-feminist yearnings, seeing the laugh as a sign of the artistic and biographical containment of Charlotte ("young, cramped, and thwarted") by historical circumstances (*A Room of One's Own* [New York and London: Harcourt, Brace, & World, 1929] 72–73). A half century later, Sandra M. Gilbert and Susan Gubar view Bertha as Jane's "truest and darkest double" who must die in order to enable Jane's narrative of empowerment to fulfill itself (*The Madwoman in the Attic: The Woman Writer and the Nineteenth-Century Literary Imagination* [New Haven: Yale UP, 1979] 360–62). Nancy Armstrong similarly views the high gothic, Romantic drama of *Jane Eyre* as precisely the sign of the ideological binding of a new privative bourgeois subjectivity defined by its mysterious, ahistorical desires (*Desire and Domestic Fiction: A Political History of the Novel* [New York and Oxford: Oxford UP, 1987] 186–213). But from another, equally well-known critical position, Cora Kaplan takes seriously the contemporaneous charge of political subversion leveled at *Jane Eyre*, seeing in the passages diminished by Woolf a revolutionary Romanticism that cannot help connect, no matter how fleetingly, political insurgency and feminist concerns (*Sea Changes: Essays on Culture and Feminism* [London: Verso, 1986] 170–75). In Gayatri Spivak's classic reading of the novel, that rebellion is itself contained by the inability of the novel to register its own gothic control over Bertha Mason and the colonial history underwriting its plot ("Three Women's Texts and a Critique of Imperialism,"

in *Race, Writing and Difference*, ed. Henry Louis Gates [Chicago: Chicago UP, 1986] 262–80).

More recently, Heather Glenn locates the exaggerated affective pitch of *Jane Eyre* not in any high elite Romantic formation but in a middle-class Byronism and, most important, the mass culture of the romance annuals saturating England during the first part of the century; in doing so, Glenn qualifies the supposed revolutionary ethos of *Jane Eyre* but also reasserts the proto-feminist concerns of the novel through its debt to a mass cultural form of Romanticism as commercial entertainment (*Charlotte Brontë: The Imagination in History* [Oxford and New York: Oxford UP, 2002] 102–43). Finally, Daniela Garofalo intriguingly argues that the gothic eros between Jane and Rochester enables a nineteenth-century sense of liberalism that appears to demand equality while actively seeking mastery and hierarchical norms (*Manly Leaders in Nineteenth-Century British Literature* (Albany: SUNY P, 2008) 137–53.

8. Anonymous, "Review," ed. Eleanor McNees, vol. 3 of *The Brontë Sisters: Critical Assessments* (Mountfield: Helm Information, 1996) 18; Lady Eastlake, "Review of *Vanity Fair* and *Jane Eyre*," also in McNees, 51. The anonymous review originally appeared in *Christian Remembrancer*, n.s. 15 (April 1848): 396–409; the one by Eastlake in *Quarterly Review* (December 1848): 153–85.

9. Daniel Cottom, "I Think, Therefore I Am Heathcliffe," *ELH* 70 (2003): 1067–88. This very scenario intriguingly resonates with the existential doubt that Heather Glenn observes one character expressing in the Brontës' juvenilia (14–17). For one example of the scholarly tradition that links the gothic to problems in epistemology, see Marshall Brown, *The Gothic Text* (Stanford: Stanford UP, 2005).

10. See, for example, Michael Gamer, "Charlotte Dacre's *Zofloya*: Two New Editions," *Romantic Circles Reviews* (December 1998) www.rc.umd.edu/reviews/zofloya.html.

11. Adriana Craciun, "Introduction: Charlotte Dacre and the 'Vivisection of Virtue,'" in *Zofloya; or, The Moor: A Romance of the Fifteenth Century*, ed. Adriana Craciun (Peterborough: Broadview, 1997) 9. See also, however, George Haggerty's argument for a strong connection between *Zofloya* and Radcliffe's *The Italian* through an erotics of maternal loss ("Mothers and Other Lovers: Gothic Fiction and the Erotics of Loss," *Eighteenth-Century Fiction* 16.2 [2004]: 157–72). In contrast to Haggerty, this chapter will focus on perhaps the more obvious divergences between Dacre's and Radcliffe's plottings, especially as exemplified in a contrast between *Zofloya* and *The Mysteries of Udolpho*.

12. See, for example, Robert Miles's comments on this distinction in *The Handbook to Gothic Literature*, ed. Marie Mulvey-Roberts (New York: NYUP, 1998) 182–83. For a Kristevan reading of the difference between male and female gothics, see Williams, *Art of Darkness*, 72–79. Other studies of the female gothic include E. J. Clery, *Women's Gothic: From Clara Reeve to Mary Shelley* (Tavistock: Northcote House, 2000); Eugenia DeLamotte, *Perils of the Night: A Feminist Study of Nineteenth-Century Gothic* (New York: Oxford UP, 1990) 149–92; Diane Long Hoeveler, *Gothic Feminism: The Professionalization of Gender from Charlotte Smith to the Brontës* (University Park, PA: Penn State UP, 1998); Tania Modeleski, *Loving with a Vengeance: Mass-Produced*

*Fantasies for Women* (New York: Methuen, 1984) 59–84; and Ellen Moers, *Literary Women: The Great Writers* (New York: Oxford UP, 1985) 90–110.

13. For the most extensive meditation of the relation of Romanticism and superstition, of Romanticism as both the overcoming of superstition and the superstition that must be overcome, see Deborah Elise White, *Romantic Returns: Superstition, Imagination, and History* (Stanford: Stanford UP, 2000).

14. David Brookshire, "*Zastrozzi: A Romance*: Paranoiac Fantasy, the Semblance of Subversion, and the Gothic Subject of Romanticism," unpublished draft, 15–16. Craciun also identifies the late eighteenth-century discourse on nymphomania as another point of reference for Victoria's deviant behavior (257–60).

15. Wollstonecraft's presence in *Zofloya* has been noticed before, although in a variety of ways. For a contrast between the writers' warnings against excessive sensibility, see Craciun, 13; for the idea that *Zofloya* might get much of its critique of court culture from Wollstonecraft, see Gary Kelly, *English Fiction of the Romantic Period, 1789–1830* (Burnt Mill, Harlow: Longman, 1989) 106; for the view that Dacre is critiquing Wollstonecraft's putative belief that women must take on masculine strength, see Beatriz González Moreno, "Gothic Excess and Aesthetic Ambiguity in Charlotte Dacre's *Zofloya*," *Women's Writing* 14, no. 3 (2007): 432; for an extended consideration of the unfortunate influence of the mother in *Zofloya* as a parody of Wollstonecraft, see Hoeveler, 143–45. Radcliffe's Laurenti is also, of course, shaped by her misbegotten upbringing.

16. For Rousseau, of course, the trick is to replace such vanities with "natural coquetry." See *Emile*, trans. Allan Bloom (New York: Basic Books, 1979) 370–73.

17. Consider also Robert Miles's description of Berenza as a "philosophical sentimentalist and moral scientist" in his *Gothic Writing 1750–1820: A Genealogy* (London and New York: Routledge, 1993) 184.

18. For Wollstonecraft, of course, young women reading romances is still better than them reading nothing at all (183–84).

19. For an extended discussion of this passage in Wollstonecraft, see Wang, *Fantastic*, 130–34. See also Craciun, 22–25, for another argument about Rousseau's presence in Dacre, although this time in terms of how Dacre rewrites Rousseau's views on female sexuality.

20. For a discussion of *Reflections* as a gothic text, see chap. 6. See also Gary Kelly's observation regarding the ubiquity of the Burkean sublime in Dacre's text (106). On the presence of Burke and Rousseau in second-generation Romantic writings, see Wang, 58–59.

21. The British association, within and beyond Burke, between the French Revolution and gender anxiety has been well documented; see Mitchell, *Iconology*, 143–44; and Neil Hertz, *The End of the Line: Essays on Psychoanalysis and the Sublime* (New York; Columbia UP, 1985) 160–91. See also Porter, *English*, 115, for an observation about the leading role of English women in bread and food riots throughout the eighteenth century. Consider also Hoeveler's intriguing claim that, in creating Victoria's mother, Dacre tempts us to think that she "blames adulterous mothers for causing all the social and political turmoil that . . . resulted in the French Revolution" (144).

22. For a survey of the generation of anti-Jacobin novels produced during the 1790s whose ideological design was much clearer, see Kelly, 59–69.

23. Perhaps predictably, the "good" characters in *Zofloya*, the noble Henriquez and the angelic Lila, are amazingly bland; as Craciun asserts, Dacre makes Lila and others like her "asexual martyrs as repugnant and inhuman as their destroyers" (28). With regard to Zofloya, it could be argued that he presents another gendered side to the racialized double bind enveloping Bertha Mason: the containment of her monstrosity and the presiding influence of his demonic intent prevent both from attaining the status of a Europeanized subjectivity. Insofar as he does acquire power and agency as the text progresses, it could still be argued that the focus remains on Victoria; there is a gravitational pull (as for Bertha with Jane) to see him as Victoria's double, even as a hyperbolic, racialized version of devious Jacobin monstrosity. (Burke, of course, did not hesitate to racialize the French revolutionaries, comparing them to "American savages" [80].) Victoria's transformation into Zofloya also arguably blunts the heterosexist, racialized frisson of her succumbing to his triumphant will; the text auto-immunizes itself, as it were, sacrificing the eros of male aggression in order to defend against a total sexual triumph by the non-European other. For our purposes, the point is how in many ways the text makes Zofloya a secondary consideration when thematizing the question of agency. For one study of race in *Zofloya*, see Hoeveler, 149–50, 156–57.

24. David Durant, "Ann Radcliffe and the Conservative Gothic," *Studies in English Literature, 1500–1900* 22 (1982): 529.

25. See Robert Miles, *Ann Radcliffe: The Great Enchantress* (New York: Manchester UP, 1995).

26. Algernon Charles Swinburne, letter to H. B. Forman, 22 November 1886, 175. Quoted in Craciun, 9.

27. Nietzsche, of course, knew something about idolatry; see his *Twilight of the Idols; or, How to Philosophize with a Hammer*, trans. Richard Polt (Indianapolis: Hackett, 1997). I am particularly thinking of the Nietzsche represented in Derrida's essay "Différance," in *Margins*, 17–19.

28. Sally Shuttleworth, *Charlotte Brontë and Victorian Psychology* (Cambridge: Cambridge UP, 1996) 149.

29. Charlotte to W. S. Williams, 11 March 1848, vol. 2 of *The Brontës: Their Lives, Friendships, and Correspondence*, ed. T. J. Wise and J. A. Symington (Oxford: Blackwell, 1933) 198. Quoted in Shuttleworth, 149.

30. Charlotte Brontë, *Jane Eyre*, ed. Q. D. Leavis (London: Penguin, 1985) 302.

31. As Glenn points out, idolatry "was a commonplace in nineteenth-century England, used—both flippantly and seriously—to denote that excessive love of the creature against which the Scripture warned" (244). This sense of the term also exists, of course, in Berenza's revolutionary attachment to Victoria. For a reading that explicitly ties the language of idolatry in *Jane Eyre* to Victorian anti-Catholic discourse, see Maria LaMonica, *Masked Atheism: Catholicism and the Victorian Secular Home* (Columbus: Ohio State UP, 2008) 33–94.

32. Perhaps complicating the text's coincidence between gender and political rebellion that Kaplan sees, Jane actually somewhat teasingly refers to Rochester's

"impetuous republican answers" (308). Trying, however, as in the case of Berenza, to turn Rochester into an example of the misguided Enlightenment *philosophe* seems much more difficult to do. Similarly, as much as Jane constantly tries to image human nature (including her own) through her drawings, it seems a stretch to equate her attempt with simply the abstract philosophizing of a Berenza, although a Victorian version of the need to moderate her own senses in some normative way does seem key to Jane's happiness.

33. Indeed, Jane actually outdoes Varens, since Varens only leads Rochester to believe that he was her "idol" (172). Varens would thus seem more agile than Jane in dealing with the idolatry of the sex-cash nexus underlying a relationship with Rochester; whether Jane and Rochester transcend that nexus at the novel's conclusion, or whether Jane's own idol breaking ultimately means something like Varens's agility—these appear to be some of the questions that the text's own ambivalent energies ask.

34. As Helena Michie argues, such dressing up was integral to the process of consumption that defined Victorian wedded feminine subjectivity: "Upper middle-class honeymoons, replete with their consuming rituals of tourism, sex, and shopping, produced, when successful, a different woman in a different body and different clothes, who answered with new knowledge to a new name" ("Under Victorian Skins: The Bodies Beneath," in *A Companion to Victorian Literature and Culture*, ed. Herbert F. Tucker [Oxford: Blackwell, 1999] 420–21). Quoted in Glenn, 94; the shadowy feminine existence that Glenn argues conduct books produce, and which the wispiness of Jane's new bridal clothing highlights, is thus very much in continuity with the real/not real existence of the commodity object. For an earlier study of the objectification of intersubjectivity in *Jane Eyre*, done within the context of gendered relations, see Margaret Homans's "Dreaming of Children: Literalization in *Jane Eyre*," in her *Bearing the Word: Language and Female Experience in Nineteenth-Century Women's Writing* (Chicago: U of Chicago P, 1986) 84–99.

35. We might also wonder from this perspective whether the novel employs such nineteenth-century scientific discourses as phrenology in order to distinguish the intimate, visual knowledge of a loved one from the *particular* abstractions of commodity reification. The scientific study of a face would thus promise a relation to the image not dominated by the forces of "glittering" exchange. See Shuttleworth, 3–4, 57–70, for an argument about how the science of phrenology ultimately led to a gothic sense of mystery about the human subject; we might wonder, then, if such sciences found themselves eventually leading back to the mystery of the commodity form, of human reification, without quite being able to articulate that fact. For another study of phrenology in other texts by Charlotte, see Nicholas Dames, *Amnesiac Selves: Nostalgia, Forgetting, and British Fiction, 1810–1870* (Oxford: Oxford UP, 2001) 76–124. See also n. 42.

36. Žižek, *Parallax*, 4–13. See also Mitchell's reading of the rhetoric of iconoclasm in Marx's analysis of both ideology and the commodity form in *Iconology*, 160–208.

37. Shuttleworth, 165; and Hermione Lee, "Emblems and Enigmas in *Jane Eyre*," *English* (Autumn 1981): 233–53. "Lurid hieroglyphs" is the term that Rochester uses to describe what his destiny writes on Thornfield (174).

38. Adela Pinch, "Thinking about the Other in Romantic Love," in *Romantic Passions*, ed. Elizabeth Fay, *Romantic Circles Praxis Series* (April 1998) www.rc.umd.edu/praxis/passions/index.html.

39. For extended discussions of *Jane Eyre* as a female gothic, see DeLamotte, 193–228; and Tamar Heller, "*Jane Eyre*, Bertha, and the Female Gothic," in *Approaches to Teaching Brontë's* Jane Eyre, ed. Diane Long Hoeveler and Beth Lau (New York: Modern Language Association of America, 1993) 49–55.

40. For the argument that Rochester's wounded body actually allows the conclusion to be read as yet another chapter of Jane's ongoing seduction, see Garofalo, 148–51.

41. For one argument about the precarious nature of the novel's ending, see Jill Matus, "'Strong Family Likeness': *Jane Eyre* and *The Tenant of Wildfell Hall*," in *The Cambridge Companion to the Brontës*, ed. Heather Glenn (Cambridge: Cambridge UP, 2002) 118–19.

42. An intriguingly alternate approach to mine would be to take this scene's references to electricity and physical occurrences seriously, and thus to consider Rochester's communication as not a supernatural event but one of early Victorian science and telepathy. It remains an open question, however, whether replacing the empirically supernatural with the empirically scientific resolves the tensions between the supernatural and religious. For an extensive discussion of the question of natural religion in the Romantic portion of the nineteenth century, see Jager, *Book of God*. For a thorough look at the trope of electricity as a socially connecting force in Victorian poetry, see Jason Rudy, *Electric Meters: Victorian Physiological Poetics* (Athens, OH: Ohio UP/Swallow, 2009). For one of the first attempts to connect Charlotte's writings to the gothic, see Robert B. Heilman, "Charlotte Brontë's 'New Gothic,'" in *From Jane Austen to Joseph Conrad: Essays Collected in Memory of James T. Hillhouse*, ed. Robert C. Rathburn and Martin Steinmann, Jr. (Minneapolis: U of Minnesota P, 1958) 118–32. Heilman doesn't read *Jane Eyre* as a gothic because of its supernatural resonances, however; he does so because of the "mysteriousness" of the emotions the novel explores (131), in a way that anticipates Armstrong's own study.

43. We might then wonder if, as scholars have recently argued, nineteenth-century Great Britain becomes increasingly beholden to the sensations of the embodied subject as the locus of social truth, whether this history is at least in part the playing out of this figured relation between perceptual and ideological deceit. See Gallagher; and William A. Cohen, *Embodied: Victorian Literature and the Senses* (Minneapolis: U of Minnesota P, 2008).

44. From a de Manian position of course, this problem replays the crucial distinction between ideological mistake and linguistic error; for a full discussion of how these choices have structured the field of Romantic studies since the 1970s, see chap. 2.

45. Jodi Dean, *Žižek's Politics* (London: Routledge, 2006) 36–37.

46. Laclau and Mouffe, *Hegemony*, 122–27. See also the discussion of antagonism in chap. 6.

47. While adamantly resisting any conflation of the historical events registered, my activation of the figure of survival very much parallels what Sara Guyer investigates

in *Romanticism after Auschwitz: Cultural Memory in the Present* (Stanford: Stanford UP, 2007) 1–23. Equally pertinent is the anecdote that Jameson uses to respond to the question of "life in Moscow during the darkest days of the 1930s and 40s," how "Abbé Siéyès's answer to an analogous question about the period of the Terror during the French Revolution might be the appropriate one. 'What did you do during the Terror?' 'I survived'" (Introduction to Lukács, *Historical*, 5).

## *Chapter 10 · Coming Attractions*

1. William Gibson and Bruce Sterling, *The Difference Engine* (New York: Bantam, 1991) 45–47.

2. See Tom Gunning, "The Cinema of Attractions: Early Film, Its Spectator, and the Avant-Garde," and "Non-Continuity, Continuity, Discontinuity: A Theory of Genres in Early Films," in *Early Cinema: Space, Frame, Narrative*, ed. Thomas Elsaesser and Adam Barker (London: BFI, 1990). See also *Cinema and the Invention of Modern Life*, ed. Leo Charney and Vanessa R. Schwartz (Berkeley: U of California P, 1995); and n. 21. While I am not claiming that visual culture did not change from the beginning to the end of the nineteenth century, I am suggesting that the social relations inherent in Gunning's sense of spectacle and attraction can be used to illumine Keats's era and poetry. The critical language of viewing publics generally informing this piece comes from the tradition of applying and complicating Jürgen Habermas in work separately done on the British Romantic period and also the history of cinema. For one foray into the use of the public and counter-public sphere during the Romantic period, see "Romanticism and Its Publics: A Forum Organized and Introduced by Jon Klancher," *Studies in Romanticism* 33 (1994): 523–88; for the application of Habermas to cinema studies, see Miriam Hansen's path-breaking *Babel and Babylon: Spectatorship in American Silent Film* (Cambridge, MA: Harvard UP, 1991). See also n. 30. For a precedent-setting meditation of not only the epistemological but institutional continuity between Romanticism and the cinema, see William Galperin, *The Return of the Visible in British Romanticism* (Baltimore: Johns Hopkins UP, 1993) 1–33.

3. The tradition of appreciating Keats's sensational nature begins with Arthur Henry Hallam's influential 1831 essay on Keats, Shelley, and Tennyson; it bifurcates in the twentieth century, with one view emblematized by Christopher Ricks's celebration of the sensual *as* gaudy sensation in Keats, and the (until recently) more influential view held by Helen Vendler, who translates Keats's sensory concerns into a more elevated experience of the poetry's formal properties. Ricks's view has gained momentum precisely to the degree that it connects Keats's oeuvre to a larger social set of meanings for sensational literature. See Arthur Henry Hallam, "On Some of the Characteristics of Modern Poetry, and on the Lyrical Poems of Alfred Tennyson," *Englishman's Magazine* 1 (August 1831): 616–21, in *Keats: The Critical Heritage*, ed. G. M. Matthews (New York: Barnes and Noble, 1971) 264–72; Ricks; and Vendler. For two more in-depth analyses of Keats criticism, see Levinson's *Keats's Life of Allegory*, 29–31; and Robert Kaufman, "Negatively Capable Dialectics: Keats, Vendler, Adorno, and the Theory of the Avant-Garde," *Critical Inquiry* 27 (2000): 357–63.

Given this chapter's attempt to consider Keats's sensational qualities in continuity with his visual culture, it is worthwhile to recall the well-known description of Keats and Shelley from Hallam: "They are both poets of sensation rather than reflection. Susceptible of the slightest impulse from external nature, their fine organs trembled into emotion at colours, and sounds, and movements, unperceived or unregarded by duller temperaments. . . . Other poets *seek* for images to illustrate their conceptions; these men had no need to seek; they lived in a world of images; for the most important and extensive portion of their life consisted in those emotions, which are immediately conversant with sensation" (Matthews, 267).

4. Byron to John Murray, 9 September 1820, in Matthews, 129.

5. Levinson, *Keats's Life*, 1–38; and James K. Chandler, "Hallam, Tennyson, and the Poetry of Sensation: Aestheticist Allegories of a Counter-Public Sphere," *Studies in Romanticism* 33 (1994): 534. For the most sustained argument for the intentionally oppositional character of the Cockney School, see Cox, particularly his point about the complications that ensue when thinking of the Hunt coterie simply in terms of class (48–49). For two different studies that both conceive of Keats's relation to the Cockney School and Leigh Hunt as the source of liberal political inspiration, see O'Rourke and Friedman. For a discussion about Keats's odes and commodity consumption, see Jones; see also chap. 7. Finally, for the suggestive argument that Keats's formal and sensational qualities speak as much to a proto-Adornoesque avant-garde position as a proto-Benjaminian modern one, see Kaufman, 354–84.

6. Derrida's famous reading in *Of Grammatology* of Rousseau and masturbation as the "dangerous supplement" can be understood as using this association to characterize the simulated nature of *écriture* (141–64).

7. John Lockhart, "Cockney School of Poetry," in Matthews, 101.

8. Richard D. Altick, *The Shows of London* (Cambridge, MA: Belknap P of Harvard UP, 1978) 95. Altick describes the cascade as "evidently . . . an offshoot of the moving picture" (95). See also Cox's point that the enemies of the Hunt circle "often used to complain that the Cockneys, as urban poets, had no sense of nature" (Cox, 30). I am indebted to both Altick and Laurent Mannoni's *The Great Art of Light and Shadow: Archaeology of the Cinema*, trans. and ed. Richard Crangle (Exeter: U of Exeter P, 2000), for much of this essay's historical adumbration. See also Galperin for a touchstone discussion of Romantic visual culture and an in-depth consideration of the uncanny "return of the visible" in the panorama and diorama shows (19–71). For two recent meditations on that culture, see Gillen D'Arcy Wood, *The Shock of the Real: Romanticism and Visual Culture 1760–1860* (New York: Palgrave, 2001); and Sophie Thomas, *Romanticism and Visuality: Fragments, History, Spectacle* (New York: Routledge, 2008). For two other accounts of nineteenth-century viewing, see Crary's *Techniques of the Observer* and his *Suspensions of Perception: Attention, Spectacle, and Modern Culture* (Cambridge, MA: MIT P, 1999); for a specific account of the pre-cinema phantasmagoria, see Terry Castle, "Phantasmagoria: Spectral Technology and the Metaphorics of Modern Reverie," *Critical Inquiry* 15 (1988): 26–61. For a suggestive application of the early history of the phantasmagoria to the British gothic novel, see Robert Miles, "The Eye of Power: Ideal Presence and Gothic Romance," *Gothic*

*Studies* 1 (1999): 17–18. Finally, see Pfau's association of Keats with the "logic of the phantasmagoria" displayed in Hazlitt's 1823 essay, "Of Londoners and Country People," which "anticipates Walter Benjamin's cinematic modernity" (354–57).

9. Edward Bulwer, *The Siamese Twins*; quoted in Altick, 1. As both the list of exhibitions and title of Bulwer's work illustrate, the London shows expressed a Foucaultian scrutiny of the body as well as a keen optic sense of colonialist empire; as the nineteenth century progressed, moreover, the display of the noble savage changed into one of the racialized, atavistic subject of anthropological science (Altick, 268–87). See also n. 26.

10. See also, however, the argument in Crary's *Techniques* that Renaissance modes of observation associated with the camera obscura differ markedly from nineteenth-century techniques of viewing, especially those associated with the 1830s stereoscope.

11. W. J. T. Mitchell, *Picture Theory: Essays on Verbal and Visual Representation* (Chicago: U of Chicago P, 1994) 114–15; Galperin, 19–33. For the argument that situates this relation within the specific historical context of the conflict between "Romantic, expressive theories of artistic production" and "a new commercial visual-cultural industry of mass reproduction, spectacle, and simulation," see Wood, 1–15. Yet see also Galperin's claim about how the traditionally "Romantic opposition of the verbal and the visual as expressive and mimetic media" actually "obfuscate[s] . . . those larger cultural imperatives (or, as the case may be, imperatives against culture) that are demonstrably cross-generic and sufficiently prolific that a literary artifact may in the end have more in common with a Diorama or a photograph than with a painting" (30). My argument about *Lamia* is that the poem takes this commonality quite seriously, especially in terms of the commercial, recreational *moving* image.

12. For one in-depth look at the Keatsian dialectic between moving word and still art, see Grant F. Scott, *The Sculpted Word: Keats, Ekphrasis, and the Visual Arts* (Hanover and London: UP of New England, 1994). See also Ian Jack, *Keats and the Mirror of Art* (Oxford: Clarendon P, 1967). Scott observes that Keats's art subjects "are not originals but reproductions, copies, restorations" but also argues that the poet's ekphrasis is "about moving the visual object from its original residence into the house of words and restoring and revivifying it." But Scott also believes that in "trying to move closer to the original works of art, Keats only establishes all the more distance from them and hence his modernity" (19). My suggestion is that for Keats the display of the "original" art piece is already to some degree informed by the visual modernity of London's shows.

13. Philip Fisher, "A Museum with One Work Inside: Keats and the Finality of Art," *Keats-Shelley Journal* 33 (1984): 85–102.

14. Great Britain thus differed greatly from both France and Italy, where the museum and art display had a much longer and more secure history. For a discussion of how the specifically English history of museum instability might have affected Keats's "Ode on a Grecian Urn," see Wang, *Fantastic*, 19–23.

15. The foregrounded center of Martini's engraving, as well as the center of the crowd's attention, is the Prince of Wales, a fact that says much about what viewing art meant for the participants at such an event.

16. Altick, 415. Haydon's attempts were less than successful, as Keats's own viewing of the Marbles was in very lowly conditions, as until 1831 the British Museum kept them "in two frame sheds adjoining Montagu House, firetraps which would have seen the precious booty destroyed if they had ignited" (Altick, 415). At one point the British zoos were the hottest tickets in town; as Altick wryly notes, Hunt's sympathy with the plight of the Regent's Park Zoo animals might have had something to do with his own two years behind bars for libeling the Prince Regent (415).

17. Benjamin Haydon, *Benjamin Robert Haydon: Correspondence and Table-Talk* (London: 1876) 2:293; quoted in Altick, 404.

18. On seeing the panorama, Keats writes, "I have been very much pleased with the Panorama of the ships at the north Pole—with the icebergs, the Mountains, the Bears the Walrus—the seals the Penguins—and a large whale floating back above the water—it is impossible to describe the place" (*The Letters of John Keats: 1814–1821*, ed. Hyder Edward Rollins [Cambridge: Harvard UP, 1958] 2:95). His 1820 citing of the phantasmagoria is especially suggestive. Writing to Fanny Brawne about his health, Keats reports, "I rest well and from last night do not remember any thing horrid in my dream, which is a capital symptom, for any organic derangement always occasions a phantasmagoria." (247). For Keats the phantasmagoria is ubiquitous enough to work as a figure for his own mental state, the "horrid" symptom of his possible "organic derangement." (Altick also mentions references to the phantasmagoria in Byron and Martineau [219, 233].) Keats's usage evinces a knowing sense of the popular phantasmagoria, whose images were oftentimes that of spirits, ghosts, and ghouls. The letter's blending of mind and phantasmagoria also has tantalizing implications for any account of Keats's imagination. When Ian Jack, for example, notes how the figures in "Ode on Indolence" differ from those on a true vase in that they move, the critic's point is that such movement could only happen in Keats's imagination (246). But what if the imagined revolution of the urn's figures knows itself through an optical toy like the rotary lantern (the *lanterne vive*) and its cut-out shadows? Keats's correspondences also refer to the days spent sleeping recovering from an accident that generated the ode's ambience, a situation that would not be the last time a psychic state was mediatized in a specific fashion, something given more edge by the poem's particular content, its putative rejection of the waking world of literary commerce and entertainment, the potential situation of the poet as "pet-lamb in a sentimental farce." Rather than simply demarcate a boundary between the waking social and dreaming interior worlds, the in-between semiconscious state of the rotary lantern would indicate a more complex, and ambiguous, dialectic between private bourgeois and commercial existence. For an extended discussion of the relation of the phantasmagoria to the Romantic and nineteenth-century mind, see Castle, 43–61. See also n. 29.

19. The Portland vase was, of course, one possible model for Keats's ode. So Lord Hamilton's proprietary relations literally connect the realms of commercial and aesthetic exhibition, as well as stress the economies of gender and sexuality involved in this type of display.

20. Cox's argument is that Keats explicitly tries in his ode to restore to art the

Benjaminian "aura of the classic . . . beyond the diminution of [art's] power through endless imitation" (155).

21. The crux of the distinction between Bordwell and Gunning is the former's teleological sense of cinematic history (with a special sense of classical cinema as the apex of that history) versus the latter's more unruly sense of that history, with the conventions of cinematic narrative caught in an ongoing dialectic with various forms of attractions, or what this chapter calls sensation. See David Bordwell, Janet Staiger, and Kristin Thompson, *The Classical Hollywood Cinema: Film Style and Mode of Production to 1960* (New York: Columbia UP, 1985). For arguments against Bordwell, see Tom Gunning, "The Aesthetic of Astonishment: Early Film and the (In)Credulous Spectactor," *Art and Text* 34 (Spring 1989); repr. in *Film Theory and Criticism: Introductory Readings*, ed. Leo Braudy and Marshall Cohen (New York: Oxford UP, 1999) 818–32; Rick Altman, "Dickens, Griffith, and Film Theory Today," in *Classical Hollywood Narrative: The Paradigm Wars*, ed. Jane Gaines (Durham: Duke UP, 1992) 9–48; Miriam Hansen, "The Mass Production of the Senses: Classical Cinema as Vernacular Modernism," in *Reinventing Film Studies*, ed. Christine Gledhill and Linda Williams (New York: Oxford UP, 2000) 332–50; and Christopher Williams, "After the Classic, the Classical and Ideology: The Differences of Realism," in Gledhill and Williams, 206–20. I'm grateful to Marianne Conroy for these references.

22. For an in-depth examination of gothic drama as "perhaps the first indisputable example of what we call 'mass culture,' an artistic configuration that becomes formulaic and gratifies a large cross-section of the population of a nation," see Paula R. Backscheider, *Spectacular Politics: Theatrical Power and Mass Culture in Early Modern England* (Baltimore: Johns Hopkins UP, 1993) xiii, 149–223. The formulaic may be construed as one of high literature's others, and Keats's virtual relation to culture as foregrounding the uncomfortable ambiguity inherent in that relationship. For one study of the relation between theater and Romanticism, see Julie A. Carlson, *In the Theater of Romanticism* (Cambridge: Cambridge UP, 1994); for ones on the relations among theater, Keats, and the Hunt circle, see Bernice Slote, *Keats and the Dramatic Principle* (Lincoln: University of Nebraska P, 1958); and Cox, 123–45.

23. See Jon Klancher, *The Making of Reading Audiences, 1790–1832* (Madison: U of Wisconsin P, 1987); and McCalman. For a study of how the Romantic poetry collection structured its audiences' reading habits, see Neil Fraistat, *The Poem and the Book: Interpreting Collections of Romantic Poetry* (Chapel Hill: U of North Carolina P, 1985).

24. The very phrase "Looking into" implies the visual nature of this mediation, as if to accomplish this literary experience Keats must first look into the physical object that is Chapman's book. This sense of mediation is already implicit in traditional praise for the allusive studiousness and technical accomplishments of Keats's verse. But see also Levinson's claim about the virtual character of Keats's literariness, the degree to which he "produces a writing which is aggressively *literary* and therefore not just 'not literature' but, in effect, *anti*-Literature: a parody" (5). Indeed, Keats's intense awareness of the different ways that culture (including "literature" but also the plastic arts) is produced further suggests reading his work as a commentary on the straddling of various forms of cultural labor. See also Pfau's overlapping argument

about how Keats's poetry can be understood as a reflexive critique of the dominant sense of the literary during his time (315).

25. See chap. 1, n. 15; see also Chandler's point about the oppositional quality of "cockney sensationalism" (534). For pertinent, earlier discussions of a sensational immediacy that connects both Romantic and present-day visual culture, see Galperin's description of the "return of the visible" as a "visible world—accessible to the material, bodily condition of sight and thus prior to idealization—[that is] manifest in certain texts, including verbal texts, of the British Romantic period" (19), as well as his elaboration of this condition in terms of both the "particular" and Walter Benjamin's ideas of "distraction" and "the archaeology of the cinema" (24–29, 32–33); and Wood's "shock of the real" (2–7, 219–23). How the issue of pornographic immediacy might comment on the debate about the relation between cinema and digital media is a highly intriguing one; it might imply more of a continuity between the two than disparities between the mediums now suggest. For two different meditations on the relation between cinema and new media, see Garrett Stewart, *Framed Time: Toward a Postfilmic Cinema* (Chicago: U of Chicago P, 2007); and D. N. Rodowick, *The Virtual Life of Film* (Cambridge, MA: Harvard UP, 2007).

26. For a study of the impact of the panorama on nineteenth-century bourgeois consciousness, see Stephan Oetterman, *The Panorama: History of a Mass Medium*, trans. Deborah Lucas Schneider (Cambridge, MA: MIT P, 1997). The panorama, with its depiction of past and current world events, is also conceivably the site of an imperialist optics. For a discussion of this specific aspect of the panorama, see Russell A. Potter's review of Oetterman's book in *Iconomania: Studies in Visual Culture* (1998) www.humnet.ucla.edu; see also n. 9. See also, however, Galperin's argument for the more indeterminate, non-hegemonic effects of the panorama and diorama (34–71).

27. Pierre Jamin and Jean François Richer, "Report of the Scientists Jamin and Richer on the Phantasmagorie of Robertson and the Phantasmaparastasie of Clisorius (17 July–2 August 1800)," in Mannoni, 480. See also Miles.

28. Ernesto Laclau, "Identity and Hegemony: The Role of Universality in the Constitution of Political Logic," in Butler, Laclau, and Žižek, 83.

29. If the figures in "Indolence" literally seem to revolve, the figures in the "Urn" are on a round, continuous surface, which when (mentally, if not actually) turned could act like a pre-cinema optic toy, giving the illusion of moving images. The eternal nature of the "mad pursuit" on the urn would then not so much be static as perpetual, a harbinger of the furious motion characterizing the large number of chase scenes reflexively allegorizing film's own kinetic abilities in early cinema. I am indebted to Jonathan Auerbach for this observation; for an exploration of such chase scenes in early film, see his "Chasing Film Narrative: Repetition, Recursion, and the Body in Early Cinema," *Critical Inquiry* 26 (2000): 798–820. See also n. 18.

30. This negotiation underpins, of course, many of our meta-narratives about the modern. Habermasian modernity, for example, depends on vehemently distinguishing between the abstraction of a disinterested public sphere and the sensation (visual or otherwise) of mass capitalist life. For a relevant critique of that distinction, see Michael Warner, "The Mass Public and the Mass Subject," in *Habermas and the Public*

*Sphere*, ed. Craig Calhoun (Cambridge, MA: MIT P, 1994) 377–401. For an intense exploration of how the opposition between sensation and abstraction, or the "tyranny of the eye" versus the "tyranny of conception," creates the reflexive space for a "subjectivity-in-default or in distraction," see Galperin, 1–33. My work abuts on but also diverges from Galperin's seminal study insofar as I use Lacan's concept of the gaze to question the reification of subjectivity that occurs when Lamia's visibility is conceived in terms of an agency.

31. Susan Wolfson, *The Questioning Presence: Wordsworth, Keats, and the Interrogative Mode in Romantic Poetry* (Ithaca: Cornell UP, 1986) 335–36.

32. Levinson makes the further distinction of seeing Lamia progress from the commodity form to, under the eyes of Apollonius, the more undifferentiated state of the money form.

33. Quoted in Stillinger, 359. For an exploration of the full social complexities of the suburb in Keats's time, see Elizabeth Jones, "Keats in the Suburbs," *Keats-Shelley Journal* 45 (1996): 23–43.

34. "The 'Enclosure of the Capucines,' under the regime of the Directoire, became the meeting place of idlers, wanderers, prostitutes, and those in search of entertainment or a pleasant rendezvous. It was a cruel irony: under the *Ancien Régime* the convent had been noted for the austerity and extreme severity of its rite" (Mannoni, 159).

35. See Judith Butler, *Gender Trouble: Feminism and the Subversion of Identity* (New York: Routledge, 1990).

36. Bruce Clarke, "Fabulous Monsters of Conscience: Anthropomorphosis in Keats's *Lamia*," *Studies in Romanticism* 23 (1984): 555–79.

37. See Mitchell, *Picture Theory*; *The Last Dinosaur Book: The Life and Times of a Cultural Icon* (Chicago: U of Chicago P, 1998); *What Do Pictures Want?* and *The Last Formalist, or W. J. T. Mitchell as Romantic Dinosaur*, ed. Orrin N. C. Wang, *Romantic Circles Praxis Series* (August 1997) www.rc.umd.edu/praxis/mitchell/index.html.

38. See, for example, Slote, 138–63; and Charles J. Rzepka, *The Self as Mind: Vision and Identity in Wordsworth, Coleridge, and Keats* (Cambridge, MA: Harvard UP, 1986) 206–24. For a discussion that connects performance in *Lamia* to public consensus, see Mark Jones, "Romantic Performativeness and Intersubjectivity," unpublished. For more general discussions of applying theatrical principles to Romantic literature, see Elizabeth A. Fay, *A Feminist Introduction to Romanticism* (Oxford: Blackwell, 1998) 188–235; and Susan Wolstenholme, *Gothic (Re) Visions: Writing Women as Readers* (Albany: State UP, 1993). Wolstenholme looks more at later nineteenth-century writers but discusses the role of the tableau vivant in women's novels. See also n. 22.

39. Insofar as theater might deconstruct this opposition, film can be said to exist already in theater.

40. *Affiches, Annonces, et Avis Divers*, 121 (20 January 1798) 2224; quoted in Mannoni, 150. The ad belonged to Étienne-Gaspard Robertson, who "was one of the earliest practitioners in France of Galvanism" (Mannoni, 150). For a treatment of the themes of animism and science in Keats's poem, see Gigante, "Monster," 433–48.

41. In that sense this passage seems to partake of a peculiar "Cockney sublime," an appropriately distorted version of the high Romantic principle in Burke and Kant. Lamia is neither large nor distant; nor is she in shadow or immediately dangerous in the manner of other forces of nature. She is entirely within Hermes's (and the reader's) frame of vision, which she does not disrupt. Seemingly well proportioned, she should be beautiful. Yet she is not. She cannot be quite seen, and attempting to do so is far from pleasant, a dynamic that very much replays the Cockney stylistics derided and applauded by different readers of Keats.

42. The light source and lenses would be on one side of the screen, while the audience would be on the other. For a full description of how the phantasmagoria worked, see Mannoni, 104–75; and Altick, 217–20. The fact that the screen separated the phantasmagoria audience from the lantern contributed to the view that the show occulted its optical techniques; see n. 58.

43. Paul Endo, "Seeing Romantically in *Lamia*," *ELH* 66 (1999): 115. Sound also works as a putative "reality" principle, as the "thrill / Of trumpets" (2:27–28) that incites Lycius to think about displaying Lamia in her wedded social form, much like the aural "bell" of the word "forlorn" that tolls the poet back to his "sole self" in Keats's "Ode to a Nightingale" (Stillinger, 281; lines 71–72).

44. See, for example, Michel Chion, *Audio-Vision: Sound on Screen*, trans. and ed. Claudia Gorbman (New York: Columbia UP, 1994). I am grateful to Celeste Langan for this reference.

45. Slavoj Žižek, "'I Hear You with My Eyes'; or The Invisible Master," in *Gaze and Voice as Love Objects*, ed. Renata Salecl and Slavoj Žižek (Durham: Duke UP, 1996) 91. See also Jacques Lacan, "Of the Gaze as *Objet Petit a*," in *The Four Fundamental Concepts of Pyscho-Analysis*, ed. Jacques-Alain Miller, trans. Alan Sheridan (New York and London: Norton, 1981) 67–119. My use of the idea of Lamia as the *objet petit a* largely comes from David Brookshire, "Fantasy and the Real in Keats's *Lamia*," unpublished. For a recent argument for Lamia's subjectivity and agency, see Endo.

46. A recent analog to both Lamia and Medusa would therefore be the little android boy in Steven Spielberg's film *A.I.*, whose gaze of loving desire unnerves both his biological mother/owner and the movie audience precisely to the degree that there is *nothing behind it*; the desire of the young protagonist is that of an inanimate object, literally a filmic image. The power of the film lies in its splendid failure at resisting this knowledge, a narrative schizophrenia that replays the dissonance between Spielberg and the film's original creator, Stanley Kubrick. Also pertinent would be Derrida's comment regarding the *pharmakon* of classical philosophy, how "bewitchment (*l'envoûtement*) is always the effect of a *representation*, pictorial or scriptural, capturing, captivating the form of the other, par excellence his face, countenance, word and look, mouth and eye, nose and ears: the *vultus*" (*Dissemination*, trans. Barbara Johnson [Chicago: U of Chicago P, 1981] 140).

47. Lamia's radical distortion would then also resonate with Lacan's more particular treatment of *anamorphosis* as the "phallic ghost," a visual sign in dialectical relation with castration, the gaze, and the *objet petit a* (Lacan, 88–89). As Lacan says

of the *objet petit a*, "this serves as a symbol of the lack, that is to say, of the phallus, not as such, but insofar as it is lacking" (103). See likewise the discussion of Lamia as the "penised lady" in Clarke, 576–77. See also n. 59.

48. Mitchell, *What Do Pictures Want?* 28–56; Galperin, 3. Galperin is, of course, citing Freud's definition of the uncanny, from *Studies in Parapsychology*, ed. Philip Rieff (New York: Collier Books, 1963) 51. Note also how Apollonius's visual aggression toward Lamia gives us one way to understand Lacan's statement "Is it not precisely because desire is established here in the domain of seeing that we can make it vanish?" (85). See also n. 59.

49. Joan Copjec, *Read My Desire: Lacan against the Historicists* (Cambridge, MA: MIT P, 1994) 34. Copjec's immediate aim is to intervene against film theory's translation of Lacan through Foucault and the all-encompassing quality of the panoptic gaze. Although she does not mention the essay specifically, Copjec's thesis would affect the assumptions behind Laura Mulvey's well-known "Visual Pleasure and Narrative Cinema," in *Visual and Other Pleasures* (London: Macmillan, 1989) 14–26. But see also n. 52.

50. Lacan's attendant notion of *mimicry* is also applicable here: "Mimicry reveals something insofar as it is distinct from what might be called an *itself* that is behind. The effect of mimicry is camouflage, in the strictly technical sense. It is not a question of harmonizing with the background but, against a mottled background, of becoming mottled—exactly like the technique of camouflage practiced in human warfare" (99). The nymph is *in*visible in that she is hidden neither by nor behind part of the visible country landscape; she is a mottled stain *on* and *of* the landscape.

51. In line with Kaufman's argument about the Adornoesque quality of Keats's formalism (380–81), one might argue that the poem's resistance, or failure, to narrate itself beyond its own reification is precisely what incites the critical thought necessary to imagine a world beyond commodification. In Adorno this reification could refer to art's resistance to commodification, but also, as in the present chapter, to its realization through the commodity form. See Theodor Adorno, "The Schema of Mass Culture," in *The Culture Industry: Selected Essays on Mass Culture*, ed. J. M. Bernstein (London: Routledge, 1991) 67. But see also nn. 58 and 61.

52. Endo applies to Lycius's actions Mulvey's associations of voyeurism with linear time, and narrative with sadism: "Sadism demands a story, depends on making something happen, forcing a change in another person, a battle or will and strength, victory/defeat" (Mulvey, 21–22).

53. "Along with motion, the spatiality and very reality of the images of these later devices can not be detected as illusions by the eye" (Tom Gunning, "Introduction," in Mannoni, xxvi). Gunning refers to the discussion of optical toys in Crary's *Techniques*.

54. For Auerbach the reflexivity of such early films comes from a "nostalgia for the autonomy of the single shot" and a resistance to the implied narrative of the films' "more dynamic linearity" (809–10).

55. For Levinson this "covert triangulated desire" is most immediately about the "monstrous collusion of Lycius's sensuous this-worldliness with Apollonius's conceptual idealism" (284). See also n. 30.

56. Quoted in Pierre Delrée, "Robertson, Physicien et Aéronaute Liégois," *La Vie Wallonne*, vol. 28 (Liége, 1954) 19; quoted in Mannoni, 149.

57. For discussions of the coining of the term *ideology* by the eighteenth-century thinker Destutt de Tracy and its later transformation into an opprobrium by Napoleon Bonaparte, see Chandler, *Wordsworth's*, 216–35; and Raymond Williams, *Marxism and Literature* (Oxford: Oxford UP, 1977) 56–59. For a study of the eighteenth- and nineteenth-century relation of images to ideology in Burke and Marx, see Mitchell, *Iconology*, 116–208. See also chaps. 6 and 9. For treatments of Louis Althusser's own problematic notion of a science of ideology, see Thomas Lewis, "Reference and Dissemination: Althusser after Derrida," *Diacritics* 15 (1985): 37–56; and Andrew Parker, "Futures for Marxism: An Appreciation of Althusser," *Diacritics* 15 (1985): 57–72.

58. Mannoni, 144; Jamin and Richer, 480. For an account of the patent battle between Robertson and Léonard André Clisorius, which tells much about the contradictory representations of the phantasmagoria as both secretive magic and open science, see Mannoni, 165–73. The association of the phantasmagoria with the secretive occultation of its own principles continued into the twentieth century with Adorno's use of the term as a figure for the mystification of the production process: the phantasmagoria is the "point at which aesthetic appearance becomes a function of the character of the commodity. As a commodity it purveys illusion. The absolute reality of the unreal is nothing but the reality of a phenomenon that not only strives unceasingly to spirit away its own origins in human labor but also, inseparably from this process and in thrall to exchange value, assiduously emphasizes its use value, stressing that this is its authentic reality, that it is 'no imitation'" (Theodor Adorno, *In Search of Wagner*, trans. Rodney Livingstone [London: Verso, 1981] 261). See Crary for a discussion of how in the 1830s the stereoscope individualized the epistemological secrecy of the phantasmagoria for separate viewers, "transforming each observer into simultaneously the magician and deceived" (*Techniques*, 133). See also nn. 51 and 61.

59. See, for example, Daniel P. Watkins, *Keats's Poetry and the Politics of the Imagination* (Rutherford: Farleigh Dickinson UP, 1989) 147. More germane to the present study is the relation between gaze and "evil eye" discussed in Lacan, 115–19. Lacan narrates a distinction (and similitude) applicable to Lamia and Apollonius, a division that the poem also temporalizes through its progression from nature to Corinthian civilization: "For it is insofar as all human desire is based on castration that the eye assumes its virulent, aggressive function, and not simply its luring function as in nature" (118). But it could also be argued that the commodity form in *Lamia* collapses this allegorized distinction between the natural and commodified realms, making the visual dialectic between Lamia as lure and Apollonius as predator the synchronic condition of capitalist modernity, rather than the diachronic progression of modernity out of nature. More precisely, Apollonius's aggressive optics would be patriarchy's own awareness of the baleful effects of the commodity form, the phallic suspicion that every Lamia might actually be a Medusa, a living thing whose lure turns men into (castrated) things—an aggressive, visual logic that patriarchy's suspicions can only compulsively anticipate and repeat.

60. Oscar Negt and Alexander Kluge, *Public Sphere and Experience: Toward an Analysis of the Bourgeois and Proletarian Public Sphere*, trans. Peter Labanyi, Jamie Oswen Daniel, and Assenka Oskiloff (Minneapolis and London: U of Minnesota P, 1992) 36; quoted in Chandler, "Hallam," 535.

61. Levinson refers to Apollonius, Lamia, and Corinth as agencies who are "producers of material" (282). But she also refers to their shared abilities as forms of magic; to the degree that labor in the poem is magic—seemingly effortless and almost immediate, at least for the agent—*Lamia* bars or demurs further inquiry into any story of production that might exist before the poem's experience of itself as a commodified image. That being said, we might also reformulate the question of production in *Lamia* as one about the resemblance between the opacity of social desire and the social materiality of the real, with materiality being equal parts de Manian and Marxist, as suggested by chap. 6. Such an equation would occasion its own choice, then, between seeing the poem's opacity as the very disruption of the symbolic of capitalist consumer modernity and viewing that same event as the symbolic limit of the dialectically materialist assertion of production as the origin of history; in *Lamia*, at least, this decision remains suspended in the very form of the commodified image that dominates the poem. But see also nn. 51 and 58.

## *Coda* · *The Embarrassment of Romanticism*

1. See Gerald Graff, *Professing Literature: An Institutional History* (Chicago: U of Chicago P, 1987) 1–15.

2. For example, the movement from print to electronic scholarly publishing could very well mean the streaming of podcasts of interviews and more polished talks, or essays. Aside from intriguingly highlighting the role of performance in our intellectual research, podcasts conceivably bring scholarly writing out of both the conference room and the confined space of activity that printed material demands into the mobile world of the MP3 player. Taking my invocation of "philosophical" writing seriously, then, what is the status of *thought* that one can engage with while driving a car, raking leaves, making dinner, or going for a run?

3. "Keats is a miserable creature, hungering after sweets which he can't get; going about saying 'I am so hungry; I should so like something pleasant!'" Quoted in Matthews, 35.

4. It should be noted that Readings's Heideggerian phrasing is neither simply nor even pessimistic, and that it doesn't imply the wished-for recovery of some prior state of non-fragmentation (166–79).

5. Along with his commitment to the sensory, this lingering over the embarrassing is precisely why it's difficult to talk consistently about Keats's Romantic sobriety.

6. Mitchell's consideration of the totemic character of Romanticism is part of a larger consideration of "bad objecthood" prevalent in Western discourses; although he doesn't pursue this line of thinking, we might then say, given its relation to "bad objecthood," that the structure of affect involved in Romanticism's persistence is at least in part embarrassment (*What Do Pictures Want?* 188).

7. See Wang, “Embarrassment,” 36–41.

8. “Poets are the hierophants of an unapprehended inspiration, the mirrors of the gigantic shadows which futurity casts upon the present, the words which express what they understand not, the trumpets which sing to battle and feel not what they inspire: the influence which is moved not, but moves” (Reiman and Fraistat, 535).

# INDEX

*Page numbers in italics refer to illustrations.*